Get the eBook FREE!

(PDF, ePub, Kindle, and liveBook all included)

We believe that once you buy a book from us, you should be able to read it in any format we have available. To get electronic versions of this book at no additional cost to you, purchase and then register this book at the Manning website.

Go to https://www.manning.com/freebook and follow the instructions to complete your pBook registration.

That's it!
Thanks from Manning!

The Java Module System

NICOLAI PARLOG

Foreword by Kevlin Henney

MANNING
SHELTER ISLAND

For online information and ordering of this and other Manning books, please visit www.manning.com. The publisher offers discounts on this book when ordered in quantity.

For more information, please contact

Special Sales Department
Manning Publications Co.
20 Baldwin Road
PO Box 761
Shelter Island, NY 11964
Email: orders@manning.com

Manning Publications Co.
20 Baldwin Road
PO Box 761
Shelter Island, NY 11964

Development editor:	Marina Michaels
Technical development editor:	Jeanne Boyarsky
Review editor:	Aleksandar Dragosavljević
Production editor:	David Novak
Copy editor:	Tiffany Taylor
Proofreader:	Melody Dolab
Technical proofreader:	Jean-François Morin
Typesetter:	Happenstance Type-O-Rama
Graphics:	Viseslav Radovic
Cover designer:	Marija Tudor

ISBN 9781617294280
Printed and bound by CPI Group (UK) Ltd, Croydon, CR0 4YY

Don't it feel right like this
All the pieces fall to his wish

—To Gabi, to Maia

brief contents

contents

foreword

The motivation and desire for modularity isn't new. In the proceedings of the 1968 NATO Software Engineering Conference, the landmark conference that played a major role in popularizing a vision of software components and the term *software engineering*, E. E. David outlined an approach for the development of large systems:

> *Define a subset of the system which is small enough to be manageable, then build on that subsystem. This strategy requires that the system be designed in modules which can be realized, tested, and modified independently, apart from conventions for intermodule communication.*

At the same conference, H. R. Gillette described how modularity supported a system's evolution:

> *Modularity helps to isolate functional elements of the system. One module may be debugged, improved, or extended with minimal personnel interaction or system discontinuity.*

Nothing new. It just took languages and practices a while to catch on and explore variations on these themes.

The story of Java modularity is scattered like pieces of a jigsaw puzzle across time and space, carefully coded into history. Java's first and most fundamental realization of a module was the *class*. In other languages, a class represents a unification of modularity and a type, affording a type, its operations, and its details some privacy and cohesion. Java took this one step further, projecting the class from source artifact into binary component.

Alas, in answering the question "How small is *small enough to be manageable?*" the class turns out to be too small. As Marx and Engels observed in 1848:

> *The history of all hitherto existing society is the history of class struggles.*
>
> —*The Communist Manifesto*

For any but the smallest of code bases or most debt-ridden of classes, the class is not the large-scale component architecture you were looking for.

Java also arrived with the false promise of the *package*, a word with all the right connotations—something that is sealed and sent, a coherent and wrapped indivisible whole ready to go—but none of the follow-through: namespaces for organizing code into folders, open plan rather than compartmentalized, more indiscreet than discrete, labeled and weighed down by trendy-at-the-time but ultimately impractical domain names.

And then came Pandora's moment, a myth made manifest. The Greek myth of Pandora, the girl with all the gifts, is typically mistold: she is described as opening a box that releases ills on all of humanity. It wasn't a box: it was a jar. What she opened was a *pithos*, a jar, but this was mistranslated to *pyxis*, a box. Just as in code, names matter.

JARs were a foot in the door of a component model, but that door had not been opened much beyond zipping class files together. To combat the resulting JAR hell, many approaches—perhaps most visibly, build tools and OSGi bundles—extended the JAR model and its manifest to take us further along the road of modularity.

But all that's past. What now? What of the future?

The answer is in front of you. That's why you're reading this book.

Java 9 brought many of the pieces of the jigsaw puzzle together in its modules, a system woven into the core of the platform rather than an extension beyond it. Java's module system has to negotiate the past. It has to retain the investment in a wealth of existing code, to not mess with an existing ecosystem, yet at the same time offer something that makes sense for code yet to be written in an ever-changing world.

At the mechanical level, you need to understand the nature of a module, the nature of dependencies, and the details of syntax and componentization. From a design perspective, you need to know the good, the bad, and the ugly of working with modules. As with any construct or concept, modularity is not a magic sauce you simply add to your development; it requires care, skill, and attention. You need answers to the question of what happens to your existing code in a more modular world, to the question of how it will affect your deployment and your development, and to the questions you have yet to discover you need answers to.

That's a lot of questions. That's why you're reading this book.

Nicolai is here to answer these questions and more. He has tracked modules since they appeared on the radar. He has dived into the depths and swum the shallows of JSRs and implementations. He has gone into details you don't want to, so you don't have to. His care and attention to detail allow you to make good on his distillation of knowledge—from theory to practice, from entry level to advanced.

This is the book with all the gifts. Open, read, enjoy.

—Kevlin Henney, Curbralan

preface

The module system and I met one early morning in April 2015. Before going to work, I checked the OpenJFX mailing list and skimmed a message from a JavaFX user who was concerned about private APIs becoming unavailable "due to modularity restrictions." No way, I remember thinking; Java would never undergo such an incompatible change. I wrote it off as a misunderstanding and headed out to work.

There, after lunch, I had a small dispute with a colleague. Nothing consequential, but it left me somewhat disgruntled, so I decided to go home early and enjoy the sunny spring day. Out on the balcony with a cool beer, I needed something to read. But what? Out of curiosity, I started going through the replies to the mail I skimmed that morning—and they sucked me right in!

Over the following weeks I devoured every piece of information I could find about *Project Jigsaw*, the roof under which the module system was being developed. It turned out that the JavaFX user's concerns were absolutely justified.

In the beginning, I mostly focused on all the things that might break on Java 9. The potential benefits, on the other hand, were a little less obvious. Fortunately, at the time, I was working on a large Java application, and it slowly began to dawn on me how the module system could be used to improve and maintain its overall structure. More and more pieces fell into place, and after a couple of weeks I was sold on the idea of introducing modules into the ecosystem—even if that meant breaking a few things.

The journey from compatibility concerns to understanding the underlying reasons to appreciating what the module system has to offer is a common one. But not the only one! Instead of worrying about existing code bases, you may want to evaluate the module system for your next greenfield Java project; or maybe you're more interested in the larger impact of modularity on the ecosystem. Wherever your journey starts, I wrote this book to be your guide.

If you wonder where the journey leads, think back to Java 8. It introduced lambda expressions—but more important than that language feature on its own is its continued effect on the community and ecosystem: it introduced millions of Java developers to the basics of functional programming and sent us on a journey that opened our eyes to new concepts, making us stronger developers in the process. It also spurred a lot of new libraries and even taught existing frameworks a thing or two.

Keep that in mind when thinking about the module system. It's more than just a language feature; it will send us on a journey to learn more about modularity in all its forms and how to properly design and maintain large software projects, and will spur better support for modularity by libraries, frameworks, and tools. It will make us stronger developers.

acknowledgments

First and foremost I thank Marina Michaels, my development editor at Manning. Without her kindness, insistence, skill, and humor, this book would never have made it into print. She made countless improvements during all stages and taught me a lot about writing. Even more importantly, time and again she helped me quit procrastinating, at least for a while, and churn out a couple new chapters.

In that vein, I want to explicitly deny any thanks to the makers of *Civilization* and *Stellaris*, of *Breaking Bad* and *The Expanse*, to the authors of the many great sci-fi books I read in recent years, and to everyone on American late-night TV—delightful as it was to enjoy the fruits of your labor, I really should've spent most of that time laboring myself, instead.

Three more people at Manning stand out: Jeanne Boyarsky, who provided important technical feedback and who carried this book through the final editing process when I couldn't; Viseslav Radovic, who showed infinite patience while creating and tweaking the diagrams to my liking; and Jean-François Morin, who tirelessly scoured the book and demo code bases for any errors I made. There are a lot more people involved in turning almost a million letters scattered around a bunch of Asciidoc files into an actual book: Cheryl Weisman, Rachael Herbert, David Novak, Tiffany Taylor, Melody Dolab, Happenstance Type-O-Rama, Aleksandar Dragosavljević, Mary Piergies, and Marija Tudor. Finally, I wish to thank all the reviewers who took the time to read my book and offer their comments: Anto Aravinth, Boris Vasile, Christian Kreutzer-Beck, Conor Redmond, Gaurav Tuli, Giancarlo Massari, Guido Pio Mariotti, Ivan Milosavljević, James Wright, Jeremy Bryan, Kathleen Estrada, Maria Gemini, Mark Dechamps, Mikkel Arentoft, Rambabu Posa, Sebastian Czech, Shobha Iyer, Steve Dawsonn-Andoh, Tatiana Fesenko, Tomasz Borek, and Tony Sweets. Thanks to all of you!

I also thank all the people from the community and at Oracle who have participated in developing the module system. Not only would there be nothing to write about without their hard work, but it was also their high-quality documentation and great talks that made me so excited about the topic. I want to especially mention Mark Reinhold, Alex Buckley, and Alan Bateman for spearheading this effort, and also for answering the many questions I posted to the Project Jigsaw mailing list. Thank you!

Among the people who might not expect it, I want to thank Robert Krüger, who, unbeknown to him, sparked my interest in the module system with that fateful mail on April 8, 2015; Christian Glökler, for the dispute that triggered my first afternoon with Project Jigsaw; and Boris Terzic, for always encouraging me to take the next step (and for letting me play with each new Java version at work). Then there are all the great people who reached out to me over the last year and provided me with feedback about what I had written so far—the overwhelming positivity gave me a lot of energy. Thank you!

To all my friends: thank you for sticking around even though I had so little time, and thank you for encouraging me during the rough patches. To my family: I tried hard not to let the work on this book bleed into the precious time we have together—thank you for forgiving me for all the times I failed. Your continued patience, love, and support made this possible. I wouldn't be who I am without you. I love you.

about this book

Java 9 introduced the Java Platform Module System (JPMS) to the language and eco-system and made modularity primitives readily available to all Java developers. For most people, me included, these concepts are new, so this book teaches them from the ground up. It goes all the way from the motivation and basics to advanced features. More than that, it also helps you migrate your existing projects to Java 9+ as well as to incrementally modularize them if you want to do that.

Note that we do not set out to study modularity per se. This is a complex topic, and entire books have been written about it (for example, *Java Application Architecture* by Kirk Knoernschild [Prentice Hall, 2012]). But while we focus on putting modularity into action with the module system, you won't be able to avoid learning about the reasons for doing so.

Who should read this book

The module system is an interesting beast. Its underlying principles and concepts are quite simple, yet its effects on the ecosystem aren't. It's not as immediately exciting as lambda expressions, but it will change the ecosystem just as thoroughly. In the end, all of that hardly matters, though. By now, it's as much a part of Java as the compiler, the `private` modifier, and the `if` statement; and just as every developer needs to know those, they need to know about the module system.

Fortunately, getting started is easy. At the module system's core lie just a few simple concepts that every developer with a minimum amount of Java knowledge can under-stand. Basically, you're good to go if you know how visibility modifiers work; have a rough idea how to use `javac`, `jar`, and `java`; and know that the JVM loads classes from JARs.

If that describes you, and you like a challenge, I encourage you to read this book—you might not be able to connect all the dots, but you'll still walk away with a strong understanding of the module system and a lot of things to follow up on to better understand the Java ecosystem.

To connect all the dots, on the other hand, you should have a couple of years of experience developing Java projects. Generally speaking, the larger they are and the more involved you are in evolving their architecture, picking the right dependencies, and fighting with them when they weren't, the more you will appreciate what the module system has to offer. It will also be easier to vet the impact the module system has on your project and the ecosystem at large.

How this book is organized: a roadmap

The book is structured on several levels. It's obviously split into chapters (and three parts), but it doesn't require you to read them linearly, so I also have a couple of proposals for what to read in which order.

Parts and chapters

This book consists of 15 chapters, organized into 3 parts.

Part 1, "*Hello, modules,*" shows the Java shortcomings that the module system was created to overcome, and explains its basic mechanisms and how to create, build, and run modular applications:

- Chapter 1, "*First piece of the puzzle,*" discusses Java's lack of support for modularity on the level of JARs, the negative effects that has, and how the module system will tackle these deficiencies.
- Chapter 2, "*Anatomy of a modular application,*" showcases how to build and run a modular application and introduces the example app that's used throughout the book. This chapter gives you the big picture but doesn't go into details—that's what the next three chapters do.
- Chapter 3, "*Defining modules and their properties,*" introduces the module declaration as the basic building block of modules and how the module system processes it to achieve its most important goals: making projects more reliable and maintainable.
- Chapter 4, "*Building modules from source to JAR,*" shows how to compile and package a modular project with the `javac` and `jar` commands.
- Chapter 5, "*Running and debugging modular applications,*" examines the many new options on the `java` command. Launching a modular application is simple, so this chapter spends most of its time giving you the tools you need to find and solve problems.

Part 2, "*Adapting real-world projects,*" turns away from the ideal case of a fully modularized project and addresses how to migrate existing projects to Java 9+ and how to modularize them incrementally:

- Chapter 6, "*Compatibility challenges when moving to Java 9 or later,*" explores the most common hurdles you'll face when migrating an existing code base to Java 9 (you're not creating any modules yet).
- Chapter 7, "*Recurring challenges when running on Java 9 or later,*" discusses two more hurdles, which are set apart because they aren't limited to migrations—you're just as likely to face them even after you've migrated and modularized your project.
- Chapter 8, "*Incremental modularization of existing projects,*" shows how to take a large code base that runs on Java 9 and start turning it into modules. The good news is that you don't have to do it all at once.
- Chapter 9, "*Migration and modularization strategies,*" reflects over the previous three chapters and develops strategies that help you migrate and modularize an existing code base.

Part 3, "*Advanced module system features,*" shows capabilities that build on the basics introduced in part 1:

- Chapter 10, "*Using services to decouple modules,*" shows how the module system supports the separation of consumers and implementers of an API.
- Chapter 11, "*Refining dependencies and APIs,*" extends the basic dependency and accessibility mechanisms introduced in chapter 3, giving you the flexibility you need to implement messy, real-world use cases.
- Chapter 12, "*Reflection in a modular world,*" discusses how reflection lost its super-powers; what application, library, and framework developers have to do to make reflecting code work; and which new, powerful features the reflection API was extended with.
- Chapter 13, "*Module versions: What's possible and what's not,*" explains why the module system mostly ignores version information, what little support it has for versions, and how it's possible, albeit complex, to run several versions of the same module.
- Chapter 14, "*Customizing runtime images with jlink,*" shows how you can benefit from the modularized JDK by creating your own runtime images with just the modules you need and how you can benefit from a modularized application by including it in that image, giving you a single deployment unit.
- Chapter 15, "*Putting the pieces together,*" shows what the application introduced in chapter 2 looks like with all the bells and whistles from part 3. It also gives advice on how to best use the module system.

Pick your own path

I want this book to be more than just a one-off device that teaches you about the module system when you read it cover to cover. Not that there's anything wrong with that, but I want it to be more. I want it to be your guide that you can use to learn what you care about the most in the order you're interested and that can stay on your desk, ready to be used as a reference whenever you need to look up a detail.

So while you're of course invited to read this book from beginning to end, you absolutely don't have to. I made sure that each mechanism and feature gets its own chapter or section, so it's introduced in all detail in one spot. If you need to read up on a concept, check the index—the page on which a term is first introduced is marked in bold.

To make jumping into a chapter easier, I often restate and cross-reference facts that are introduced in other parts of the book so that you're aware of them if you haven't read the corresponding part. I hope you forgive me if, at times, you feel that I'm repeating myself or putting up too many signposts.

In case you're not a cover-to-cover person, here are a few paths you could take:

I HAVE TWO HOURS—SHOW ME WHAT YOU'VE GOT:

- *"Goals of the module system,"* section 1.6.
- *"Anatomy of a modular application,"* chapter 2.
- *"Defining modules and their properties,"* chapter 3.
- *"Tips for a modular application,"* section 15.2.

I WANT MY EXISTING PROJECT TO RUN ON JAVA 9:

- *"First piece of the puzzle,"* chapter 1.
- *"Defining modules and their properties,"* chapter 3.
- *"Compatibility challenges when moving to Java 9 or later,"* chapter 6.
- *"Recurring challenges when running on Java 9 or later,"* chapter 7.
- *"The unnamed module, aka the class path,"* section 8.2.
- *"Migration strategies,"* section 9.1.

I'M CONSIDERING STARTING A NEW PROJECT WITH MODULES:

- *"Hello, modules,"* part 1.
- *"Using services to decouple modules,"* chapter 10.
- *"Refining dependencies and APIs,"* chapter 11.
- *"Putting the pieces together,"* chapter 15.

HOW DOES THE MODULE SYSTEM CHANGE THE JAVA ECOSYSTEM?

- *"First piece of the puzzle,"* chapter 1.
- *"Anatomy of a modular application,"* chapter 2.
- *"Defining modules and their properties,"* chapter 3.
- Skim *"Compatibility challenges when moving to Java 9 or later,"* chapter 6 and *"Recurring challenges when running on Java 9 or later,"* chapter 7.
- *"Advanced module system features,"* part 3, except possibly chapters 10 and 11.

I'M INVITED TO A PARTY AND NEED TO KNOW SOME ODDITIES OF THE MODULE SYSTEM TO MAKE CONVERSATION:

- *"Bird's-eye view of the module system,"* section 1.4.
- *"Goals of the module system,"* section 1.6.
- *"Organizing your project in a directory structure,"* section 4.1.
- *"Loading resources from modules,"* section 5.2.
- *"Debugging modules and modular applications,"* section 5.3.

- Anything from "*Compatibility challenges when moving to Java 9 or later,*" chapter 6; and "*Recurring challenges when running on Java 9 or later,*" chapter 7 makes a great conversation starter.
- "*Module versions: What's possible and what's not,*" chapter 13.
- "*Customizing runtime images with jlink,*" chapter 14.

THIS IS AWESOME. I WANT TO KNOW EVERYTHING!

- Read everything. Maybe leave part 2, "*Adapting real-world projects,*" for the end if you don't have an existing project to worry about.

Whichever path you take, look out for signposts, particularly at the beginning and end of each chapter, to decide where to go next.

Watch out for these

This book is full of new terms, examples, tips, and things to keep in mind. To make it easier for you to find what you're looking for, I explicitly highlighted two kinds of information:

Definitions of a **new concept**, **term**, **module property**, or **command-line option** are in italics. The most important ones are set in a grey box with a header. All these are the most essential paragraphs in the book—search for them if you need to look up how exactly a specific mechanism works.

ESSENTIAL INFO Paragraphs marked with this icon give you the most relevant information on the concept that's currently being discussed or point out some non-obvious fact that's worth keeping in mind—commit them to memory!

About the code

The entire book uses the *ServiceMonitor* application to demonstrate the module system's features and behavior. You can find it at www.manning.com/books/the-java-module-system and also at https://github.com/CodeFX-org/demo-jpms-monitor.

In slight variations, it's used in almost all chapters. The Git repository has a few branches that specifically show the features presented in part 1 (mostly `master` and a few of the `break-...` branches) and part 3 (separate `feature-...` and the other `break-...` branches).

Part 2, which tackles migration and modularization challenges, also occasionally uses *ServiceMonitor* as an example, but there are no specific branches for that. Another variant of the application showcases a couple of the migration problems, though: https://github.com/CodeFX-org/demo-java-9-migration.

All you need to code along with the book or experiment with the examples is Java 9 or later (see the next section), a text editor, and minimal command-line skills. If you decide to work with the code in an IDE, pick one that has proper Java 9 support (*at least* IntelliJ IDEA 2017.2, Eclipse Oxygen.1a, or NetBeans 9). I recommend either typing the commands yourself or running the `.sh` or `.bat` scripts, but for some use cases you can use Maven—if you want to build projects with it, you need at least 3.5.0.

You can find more setup details in each project's README.

About the Java version

> ### Java EE becomes Jakarta EE
>
> The module system is part of the *Java Standard Edition 9* (*Java SE 9*). Besides Java SE, there is the *Java Enterprise Edition* (*Java EE*); its current release is Java EE 8. In the past, Java SE and EE were governed by the same process and under the roof of the same guardian: first Sun, then Oracle.
>
> That changed in 2017. Oracle transferred the Java EE technologies to the Eclipse Foundation, which founded the project *Eclipse Enterprise for Java* (*EE4J*) to govern it. The Java EE platform will henceforth be called *Jakarta EE*, and its first release is Jakarta EE 8.
>
> I will occasionally reference Java EE and Jakarta EE in this book, particularly in section 6.1. To avoid confusion between the two projects and whether a technology is formally still Java EE or already Jakarta EE, I will use the abbreviation *JEE*.

This book was written when Java 9 was still fresh, and all code is guaranteed to work on it—more precisely, on version 9.0.4. It has also been tested on and updated for Java 10 and 11. When the book was going to print, 11 was still in early access, though, and it's possible that there will be small changes before the release that aren't reflected in this book.

Java 9 not only introduced the module system, though; it was also the starting point of the six-month release cycle. So Java 10 and 11 are already out, and even Java 12 will be soon (depending on when you read this, it very well might already have been released). Does that mean this book is already dated?

Fortunately, not at all. Except for a few details, Java 10 and 11 don't change anything about the module system; and even if we look further into the future, no major changes are planned. So while this book mostly mentions Java 9, all of that also applies to 10, 11, and probably a few more versions to come.

That's particularly true for the compatibility challenges laid out in part 2. You can't forego them by jumping from 8 to 10 or later. At the same time, once you've mastered Java 9, the rest will be a piece of cake, as Java 10 and 11 are much smaller releases with no compatibility problems.

Code formatting conventions

This book contains many examples of source code, both in numbered listings and in line with normal text. In both cases, source code is formatted in a `fixed-width font like this` to separate it from ordinary text. (Module names are *italicized*, though—see below.)

In many cases, the original source code and the compiler's or JVM's output have been reformatted to accommodate the available page space in the book:

- Added line breaks and reworked indentation
- Truncated output, for example by removing package names
- Shortened error messages

In rare cases, even this was not enough, and listings include line-continuation markers (➡). Additionally, comments in the source code have often been removed from the listings when the code is described in the text. Code annotations accompany many of the listings, highlighting important concepts.

Since Java 8, it's common to use the method reference syntax to refer to methods on a class, so `add` on `List` is `List::add`. Unlike `List.add`, it doesn't look similar to an actual method call (but where did the parenthesis go?) and doesn't beg the question about the number of parameters. In fact `List::add` refers to all the `add` overloads, not just one of them. I use that syntax throughout the book.

Module name conventions

ESSENTIAL INFO Module names are about as long as package names, which can bloat code snippets and diagrams. I opted against that, so all self-made modules in this book have dangerously short names—don't do that in a real project! Instead, go with the guidelines laid out in section 3.1.3, "*Module declarations: Defining a module's properties.*"

Because package and module names are so similar, I decided to italicize module names *like so*, whereas package names are in a `fixed-width` font. This lets you tell them apart, and I encourage you to use the same style if you write about modules.

Placeholders in code snippets

New features, like command-line flags and what goes into `module-info.java`, are defined in general terms. This makes it necessary to use `${placeholders}` to point out where your specific values go. You can recognize them by the dollar sign, followed by curly braces.

This syntax is exclusively used in that context, and its similarity to how some operating systems and programming languages reference arguments or variables is not accidental. But it never refers to any specific mechanism, and placeholders are never meant to be filled in by the operating system or JVM. You will have to do that yourself, and you can usually spot an explanation of what to put into a `${placeholder}` somewhere close by.

EXAMPLE

From section 4.5.3:

> When `jar` *is used to package class files into an archive, it's possible to define a main class with* `--main-class ${class}`*, where* `${class}` *is the fully qualified name (meaning the package name appended with a dot and the class name) of the class with the* `main` *method.*

Easy, right?

Commands and their output

The best way to get to know the module system is to use it directly by issuing `javac`, `java`, and other commands and read the messages Java prints back to the command line. Consequently, this book contains a lot of back and forth between commands and messages. In code snippets, commands are always prefixed with $, messages with >, and my comments with #.

EXAMPLE

Here's a command issued in section 5.3.2:

```
$ java
    --module-path mods
    --validate-modules

# truncated standardized Java modules
# truncated non-standardized JDK modules
> file:.../monitor.rest.jar monitor.rest
> file:.../monitor.observer.beta.jar monitor.observer.beta
```

liveBook discussion forum

Purchase of *The Java Module System* includes free access to a private web forum run by Manning Publications where you can make comments about the book, ask technical questions, and receive help from the author and from other users. To access the forum, go to https://livebook.manning.com/#!/book/the-java-module-system/discussion. You can also learn more about Manning's forums and the rules of conduct at https://livebook.manning.com/#!/discussion.

Manning's commitment to our readers is to provide a venue where a meaningful dialogue between individual readers and between readers and the author can take place. It is not a commitment to any specific amount of participation on the part of the author, whose contribution to the forum remains voluntary (and unpaid). We suggest you try asking the author some challenging questions lest his interest stray! The forum and the archives of previous discussions will be accessible from the publisher's website as long as the book is in print.

about the author

 **Nicolai Parlog** is a thirty-year-old boy, as the narrator would put it (if he squints), who has found his passion in software development. He constantly reads, thinks, and writes about it, and codes for a living as well as for fun.

Nicolai has been a professional Java developer since 2011 and has turned into a freelance developer, trainer, and long-tail contributor to several open source projects. He also blogs, newsletters, speaks, chats, records, and streams about software development—not all at the same time, but in prolific fits and starts with high throughput and long latencies. His home is at https://codefx.org, where you'll find links to all his activities.

about the cover illustration

The figure on the cover of *The Java Module System* is captioned "Habitant de la Floride" and shows a Native American man from Florida. The illustration is taken from a collection of dress costumes from various countries by Jacques Grasset de Saint-Sauveur (1757–1810), titled *Costumes civils actuels de tous les peuples connus,* published in France in 1788. Each illustration is finely drawn and colored by hand. The rich variety of Grasset de Saint-Sauveur's collection reminds us vividly of how culturally apart the world's towns and regions were just 200 years ago. Isolated from each other, people spoke different dialects and languages. In the streets or in the countryside, it was easy to identify where they lived and what their trade or station in life was just by their dress.

The way we dress has changed since then and the diversity by region, so rich at the time, has faded away. It is now hard to tell apart the inhabitants of different continents, let alone different towns, regions, or countries. Perhaps we have traded cultural diversity for a more varied personal life—certainly for a more varied and fast-paced technological life.

At a time when it is hard to tell one computer book from another, Manning celebrates the inventiveness and initiative of the computer business with book covers based on the rich diversity of regional life of two centuries ago, brought back to life by Grasset de Saint-Sauveur's pictures.

Part 1

Hello, modules

Java 9 makes modularity a first-class concept. But what *are* modules? Which problems do they solve, and how can you benefit from them? And what does *first-class* mean?

The book you're reading will answer all of these questions and more. It teaches you how to define, build, and run modules, what impact they have on existing projects, and what benefits they provide.

All in due time, though. This part of the book starts by explaining what *modularity* means, why it's direly needed, and what the module system's goals are (chapter 1). Chapter 2 throws you into the deep end and shows code that defines, builds, and runs modules, before chapters 3–5 explore those three steps in detail. Chapter 3 is particularly important because it introduces the basic concepts and mechanisms underlying the module system.

Part 2 of the book discusses the challenges Java 9 incurs for existing applications, and part 3 introduces more-advanced features.

First piece of the puzzle

This chapter covers

- Modularity and how it shapes a system
- Java's inability to enforce modularity
- How the new module system aims to fix these issues

We've all been in situations where the software we've deployed refuses to work the way we want it to. There are myriad possible reasons, but one class of problems is so obnoxious that it earned a particularly gracious moniker: *JAR hell.* Classic aspects of JAR hell are misbehaving dependencies: some may be missing but, as if to make up for it, others may be present multiple times, likely in different versions. This is a surefire way to crash or, worse, subtly corrupt running applications.

The root problem underpinning JAR hell is that we see JARs as artifacts with identities and relationships to one another, whereas Java sees JARs as simple class-file containers without any meaningful properties. This difference leads to trouble.

One example is the lack of meaningful encapsulation across JARs: all public types are freely accessible by all code in the same application. This makes it easy to inadvertently depend on types in a library that its maintainers considered implementation details and never polished for public use. They likely hid the types in a package called `internal` or `impl`, but that doesn't stop us from importing them anyway.

3

Then, when the maintainers change these internals, our code breaks. Or, if we hold enough sway in the library's community, the maintainers may be forced to leave untouched code they consider internal, preventing refactoring and code evolution. Lacking encapsulation leads to reduced maintainability—for libraries as well as for applications.

Less relevant for everyday development, but even worse for the ecosystem as a whole, is that it's hard to manage access to security-critical code. In the Java Development Kit (JDK), this led to a number of vulnerabilities, some of which contributed to Java 8's delayed release after Oracle bought Sun.

These and other problems have haunted Java developers for more than 20 years, and solutions have been discussed for almost as long. Java 9 was the first version to present one that's built into the language: the Java Platform Module System (JPMS), developed since 2008 under the umbrella of Project Jigsaw. It allows developers to create modules by attaching metainformation to JARs, thus making them more than mere containers. From Java 9 on, the compiler and runtime understand the identity of and relationship between modules and can thus address problems like missing or duplicate dependencies and the lack of encapsulation.

But the JPMS is more than just a Band-Aid. It comes with a number of great features we can use to develop more beautiful, maintainable software. Maybe the biggest benefit is that it brings every individual developer and the community at large face-to-face with the essential concept of modularity. More knowledgeable developers, more modular libraries, better tool support—we can expect these and more from a Java world where modularity is a first-class citizen.

I recognize that many developers will skip past multiple versions of Java when upgrading. For example, it's common to go straight from Java 8 to Java 11. I'll call attention to differences between Java 9, 10, or 11 where they occur. Most of the material in the book is the same for all versions of Java, starting with Java 9. In some cases, I write Java 9+ as shorthand for Java 9 or later.

This chapter starts in section 1.1 by exploring what modularity is all about and how we commonly perceive a software system's structure. The crux is that, at a specific level of abstraction (JARs), the JVM doesn't see things like we do (section 1.2). Instead, it erases our carefully created structure! This impedance mismatch causes real problems, as we'll discuss in section 1.3. The module system was created to turn artifacts into modules (section 1.4) and solve the issues arising from the impedance mismatch (section 1.5).

1.1   *What is modularity all about?*

How do you think about software? As lines of code? As bits and bytes? UML diagrams? Maven POMs?

I'm not looking for a definition but an intuition. Take a moment and think about your favorite project (or one you're being paid to work on): What does it feel like? How do you visualize it?

1.1.1 Visualizing software as graphs

I see code bases I'm working on as systems of interacting parts. (Yes, *that* formal.) Each part has three basic properties: a name, dependencies on other parts, and features it provides to other parts.

This is true on every level of abstraction. On a very low level, a part maps to an individual method, where its name is the method's name, its dependencies are the methods it calls, and its features are the return value or state change it triggers. On a very high level, a part corresponds to a service (did anyone say micro?) or even a whole application.

Imagine a checkout service: as part of an e-shop, it lets users buy the goods they picked out. In order to do that, it needs to call the login and shopping cart services. Again we have all three properties: a name, dependencies, and features. It's easy to use this information to draw the diagram shown in figure 1.1.

We can perceive parts on different levels of abstraction. Between the extremes of methods and entire applications, we can map them to classes, packages, and JARs. They also have names, dependencies, and features.

What's interesting about this perspective is how it can be used to visualize and analyze a system. If we imagine, or even draw, a node for every part we have in mind and then connect them with edges according to their dependencies, we get a graph.

This mapping comes so naturally that the e-shop example already did it, and you probably didn't notice. Take a look at other common ways to visualize software systems, such as those shown in figure 1.2, and graphs pop up everywhere.

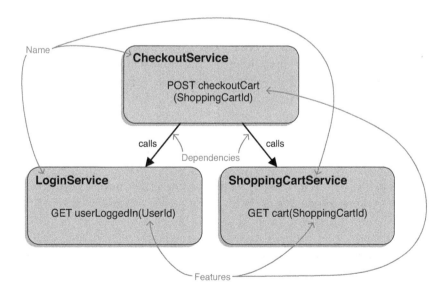

Figure 1.1 If the checkout service and its dependencies are jotted down, they naturally form a small graph that shows their names, dependencies, and features.

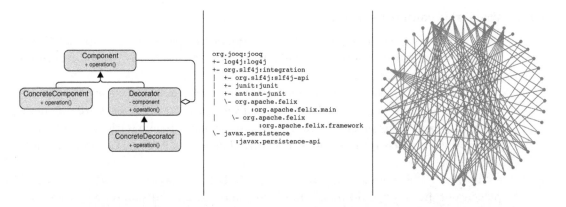

Figure 1.2   **In software development, graphs are ubiquitous. They come in all shapes and forms: for example, UML diagrams (left), Maven dependency trees (middle), and microservice connectivity graphs (right).**

Class diagrams are graphs. Build tools' dependency output is structured like trees (if you use Gradle or Maven, try `gradle dependencies` or `mvn dependency:tree`, respectively), which are a special type of graph. Have you ever seen those crazy microservice diagrams, where you can't understand anything? Those are graphs, too.

These graphs look different, depending on whether we're talking about compile-time or run-time dependencies, whether we look at only one level of abstraction or mix them, whether we examine the system's entire lifetime or a single moment, and many other possible distinctions. Some of the differences will become important later, but for now we don't need to go into that. For now, any of the myriad of possible graphs will do—just imagine the one you're most comfortable with.

1.1.2   *The impact of design principles*

Visualizing a system as a graph is a common way to analyze its architecture. Many of the principles of good software design directly impact how it looks.

Take, for example, the principle that says to separate concerns. Following it, we strive to create software in which each individual part focuses on one task (like "log user in" or "draw map"). Often, tasks are made up of smaller tasks (like "load user" and "verify password" to log in the user) and the parts implementing them should be separated as well. This results in a graph where individual parts form small clusters that implement clearly separated tasks.

Conversely, if concerns are poorly separated, the graph has no clear structure and looks like everything connects to everything else. As you can see in figure 1.3, it's easy to distinguish the two cases.

Another example of a principle that impacts the graph is *dependency inversion*. At run time, high-level code always calls into low-level code, but a properly designed system inverts those dependencies at compile time: high-level code depends on interfaces and low-level code implements them, thus inverting the dependencies upward toward

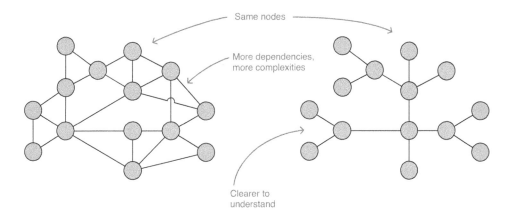

Figure 1.3 Two systems' architectures depicted as graphs. Nodes could be JARs or classes, and edges are dependencies between them. But the details don't matter: all it takes is a quick glance to answer the question of whether there is good separation of concerns.

interfaces. Looking at the right variant of the graph (see figure 1.4), you can easily spot these inversions.

The goal of principles like separation of concerns and dependency inversion is to disentangle the graph. If we ignore them, the system becomes a mess, where nothing can be changed without potentially breaking something seemingly unrelated. If we follow them, the system can be organized well.

1.1.3 What modularity is all about

The principles of good software design guide us toward disentangled systems. Interestingly, although maintainable *systems* are the goal, most principles lead us there on paths that allow us to concentrate on individual *parts*. The principles focus not on the entire code base, but on single elements, because in the end their characteristics determine the properties of the systems they constitute.

We already glanced at how separation of concerns and dependency inversion provide two positive characteristics: focused on a single task and depending on interfaces,

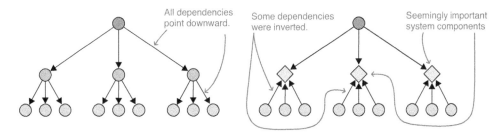

Figure 1.4 A system where high-level code depends on low-level code creates a different graph (left) than one where interfaces are used to invert dependencies upward (right). This inversion makes it easier to identify and understand meaningful components within the system.

not implementations. The most desirable traits of a system's parts can be summarized as follows.

 ESSENTIAL INFO   Each module, what I've called a *part* up to now, has clear responsibilities and a well-defined contract it implements. It's self-contained, it's opaque to its clients, and it can be replaced by a different module as long as that one implements the same contract. Its few dependencies are APIs, not implementations.

Systems built from such modules are more amenable to changes and, depending on how dependencies are realized, more flexible at launch and maybe even run time. And this is what modularity is all about: achieving maintainability and flexibility as emergent properties of well-designed modules.

1.2   *Module erasure before Java 9*

You've seen how the graph of interacting parts connects to a couple of nice properties that are generally summarized as modularity. But in the end, these are just ideas— ways to talk about software. The graph is just lines of code that, in the case of Java, are eventually compiled to bytecode instructions and executed by the Java Virtual Machine (JVM). It would be great if language, compiler, and JVM (which I'll crudely and incorrectly summarize under the term *Java*) could see things like we do.

And often, they do! If you design a class or an interface, then the name you give it is what Java uses to identify it. The methods you define as its API are exactly what other code can call—with the exact method names and parameter types you define. Its dependencies are clearly visible, either as import statements or fully qualified class names, and the compiler and JVM will use classes with those names to fulfill them.

As an example, let's look at the interface Future, which represents the result of a computation that might or might not yet be finished. The type's functionality isn't important, though, because we're only interested in its dependencies:

```
public interface Future<V> {

  boolean cancel(boolean mayInterruptIfRunning);
  boolean isCancelled();
  boolean isDone();
  V get() throws InterruptedException, ExecutionException;
  V get(long timeout, TimeUnit unit)
    throws InterruptedException,
      ExecutionException,
      TimeoutException;
}
```

Going through the methods Future declares, it's easy to enumerate the dependencies:

- InterruptedException
- ExecutionException
- TimeUnit
- TimeoutException

Applying the same analysis to the types just identified, we can create the dependency graph in figure 1.5. The exact form of the graph isn't relevant here. What's important is that the dependency graph we have in mind when we talk about a type and the one Java implicitly creates for it are identical.

Because of Java's strongly and statically typed nature, it will tell you immediately if something breaks. A class's name is illegal? One of your dependencies is gone? A method's visibility changed, and now callers can't see it? Java will tell you—the compiler during compilation, and the JVM during execution.

Compile-time checks can be bypassed with reflection (see appendix B for a quick introduction). For this reason, it's considered a sharp, potentially dangerous tool, only to be used for special occasions. We're going to ignore it for now but will come back to it in later chapters.

As an example of where Java's perception of dependencies and ours diverge, let's look at the service or application level. This is outside Java's scope: it has no idea what an application is called, can't tell you there's no "GitHab" service or "Oracel" database (oops), and doesn't know you changed your service's API and broke your clients. It has no constructs that map to the collaboration of applications or services. And that's fine, because Java operates on the level of an *individual* application.

But one level of abstraction clearly lies within Java's scope, although before Java 9, it was very poorly supported—so poorly that modularization efforts were effectively undone, leading to what has been called *module erasure*. That level is the one dealing with artifacts, or *JARs* in Java's parlance.

If an application is modularized on this level, it consists of several JARs. Even if it isn't, it depends on libraries, which might have their own dependencies. Jotting these down, you'll end up with the already familiar graph, but this time for JARs, not classes.

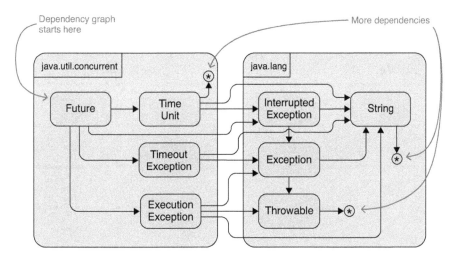

Figure 1.5 The dependency graph Java operates on for any given type coincides with our perception of the type's dependencies. This graph shows the dependencies of the interface `Future` **across the packages** `java.util.concurrent` **and** `java.lang`**.**

As an example, let's consider an application called *ServiceMonitor*. Without going into too much detail, it behaves as follows: it checks availability of other services on the network and aggregates statistics. Those are written to a database and made available via a REST API.

The application's authors created four JARs:

- *observer*—Observes other services and checks availability
- *statistics*—Creates statistics from availability data
- *persistence*—Reads and writes statistics to the database with *hibernate*
- *monitor*—Triggers data collection and pipes the data through *statistics* into *persistence*; implements the REST API with *spark*

Each JAR has its own dependencies, all of which can be seen in figure 1.6.

The graphs include everything we discussed earlier: the JARs have names, they depend on each other, and each offers specific features by providing public classes and methods that other JARs can call.

When starting an application, you must list on the class path all the JARs you want to use:

```
$ java
  --class-path observer.jar:statistics.jar:persistence.jar:monitor.jar
  org.codefx.monitor.Monitor
```

Explicitly list required JAR files with the --class-path option (a new alternative for -cp and -classpath, which also works with javac).

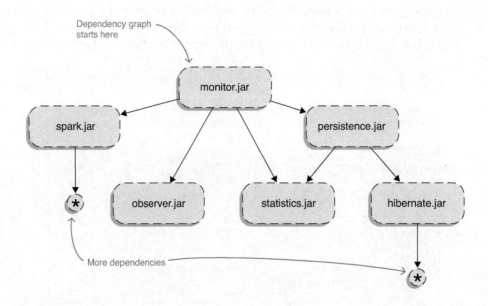

Figure 1.6 Given any application, you can draw a dependency graph for its artifacts. Here the *ServiceMonitor* application is split into four JARs, which have dependencies between them but also on third-party libraries.

ESSENTIAL INFO And this is where things go awry—at least, before Java 9. The JVM launches without knowledge of your classes. Every time it encounters a reference to an unknown class, starting with the main class specified on the command line, it goes through all JARs on the class path, looking for a class with that fully qualified name. If it finds one, it loads the class into a huge set of all classes and is finished. As you can see, there's no run-time concept in the JVM that corresponds to JARs.

Without run-time representation, JARs lose their identity. Although they have filenames, the JVM doesn't much care about them. Wouldn't it be nice if exception messages could point to the JAR the problem occurred in, or if the JVM could name a missing dependency?

Talking about dependencies—these become invisible as well. Operating on the level of classes, the JVM has no concept for dependencies between JARs. Ignoring the artifacts that contained the classes also means encapsulation of those artifacts is impossible. And indeed, every public class is visible to all other classes.

Names, explicit dependencies, clearly defined APIs—neither compiler nor JVM cares much about any of the things we value in modules. This erases the modular structure and turns that carefully designed graph into a big ball of mud, as shown in figure 1.7. This is not without consequences.

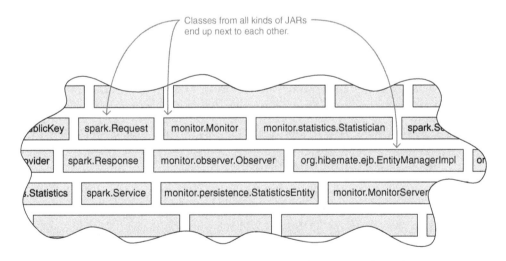

Figure 1.7 **Neither Java's compiler nor its virtual machine has concepts for artifacts or the dependencies between them. Instead, JARs are treated as simple containers, out of which classes are loaded into a single namespace. Eventually, the classes end up in a kind of primordial soup, where every public type is accessible to every other.**

1.3   *Complications before Java 9*

As you've seen, Java before version 9 lacked the concepts to properly support modularity across artifacts. And although this causes problems, they obviously aren't prohibitive (or we wouldn't use Java). But when they *do* rear their ugly heads, typically in larger applications, they can be hard or even impossible to solve.

As I mentioned at the beginning of the chapter, the complications that are most likely to affect application developers are commonly summarized under the endearing term *JAR hell*, but they aren't the only ones. Security and maintenance problems, more of an issue for JDK and library developers, are also consequences.

I'm sure you've seen quite a few of these complications yourself, and over the course of this section we'll look at them one by one. Don't worry if you're not familiar with all of them—quite the opposite, consider yourself lucky that you haven't had to deal with them yet. If you're familiar with JAR hell and related problems, feel free to skip to section 1.4, which introduces the module system.

In case you're getting frustrated with this seemingly endless stream of problems, relax—there will be a catharsis: section 1.5 discusses how the module system overcomes most of these shortcomings.

1.3.1   *Unexpressed dependencies between JARs*

Has an application of yours ever crashed with a `NoClassDefFoundError`? This occurs when the JVM can't find a class on which the code that's currently being executed depends. Finding the depending code is easy (a look at the stack trace will reveal it), and identifying the missing dependency usually doesn't require much more work (the missing class's name often gives it away), but determining *why* the dependency isn't present can be tough. Considering the artifact dependency graph, though, the question arises why we're only finding out at run time that something's missing.

 ESSENTIAL INFO   The reason is simple: *a JAR can't express which other JARs it depends on* in a way the JVM will understand. An external entity is required to identify and fulfill the dependencies.

Before build tools gained the ability to identify and fetch dependencies, that external entity was us. We had to scan the documentation for dependencies, find the correct projects, download the JARs, and add them to the project. Optional dependencies, where a JAR might require another JAR only if we wanted to use certain features, further complicated the process.

For an application to work, it might only need a handful of libraries. But each of those in turn might need a handful of other libraries, and so on. As the problem of unexpressed dependencies is compounded, it becomes exponentially more labor-intensive and error-prone.

ESSENTIAL INFO   Build tools like Maven and Gradle largely solved this problem. They excel in making dependencies explicit so they can hunt down each required JAR along the myriad edges of the transitive dependency tree. Still, having the JVM understand the concept of artifact dependencies would increase robustness and portability.

1.3.2   *Shadowing classes with the same name*

Sometimes, different JARs on the class path contain classes with the same fully qualified name. This can happen for a number of reasons:

- There may be two different versions of the same library.
- A JAR may contain its own dependencies—it's called a *fat JAR* or an *uber JAR*—but some of them are also pulled in as standalone JARs because other artifacts depend on them.
- A library may have been renamed or split, and some of its types are unknowingly added to the class path twice.

> **Definition: Shadow**
>
> Because a class will be loaded from the first JAR on the class path that contains it, it makes all other classes of the same name unavailable—it's said to *shadow* them.

If the variants differ semantically, this can lead to anything from too-subtle-to-notice-misbehavior to havoc-wreaking errors. Even worse, the form in which the problem manifests itself can seem nondeterministic. It depends on the order in which the JARs are searched, which may differ across different environments: for example, between your IDE (such as IntelliJ, Eclipse, or NetBeans) and the production machine where the code will eventually run.

Take the example of Google's widely used *Guava* library, which contains a utility class `com.google.common.collect.Iterators`. From Guava version 19 to version 20, the method `emptyIterator()` was removed. As figure 1.8 shows, if both versions end up on the class path *and* if version 20 comes first, then any code that depends on `Iterators` will use the new version, thus ending up unable to call 19's `Iterators::emptyIterator`. Even though a class containing the method is on the class path, it's effectively invisible.

Shadowing mostly happens by accident. But it's also possible to purposely use this behavior to override specific classes in third-party libraries with handcrafted implementations, thus patching the library. Although build tools might reduce the chance of this happening accidentally, they generally can't prevent it.

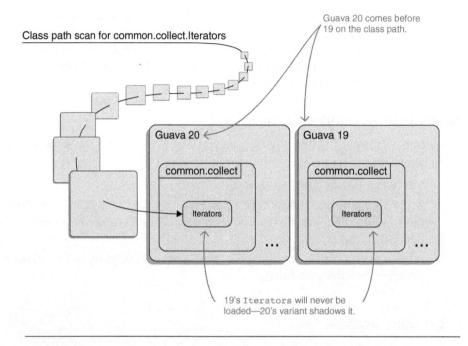

Class path scan for common.collect.Iterators

Guava 20 comes before 19 on the class path.

Guava 20

common.collect

Iterators

...

Guava 19

common.collect

Iterators

...

19's Iterators will never be loaded—20's variant shadows it.

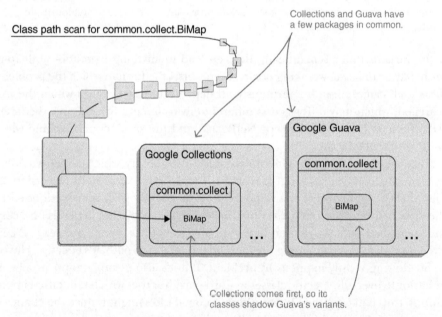

Class path scan for common.collect.BiMap

Collections and Guava have a few packages in common.

Google Collections

common.collect

BiMap

...

Google Guava

common.collect

BiMap

...

Collections comes first, so its classes shadow Guava's variants.

Figure 1.8   It's possible that the class path contains the same library in two different versions (top) or two libraries that have a set of types in common (bottom). In both cases, some types are present more than once. Only the first variant encountered during the class path scan is loaded (it shadows all the others), so the order in which the JAR files are scanned determines which code runs.

1.3.3 *Conflicts between different versions of the same project*

Version conflicts are the bane of any large software project. Once the number of dependencies is no longer a single digit, the likelihood of conflicts occurring converges to 1 with alarming speed.

> **Definition: Version conflict**
>
> *Version conflicts* arise when two required libraries depend on different, incompatible versions of a third library.

If both versions are present on the class path, the behavior will be unpredictable. Because of shadowing, classes that exist in both versions will only be loaded from one of them. Worse, if a class that exists in one version but not the other is accessed, that class will be loaded as well. Code calling into the library may find a mix of both versions.

On the other hand, if one of the versions is missing, the program most likely won't function correctly because both versions are required and by assumption not compatible, which means they can't stand in for each other (see figure 1.9). As with missing dependencies, this manifests as unexpected behavior or as a `NoClassDefFoundError`.

Continuing the Guava example from the section on shadowing, imagine some code depends on `com.google.common.io.InputSupplier`, a class that was present in 19 but removed in 20. The JVM would first scan Guava 20 and, after not finding the class, load it from Guava 19. Suddenly an amalgam of both Guava versions is running! As a

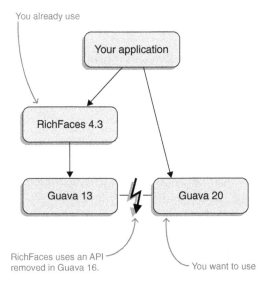

Figure 1.9 Transitive dependencies on conflicting versions of the same library often aren't resolvable—one dependency must be eliminated. Here, an old version of `RichFaces` depends on a different version of Guava than the application wants to use. Unfortunately, Guava 16 removed an API that `RichFaces` relies on.

finishing move, imagine `InputSupplier` calling `Iterators::emptyIterator`. What do you think—how much fun would it be to debug that?

 ESSENTIAL INFO   There's no technical solution for this issue that doesn't involve existing module systems or manually fiddling with class loaders. Build tools are generally able to detect this scenario. They may warn about it and usually resolve it with simple mechanisms like picking the most current version.

1.3.4   *Complex class loading*

Our examination of the class-loading mechanism in section 1.2 wasn't complete. The described behavior is the default, where all application classes are loaded by the same class loader. But developers are free to add additional class loaders, delegating from one to the other to solve some of the problems we're discussing here.

This is typically done by containers like component systems and web servers. Ideally this implicit use is hidden from application developers; but as we know, all abstractions are leaky. And in some circumstances, developers may explicitly add class loaders to implement features: for example, to allow users to extend the application by loading new classes, or to be able to use conflicting versions of the same dependency.

Regardless of how multiple class loaders enter the picture, they require you to take a deeper dive into this topic. And they can quickly lead to a complex delegation mechanism that exhibits unexpected, hard-to-understand behavior.

1.3.5   *Weak encapsulation across JARs*

Java's visibility modifiers are great to implement encapsulation between classes in the same package. But across package boundaries, there's only one visibility for types: `public`.

As you've seen, a class loader folds all loaded packages into one *big ball of mud*—with the consequence that all public classes are visible to all other classes. Due to this *weak encapsulation*, there's no way to create functionality that's visible throughout an entire JAR but not outside of it.

This makes it difficult to properly modularize a system. If some functionality is required by different parts of a module (such as a library or a subproject of your system) but shouldn't be visible outside of it, the only way to achieve this is to put them all into one package and use package visibility. In an act of preemptive obedience, you erase the code's structure instead of leaving this task to the JVM. Even in cases where package visibility solves this problem, there's still reflection to get around that.

Weak encapsulation lets clients of an artifact break into its internals (see figure 1.10). This can happen accidentally if an IDE suggests importing classes from packages that documentation marks as being internal. More often, it's done purposefully to overcome problems that seem to have no other solution (which is sometimes the case and sometimes not). But it comes at a high price!

Now the clients' code is coupled to the artifact's implementation details. This makes updates risky for the clients and, if the maintainers decide to take this coupling into

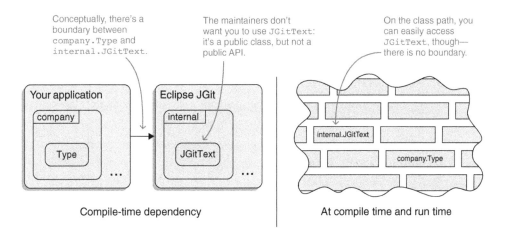

Compile-time dependency   At compile time and run time

Figure 1.10 **The maintainers of Eclipse JGit didn't intend the types in** `org.eclipse.`
`jgit.internal` **for public consumption. Unfortunately, because Java has no concept of JAR internals,
there's nothing the maintainers can do to stop any** `com.company.Type` **from compiling against it.
Even if it were only package visible, it could still be accessed via reflection.**

consideration, impedes changing those internals. It can go as far as to slow or even prevent meaningful evolution of the artifact.

In case this sounds like an edge case, it isn't. The most notorious example is `sun.misc.Unsafe`, a JDK-internal class that lets us do crazy things (by Java standards) like directly allocating and freeing memory. Many critical Java libraries and frameworks like Netty, PowerMock, Neo4J, Apache Hadoop, and Hazelcast use it. And because many applications depend on those libraries, they also depend on these internals. That way, `Unsafe` became a critical piece of infrastructure even though it was neither intended nor designed to be.

Another example is JUnit 4. Many tools, especially IDEs, have all kinds of nice features that make testing easier for developers. But because JUnit 4's API isn't rich enough to implement all these features, tools break into its internals. This coupling considerably slowed JUnit 4's development, eventually becoming an important reason to completely start over with JUnit 5.

1.3.6 *Security checks have to be handcrafted*

An immediate consequence of weak encapsulation across package boundaries is that security-relevant functionality is exposed to all code running in the same environment. This means malicious code can access critical functionality, and the only way to combat that is to *manually implement security checks* on critical execution paths.

Since Java 1.1, this has been done by invoking `SecurityManager::checkPackage-Access`—which checks whether the calling code is allowed to access the called package—on every code path into security-relevant code. Or rather, it *should* be invoked on every such path. Forgetting these calls led to some of the vulnerabilities that plagued Java in the past, particularly during the transition from Java 7 to 8.

It can, of course, be argued that security-relevant code should be double, triple, or quadruple checked. But to err is human, and requiring us to manually insert security checks at module boundaries poses a higher risk than a well-automated variant.

1.3.7 Poor startup performance

Did you ever wonder why many Java applications, particularly web backends that use powerful frameworks like Spring, take so long to load?

> **Definition: Slow startup**
>
> As you saw earlier, the JVM will *lazily load* classes as they're required. Most commonly, many classes are first accessed immediately during startup (as opposed to later when the application has run for a while). And it takes a while for the Java runtime to load them all.

One reason is that the class loader has no way to know which JAR a class comes from, so it must execute a linear scan of all JARs on the class path. Similarly, identifying all occurrences of a specific annotation requires the inspection of all classes on the class path.

1.3.8 Rigid Java runtime

This isn't really a consequence of the JVM's big-ball-of-mud approach, but as long as I'm ranting, I'll get it out there.

> **Definition: Rigid runtime**
>
> Before Java 8, there was *no way to install a subset of the JRE*. All Java installations had support for, for example, XML, SQL, and Swing, which many use cases don't require.

Although this may be of little relevance for medium-sized computing devices (such as desktop PCs and laptops), it's obviously important for the smallest devices like routers, TV boxes, cars, and all the other nooks and crannies where Java is used. With the current trend of containerization, it also gains relevance on servers, where reducing an image's footprint will reduce costs.

Java 8 brought compact profiles, which define three subsets of Java SE. They alleviate the problem but don't solve it. Compact profiles are fixed and hence unable to cover all current and future needs for partial JREs.

1.4 Bird's-eye view of the module system

We've just discussed quite a few problems. How does the Java Platform Module System address them? The principal idea is pretty simple!

ESSENTIAL INFO Modules are the basic building block of the JPMS (surprise). Like JARs, they're containers for types and resources; but unlike JARs, they have additional characteristics. These are the most fundamental ones:

- A name, preferably one that's globally unique
- Declarations of dependencies on other modules
- A clearly defined API that consists of exported packages

1.4.1 Everything is a module

There are different kinds of modules, and section 3.1.4 categorizes them, but it makes sense to take a quick look at them now. During work on Project Jigsaw, the OpenJDK was split up into about 100 modules, the so-called *platform modules*. Roughly 30 of them have names beginning with `java.*`; they're the standardized modules that every JVM must contain (figure 1.11 shows a few of them).

These are some of the more important ones:

- *java.base*—The module without which no JVM program functions. Contains packages like `java.lang` and `java.util`.
- *java.desktop*—Not only for those brave desktop UI developers out there. Contains the Abstract Window Toolkit (AWT; packages `java.awt.*`), Swing (packages `javax.swing.*`), and more APIs, among them JavaBeans (package `java.beans.*`).
- *java.logging*—Contains the package `java.util.logging`.
- *java.rmi*—Remote Method Invocation (RMI).

This is not merely a conceptual diagram, it's how the module system actually sees things.

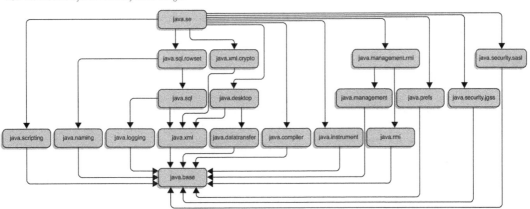

Figure 1.11 A selection of platform modules. The arrows show their dependencies, but some aren't depicted to keep the graph simpler: The aggregator module *java.se* directly depends on each module, and each module directly depends on *java.base*.

- *java.xml*—Contains most of the XML API word salad: Java API for XML Processing (JAXP), Streaming API for XML (StAX), Simple API for XML (SAX), and the document object model (DOM).
- *java.xml.bind*—Java Architecture for XML Binding (JAXB).
- *java.sql*—Java Database Connectivity (JDBC).
- *java.sql.rowset*—JDBC RowSet API.
- *java.se*—References the modules making up the core Java SE API. (This is a so-called *aggregator module*; see section 11.1.5.)
- *java.se.ee*—References the modules making up the full Java SE API (another aggregator).

Then there's JavaFX. A telltale sign that its high-level architecture is superior to AWT's and Swing's is that not only was it sufficiently decoupled from the rest of the JDK to get its own module, it was actually split into seven: bindings, graphics, controls, web view, FXML, media, and Swing interop. All of these module names begin with *javafx.*.

Finally, there are about 60 modules whose names begin with *jdk*. They contain API implementations, internal utilities, tools (such as the compiler, JAR, Java Dependency Analysis Tool [JDeps], and Java Shell Tool [JShell]), and more. They may differ across JVM implementations, so using them is akin to using code from sun. packages: not a future-proof choice but sometimes the only option available.

You can see a list of all modules contained in a JDK or JRE by running java --list-modules. To get details for a single module, execute java --describe-module ${module-name}. (${module-name} is a placeholder, not valid syntax—replace it with your module of choice.)

Platform modules are packed into JMOD files, a new format created specifically for this purpose. But code outside the JDK can create modules just as well. In that case, they're *modular JARs*: plain JARs that contain a new construct, the *module descriptor*, which defines the module's name, dependencies, and exports. Finally, there are modules the module system creates on the fly from JARs that weren't yet transformed into modules.

 ESSENTIAL INFO This leads to a fundamental aspect of the module system: *everything is a module!* (Or, more precisely, no matter how types and resources are presented to the compiler or the virtual machine, they will end up in a module.) Modules are at the heart of the module system and hence of this book. Everything else can ultimately be traced back to them and their name, their declaration of dependencies, and the API they export.

1.5 *Your first module*

That the JDK was modularized is fine and dandy, but what about your code? How does it end up in modules? That's fairly simple.

The only thing you need to do is add a file called `module-info.java`, a *module declaration*, to your source folder and fill it with your module's name, dependencies on other modules, and the packages that make up its public API:

```
module my.xml.app {
    requires java.base;      ◄────────┐  You'll see later that requiring java.base
    requires java.xml;                │  isn't actually necessary.
    exports my.xml.api;
}
```

Looks like the *my.xml.app* module uses the platform modules *java.base* and *java.xml* and exports a package `com.example.xml`. So far, so good. Now you compile `module-info.java` with all other sources to `.class` files and package it into a JAR. (The compiler and the `jar` tool will automatically do the right thing.) Et voilà, you've created your first module.

1.5.1 *The module system in action*

Let's launch the XML application and observe the module system in action. To do so, fire off the following command:

```
java
    --module-path mods
    --module my.xml.app
```

The module system picks it up from here. It takes a number of steps to improve the situation over the ball of mud you saw in sections 1.2 and 1.3:

1. Bootstraps itself
2. Verifies that all required modules are present
3. Builds internal representation of application architecture
4. Launches the initial module's `main` method
5. Stays active while the application is running, to protect the module internals

Figure 1.12 captures all the steps. But let's not get ahead of ourselves, and study each step in turn.

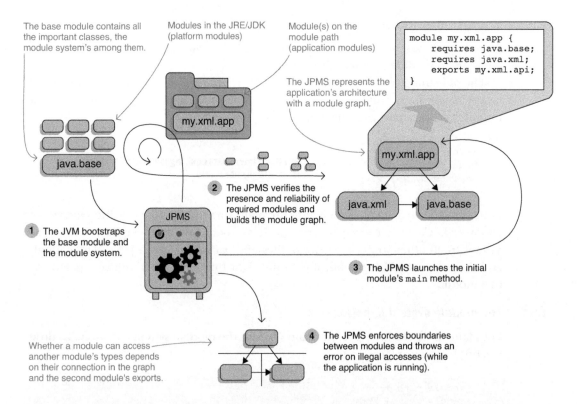

The base module contains all
the important classes, the
module system's among them.

Modules in the JRE/JDK
(platform modules)

Module(s) on the
module path
(application modules)

```
module my.xml.app {
    requires java.base;
    requires java.xml;
    exports my.xml.api;
}
```

The JPMS represents the
application's architecture
with a module graph.

my.xml.app

java.base

my.xml.app

2 The JPMS verifies the
presence and reliability of
required modules and
builds the module graph.

java.xml → java.base

JPMS

1 The JVM bootstraps
the base module and
the module system.

3 The JPMS launches the initial
module's `main` method.

Whether a module can access
another module's types depends
on their connection in the graph
and the second module's exports.

4 The JPMS enforces boundaries
between modules and throws an
error on illegal accesses (while
the application is running).

Figure 1.12   The Java Platform Module System (JPMS) in action. It does most of its work at launch time: after (1) bootstrapping, it (2) makes sure all modules are present while building the module graph, before (3) handing control over to the running application. At run time, it (4) enforces that each module's internals are protected.

LOADING THE BASE MODULE

The module system is just code, and you've learned that everything is a module, so which one contains the JPMS? That would be *java.base*, the base module. In a considerable hen-and-egg mind-boggler, the module system and the base module bootstrap each other.

The base module is also the first node in the module graph that the JPMS builds. That's exactly what it does next.

MODULE RESOLUTION: BUILDING A GRAPH THAT REPRESENTS THE APPLICATION

The command you issued ended with `--module my.xml.app`. This tells the module system that *my.xml.app* is the application's main module and that dependency resolution needs to start there. But where can the JPMS find the module? That's where `--module-path` mods comes in. It tells the module system that it can find application modules in the folder mods, so the JPMS dutifully looks there for the *my.xml.app* module.

Folders don't contain modules, though: they contain JARs. So the module system scans all JARs in mods and looks for their module descriptors. In the example, mods contains my.xml.app.jar, and its descriptor claims it contains a module named *my.xml.app*. Exactly what the module system has been looking for! The JPMS creates an internal representation of *my.xml.app* and adds it to the module graph—so far, not connected to anything else.

The module system found the initial module. What's next? Searching for its dependencies. The descriptor of *my.xml.app* states that it requires the modules *java.base* and *java.xml*. Where can the JPMS find those?

The first one, *java.base*, is already known, so the module system can add a connection from *my.xml.app* to *java.base*—the first edge in the graph. Next up is *java.xml*. It begins with *java*, which tells the module system it's a platform module; so the JPMS doesn't search the module path for it, but instead searches its own module storage. The JPMS finds *java.xml* there and adds it to the graph with a connection from *my.xml.app* to it.

Now you have three nodes in the graph, but only two were resolved. The dependencies of *java.xml* are still unknown, so the JPMS checks them next. It doesn't have any dependencies other than *java.base*, though, so module resolution concludes. Starting with *my.xml.app* and the omnipresent base module, the process built a small graph with three nodes.

If the JPMS can't find a required module, or if it encounters any ambiguities (like two JARs containing modules with the same name), it will quit with an informative error message. This means you can discover problems at launch time that would otherwise crash the running application at some arbitrary point in the future.

LAUNCHING THE INITIAL MODULE

How did this process start, again? Ah yes, with the command ending in `--module my.xml.app`. The module system fulfilled one of its core functions—verifying the presence of all required dependencies—and can now hand control over to the application.

The initial module *my.xml.app* is not only the one where module resolution starts, it must also contain a `public static void main(String[])` method. But you don't necessarily have to specify the class containing that method when launching the app. I skipped past this, but you were diligent when packaging the `.class` files into a JAR and specified the main class then. That information was embedded in the module descriptor, which is where the JPMS can read it from now.

Because you used `--module my.xml.app` without specifying a main class, the module system expects to find that information in the module descriptor. Fortunately it does, and it calls `main` on that class. The application launches, but the JPMS's work isn't over yet!

GUARDING MODULE INTERNALS

Even with the application successfully launched, the module system needs to stay active to fulfill its second essential function: guarding module internals. Remember the line `exports my.xml.api` in *my.xml.app*'s module declaration? This is where it and others like it come into play.

Whenever a module first accesses a type in another module, the JPMS verifies that three requirements are met:

- The accessed type needs to be public.
- The module owning that type must have exported the package containing it.
- In the module graph, the accessing module must be connected to the owning one.

When *my.xml.app* first uses `javax.xml.XMLConstants` (for example), the module system checks whether `XMLConstants` is public (✔), whether *java.xml* exports `javax.xml` (✔), and whether *my.xml.app* is connected to *java.xml* in the module graph (✔). Because all three pan out, *my.xml.app* can do its thing with `XMLConstants`.

This behavior fixes a critical deficiency of the ball-of-mud approach Java used to take with artifact relationships: that there was no way to distinguish code that's internal to an artifact from code that can be used publicly. With `exports` in play, a module can clearly define which parts of its API are public and which are internal and can depend on the module system to enforce its decision.

A MORE COMPLEX EXAMPLE

As a less trivial example, figure 1.13 shows the module graph for the *ServiceMonitor* application introduced in section 1.2. Its four JARs—*monitor, observer, statistics*, and *persistence*—as well as its two dependencies—*spark* and *hibernate*—were turned into modules. JDK modules like *java.xml* and *java.base* are visible as well, because the application depends on some of them, too.

I find the comparison with figure 1.6, which depicts the dependencies between *ServiceMonitor*'s JARs, striking. Figure 1.6 shows *our* understanding of how the application is organized on an artifact level, whereas figure 1.13 shows how *the module system* sees it. That they're so similar demonstrates how well the module system can be used to express an application's architecture.

1.5.2 *Your non-modular project will be fine—mostly*

Developers of existing projects, particularly with large code bases, will be interested in migration paths. Although other module systems are usually "in or out," meaning in order to use them, everything must be a module, this isn't an option for the JPMS. To uphold backward compatibility, a regular application running from the class path on Java 8 or earlier must do the same on Java 9. Thus unmodularized applications must run on top of the modularized JDK, which implies that the module system must handle that case.

And it does. I already mentioned in passing that the module system handles JARs that weren't yet turned into modules. This is the case precisely because of backward compatibility. Although migrating to the module system is beneficial, it's *not compulsory*.

As a consequence, the class path, used to specify JARs or plain `.class` files for the compiler and JVM, works as on Java 8 and before. Even modules on the class path behave just like non-modular JARs. The underlying assumption is that the class path is in charge of accessing artifacts that want to be turned into the ball of mud discussed in section 1.3.

Parallel to that, a new concept was created: the *module path*. Here, the underlying assumption is that it treats all artifacts as modules. Interestingly, this is true even for plain JARs.

 ESSENTIAL INFO The coexistence of the class path and the module path and their respective treatment of plain and modular artifacts is the key to incremental migrations of large applications to the module system. Chapter 8 explores this important topic in depth.

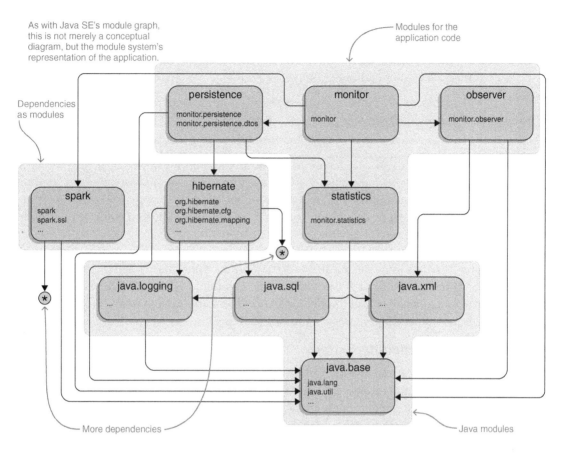

As with Java SE's module graph, this is not merely a conceptual diagram, but the module system's representation of the application.

Modules for the application code

Dependencies as modules

More dependencies

Java modules

Figure 1.13 The module graph for the *ServiceMonitor* application is very similar to the architecture diagram in figure 1.6. The graph shows the four modules containing the application's code, the two libraries it uses to implement its feature set, and the involved modules from the JDK. Arrows depict the dependencies between them. Each module lists some of the packages it exports.

Another aspect of the module system that's important, particularly to legacy projects, is compatibility. The JPMS entails a lot of changes under the hood, and although almost all of them are backward-compatible in the strict meaning of the word, some interact badly with existing code bases. For example:

- Dependencies on JDK-internal APIs (for example, those in `sun.*` packages) cause compile-time errors and run-time warnings.
- JEE APIs must be resolved manually.
- Different artifacts that contain classes in the same package can cause problems.
- Compact profiles, the extension mechanism, the endorsed-standards-override mechanism, and similar features were removed.
- The run-time image layout changed considerably.
- The application class loader is no longer a `URLClassLoader`.

In the end, regardless of whether an application is modularized, running on Java 9 or later may break it. Chapters 6 and 7 are dedicated to identifying and overcoming the most common challenges.

At this point, you may have questions like these:

- Don't Maven, Gradle, and others already manage dependencies?
- What about Open Service Gateway Initiative (OSGi)? Why don't I just use that?
- Isn't a module system overkill in times when everybody writes microservices?

And you're right to ask. No technology is an island, and it's worth looking at the Java ecosystem as a whole and examining how existing tools and approaches are related to the module system and what their relation might be in the future. I do this in section 15.3; you already know everything you need to understand it, so if you can't let those questions go, why not read it now?

Section 1.5 describes the high-level goals the module system wants to achieve, and chapter 2 shows a longer example of what a modular application might look like. Chapters 3, 4, and 5 explore in detail how to write, compile, package, and run such applications from scratch. Part 2 of this book discusses compatibility and migration before part 3 turns to advanced features of the module system.

1.6   Goals of the module system

In essence, the Java Platform Module System was developed to teach Java about the dependency graph between artifacts. The idea is that if Java stops erasing the module structure, most of the ugly consequences of that erasure disappear as well.

First and foremost, this should alleviate many of the pain points the current state of affairs is causing. But more than that, it introduces capabilities, new to most developers who haven't used other module systems, that can further improve the modularization of software. What does this mean on a more concrete level?

Before we come to that, it's important to note that not all of the module system's goals are equally important to all kinds of projects. Many predominantly benefit large, long-lived projects like the JDK, for which the JPMS was primarily developed. Most of the goals won't have a huge impact on day-to-day coding, unlike, for example, lambda expressions in Java 8 or var in Java 10. They will, however, change the way projects are developed and deployed—something we all do on a daily basis (right?).

Among the module system's goals, two stand out as particularly important: reliable configuration and strong encapsulation. We'll look at them more closely than the others.

1.6.1   Reliable configuration: Leaving no JAR behind

As you saw in section 1.4.3 when observing the module system in action, individual modules declare their dependencies on other modules and the JPMS analyzes these dependencies. Although we only looked at a JVM launch, the same mechanism is at play at compile time and link time (yep, that's new; see chapter 14). These operations can thus fail fast when dependencies are missing or conflicting. The fact that dependencies can be found missing at launch time, as opposed to only when the first class is needed, is a big win.

Before Java 9, JARs with the same classes weren't identified as being in conflict. Instead, the runtime would choose an arbitrary class, thus shadowing the others, which led to the complications described in section 1.3.2. Starting with Java 9, the compiler and JVM recognize this and many other ambiguities that can lead to problems early on.

> **Definition: Reliable configuration**
>
> Together, this makes a *system's configuration more reliable* than it used to be, because only well-formed launch configurations will pass these tests. If they do, the JVM can turn the conceptual dependency graph into a module graph, which replaces the ball of mud with a structured view of the running system, much like we may have it.

1.6.2 *Strong encapsulation: Making module-internal code inaccessible*

Another key goal of the module system is to *enable modules to strongly encapsulate their internals* and export only specific functionality.

> *A class that is private to a module should be private in exactly the same way that a private field is private to a class. In other words, module boundaries should determine not just the visibility of classes and interfaces but also their accessibility.*
>
> —Mark Reinhold, *"Project Jigsaw: Bringing the Big Picture into Focus"*
> (https://mreinhold.org/blog/jigsaw-focus)

To achieve this goal, both compiler and JVM enforce strict accessibility rules across module boundaries: only access to public members (meaning fields and methods) of public types *in exported packages* is allowed. Other types aren't accessible to code outside the module—not even via reflection. Finally we can strongly encapsulate libraries' internals and be sure applications don't accidentally depend on implementation details.

This also applies to the JDK, which, as described in the previous section, was turned into modules. As a consequence, the module system prevents access to JDK-internal APIs, meaning packages starting with `sun.` or `com.sun.`. Unfortunately, many widely used frameworks and libraries like Spring, Hibernate, and Mockito use such internal APIs, so many applications would break on Java 9 if the module system were that strict. To give developers time to migrate, Java is more lenient: the compiler and JVM have command-line switches that allow access to internal APIs; and, on Java 9 to 11, run-time access is allowed by default (more on that in section 7.1).

To prevent code from accidentally depending on types in indirect dependencies, which may change from one run to the next, the situation is even stricter: in general, a module can only access types of modules that it requires as a dependency. (Some advanced features create deliberate exceptions to that rule.)

1.6.3   *Automated security and improved maintainability*

The strong encapsulation of module-internal APIs can greatly improve security and maintainability. It helps with security because critical code is effectively hidden from code that doesn't require its use. It also makes maintenance easier, because a module's public API can more easily be kept small.

> *Casual use of APIs that are internal to Java SE Platform implementations is both a security risk and a maintenance burden. The strong encapsulation provided by the proposed specification will allow components that implement the Java SE Platform to prevent access to their internal APIs.*
>
> —*Java Specification Request (JSR) 376*

1.6.4   *Improved startup performance*

With clearer bounds of where code is used, existing optimization techniques can be used more effectively.

> *Many ahead-of-time, whole-program optimization techniques can be more effective when it is known that a class can refer only to classes in a few other specific components rather than to any class loaded at run time.*
>
> —*JSR 376*

It's also possible to index classes and interfaces by their annotations, so that such types can be found without a full class path scan. That wasn't implemented in Java 9 but may come in a future release.

1.6.5   *Scalable Java platform*

A beautiful consequence of modules with clearly defined dependencies is that it's easy to determine running subsets of the JDK. Server applications, for example, don't use AWT, Swing, or JavaFX and can thus run on a JDK without that functionality. The new tool `jlink` (see chapter 14) makes it possible to create run-time images with exactly the modules an application needs. We can even include library and application modules, thereby creating a self-contained program that doesn't require Java to be installed on the host system.

> **Definition: Scalable platform**
>
> With the JDK being modularized, we can *cherry-pick the functionality* we need and *create JREs* consisting of only the required modules.

This will maintain Java's position as a key player for small devices as well as for containers.

1.6.6 Non-goals

Unfortunately, the module system is no panacea, and a couple of interesting use cases aren't covered. First, the JPMS has no concept of versions. You can't give a module a version or require versions for dependencies. That said, it's possible to embed such information in the module descriptor and access it using the reflection API, but that's just metainformation for developers and tools—the module system doesn't process it.

That the JPMS doesn't "see" versions also means it won't distinguish two different versions of the same module. On the contrary, and in line with the goal of reliable configuration, it will perceive this situation as a classic ambiguity—the same module present twice—and refuse to compile or launch. For more on module versions, see chapter 13.

The JPMS offers no mechanism to search for or download existing modules from a centralized repository or to publish new ones. This task is sufficiently covered by existing build tools.

It's also not the goal of the JPMS to model a dynamic module graph, where individual artifacts can show up or disappear at run time. It's possible, though, to implement such a system on top of one of the advanced features: layers (see section 12.4).

1.7 Skills, old and new

I've described a lot of promises, and the rest of the book explains how the Java Platform Module System aims to achieve them. But make no mistake, these benefits aren't free! To build applications on top of the module system, you'll have to think harder than before about artifacts and dependencies, and commit more of those thoughts to code. Certain things that used to work will stop doing so on Java 9, and using certain frameworks will require a little more effort than before.

You can view this as similar to how a statically and strongly typed language requires more work than a dynamic one—at least, while the code is being written. All those types and generics—can't you just use `Object` and casts everywhere? Sure, you could, but would you be willing to give up the safety the type system provides, just to save some brain cycles while writing code? I don't think so.

1.7.1 What you'll learn

New skills are required! Luckily, this book teaches them. When all is said and done, and you've mastered the mechanisms laid out in the following chapters, neither new nor existing applications will defy you.

Part 1, particularly chapters 3–5, goes through the basics of the module system. In addition to practical skills, they teach underlying mechanisms to give you deeper understanding. Afterward, you'll be able to describe modules and their relationships by encapsulating a module's internals and expressing its dependencies. With `javac`, `jar`, and `java`, you'll compile, package, and run modules and the applications they form.

Part 2 of the book builds on the basics and extends them to cover more complex use cases. For existing applications, you'll be able to analyze possible incompatibilities with Java 9 to 11 and create a migration path to the module system using the various features it offers for that purpose. Toward that end, and also to implement less straightforward module relationships, you can use advanced features like qualified exports, open modules, and services as well as the extended reflection API. With `jlink`, you'll create pared-down JREs, optimized for a particular use case, or self-contained application images that ship with their own JREs. Finally, you'll see the bigger picture, including how the module system interacts with class loading, reflection, and containers.

1.7.2 *What you should know*

The JPMS has an interesting character when it comes to skill requirements. Most of what it does is brand-new and comes with its own syntax partitioned off in the module declaration. Learning that is relatively easy, if you have basic Java skills. So if you know that code is organized in types, packages, and ultimately JARs; how visibility modifiers, particularly `public`, work across them; and what `javac`, `jar`, and `java` do, and have a rough idea of how to use them, then you have all it takes to understand part 1 as well as many of the more advanced features introduced in part 3.

But to really understand the problems the module system addresses and to appreciate the solutions it proposes requires more than that. Familiarity with the following and experience working with large applications make it easier to understand the motivation for the module system's features and their benefits and shortcomings:

- How the JVM, and particularly the class loader, operates
- The trouble that mechanism causes (think JAR hell)
- More advanced Java APIs like the service loader and reflection API
- Build tools like Maven and Gradle and how they build a project
- How to modularize software systems

But however knowledgeable you are, you may encounter references or explanations that don't connect with something you know. For an ecosystem as gigantic as Java's, that's natural, and everybody learns something new wherever they turn (believe me, I know that first hand). So, never despair! If some fluff doesn't help, chances are you can understand the technicalities purely by looking at the code.

With the background colored in, it's time to get your hands dirty and learn the JPMS basics. I recommend you continue with chapter 2, which cuts across the rest of part 1 and shows code that defines, builds, and runs modular JARs. It also introduces the demo application that appears throughout the rest of the book. If you prefer learning the underlying theory first, you can skip to chapter 3, which teaches the module system's fundamental mechanisms. If you're driven by worry about your project's compatibility with Java 9, chapters 6 and 7 cover that in detail, but those chapters will be hard to understand without a good grasp of the basics.

Summary

- A software system can be visualized as a graph, which often shows (un)desired properties of the system.
- On the level of JARs, Java used to have no understanding of that graph. This led to various problems, among them JAR hell, manual security, and poor maintainability.
- The Java Platform Module System exists to make Java understand the JAR graph, which brings artifact-level modularity to the language. The most important goals are reliable configuration and strong encapsulation as well as improved security, maintainability, and performance.
- This is achieved by introducing modules: basically, JARs with an additional descriptor. The compiler and runtime interpret the described information in order to build the graph of artifact dependencies and provide the promised benefits.

Anatomy of a modular application

This chapter covers

- Laying out a modular application's source code
- Creating module declarations
- Compiling modules
- Running a modular application

This chapter introduces you to the overall workflow of creating modular applications, but it doesn't explain these topics in all detail. Chapters 3, 4, and 5 do that—they explore these subjects in depth. But with a topic as encompassing as the module system, it can be easy to miss the forest for the trees. That's why this chapter shows you the big picture. It gives you an impression of how the different pieces of the puzzle fit together by presenting a simple modular application, how its modules are defined and compiled, and how the application is executed.

That means I make you jump into the deep end: not everything that follows may be immediately obvious. But don't worry if something's unclear—it will be thoroughly explained soon. When you're done with part 1 of this book, everything in the example will make perfect sense. So dog-ear these pages, because you may want to refer back to them.

Section 2.1 explains what the hypothetical application does, what types it consists of, and what their responsibilities are. The module system comes into play in section 2.2, which discusses how to organize the files and folders, describe the modules, and compile and run the application. That brief encounter will demonstrate many of the module system's core mechanisms as well as some instances where basic features don't suffice to modularize a complex application—topics that section 2.3 discusses. You can find the application online at www.manning.com/books/the-java-module-system and https://github.com/CodeFX-org/demo-jpms-monitor. The master branch contains the variant described in section 2.2.

2.1 *Introducing ServiceMonitor*

To see the module system in action, you need an example project you can apply it to. It isn't terribly important exactly what the project does, so don't fret over its details.

Let's imagine a network of services that cooperate to delight users—maybe a social network or a video platform. You want to monitor those services to determine how healthy the system is and spot problems when they occur (instead of when customers report them). This is where the example application comes in.

The example application is called *ServiceMonitor*. It contacts individual services, collects and aggregates diagnostic data, and makes that data available via REST.

> **NOTE** You might recall the application from section 1.2 or figure 1.10, where it's split into four different JARs. We'll eventually come to an even more detailed modularization, but that's for section 2.2 to explore. Before doing that, let's think about how you'd implement such a system in a single artifact (let's call that the *monolithic* approach). Never mind if it doesn't line up 100% with chapter 1—new chapter, new details.

As luck would have it, the services already collect the data you want, so all *ServiceMonitor* needs to do is query them periodically. This is the job of the `ServiceObserver` implementations. Once you have the diagnostic data in the form of `DiagnosticData-Point`, it can be fed to `Statistician`, which aggregates it to `Statistics`. The statistics, in turn, are stored in `StatisticsRepository` as well as made available via REST. The `Monitor` class ties everything together.

Figure 2.1 shows how these types relate to each other. To get a better feeling for how this works, let's look at the code, starting with the `ServiceObserver` interface.

Listing 2.1 `ServiceObserver` **interface**

```java
public interface ServiceObserver {

 DiagnosticDataPoint gatherDataFromService();

}
```

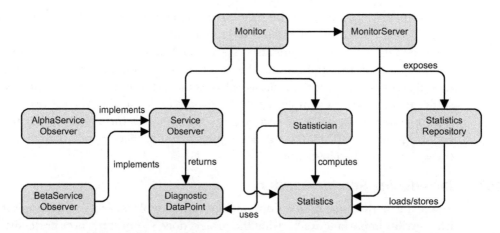

Figure 2.1   **The classes making up the *ServiceMonitor* application. Two** `ServiceObserver`
implementations query services with Alpha and Beta APIs and return diagnostic data, which
`Statistician` **aggregates into** `Statistics`. **The statistics are stored and loaded by a repository as**
well as exposed via a REST API. `Monitor` **orchestrates all this.**

Looks simple enough, but unfortunately, not all services expose the same REST API. Two generations are in use: Alpha and Beta. That's why `ServiceObserver` is an interface with two implementations (see figure 2.2): each implementation connects to a different API generation and makes sure to expose the data to your application via the same interface.

`Statistician` has no state of its own—it just offers two methods that either create a new `Statistics` instance or combine existing statistics and new data points into updated statistics.

Listing 2.2   `Statistician` class

```
public class Statistician {

 public Statistics emptyStatistics() {
  return Statistics.empty();
 }

 public Statistics compute(
    Statistics currentStats,
    Iterable<DiagnosticDataPoint> dataPoints) {
  Statistics finalStats = currentStats;
  for (DiagnosticDataPoint dataPoint : dataPoints)
    finalStats = finalStats.merge(dataPoint);
  return finalStats;
 }

}
```

`StatisticsRepository` doesn't do anything fancy—it loads and stores statistics. Whether that's done via serialization, JSON files, or a backing database is irrelevant for this example.

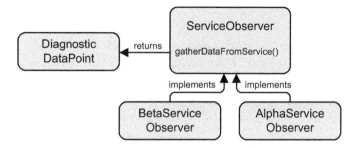

Figure 2.2 The observed services use two different API generations to expose the diagnostic data. Accordingly, the `ServiceObserver` **interface has two implementations.**

Listing 2.3 `StatisticsRepository` **class**

```
public class StatisticsRepository {

  public Optional<Statistics> load() { /* ... */ }

  public void store(Statistics statistics) { /* ... */ }

}
```

This leaves you with a type that collects data points, another that converts them to statistics, and a third that stores stats. What's missing is a class that binds them together by regularly polling data and pushing it through the statistician into the repository. That's what `Monitor` is there for. The following listing shows its fields and the `updateStatistics()` method, which implements its core responsibility. (The code that makes sure the task is run regularly is omitted.)

Listing 2.4 `Monitor` **class and its** `updateStatistics()` **method**

```
public class Monitor {

 private final List<ServiceObserver> serviceObservers;
 private final Statistician statistician;
 private final StatisticsRepository repository;
 private Statistics currentStatistics;
 // [...]

 private void updateStatistics() {
  List<DiagnosticDataPoint> newData = serviceObservers
    .stream()
    .map(ServiceObserver::gatherDataFromService)
    .collect(toList());
  Statistics newStatistics = statistician
    .compute(currentStatistics, newData);
  currentStatistics = newStatistics;
  repository.store(newStatistics);
 }

 // [...]
}
```

Monitor stores the most recent statistics in a `currentStatistics` field (of type `Statistics`).

Upon requests, `MonitorServer`, which exposes the REST API, asks the monitor to provide the statistical data—either from memory or from persistence—and then extracts the requested bits and returns them.

Listing 2.5   `MonitorServer` class

```
public class MonitorServer {

 private final Supplier<Statistics> statistics;

 public MonitorServer(Supplier<Statistics> statistics) {
  this.statistics = statistics;
 }

 // [...]

 private Statistics getStatistics() {
  return statistics.get();
 }

 // [...]

}
```

An interesting detail to note is that although `MonitorServer` calls `Monitor`, it doesn't depend on it. That's because `MonitorServer` doesn't get a reference to a monitor but rather a supplier for the data that forwards calls to the monitor. The reason is pretty simple: `Monitor` orchestrates the entire application, which makes it a class with a lot going on inside. I didn't want to couple the REST API to such a heavyweight object just to call a single getter. Before Java 8, I might have created a dedicated interface to get the statistics and make `Monitor` implement it; but since Java 8, lambda expressions and the existing functional interfaces make ad hoc decoupling much easier.

All in all, you end up with these types:

- `DiagnosticDataPoint`—Availability data for a service in a time interval.
- `ServiceObserver`—Interface for service observation that returns `Diagnostic-DataPoint`.
- `AlphaServiceObserver` and `BetaServiceObserver`—Each observes a variant of services.
- `Statistician`—Computes statistics from `DiagnosticDataPoint`.
- `Statistics`—Holds the computed statistics.
- `StatisticsRepository`—Stores and retrieves statistics.
- `MonitorServer`—Answers REST calls for the statistics.
- `Monitor`—Ties everything together.

2.2   *Modularizing ServiceMonitor*

If you were to implement the *ServiceMonitor* application as it was just described as a real-life project, bringing the module system into play with full force would be like using a sledgehammer to crack a nut. But it's just an example, and it's here to show you a modularized project's anatomy, so you'll structure it as if it were a much larger project.

Talking about structure, let's start by cutting the application into modules before discussing how the source code is laid out on the filesystem. Then come the most interesting steps: how to declare and compile the modules and run the application.

2.3   *Cutting ServiceMonitor into modules*

The most common way to modularize applications is by a separation of concerns. *ServiceMonitor* has the following, with the related types in parentheses:

- Collecting data from services (`ServiceObserver`, `DiagnosticDataPoint`)
- Aggregating data into statistics (`Statistician`, `Statistics`)
- Persisting statistics (`StatisticsRepository`)
- Exposing statistics via a REST API (`MonitorServer`)

But not only the domain logic generates requirements. There are also technical ones:

- Data collection must be hidden behind an API.
- The Alpha and Beta services each require a separate implementation of that API (`AlphaServiceObserver` and `BetaServiceObserver`).
- All concerns must be orchestrated (`Monitor`).

 ESSENTIAL INFO   This results in the following modules with the mentioned publicly visible types:

- *monitor.observer* (`ServiceObserver`, `DiagnosticDataPoint`)
- *monitor.observer.alpha* (`AlphaServiceObserver`)
- *monitor.observer.beta* (`BetaServiceObserver`)
- *monitor.statistics* (`Statistician`, `Statistics`)
- *monitor.persistence* (`StatisticsRepository`)
- *monitor.rest* (`MonitorServer`) * *monitor* (`Monitor`)

Superimposing these modules over the class diagram in figure 2.3, it's easy to see the module dependencies emerge.

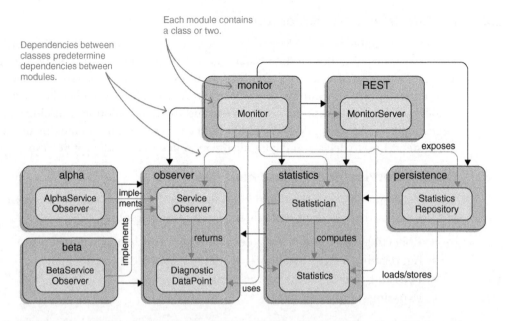

Figure 2.3   The *ServiceMonitor* application's modules (bold) overlaying the class structure (regular). Note how class dependencies across module boundaries determine module dependencies.

2.4   Laying out files in a directory structure

Figure 2.4 shows the application's directory structure. Each module will be its own project, which means each can have an individual directory structure. There's no reason to complicate things, though, so you'll use the same structure for all. If you've been involved in different projects or have been using Maven, Gradle, or other build tools, you'll recognize this as the default one.

The first thing to note is the mods folder. Later, when you're creating modules, this is where they'll end up. Section 4.1 goes into more detail about the directory structure.

Then there's the slightly unusual libs folder, which contains third-party dependencies. In a real-life project, you wouldn't need it, because your build tool manages dependencies. But you're going to compile and launch by hand, and having all dependencies in one place greatly simplifies that. So this isn't a recommendation or even a requirement—it's just a simplification.

The other uncommon thing is module-info.java. It's called a *module declaration* and is in charge of defining a module's properties. This puts it right at the center of the module system and hence this book, particularly of section 3.1. Nonetheless, we'll have a quick look at it in the following section.

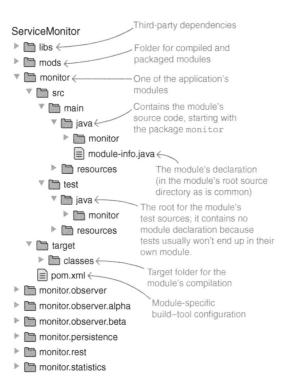

Figure 2.4 Each module of the *ServiceMonitor* application is its own project with the well-known directory structure. New are the `mods` folder, which collects the modular JARs once they're built, and the module declarations `module-info.java` file in each project's root source directory.

2.5   *Declaring and describing modules*

 ESSENTIAL INFO   Each module has a module declaration. By convention, this is a `module-info.java` file in the project's root source folder. From this, the compiler creates a module descriptor, `module-info.class`. When the compiled code is packaged into a JAR, the descriptor must end up in the root folder for the module system to recognize and process it.

As discussed in section 2.2.1, the application consists of seven modules, so there must be seven module declarations. Listing 2.6 shows all of them. Even without knowing any details yet, you can glimpse what's going on.

A `module the.name { }` block defines a module. The name typically follows the package-naming convention: it should be globally unique by reverting a domain name, it's all lowercase, and sections are separated by dots (see section 3.1.3 for more—I use shorter names only to make them more amenable for this book). Inside the module block, `requires` directives express the dependencies between modules, and `exports` directives define each module's public API by naming the packages whose public types are to be exported.

Listing 2.6   Declarations for all *ServiceMonitor* modules

```
module monitor.observer {
 exports monitor.observer;
}

module monitor.observer.alpha {
 requires monitor.observer;
 exports monitor.observer.alpha;
}

module monitor.observer.beta {
 requires monitor.observer;
 exports monitor.observer.beta;
}

module monitor.statistics {
 requires monitor.observer;
 exports monitor.statistics;
}

module monitor.persistence {
 requires monitor.statistics;
 requires hibernate.jpa;
 exports monitor.persistence;
 exports monitor.persistence.entity;
}

module monitor.rest {
 requires spark.core;
 requires monitor.statistics;
 exports monitor.rest;
}

module monitor {
 requires monitor.observer;
 requires monitor.observer.alpha;
 requires monitor.observer.beta;
 requires monitor.statistics;
 requires monitor.persistence;
 requires monitor.rest;
}
```

2.5.1   *Declaring dependencies on other modules*

 ESSENTIAL INFO   A requires directive contains a module name and tells the JVM that the declaring module depends on the one given by the directive.

You see that the observer implementations depend on the observer API, which immediately makes sense. The *statistics* module also depends on the observer API because Statistician::compute uses the type DiagnosticDataPoint, which is part of the API.

Similarly, the *persistence* module needs statistics, so it depends on the *statistics* module. It also depends on Hibernate because it uses Hibernate to talk to the database.

Then you have *monitor.rest*, which also depends on the *statistics* module because it handles statistics. Beyond that, it uses the Spark micro framework to create the REST endpoint. When modularizing the application in section 2.2.1, I made a point that `MonitorServer` doesn't depend on `Monitor`. That comes in handy now because it means *monitor.rest* doesn't depend on *monitor*; this is great because *monitor* depends on *monitor.rest*, and the module system forbids declaring cyclic dependencies. Finally, *monitor* depends on all the other modules because it creates most instances and pipes the results from one into the other.

2.5.2 Defining a module's public API

 ESSENTIAL INFO An `exports` directive contains a package name and informs the JVM that other modules depending on the declaring one can see public types in that package.

Most of the modules export a single package: the one that contains the types listed when the modules were determined. You may have noticed that the package names are always prefixed with the module names—often they're identical. This isn't mandatory, but because both module and package names follow the reverse-domain naming scheme, this is the common case.

The persistence module is the only one that exports more than one package. In addition to *monitor.persistence*, which contains its core feature (`StatisticsRepository`), it also exports *monitor.persistence.entity*. That package defines a set of classes that are annotated so Hibernate understands how to store and load them (these are commonly called entities). This means Hibernate has to access them, which in turn implies that the module has to export the package containing them. (If you rely on Hibernate reflecting over private fields or constructors, exporting won't suffice—see section 12.2 for a solution.)

The other exception is *monitor*, which exports no packages. This makes sense because it sits, like a spider in a web, in the center of the module graph and coordinates the execution flow. As such, it has no API of its own that anybody else might want to call. Having the main module—which usually and fittingly contains the program's main method—not export any packages is typical.

2.5.3 Visualizing ServiceMonitor with the module graph

With the modules' dependencies and exports neatly defined, let's look at the resulting module graph in figure 2.5. Although it looks like it's just a cleaned-up version of figure 2.3, it's much more than that! Figure 2.3 is a diagram that the application's architects might have drawn on a whiteboard. It shows modules and their relations, but those were just figments of your imagination—nothing that mattered to the compiler or virtual machine. Figure 2.5, on the other hand, is the module system's interpretations of your architecture.

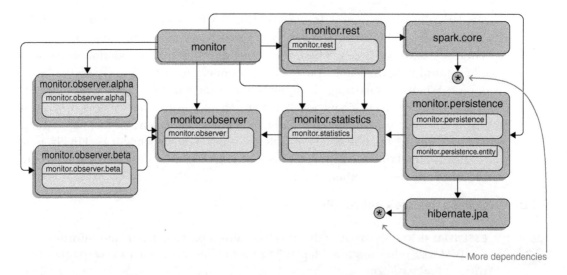

Figure 2.5   The application's module graph, showing modules with their exported packages and the dependencies between them. Unlike figure 2.3, this is not merely an architecture diagram; it's how the module system sees the application.

That the modular aspects in both diagrams look so similar, to the point of being almost interchangeable, means you can express your vision of the application's architecture fairly precisely in code: namely, in module declarations. Isn't that something?

Writing code is much like before

You may wonder if writing code will be different than before Java 9. The answer is no, in the overwhelming majority of cases. A few details have changed, though, and to prepare you, chapters 6 and 7 cover them in detail.

Other than properly modularizing a project and occasionally having to think about which package to place classes in or whether to modify a dependency or an export, the day-to-day work to model the domain and solve the problems at hand will remain the same. With IDE support, modifying dependencies or exports is as easy as managing package imports.

The big-picture work of how to organize a larger code base will get easier, though. Adding dependencies, particularly ones that were already transitively present, becomes more explicit and thus more readily a matter of discussion during pair programming, code reviews, or architecture reviews—this will make sure that perceived and real architecture can't easily drift apart. Prominent features like services (see chapter 10) and aggregator modules (see section 11.1.5) will enhance the modularity tool box, leading to better design if used well.

2.6 Compiling and packaging modules

Now that you've neatly organized the project in module-specific folders, created module declarations, and written the code, you're ready to build and (later) run the application. To build it, you'll create module artifacts, which is a two-step process: compilation and packaging.

When compiling, you need the compiler to know where to find the modules the declarations are referencing. This is trivial for dependencies on Java modules, because the compiler knows where to find them (in the run-time environment's libs/modules file).

 ESSENTIAL INFO For your own module to be found, you have to use the *module path*, a concept paralleling the class path but, as the name suggests, expecting modular JARs instead of plain JARs. It will be scanned when the compiler searches for referenced modules. To define the module path, `javac` has a new option: `--module-path`, or `-p` for short. (The same line of thought is true for launching the application with the JVM. Accordingly, the same options, `--module-path` and `-p`, were added to `java` as well, where they function just the same.)

You chose the `mods` folder to store your modules, which means two things:

- The module path will contain `mods`.
- The packaged artifacts will be created in `mods`.

Some of your modules have external dependencies: the persistence module requires Hibernate (`hibernate.jpa`), and the REST module requires Spark (`spark.core`). For now, it's easiest to assume that their artifacts are also already modularized JARs and that you or a tool placed them and their dependencies in the `mods` folder.

What happens if you place plain JARs on the module path, place modular JARs on the class path, or mix and match? And what can you do if a dependency isn't yet modularized but you want to use it anyway? All of that is part of the migration story and covered in chapter 8.

With all the prerequisites in `mods`, you can compile and package the modules. You start with *monitor.observer*, which has no dependencies. It contains nothing new—executed with an older version of Java, these commands would lead to the exact same result:

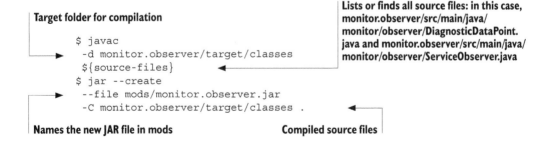

Target folder for compilation

Lists or finds all source files: in this case, monitor.observer/src/main/java/monitor/observer/DiagnosticDataPoint.java and monitor.observer/src/main/java/monitor/observer/ServiceObserver.java

```
$ javac
  -d monitor.observer/target/classes
  ${source-files}
$ jar --create
  --file mods/monitor.observer.jar
  -C monitor.observer/target/classes .
```

Names the new JAR file in mods

Compiled source files

The *monitor.alpha* module does have a dependency, so you have to use the module path to tell the compiler where to find the required artifacts. Packaging with `jar` of course isn't impacted by that:

```
$ javac --module-path mods
 -d monitor.observer.alpha/target/classes
 ${source-files}
$ jar --create
 --file mods/monitor.observer.alpha.jar
 -C monitor.observer.alpha/target/classes .
```

Folder in which javac will search for modules that the code depends on

Most other modules work much the same. One exception is *monitor.rest*, which has third-party dependencies in the `libs` folder, so you need to add that to the module path:

```
$ javac --module-path mods:libs
 -d monitor.rest/target/classes
 ${source-files}
```

The module has dependencies in two folders, so both are added to the module path.

Another exception is *monitor*. You take the opportunity to inform the module system that it has a `main` method that can be used as an entry point into the application:

```
$ javac --module-path mods
 -d monitor/target/classes
 ${source-files}
$ jar --create
 --file mods/monitor.jar
 --main-class monitor.Monitor
 -C monitor/target/classes .
```

Class that contains the application's main method

Figure 2.6 shows what you end up with. These JAR files are just like plain old JARs, with one exception: each contains a module descriptor `module-info.class` that marks it as a modular JAR.

2.7 Running ServiceMonitor

With all the modules compiled into the `mods` folder, you're finally ready to launch the application. As you can see in the following one-liner, this is where some of the hard work that you put into the module declarations pays off:

```
$ java
 --module-path mods:libs
 --module monitor
```

Folders in which java searches for modules

Name of the module to launch

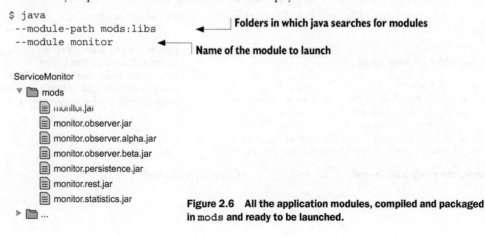

Figure 2.6   All the application modules, compiled and packaged in `mods` and ready to be launched.

ESSENTIAL INFO All you need to do is to call `java`, specify the module path so `java` knows where to find the artifacts your application consists of, and tell it which module to launch. Resolving all dependencies, making sure there are no conflicts or ambiguous situations, and launching with just the right set of modules are handled by the module system.

2.8 Extending a modular code base

Of course, no software project is ever finished (unless it's dead), so change is inevitable. What happens, for example, if you want to add another observer implementation? Usually you'd take these steps:

1 Develop the subproject.
2 Make sure it builds.
3 Use it in existing code.

And this is exactly what you'll do now. For the new module, the module system is content if you add a declaration:

```
module monitor.observer.gamma {
 requires monitor.observer;
 exports monitor.observer.gamma;
}
```

You compile and package the new module just like the others:

```
$ javac --module-path mods
 -d monitor.observer.gamma/target/classes
 ${source-files}
$ jar --create
 --file mods/monitor.observer.gamma.jar
 -C monitor.observer.gamma/target/classes .
```

Then you can add it as a dependency to your existing code:

```
module monitor {
 requires monitor.observer;
 requires monitor.observer.alpha;
 requires monitor.observer.beta;
 requires monitor.observer.gamma;
 requires monitor.statistics;
 requires monitor.persistence;
 requires monitor.rest;
}
```

And you're finished. Assuming a build takes care of compilation and packaging, all you really had to do was add or edit module declarations. This is also true for removing or refactoring modules: beyond the usual work you have to put in, you need to spend a little extra thought on how this impacts your module graph and update the declarations accordingly.

2.9   *Post mortem: Effects of the module system*

All in all, that went pretty well, don't you think? Before exploring the details in the following chapters, let's take some time to look at two of the benefits the module system promises as well as some of the rough edges you can hope to smooth out with more advanced features.

2.9.1   *What the module system does for you*

When discussing the goals of the module system in section 1.5, we talked about the two most important ones: reliable configuration and strong encapsulation. Now that you've built something more concrete, we can revisit those goals and see how they're going to help you deliver robust, maintainable software.

RELIABLE CONFIGURATION

What happens if a dependency is missing from mods? What happens if two dependencies require different versions of the same project—maybe Log4j or Guava? What happens if two modules export the same types, inadvertently or on purpose?

With the class path, these problems would manifest at run time: some would crash the application, whereas others would be more subtle, and arguably more devious, and lead to corrupted application behavior. With the module system in play, many of these unreliable situations, particularly those I just mentioned, would be recognized much earlier. The compiler or JVM would abort with a detailed message and give you a chance to fix the mistake.

This, for example, is the message you get if the application is launched but *monitor .statistics* is missing:

```
> Error occurred during initialization of boot layer
> java.lang.module.FindException:
>     Module monitor.statistics not found,
>     required by monitor
```

Similarly, this is the result of launching the *ServiceMonitor* application with two SLF4J versions present on the module path:

```
> Error occurred during initialization of boot layer
> java.lang.module.FindException:
>     Two versions of module org.slf4j.api found in mods
>     (org.slf4j.api-1.7.25.jar and org.slf4j.api-1.7.7.jar)
```

You can also no longer accidentally depend on your dependencies' dependencies. Hibernate uses SLF4J, which means the library is always present when your application is launched. But as soon as you start importing types from SLF4J (which you don't require in any module declaration), the compiler will stop you, informing you that you're using code from a module you don't explicitly depend on:

```
> monitor.persistence/src/main/java/.../StatisticsRepository.java:4:
>     error: package org.slf4j is not visible
>     (package org.slf4j is declared in module org.slf4j.api,
>      but module monitor.persistence does not read it)
```

Even if you were to trick the compiler, the module system executes the same checks at launch time.

STRONG ENCAPSULATION

Now let's change perspective from being a module's user to being its maintainer. Imagine refactoring code in *monitor.observer.alpha*, maybe in preparation for fixing a bug or to improve performance. After releasing a new version, you find out that you broke some code in *monitor* and made the application unstable. If you changed a public API, it's your fault.

But what if you changed an internal implementation detail in a type that was accessed despite being marked as unsupported? Maybe the type had to be public because you wanted to use it in two packages, or perhaps the authors of *monitor* accessed it via reflection. In that case, there's nothing you could have done to prevent users from depending on your implementation.

With the help of the module system, you can avoid this situation. You already did! Only types in the packages you export are visible. The rest are safe—even from reflection.

> **NOTE** In case you're wondering what you can do if you really need to break into a module, check out sections 7.1 and 12.2.2.

2.9.2 *What else the module system can do for you*

Although the modularization of *ServiceMonitor* went pretty well, there are a couple of rough edges we need to discuss. You won't be able to do anything about them now, but the advanced features presented throughout part 3 of this book will enable you to smooth them out. This section gives you a preview of what's to come.

MARKING INDISPENSABLE MODULE DEPENDENCIES

The modules *monitor.observer.alpha* and *monitor.observer.beta* declare a dependency on *monitor.observer*, which makes sense because they implement the `ServiceObserver` interface that the latter exposes. They also return instances of `DiagnosticDataPoint`, which belongs to the same module.

This has interesting consequences for any code using the implementation modules:

```
ServiceObserver observer = new AlphaServiceObserver("some://service/url");
DiagnosticDataPoint data = observer.gatherDataFromService();
```

The module containing these lines needs to depend on *monitor.observer* as well; otherwise it couldn't see the types `ServiceObserver` and `DiagnosticDataPoint`. The entire *monitor.observer.alpha* module becomes pretty much useless to clients that don't also depend on *monitor.observer*.

Having a module that's usable only if clients remember to explicitly depend on another module is clumsy. Good thing there's a way around that! You'll read about implied readability in section 11.1.

DECOUPLING IMPLEMENTATIONS AND CONSUMERS OF AN API

Thinking about the relationship between *monitor.observer* and the implementing modules, *monitor.observer.alpha* and *monitor.observer.beta*, something else comes to mind. Why does *monitor* have to know the implementations?

As it stands, *monitor* needs to instantiate the concrete classes, but from then on it only interacts with them through the interface. Depending on an entire module to call one constructor seems excessive. And indeed, any time a deprecated `ServiceObserver` implementation is phased out or a new implementation is introduced, you'd have to update *monitor*'s module dependencies and then recompile, package, and redeploy the artifact.

To enable a looser coupling between implementations and consumers of an API, where consumers like *monitor* don't need to depend on implementations like *monitor. observer.alpha* and *monitor.observer.beta*, the module system offers services. They're discussed in chapter 10.

MAKING EXPORTS MORE TARGETED

Remember how the persistence module exported the package that contains the data-transfer objects annotated for use by Hibernate?

```
module monitor.persistence {
  requires monitor.statistics;
  requires hibernate.jpa;
  exports monitor.persistence;
  exports monitor.persistence.entity;
}
```

This doesn't look right—only Hibernate needs to see those entities. But now other modules that depend on *monitor.persistence*, such as *monitor*, can see them, too.

Again, an advanced module system feature has you covered. Qualified exports allow a module to export a package not to everybody, but just to a select list of modules. Section 11.3 introduces that mechanism.

MAKING PACKAGES AVAILABLE TO REFLECTION ONLY

Even exporting a package only to selected modules can be too much:

- You might compile your module against an API (such as the Java Persistence API [JPA]) and not against a concrete implementation (for example, Hibernate), so you're understandably wary of mentioning the implementing module in your qualified exports.
- You might be using a reflection-based tool (like Hibernate or Guice) that only accesses your code at run time via reflection, so why make it accessible at compile time?
- You might be relying on reflection over private members (Hibernate does it when configured for field injection), which doesn't work in exported packages.

A solution is presented in section 12.2, which introduces *open modules* and *open packages*. They make packages available at run time only. In exchange, they allow reflection over private members as is often required by reflection-based tools. Similar to exports, there are *qualified opens*, with which you can open a package to just a selected module.

If you've been using, for example, Hibernate as a JPA provider, you may have worked hard to prevent direct dependencies on Hibernate. In that case, hard-coding a dependency into a module declaration won't be something you look forward to. Section 12.3.5 discusses that scenario in detail.

2.9.3 Allowing optional dependencies

It isn't uncommon for a project to contain code that's executed only if a specific dependency is present in the running application. The module *monitor.statistics*, for example, might contain code using a fancy statistics library that—perhaps due to licensing issues—isn't always present when *ServiceMonitor* launches. Another example is a library with certain features that are interesting to users only if a third dependency is present—maybe a testing framework that cooperates with some assertion library if it's used with the framework.

In such cases, according to what was discussed earlier, the dependency must be required in the module declaration. This forces it to be present at compile time for a successful compilation. Unfortunately, the same `requires` directive means the dependency must also be present at launch time, or the JVM will refuse to run the application.

This is unsatisfactory. But as expected, the module system presents an out: optional dependencies, which must be present at compile time but aren't required at run time. They're discussed in section 11.2. After we've discussed all of these and other advanced features, section 15.1 shows a variant of *ServiceMonitor* that uses most of them.

Each of the three steps of defining, building, and running a modular application has its own chapter: 3, 4, and 5, respectively. All of them are important, but chapter 3 is particularly so because it introduces the fundamental concepts and mechanisms underlying the module system.

Summary

- When you're modularizing an application, you can deduce the module dependencies from type dependencies across module boundaries. This makes creating an initial module-dependency graph a straightforward procedure.
- The directory structure of a multimodule project can be similar to what it would have been before Java 9, so existing tools and approaches will continue to work.
- The module declaration—a `module-info.java` file in the project's root directory—is the most obvious change that the module system brings to coding. It names the module and declares dependencies as well as the public API. Other than that, the way code is written is virtually unchanged.
- The commands `javac`, `jar`, and `java` have been updated to work with modules. The most obvious and relevant change is the module path (command-line option `--module-path` or `-p`). It parallels the class path but is used for modules.

Defining modules and their properties

This chapter covers

- What modules are, and how module declarations define them
- Discerning different types of modules
- Module readability and accessibility
- Understanding the module path
- Building module graphs with module resolution

We've talked a lot about modules already. They're the core building blocks not only of modular applications, but also of a true comprehension of the module system. As such, it's important to build a deeper understanding of what they are and how their properties shape a program's behavior.

Of the three essential steps of defining, building, and running modules, this chapter explores the first (for the other two, see chapters 4 and 5). This chapter explains in detail what a module is and how a module's declaration defines its name, dependencies, and API (section 3.1). Some examples from the JDK give you a first look at the module landscape we're going to explore from Java 9 on and categorize the kinds of modules to help you navigate.

We also discuss how the module system—and, by extension, the compiler and runtime—interact with modules (sections 3.2 and 3.3). Last but not least, we examine the module path and how the module system resolves dependencies and builds a graph from them (section 3.4).

If you want to code along, check out *ServiceMonitor*'s master branch. It contains most of the module declarations shown in this chapter. By the end of the chapter, you'll know how to define a module's name, dependencies, and API and how the module system behaves based on that information. You'll understand the error messages the module system may throw at you and be able to analyze and fix their root cause.

> **Signposts**
>
> This chapter lays the groundwork for everything to come, and thus the rest of the book is connected to it. To make those connections apparent, the chapter includes a lot of forward references. If they bother you, you can ignore them—they will become important when you open this chapter to look something up.

3.1 Modules: The building blocks of modular applications

After all that lofty talk about modules, it's time to get your hands dirty. We'll first look at the two file formats in which you may encounter modules (JMODs and modular JARs) before turning to how you declare a module's properties. Laying some groundwork for easier discussions in the rest of this book, we'll categorize the different kinds of modules.

3.1.1 Java modules (JMODs), shipped with the JDK

During the work on Project Jigsaw, the Java code base was split into about 100 modules, which are delivered in a new format called *JMOD*. It's deliberately unspecified to allow a more aggressive evolution than was possible with the JAR format (which is essentially a ZIP file). It's reserved for use by the JDK, which is why we won't discuss it in depth.

Although we aren't supposed to create JMODs, we can examine them. To see the modules contained in a JRE or JDK, call `java --list-modules`. The information comes from an optimized module storage, the `modules` file in the runtime install's `libs` folder. JDKs (not JREs) also contain the raw modules in a `jmods` folder; and the new `jmod` tool, which you can find in the `bin` folder next to `jmods`, can be used to output their properties with the `describe` operation.

The following snippet shows an example of examining a JMOD file. Here, `jmod` is used to describe *java.sql* on a Linux machine, where JDK 9 is installed in `/opt/jdk-9`. Like most Java modules, *java.sql* uses several of the module system's advanced features, so not all details will be clear by the end of the chapter:

```
$ jmod describe /opt/jdk-9/jmods/java.sql.jmod

> java.sql@9.0.4    ◄─────────────────────────
```

The module's version is recorded in the file as a simple string: here, 9.0.4.

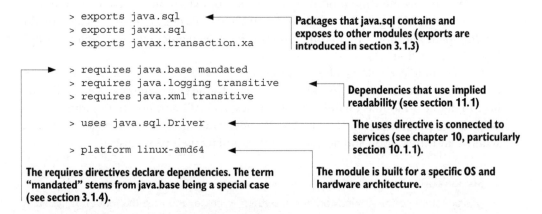

```
> exports java.sql
> exports javax.sql
> exports javax.transaction.xa
```
Packages that java.sql contains and exposes to other modules (exports are introduced in section 3.1.3)

```
> requires java.base mandated
> requires java.logging transitive
> requires java.xml transitive
```
Dependencies that use implied readability (see section 11.1)

```
> uses java.sql.Driver
```
The uses directive is connected to services (see chapter 10, particularly section 10.1.1).

```
> platform linux-amd64
```
The module is built for a specific OS and hardware architecture.

The requires directives declare dependencies. The term "mandated" stems from java.base being a special case (see section 3.1.4).

3.1.2   Modular JARs: Home-grown modules

We aren't supposed to create JMODs, so how do we deliver the modules we create? This is where modular JARs come in.

> **Definition: Modular JAR and module descriptor**
>
> A *modular JAR* is just a plain JAR, except for one small detail. Its root directory contains a *module descriptor*: a `module-info.class` file. (This book calls JARs without a module descriptor *plain JARs*, but that isn't an official term.)

The module descriptor holds all the information needed by the module system to create a run-time representation of the module. All properties of an individual module are represented in this file; consequently, many of the features discussed throughout this book have their counterpart in it, too. Creating such a descriptor from a source file, as covered in the next section, and including it in a JAR allow developers and tools to create modules.

Although the module descriptor allows a modular JAR to be more than a mere class file archive, using it that way isn't mandatory. Clients can choose to use it as a simple JAR, ignoring all module-related properties, by placing it on the class path. This is indispensable for incremental modularizations of existing projects. (Section 8.2 introduces the *unnamed module*.)

3.1.3   Module declarations: Defining a module's properties

So a module descriptor, `module-info.class`, is all you need to turn any old JAR into a module. That begs the question, though, of how you create a descriptor. As the file extension `.class` suggests, it's the result of compiling a source file.

Definition: Module declaration

A module descriptor is compiled from a *module declaration*. By convention, this is a `module-info.java` file in the project's root source folder. The declaration is the pivotal element of modules and thus the module system.

Declaration vs. description

You may be worried that you'll confuse the terms *module declaration* and *module descriptor*. If you do, that's usually not a big deal. The former is source code and the latter bytecode, but they're just different forms of the same idea: something that defines a module's properties. The context often leaves only one option, so it's usually clear which form is meant.

If that doesn't satisfy you, and you want to always get it right, I can help by sharing my mnemonic: lexicographically speaking, *declaration* comes before *descriptor*, which is neat because temporally speaking, you first have the source code and then the bytecode. Both orderings align: first declaration/source, then descriptor/bytes.

The module declaration determines a module's identity and behavior in the module system. Many of the features the following chapters introduce have corresponding directives in the module declaration, presented in due time. For now, let's look at the three basic properties lacking in JARs: a name, explicit dependencies, and encapsulated internals.

 ESSENTIAL INFO This is the structure of a simple `module-info.java` file that defines these three properties:

```
module ${module-name} {
  requires ${module-name};
  exports ${package-name};
}
```

Of course, `${module-name}` and `${package-name}` need to be replaced with actual module and package names.

Take the descriptor of *ServiceMonitor*'s *monitor.statistics* module as an example:

```
module monitor.statistics {
  requires monitor.observer;
  exports monitor.statistics;
}
```

You can easily recognize the structure I just described: the `module` keyword is followed by the module's name, and the body contains `requires` and `exports` directives. The following sections look at the details of declaring these three properties.

> **New keywords?**
>
> You may wonder what the new keywords `module`, `requires`, `exports`, and others in later chapters mean for code that already uses these terms as names for fields, parameters, variables, and other named entities. Fortunately, there's nothing to worry about. These are *restricted keywords*, meaning they act as a keyword only if used in a position where the syntax expects them. So although you can't have a variable named `package` or a module named `byte`, you can have a variable and even a module named `module`.

NAMING MODULES

The most basic property that JARs are missing is a name that the compiler and JVM can use to identify them. So, this is the most prominent characteristic of a module. You'll have the opportunity and even the obligation to give every module you create a name.

 ESSENTIAL INFO   In addition to the `module` keyword, a declaration starts by giving the module a name. This has to be an *identifier*, meaning it must adhere to the same rules as, for example, a package name. Module names are usually lowercase and hierarchically structured with dots.

Naming a module will be fairly natural, because most tools you use on a daily basis already have you name your projects. But although it makes sense to take the project name as a springboard on the search for a module name, it's important to choose wisely!

As you'll see in section 3.2, the module system leans heavily on a module's name. Conflicting or evolving names in particular cause trouble, so it's important that the name is

- Globally unique
- Stable

The best way to achieve this is to use the reverse-domain naming scheme that's commonly used for packages. Together with the limitations for identifiers, this often leads to a module's name being a prefix of the packages it contains. That isn't mandatory, but it's a good sign that both were chosen deliberately.

Keeping the module name and package name prefix in sync emphasizes that a module name change (which would imply a package name change) is one of the most severe breaking changes possible. In the interest of stability, it should be an exceedingly rare event.

For example, the following descriptor names the module *monitor.statistics* (to keep names succinct, the modules making up the *ServiceMonitor* application don't follow the reverse-domain naming scheme):

```
module monitor.statistics {
  // requires and exports truncated
}
```

All other properties are defined within the curly braces following the module's name. No particular order is enforced, but it's common to start off with dependencies before coming to exports.

REQUIRING MODULES TO EXPRESS DEPENDENCIES

Another thing we miss in JARs is the ability to declare dependencies. With JARs, we never know what other artifacts they need to run properly, and we depend on build tools or documentation to determine that. With the module system, dependencies have to be made explicit. (See figure 3.1 for how this plays out.)

> ### Definition: Dependencies
> *Dependencies* are declared with `requires` directives, which consist of the keyword followed by a module name. The directive states that the declared module depends on the named one and requires it during compilation and at run time.

The *monitor.statistics* module has a compile-time and run-time dependency on *monitor.observer*, which is declared with a `requires` directive:

```
module monitor.statistics {
 requires monitor.observer;
 // exports truncated
}
```

If a dependency is declared with a `requires` directive, the module system will throw an error if it can't find a module with that exact name. Compiling as well as launching an application will fail if modules are missing (see section 3.2).

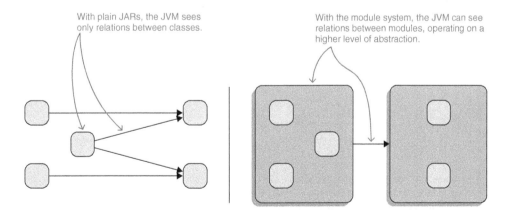

With plain JARs, the JVM sees only relations between classes.

With the module system, the JVM can see relations between modules, operating on a higher level of abstraction.

Figure 3.1   Being able to express dependencies between modules introduces a new layer of abstraction the JVM can reason about. Without them (left), it only sees dependencies between types; but with them (right), it sees dependencies between artifacts much as we tend to.

EXPORTING PACKAGES TO DEFINE A MODULE'S API

Last up are exports, which define a module's public API. Here you can pick and choose which packages contain types that should be available outside the module and which packages are only meant for internal use.

> **Definition: Exported packages**
>
> The keyword `exports` is followed by the name of a package the module contains. Only *exported packages* are usable outside the module; all others are strongly encapsulated within it (see section 3.3).

The module *monitor.statistics* exports a package of the same name:

```
module monitor.statistics {
  requires monitor.observer;
  exports monitor.statistics;
}
```

Note that even though we like to think they are, packages aren't hierarchical! The package `java.util` doesn't contain `java.util.concurrent`; accordingly, exporting the former doesn't expose any types in the latter. This is in line with imports, where `import java.util.*` will import types all from `java.util` but none from `java.util.concurrent` (see figure 3.2).

This implies that if a module wants to export two packages, it always needs two `exports` directives. The module system also offers no wildcards like `exports java.util.*` to make that easier—exposing an API should be a deliberate act.

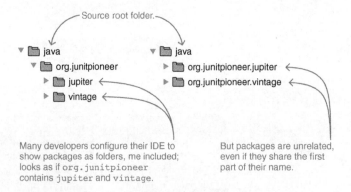

Figure 3.2 **We like to think of packages as hierarchical, where `org.junitpioneer` contains `extension` and `vintage` (left). But that isn't the case! Java is only concerned with full package names and sees no relation between the two (right). This has to be considered when exporting packages. For example, `exports org.junitpioneer` won't export any of the types in `jupiter` or `vintage`.**

EXAMPLE MODULE DECLARATIONS

To get your feet wet, let's look at some real-life module declarations. The most fundamental module is *java.base*, because it contains `java.lang.Object`, a class without which no Java program could function. It's the dependency to end all dependencies: all other modules require it, but it requires nothing else. The dependency on *java.base* is so fundamental that modules don't even have to declare it as the module system fills it in automatically (the following section goes into more detail). Although it depends on nothing, it exports a whopping 116 packages, so I'll only show a heavily truncated version of it:

```
module java.base {
 exports java.lang;
 exports java.math;
 exports java.nio;
 exports java.util;
 // many, many more exports
 // use of fancy features is truncated
}
```

A much simpler module is *java.logging*, which exposes the `java.util.logging` package:

```
module java.logging {
 exports java.util.logging;
}
```

To see a module that requires another, let's turn to *java.rmi*. It creates log messages and accordingly depends on *java.logging* for that. The API it exposes can be found in `java.rmi` and other packages with that prefix:

```
module java.rmi {
 requires java.logging;
 exports java.rmi;
 // exports of other `java.rmi.*` packages
 // use of fancy features is truncated
}
```

For more examples, flip back to section 2.2.3, particularly the code that declares the modules of the *ServiceMonitor* applications.

3.1.4 *The many types of modules*

Think of an application you're working on at the moment. There's a good chance it consists of a number of JARs, which, at some point in the future, will likely all be modules. They aren't the only ones making up the application, though. The JDK was also split into modules, and they will become part of your consideration, as well. But wait, there's more! In this set of modules, some have characteristics that make it necessary to call them out specifically.

- *Application modules*—A non-JDK module; the modules Java developers create for their own projects, be they libraries, frameworks, or applications. These are found on the module path. For the time being, they will be modular JARs (see section 3.1.2).
- *Initial module*—Application module where compilation starts (for `javac`) or containing the `main` method (for `java`). Section 5.1.1 shows how to specify it when launching the application with the `java` command. The compiler also has a use for the concept: as explained in section 4.3.5, it defines which module the compilation starts with.
- *Root modules*—Where the JPMS starts resolving dependencies (a process explained in detail in section 3.4.1). In addition to containing the main class or the code to compile, the initial module is also a root module. In tricky situations you'll encounter further into the book, it can become necessary to define root modules beyond the initial one (as explained in section 3.4.3).
- *Platform modules*—Modules that make up the JDK. These are defined by the Java SE Platform Specification (prefixed with *java.*) as well as JDK-specific modules (prefixed with *jdk.*). As discussed in section 3.1.1, they're stored in optimized form in a `modules` file in the runtime's `libs` directory.
- *Incubator modules*—Nonstandard platform modules whose names always start with *jdk.incubator*. They contain experimental APIs that could benefit from being tested by adventurous developers before being set in stone.
- *System modules*—In addition to creating a run-time image from a subset of platform modules, `jlink` can also include application modules. The platform and application modules found in such an image are collectively called its *system modules*. To list them, use the `java` command in the image's `bin` directory and call `java --list-modules`.
- *Observable modules*—All platform modules in the current runtime as well as all application modules specified on the command line; modules that the JPMS can use to fulfill dependencies. Taken together, these modules make up the *universe of observable modules*.
- *Base module*—The distinction between application and platform modules exists only to make communication easier. To the module system, all modules are the same, except one: the platform module *java.base*, the so-called base module, plays a particular role.

Platform modules and most application modules have module descriptors that are given to them by the module's creator. Do other modules exist? Yes:

- *Explicit modules*—Platform modules and most application modules that have module descriptors given to them by the module's creator.
- *Automatic modules*—Named modules without a module description (spoiler: plain JARs on the module path). These are application modules created by the runtime, not a developer.
- *Named modules*—The set of explicit modules and automatic modules. These modules have a name, either defined by a descriptor or inferred by the JPMS.
- *Unnamed modules*—Modules that aren't named (spoiler: class path content) and hence aren't explicit.

Both automatic and unnamed modules become relevant in the context of migrating an application to the module system—a topic discussed in depth in chapter 8. To get a better sense of how these types of modules relate to one another, see figure 3.3.

To apply these terms to an example, let's turn to the *ServiceMonitor* application we explored in chapter 2. It consists of seven modules (*monitor, monitor.observer, monitor.rest,* and so forth) plus the external dependencies Spark and Hibernate and their transitive dependencies.

When it's launched, the folders containing its seven modules and its dependencies are specified on the command line. Together with the platform modules in the JRE or

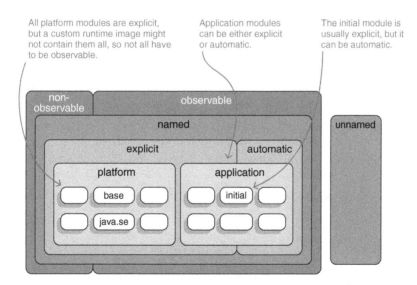

Figure 3.3 **Most types of modules, organized in a handy diagram. The modules shipped with the JDK are called platform modules, with the base module at their center. Then there are application modules, one of which must be the initial module, which contains the application's** `main` **method. (Root, system, and incubator modules aren't shown.)**

JDK that's running the application, they form the universe of observable modules. This is the pool of modules from which the module system will try to fulfill all dependencies.

ServiceMonitor's modules as well as those making up its dependencies, Hibernate and Spark, are the application modules. Because it contains the main method, *monitor* is the initial module—no other root modules are required. The only platform module the program depends on directly is the base module *java.base*, but Hibernate and Spark pull in further modules like *java.sql* and *java.xml*. Because this is a brand-new application and all dependencies are assumed to be modularized, this isn't a migration scenario; hence, no automatic or unnamed modules are involved.

Now that you know what types of modules exist and how to declare them, it's time to explore how Java processes this information.

3.2   *Readability: Connecting the pieces*

Modules are the atomic building blocks: the nodes in a graph of interacting artifacts. But there can be no graph without edges connecting the nodes! This is where *readability* comes in, based on which the module system will create connections between nodes.

> **Definition: Readability edge**
>
> When a module *customer* requires a module *bar* in its declaration, then at run time *customer* will *read bar* or, conversely, *bar* will be readable by *customer* (see figure 3.4). The connection between the two modules is called a *readability edge*, or *reads edge* for short.

Whereas phrases like "*customer* requires *bar*" and "*customer* depends on *bar*" mirror a static, compile-time relationship between *customer* and *bar*, readability is its more dynamic, run-time counterpart. Why is it more dynamic? The requires directive is the primal originator of reads edges, but it's by no means the only one. Others are command-line options (see --add-reads in section 3.4.4) and the reflection API (see section 12.3.4), both of which can be used to add more; in the end, it's irrelevant. Regardless of how reads edges come to be, their effects are always the same: they're the basis for reliable configuration and accessibility (see section 3.3).

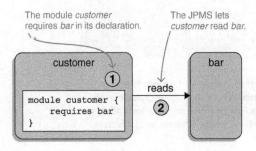

Figure 3.4   **The module *customer* requires the module *bar* in its descriptor (1). Based on that, the module system will let *customer* read *bar* at run time (2).**

3.2.1 Achieving reliable configuration

As described in section 1.5.1, reliable configuration aims to ensure that the particular configuration of artifacts a Java program is compiled against or launched with can sustain the program without spurious run-time errors. To this end, it performs a couple of checks (during module resolution, a process explained in section 3.4.1).

 ESSENTIAL INFO The module system checks whether the universe of observable modules contains all required dependencies, direct and transitive, and reports an error if something's missing. There must be no ambiguity: no two artifacts can claim they're the same module. This is particularly interesting in the case where two versions of the same module are present—because the module system has no concept of versions (see chapter 13), it treats this as a duplicate module. Accordingly, it reports an error if it runs into this situation. There must be no static dependency cycles between modules. At run time, it's possible and even necessary for modules to access each other (think about code using Spring annotations and Spring reflecting over that code), but these must not be *compile* dependencies (Spring is obviously not compiled against the code it reflects over). Packages should have a unique origin, so no two modules must contain types in the same package. If they do, this is called a *split package*, and the module system will refuse to compile or launch such configurations. This is particularly interesting in the context of migration because some existing libraries and frameworks split packages on purpose (see section 7.2).

This verification of course isn't airtight, and it's possible for problems to hide long enough to crash a running application. If, for example, the wrong version of a module ends up in the right place, the application will launch (all required modules are present) but will crash later, when, for example, a class or method is missing.

Because the module system is developed to exhibit consistent behavior across compile time and run time, these errors can be further minimized by basing compilation and launch on the same artifacts. (In the example, the compilation against the module with the wrong version would have failed.)

3.2.2 Experimenting with unreliable configurations

Let's try to break things! What are some unreliable configurations the module system detects? To investigate, we'll turn to the *ServiceMonitor* application introduced in chapter 2.

MISSING DEPENDENCIES

Consider *monitor.observer.alpha* and its declaration:

```
module monitor.observer.alpha {
  requires monitor.observer;
  exports monitor.observer.alpha;
}
```

This is what it looks like to try to compile it with *monitor.observer* missing:

```
> monitor.observer.alpha/src/main/java/module-info.java:2:
>     error: module not found: monitor.observer
>         requires monitor.observer
>                                ^
> 1 error
```

If the module is present at compile time but gets lost on the way to the launch pad, the JVM will quit with the following error:

```
> Error occurred during initialization of boot layer
> java.lang.module.FindException:
>     Module monitor.observer not found,
>     required by monitor.observer.alpha
```

Although it makes sense to enforce the presence of all transitively required modules at launch time, the same can't be said for the compiler. Accordingly, if an indirect dependency is missing, the compiler emits neither a warning nor an error, as you can see in the following example.

These are the module declarations of *monitor.persistence* and *monitor.statistics*:

```
module monitor.persistence {
  requires monitor.statistics;
  exports monitor.persistence;
}

module monitor.statistics {
  requires monitor.observer;
  exports monitor.statistics;
}
```

It's clear that *monitor.persistence* doesn't require *monitor.observer* directly, so compilation of *monitor.persistence* succeeds even if *monitor.observer* isn't on the module path.

Launching an application with a missing transitive dependency won't work. Even if the initial module doesn't directly depend on it, some other module does, so it will be reported as missing. The branch break-missing-transitive-dependency in the *ServiceMonitor* repository creates a configuration where a missing module leads to an error message.

DUPLICATE MODULES

Because modules reference one another by name, any situation where two modules claim to have the same name is ambiguous. Which one is correct to pick is highly dependent on the context and not something the module system can generally decide. So instead of making a potentially bad decision, it makes none at all, and instead produces an error. Failing fast like this allows the developer to notice the problem and fix it before it causes any more issues.

This is the compile error the module system produces when trying to compile a module with two variants of *monitor.observer.beta* on the module path:

```
> error: duplicate module on application module path
```

```
>      module in monitor.observer.beta
> 1 error
```

Note that the compiler can't link the error to one of the files under compilation because they aren't the reason for the problem. Instead, the artifacts on the module path are causing the error.

When the error goes undetected until the JVM is launched, it gives a more precise message that lists the JAR filenames as well:

```
> Error occurred during initialization of boot layer
> java.lang.module.FindException:
>     Two versions of module monitor.observer.beta found in mods
>     (monitor.observer.beta.jar and monitor.observer.gamma.jar)
```

As we discussed in section 1.5.6 and further explored in section 13.1, the module system has no concept of versions, so in this case the same error will occur. I'd say it's a good guess that the vast majority of duplicate-module errors will be caused by having the same module in several versions on the module path.

 ESSENTIAL INFO Ambiguity checks are only applied to individual module path entries! (That sentence may leave you scratching your head—I'll explain what I mean in section 3.4.1, but I wanted to mention it here so this important fact isn't left out.)

The module system also throws the duplicate module error if the module isn't actually required. It suffices that the module path *contains* it! Two of the reasons for that are services and optional dependencies, which are presented in chapter 10 and section 11.2. The *ServiceMonitor* branch break-duplicate-modules-even-if-unrequired creates an error message due to a duplicate module even though it isn't required.

DEPENDENCY CYCLES

Accidentally creating cyclic dependencies isn't hard, but getting them past the compiler is. It isn't even straightforward to *present* them to the compiler. In order to do that, you'd have to solve the chicken-and-egg problem that if two projects depend on each other, it isn't possible to compile one without the other. If you tried, you'd have missing dependencies and get the corresponding errors.

One way to get past this is to compile both modules at once, starting with both the chicken and the egg at the same time, so to speak; section 4.3 explains how. Suffice it to say, if there's a cyclic dependency between the modules being compiled, the module system recognizes that and causes a compile error. This is how it looks if *monitor.persistence* and *monitor.statistics* depend on each other:

```
> monitor.statistics/src/main/java/module-info.java:3:
>     error: cyclic dependence involving monitor.persistence
>         requires monitor.persistence;
>                          ^
> 1 error
```

Another way to go about this is to establish the cyclic dependency not at once but over time, *after* a valid configuration is already built. Let's once more turn to *monitor.persistence* and *monitor.statistics*:

```
module monitor.persistence {
 requires monitor.statistics;
 exports monitor.persistence;
}

module monitor.statistics {
 requires monitor.observer;
 exports monitor.statistics;
}
```

This configuration is fine and compiles without problems. Now the trickery begins: compile the modules and keep the JARs around. Then change the module declaration of *monitor.statistics* to require *monitor.persistence*, which creates a cyclic dependency (the change doesn't make much sense in this example, but in more-complex applications it often does):

```
module monitor.statistics {
 requires monitor.observer;
 requires monitor.persistence;
 exports monitor.statistics;
}
```

The next step is to compile just the changed *monitor.statistics* with the already-compiled modules on the module path. This must include *monitor.persistence*, because the statistics module now depends on it. In turn, the persistence module still declares its dependency on *monitor.statistics*, which is the second half of the dependency cycle. Unfortunately, for this round of hacking, the module system recognizes the cycle and causes the same compile error as before.

Taking the shell game to the next level finally tricks the compiler. In this scenario, two completely unrelated modules—let's pick *monitor.persistence* and *monitor.rest*—are compiled into modular JARs. Then comes the sleight of hand:

One dependency is added, say from *persistence* to *rest*, and the changed *persistence* is compiled against the original set of modules. This works because the original *rest* doesn't depend on *persistence*.

The second dependency, *rest* to *persistence*, is added, but *rest* is also compiled against the original set of modules, including the version of *persistence* that doesn't yet depend on it. As a consequence, it can be compiled as well.

Confused? Look at figure 3.5 to get another perspective.

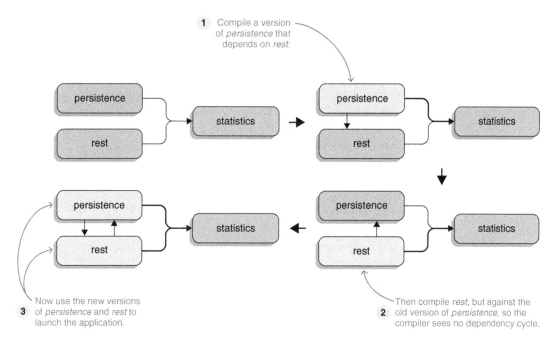

Figure 3.5 Getting dependency cycles past the compiler isn't easy. Here it's done by picking two unrelated modules, *persistence* and *rest* (both depend on *statistics*), and then adding dependencies from one to the other. It's important to compile rest against the old *persistence* so the cycle doesn't show and compilation passes. In a final step, both original modules can be replaced with the newly compiled ones that have the cyclic dependency between them.

Now there are versions of *monitor.persistence* and *monitor.rest* that depend on each other. For this to happen in real life, the compilation process—maybe managed by a build tool—must be in serious disarray (but that isn't unheard of). Luckily, the module system has your back and reports the error when the JVM is launched with such a configuration:

```
> Error occurred during initialization of boot layer
> java.lang.module.FindException:
>       Cycle detected:
>           monitor.persistence
>               -> monitor.rest
>               -> monitor.persistence
```

All the examples show a cyclic dependency between two artifacts, but the module system detects cycles of all lengths. It's good that it does! Changing code always risks breaking upstream functionality, meaning other code that uses the code that's being changed—either directly or transitively.

If dependencies go in one direction, there's only so much code a change can impact. On the other hand, if dependencies can form cycles, then all code in that cycle and all that depends on it can be affected. Particularly if cycles are large, this can quickly turn into *all* the code being affected, and I'm sure you agree you want to avoid that. And the module system isn't alone in helping you here—so is your build tool, which also bristles at dependency cycles.

SPLIT PACKAGES

A split package occurs when two modules contain types in the same package. For example, recall that the *monitor.statistics* module contains a class `Statistician` in the `monitor.statistics` package. Now let's assume the monitor module contained a simple fallback implementation, `SimpleStatistician`, and to promote uniformity, it's in monitor's own `monitor.statistics` package.

When trying to compile *monitor*, you get the following error:

```
> monitor/src/main/java/monitor/statistics/SimpleStatistician.java:1:
>     error: package exists in another module: monitor.statistics
>         package monitor.statistics;
>         ^
> 1 error
```

 ESSENTIAL INFO   Interestingly, the compiler shows an error only if the module under compilation can access the split package in the other module. That means the split package must be exported.

To try this, let's go a different route: `SimpleStatistician` is gone, and this time it's *monitor.statistics* that creates the split package. In an attempt to reuse some utility methods, it creates a `Utils` class in the `monitor` package. It has no desire to share that class with other modules, so it continues to only export the `monitor.statistics` package.

Compiling *monitor.statistics* is error-free, which makes sense because it doesn't require *monitor* and is hence unaware of the split package. It gets interesting when the time comes to compile *monitor*. It depends on *monitor.statistics*, and both contain types in the package monitor. But, as I just mentioned, because *monitor.statistics* doesn't export the package, compilation works.

Great! Now it's time to launch:

```
> Error occurred during initialization of boot layer
> java.lang.reflect.LayerInstantiationException:
>     Package monitor in both module monitor.statistics and module monitor
```

That didn't go well. The module system checks for split packages on launch, and here it doesn't matter whether they're exported or not: no two modules can contain types in the same package. As you'll see in section 7.2, this can turn into a problem when migrating code to Java 9.

The *ServiceMonitor* repository demonstrates the split-package problem at compile and at run time in the branches `break-split-package-compilation` and `break-split-package-launch`.

THE MODULAR DIAMOND OF DEATH

A particularly devious mixture of split packages and missing dependencies is the *modular diamond of death* (see figure 3.6). Assume a module changed its name between two

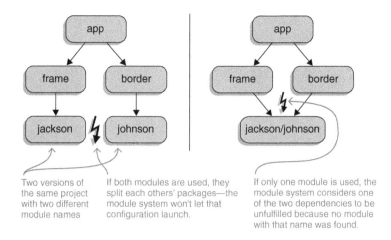

Figure 3.6 **If a module changes its name (here, *jackson* to *johnson*), projects that depend on it twice (here, app via frame and border) can end up facing the modular diamond of death: They depend on the same project but by two different names.**

releases: one of your dependencies requires it by its old name, and another dependency requires it by its new name. Now you need the same code to appear under two different module names, but the JPMS isn't going to let that happen.

You'll have one of the following situations:

- One modular JAR, which can only appear as one module with one name and will thus trigger an error because one dependency couldn't be fulfilled
- Two modular JARs with different names but the same packages, which will cause the split-package error you just observed

 ESSENTIAL INFO You should avoid this situation at all costs! If you're publishing artifacts to a public repository, you should carefully consider whether renaming your module is necessary. If it is, you may also want to change the package names, so people can use old and new modules side by side. If you end up in this situation as a user, you may be lucky to get away with creating an aggregator module (see section 11.1.5) or editing module descriptors (see section 9.3.3).

3.3 *Accessibility: Defining public APIs*

With modules and the read edges in place, you know how the module system constructs the graph you have in mind. To keep that graph from behaving like the ball of mud you wanted to escape, there's one more requirement: the ability to hide a module's internals so no outside code can access it. This is where *accessibility* comes in.

Definition: Accessibility

A type `Drink` in a module *bar* is *accessible* to code in a module *customer* if all of the following conditions are fulfilled (see figure 3.7):

- `Drink` is public.
- `Drink` belongs to a package that *bar* exports.
- *customer* reads *bar*.

For an accessible type's members (meaning its fields, methods, and nested classes), the usual visibility rules hold: public members are fully accessible, and protected members only to inheriting classes. Technically, package-private members are accessible in the same package, but as you saw in the previous section, that isn't helpful due to the rule against split packages across modules.

NOTE   The definition of accessibility includes the module that wants to access the type. In this sense, a type is never "accessible" but only "accessible to a particular module." It's common, though, to use the same term even if no other module is in sight and say that a type is *accessible* if it's public and in an exported package. Any module is then free to access the type by reading the module that contains it.

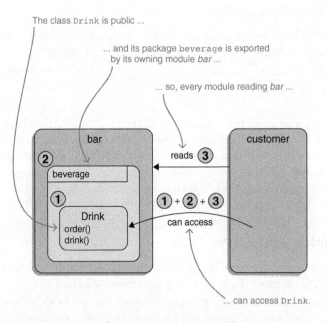

Figure 3.7   The module *bar* contains a public type `Drink` (1) in an exported package (2). The module *customer* reads the module *bar* (3), so all requirements are fulfilled for code in customer to access `Drink`. Want to know what happens if some aren't fulfilled? Check section 3.3.3.

To understand how accessibility shapes a module's public API, it's important to understand that term first: what is the *public API?*

> ### Definition: Public API
>
> In nontechnical terms, a module's *public API* is everything that can't be changed without causing compile errors in code that uses it. (In general, the term also includes a specification of run-time behavior, but because the module system doesn't operate in that dimension, I'll ignore it in this book.) More technically speaking, a module's public API consists of the following:
>
> - Names of all public types in exported packages
> - Names and type names of public and protected fields
> - Names, argument type names, and return type names of all public and protected methods (called *method signatures*)

In case you find it weird that I'm suddenly talking about names, think about what you can change in a type while keeping dependent code from outside the package compiling. Private and package-visible fields? Definitely! Private and package-visible methods? Sure. Bodies of public methods? Yes. What needs to stay untouched are the names of everything that other code may be compiled against: the type's name, the signature of public methods, and so forth.

Looking over the definition of what makes a public API, it becomes clear that the module system changes things from before Java 9 on the level of packages (must be exported) and types (must be public). Within a type, on the other hand, nothing changed, and a type's public API is the same in Java 8 as in Java 9 and later.

3.3.1 Achieving strong encapsulation

 ESSENTIAL INFO If a type isn't accessible, it isn't possible to interact with it in any way specific to that type: you can't instantiate it, access its fields, invoke methods, or use nested classes. The phrase "specific to that type" is a little unusual—what does it mean? That it's possible to interact with a type's members if they're defined in an accessible supertype like an interface the type implements or, ultimately, `Object`. This is much like before Java 9, where a non-public implementation of a public interface could be used, but only through that interface.

As an example, consider a high-performance library *superfast* with custom implementations of the known Java collections. Let's focus on a hypothetical `SuperfastHashMap` class, which implements Java's `Map` interface and is not accessible (maybe it is package visible in an exported package, maybe the package is not exported at all).

If code outside the *superfast* module gets a `SuperfastHashMap` instance (maybe from a factory), then it's limited to using it as a `Map`. It can't assign it to a variable of type `SuperfastHashMap` and can't call `superfastGet` on it (even if that method is public) but everything that's defined on accessible supertypes like `Map` and `Object` is no problem. (See figure 3.8.)

The accessibility rules make it possible to expose carefully selected features while strongly encapsulating a module's internals, making sure no outside code can depend on implementation details. Interestingly, this includes reflection, which can't bypass the rules either if used across module boundaries! (We're going to talk about reflection throughout the rest of the chapter—if you need to catch up on the basics, see appendix B.)

Maybe you're wondering how reflection-based libraries like Spring, Guice, Hibernate, and others will work in the future, or how code will be able to break into a module if it absolutely has to. There are a few ways to give or gain access:

- Regular exports (see section 3.1)
- Qualified export (see section 11.3)
- Open modules and open packages (see section 12.2)
- Command-line options (summarized in section 7.1)

Chapter 12 explores reflection in more depth.

But let's go back to the three conditions that are the premise for accessibility (public type, exported package, reading module). They have interesting consequences.

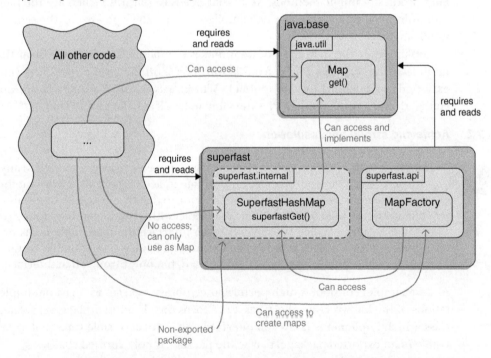

Figure 3.8   The inaccessible type `SuperfastHashMap` implements the accessible `Map` interface.
Code outside of the *superfast* module, if it gets hold of an instance, can use it as a `Map` and as an
`Object`, but never in ways specific to that type: for example, by calling `superfastGet`. Code in the
***superfast* module is unrestricted by accessibility and can use the type as usual: for example, to create**
instances and return them.

ESSENTIAL INFO For one, `public` is no longer *public*. It's no longer possible to tell by looking at a type whether it will be visible outside of the module—for that, it's necessary to check `module-info.java` or trust the IDE to highlight exported packages or types. Without `requires` directives, *all* types in a module are inaccessible to the outside. Encapsulation is the new default!

The three conditions also imply that you can also no longer accidentally rely on transitive dependencies. Let's see why.

3.3.2 *Encapsulating transitive dependencies*

Without the module system, it's possible to use types from a JAR that a dependency draws in but that isn't declared as a dependency. Once a project uses types this way, the build configuration no longer reflects the true set of dependencies, which can lead to anything from uninformed architectural decisions to run-time errors.

As an example, let's say a project is using Spring, which depends on OkHttp. Writing code that uses types from OkHttp is as easy as letting the IDE add the import statements it helpfully suggests. The code will compile and run because the build tool will make sure Spring and all its dependencies, including OkHttp, are present at all times. This makes it unnecessary to declare the dependency on OkHttp, so it's easily forgotten. (See figure 3.9.)

As a consequence, a dependency analysis of the project would deliver misleading results, based on which problematic decisions could be made. The OkHttp version also isn't fixed and depends entirely on what Spring uses. If that version is updated, the code depending on OkHttp is silently running on a different version, creating the real risk that the program will misbehave or crash at run time.

Due to the module system's requirement that the accessing module must read the accessed module, this can no longer happen. Unless the project declares its dependency on OkHttp by using a `requires` directive, the module system won't allow it to access OkHttp's classes. This way it forces you to keep your configuration up to date.

Note that modules have the ability to pass their own dependencies on to modules that depend on them with a feature called *implied readability*. Check section 11.11 for details.

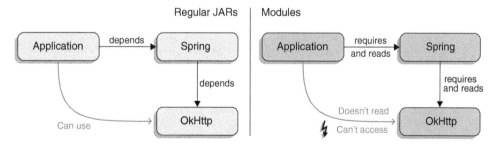

Figure 3.9 Without modules, it's easy to accidentally depend on transitive dependencies as in this example, where the application depends on OkHttp, which is pulled in by Spring. With modules, on the other hand, dependencies have to be declared with `requires` directives to be able to access them. The application doesn't require OkHttp and so can't access it.

3.3.3 *Encapsulation skirmishes*

As we did with readability, let's break things! But before we do so, I want to show a scenario that follows all the rules and works. Once again, it's based on the *ServiceMonitor* application introduced in chapter 2.

For the sake of these examples, assume that the module *monitor.observer* contained in its package `monitor.observer` a class `DisconnectedServiceObserver`. What it does is irrelevant: what counts is that it implements `ServiceObserver`, that it has a constructor that doesn't require any arguments, and that the monitor module uses it.

The module *monitor.observer* exports `monitor.observer` and `DisconnectedService-Observer` is public. This fulfills the first two accessibility requirements, so other modules can access it *if* they read *monitor.observer*. The module *monitor* fulfills that precondition, too, because it requires *module.observer* in its module declaration. Taken together (figure 3.10 and listing 3.1), all requirements are fulfilled, and code in *monitor* can access `DisconnectedServiceObserver`. Accordingly, compilation and execution are error-free. Let's fiddle with the details and watch how the module system reacts.

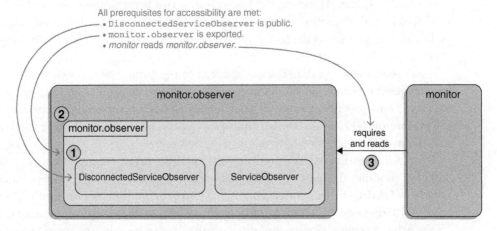

Figure 3.10 `DisconnectedServiceObserver` **is public (1) and in a package exported by** `monitor.observer` **(2). Because the monitor module reads** `monitor.observer` **(3), code in it can use** `DisconnectedServiceObserver`**.**

Listing 3.1 `DisconnectedServiceObserver`, **accessible by** *monitor*

```
// --- TYPE DisconnectedServiceObserver ---
package monitor.observer;

public class DisconnectedServiceObserver   //
  implements ServiceObserver {
 // class body truncated
}

// --- MODULE DECLARATION monitor.observer ---
module monitor.observer {
  exports monitor.observer;   //
}
```

Public monitor.observer.
DisconnectedServiceObserver

The module monitor.observer exports
the package monitor.observer.

```
// --- MODULE DECLARATION monitor ---
module monitor {
 requires monitor.observer;  //
 // other requires directives truncated
}
```

The module monitor requires and thus eventually reads monitor.observer.

TYPE NOT PUBLIC

If `DisconnectedServiceObserver` is made package-visible, compilation of *monitor* fails. More precisely, the import causes the first error:

```
> monitor/src/main/java/monitor/Monitor.java:4: error:
>     DisconnectedServiceObserver is not public in monitor.observer;
>     cannot be accessed from outside package
> import monitor.observer.DisconnectedServiceObserver;
>                         ^
```

Accessing package-visible types from another package wasn't possible before Java 9, either, and for that reason the error message is nothing new—you'd get the same one without the module system in play.

Similarly, if you bypass the compiler checks by recompiling just the *monitor.observer* module after `DisconnectedServiceObserver` is made package-visible and then launching the entire application, the error is the same as without the module system:

```
> Exception in thread "main" java.lang.IllegalAccessError:
>     failed to access class monitor.observer.DisconnectedServiceObserver
>     from class monitor.Monitor
```

Before Java 9, it was possible to use the reflection API to access the type at run time, and this is something strong encapsulation prevents. Consider the following code:

```
Constructor<?> constructor = Class
 .forName("monitor.observer.DisconnectedServiceObserver")
 .getDeclaredConstructor();
constructor.setAccessible(true);
ServiceObserver observer = (ServiceObserver) constructor.newInstance();
```

In Java 8 and before, this works regardless of whether `DisconnectedServiceObserver` is public or package-visible. In Java 9 and later, the module system prevents access if `DisconnectedServiceObserver` is package-visible, and the call to `setAccessible` causes an exception:

```
> Exception in thread "main" java.lang.reflect.InaccessibleObjectException:
>     Unable to make monitor.observer.DisconnectedServiceObserver()
>     accessible: module monitor.observer does not "opens monitor.observer"
>     to module monitor
```

The *ServiceMonitor* repository's branch `break-reflection-over-internals` demonstrates the behavior shown here. The complaint that *monitor.observer* doesn't open *monitor.observer* points toward one solution for this problem—something section 12.2 explores.

PACKAGE NOT EXPORTED

Next on the list of requirements is that the package containing the accessed type must be exported. To toy with that, let's make `DisconnectedServiceObserver` public again but move it into another package *monitor.observer.dis*, which *monitor.observer* doesn't export. The imports in *monitor* are updated to the new package:

```
> monitor/src/main/java/monitor/Monitor.java:4: error:
>     package monitor.observer.dis does not exist
> import monitor.observer.dis.DisconnectedServiceObserver;
>                            ^
> (package monitor.observer.dis is declared in module
>  monitor.observer, which does not export it)
```

That's pretty straightforward.

To see how the runtime fares in this case, you need to bypass the compiler checks. To that end, edit *monitor.observer* to export *monitor.observer.dis*, compile all modules, and then compile *monitor.observer* once again without that export. You can launch the application as before and provoke a run-time error:

```
> Exception in thread "main" java.lang.IllegalAccessError:
>     class monitor.Monitor (in module monitor) cannot access class
>     monitor.observer.dis.DisconnectedServiceObserver (in module
>     monitor.observer) because module monitor.observer does not export
>     monitor.observer.dis to module monitor
```

Like the compiler, the runtime is pretty talkative and explains what the problem is. The same is true for the reflection API when you try to make the constructor accessible, so you can create an instance of `DisconnectedServiceObserver`:

```
> Exception in thread "main" java.lang.reflect.InaccessibleObjectException:
>     Unable to make public
>     monitor.observer.dis.DisconnectedServiceObserver() accessible:
>     module monitor.observer does not "exports monitor.observer.dis"
>     to module monitor
```

If you look closely, you'll see that both the runtime and the reflection API talk about exporting a package *to* a module. That's called a *qualified export* (explained in section 11.3).

MODULE NOT READ

The last requirement on the list is that the exporting module must be read by the one accessing the type. Removing the `requires monitor.observer` directive from *monitor*'s module declaration leads to the expected compile-time error:

```
> monitor/src/main/java/monitor/Monitor.java:3: error:
>     package monitor.observer is not visible
> import monitor.observer.DiagnosticDataPoint;
>                        ^
> (package monitor.observer is declared in module
>  monitor.observer, but module monitor does not read it)
```

To see how the runtime reacts to a missing `requires` directive, first compile the entire application with a working configuration, meaning *monitor* reads *monitor.observer*. Then remove the `requires` directive from monitor's `module-info.java`, and recompile just that file. This way, the module's code is compiled with a module declaration that still requires *monitor.observer*, but the runtime will see a module description that claims nothing of the kind. As expected, the result is a run-time error:

```
> Exception in thread "main" java.lang.IllegalAccessError:
>     class monitor.Monitor (in module monitor) cannot access class
>     monitor.observer.DisconnectedServiceObserver (in module
>     monitor.observer) because module monitor does not read module
>     monitor.observer
```

Again, the error message is pretty clear.

Finally, let's turn to reflection. You can use the same compilation trick to create a monitor module that doesn't read *monitor.observer*. And reuse the reflection code from earlier when `DisconnectedServiceObserver` wasn't public but you wanted to create an instance anyway.

Surely running these modules together fails as well, right? Yes, it does, but not the way you may have expected:

```
> Exception in thread "main" java.lang.IllegalAccessError:
>     class monitor.Monitor (in module monitor) cannot access class
>     monitor.observer.ServiceObserver (in module monitor.observer)
>     because module monitor does not read module monitor.observer
```

Why is the error message complaining about `ServiceObserver`? Because that type is also in *monitor.observer*, which *monitor* no longer reads. Let's change the reflection code to only use `Object`:

```
Constructor<?> constructor = Class
  .forName("monitor.observer.DisconnectedServiceObserver")
  .getDeclaredConstructor();
constructor.setAccessible(true);
Object observer = constructor.newInstance();
```

Run this—it works! But what about the missing read edge, you may ask? The answer is simple but a little surprising at first: the reflection API fills it in automatically. Section 12.3.1 explores the reasons behind that.

3.4 The module path: Letting Java know about modules

You now know how to define modules and their essential properties. What's still a little unclear is how you tell the compiler and runtime about them. Chapter 4 looks into building modules from source to JAR, and you'll quickly run into the situation where you need to reference existing modules the code under compilation depends on. The situation is the same in chapter 5, where the runtime needs to know about the application modules, so you can launch one of them.

Before Java 9, you would have used the class path, which had plain JARs on it (see appendix A for a quick class-path recap), to inform compiler and runtime where to find artifacts. They search it when they're looking for individual types required during compilation or execution.

The module system, on the other hand, promises not to operate on types, but to go one level above them and manage modules instead. One way this approach is expressed is a new concept that parallels the class path but expects modules instead of bare types or plain JARs.

Definition: Module path

The *module path* is a list whose elements are artifacts or directories that contain artifacts. Depending on the OS, module path elements are separated by : (Unix-based) or ; (Windows). It's used by the module system to locate required modules that aren't found among the platform modules. Both `javac` and `java` as well as other module-related commands can process it—the command-line options are `--module-path` and `-p`.

Listing 3.2 shows how the *ServiceMonitor* application's monitor module could be compiled, packaged, and launched. It uses `--module-path` to point to the directory mods, which you assume contains all required dependencies as modular JARs. For details on compilation, packaging, and launching, see sections 4.2, 4.5, and 5.1.

Listing 3.2   Compiling, packaging, and launching *monitor*

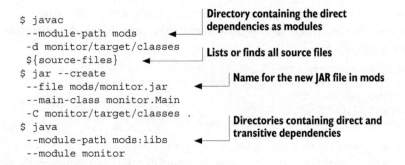

```
$ javac
  --module-path mods          ◄─── Directory containing the direct
  -d monitor/target/classes        dependencies as modules
  ${source-files}             ◄─── Lists or finds all source files
$ jar --create
  --file mods/monitor.jar     ◄─── Name for the new JAR file in mods
  --main-class monitor.Main
  -C monitor/target/classes .
$ java                        ◄─── Directories containing direct and
  --module-path mods:libs          transitive dependencies
  --module monitor
```

 ESSENTIAL INFO   It's important to clarify that *only the module path* processes artifacts as modules. Armed with that knowledge, you can be a little more precise about what constitutes the universe of observable modules. In section 3.1.4, it's defined as follows: all platform modules in the current runtime as well as all application modules specified on the command line are called *observable*, and together they make up the *universe of observable modules*.

The phrase "modules specified on the command line" is a little vague. Now you know that they're artifacts that can be found on the module path.

Note that I said *artifacts*, not *modules*! Not only modular JARs but also plain ones will, when placed on the module path, be turned into modules and become part of the universe of observable modules. This somewhat surprising behavior is part of the migration story, and discussing it here would derail our exploration of the module path, so let me defer explaining it to section 8.3. What I want to mention now is that symmetrical to the module path interpreting every artifact as a module, the class path treats all artifacts as plain JARs, regardless of whether they contain a module descriptor.

Annotation processors

If you're using annotation processors, you've been placing them on the class path together with the application's artifact. Java 9 suggests to separate by concerns and use `--class-path` or `--module-path` for application JARs and `--processor-path` or `--processor-module-path` for processor JARs. For unmodularized JARs, the distinction between the application and processor paths is optional: placing everything on the class path is valid, but for modules it's binding; processors on the module path won't be used.

Because the module path is used by several tools, most notably the compiler and the virtual machine, it makes sense to look at the concept in general. Unless otherwise noted, the described mechanisms work the same in all environments.

3.4.1 *Module resolution: Analyzing and verifying an application's structure*

What happens after calling `javac` or `java` with a bunch of modules on the module path? This is when the module system starts checking the launch configuration, meaning the modules and their declared dependencies, for reliability.

The process has to start somewhere, so the module system's first order of business is to decide on the set of root modules. There are several ways to make a module a root, and we'll discuss them all in due time, but the most prominent is specifying the initial module. For the compiler, that's either the module under compilation (if a module declaration is among the source files) or the one specified with `--module` (if the module source path is used). In the case of launching the virtual machine, only the `--module` option remains.

Next, the module system *resolves* dependencies. It checks the root modules' declarations to see which other modules they depend on and tries to satisfy each dependency with an observable module. It then goes on to do the same with those modules and so forth. This continues until either all transitive dependencies of the initial module are fulfilled or the configuration is identified as unreliable.

Resolving services and optional dependencies

Two aspects of module resolution add a little to the process discussed so far:

- Services (see chapter 10, particularly section 10.1.2)
- Optional dependencies (see section 11.2, particularly 11.2.3)

I won't go into them here because you lack the prerequisites, but I want to mention them, so you know more is coming. Suffice it to say, they don't void anything I've described—they just add bits and pieces.

ESSENTIAL INFO Regarding unreliable configurations, section 3.2.2 explores the kinds of things that can go wrong during this phase and how the module system reacts to them. There's one noteworthy detail to add: if the module path consists of several entries (directories or individual JARs), ambiguity checks aren't applied across them! Each individual entry must contain a module only once; but if several different entries contain the same module, the first one (in the order in which they were named on the module path) is picked—it shadows the other modules.

The easiest way to demonstrate that modules can be duplicated across folders is to pick a project that's ready to be launched and has all its modules in a folder (say, mods). Then create a copy of the entire folder (say, mods-copy) and place both on the module path:

```
$ java
 --module-path mods:mods-copy:libs
 --module monitor
```

All modules appear once in each folder, but the application starts nonetheless.

Now consider that build tools usually create a module path that lists each dependency individually. That means that as long as the build tool is in control, for example during compilation and testing, ambiguity checks aren't applied across all dependencies.

I find this unfortunate, because it voids a part of the promise of reliable configuration. On the other hand, it does have the upside that you can purposely shadow modules with versions you like better as long as you put yours first. Just remember that unlike in class-path times, different JARs are never "mixed." If the module system picks one module as a package's origin, it will look up all classes from that package in that JAR and *never* look in other JARs (this is related to split packages, discussed in sections 3.2.2 and 7.2).

Next, let's assume all modules were resolved. If no errors were found, the module system guarantees that each required module is present. Or rather, that modules with the right names are present.

There are no additional checks during this phase, so if a module depends on, for example, *com.google.common* (the module name for Google's Guava library) and an empty module with that name was found, the module system is content. But the missing types will still cause trouble down the road, in the form of compile-time or run-time errors. While empty modules are unlikely, a module with a different version than expected, missing a couple of types, isn't implausible. Still, a reliable configuration will greatly reduce the number of NoClassDefFoundErrors that crop up during execution.

3.4.2 *Module graph: Representation of an application's structure*

One of this book's first headings is "Visualizing software as graphs" (section 1.1.1). The ensuing paragraphs explain how developers and tools tend to see code in general but particularly dependencies between artifacts as graphs. The rest of chapter 1 illustrates that Java instead sees them as mere containers for types it consequently rolls into a ball of mud and how that mismatch is the root of a few hard problems plaguing the ecosystem.

The module system promises to solve many of those issues by aligning Java's perception with yours. All of this builds up to one revelation: the module system also sees a graph of artifacts. So here it is: the module graph!

> ### Definition: Module graph
>
> In a *module graph*, modules (as nodes) are connected according to their dependencies (with directed edges). The edges are the basis for readability (described in section 3.2). The graph is constructed during module resolution and available at run time via the reflection API (explained in section 12.4.2).

Figure 3.11 shows how module resolution creates the module graph for a simplified *ServiceMonitor* application. You don't have to leave everything up to the JPMS, though. With the right command-line options, you can add more modules and reads edges to the graph; we'll explore that next.

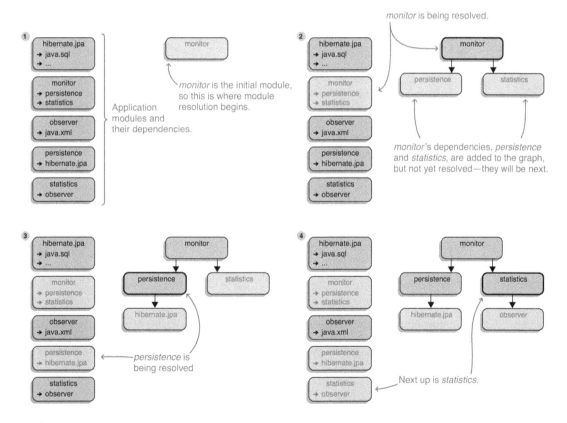

Figure 3.11a   Module resolution builds the module graph for a simplified *ServiceMonitor* application. In each step, one module is resolved, meaning it's located in the universe of observable modules and its dependencies are added to the module graph. Step by step, all transitive dependencies are resolved, at some point going from application to platform modules.

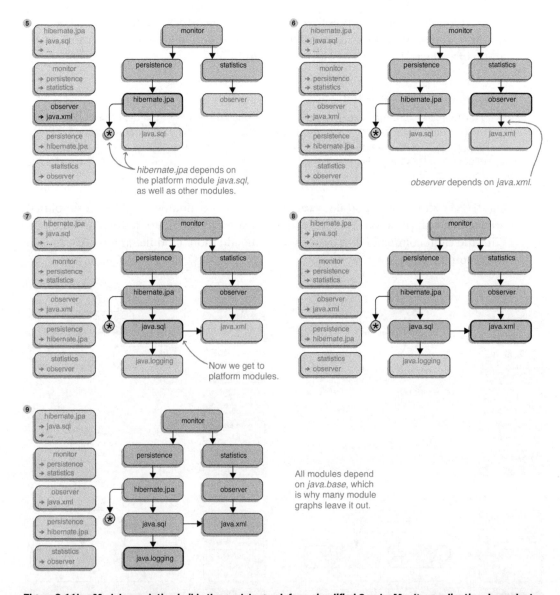

Figure 3.11b   Module resolution builds the module graph for a simplified *ServiceMonitor* application. In each step, one module is resolved, meaning it's located in the universe of observable modules and its dependencies are added to the module graph. Step by step, all transitive dependencies are resolved, at some point going from application to platform modules.

3.4.3   *Adding modules to the graph*

It's important to note that modules that didn't make it into the module graph during resolution aren't available later during compilation or execution, either. For cases where all application code is in modules, this is often irrelevant. After all, following the rules for readability and accessibility, even if such modules *were* available, their types would be inaccessible because nobody reads the modules. But there are scenarios using more advanced features where this may pop up as a compile-time or run-time error or even as an application that doesn't behave the way it's supposed to.

Various use cases can lead to the scenario of modules not making it into the graph. One of them is reflection. It can be used to have code in one module call code in another without explicitly depending on it. But without that dependency, the depended-on module may not make it into the graph.

Assume there was some alternative statistics module, *monitor.statistics.fancy*, that couldn't be present on the module path for each deployment of the service. (The reason is irrelevant, but let's go with a license that prevents the fancy code from being used "for evil." Evil masterminds that we are, we occasionally want to do just that.) So the module may sometimes be present and sometimes not, and hence no other module can require it because then the application couldn't launch if the module was missing.

How could the application handle that? The code depending on the fancy statistics library could use reflection to check whether the library is present and only call it if it is. But according to what you just learned, *that will never be the case!* By necessity, the fancy statistics module isn't required by any other module and hence won't end up in the module graph, meaning it can never be called. For these and other scenarios that pop up throughout the book, the module system offers a solution.

> **Definition: --add-modules**
>
> The option `--add-modules ${modules}`, available on `javac` and `java`, takes a comma-separated list of module names and defines them as root modules beyond the initial module. (As explained in section 3.4.1, root modules form the initial set of modules from which the module graph is built by resolving their dependencies.) This enables users to add modules (and their dependencies) to the module graph that would otherwise not show up because the initial module doesn't directly or indirectly depend on them.
>
> The `--add-modules` option has three special values: `ALL-DEFAULT`, `ALL-SYSTEM`, and `ALL-MODULE-PATH`. The first two only work at run time and are used for edge cases this book doesn't discuss. The last one can be useful, though: with it, all modules on the module path become root modules, and hence all of them make it into the module graph.

In the case of the *ServiceMonitor* application having an optional dependency on *monitor.statistics.fancy*, you have to make sure the module shows up in the module graph for those deployments that ship with it. In such cases, you'd use `--add-modules monitor.statistics.fancy` to make it a root module, causing the module system to add it and its dependencies to the module graph:

```
$ java
 --module-path mods:libs
 --add-modules monitor.statistics.fancy
 --module monitor
```

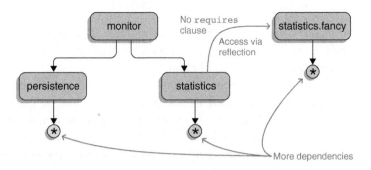

**Figure 3.12   The module graph for the simplified *ServiceMonitor*
application from figure 3.10, with the additional root module *monitor*.
statistics.fancy defined with `--add-modules`. Neither the monitor
module nor any of its dependencies depend on it, so it wouldn't make it
into the module graph without that option.**

You can see the resulting module graph in figure 3.12.

A particularly important use case for `--add-modules` are JEE modules, which, as section 6.1 explains, aren't resolved by default when running an application from the class path. Because you can add modules to the graph, it's only natural to wonder whether you also can remove them. The answer is yes, kind of: the option `--limit-modules` goes in that direction, and section 5.3.4 shows how it works.

Unfortunately, it isn't possible to let the module system know a specific dependency won't be fulfilled and you're OK with that. That would allow you to exclude (transitive) dependencies you don't need. Judging by the number of exclusions I see in typical Maven POMs, this is common, but, alas, the module system's strictness doesn't allow it.

3.4.4   *Adding edges to the graph*

When a module is added explicitly, it's on its own in the module graph, without any incoming reads edges. If access to it is purely reflective, that's fine, because the reflection API implicitly adds a reads edge. But for regular access, such as when importing a type from it, accessibility rules require readability.

> **Definition: --add-reads**
>
> The compiler-time and run-time option `--add-reads ${module}=${targets}` adds reads edges from `${module}` to all modules in the comma-separated list `${targets}`. This allows `${module}` to access all public types in packages exported by those modules even though it has no `requires` directives mentioning them. If `${targets}` includes `ALL-UNNAMED`, `${module}` can read the class-path content (that's a little handwavy— see section 8.2 for details).

Back to *monitor.statistics.fancy*, you can use `add-reads` to allow *monitor.statistics* to read it:

```
$ java
  --module-path mods:libs
```

```
--add-modules monitor.statistics.fancy
--add-reads monitor.statistics=monitor.statistics.fancy
--module monitor
```

The resulting module graph is the same as in figure 3.12, except the dashed line is now replaced by a proper reads edge. Toward the end of section 8.3.2 is a case where `--add-reads … =ALL-UNNAMED` saves the day.

3.4.5 Accessibility is an ongoing effort

Once the module system has resolved all dependencies, built the module graph, and established readability between modules, it stays active by checking the accessibility rules section 3.3 defines. If these rules are broken, compile-time or run-time errors ensue, as shown in section 3.3.3. If you encounter a problem with the module system and can't tell from the error message what went wrong, see section 5.3 for advice on how to debug the situation.

If you're interested in learning more about building and running modular applications, such as your own green-field projects, chapters 4 and 5 go deeper into that. Alternatively, you can check out the module system's effects on your existing project in chapters 6 and 7. You're also well-prepared to go deeper and check out the advanced features, particularly chapters 10 and 11.

> **NOTE** You've hit a milestone! You now understand how modules are defined, which mechanisms operate on that definition, and what effects they have—generally speaking, how Java works with modules.

Summary

- Modules come in two forms:
  - The ones shipped with the Java runtime are *platform modules*. They're merged into a `modules` file in the runtime's `libs` directory. A JDK also holds them in raw form as JMOD files in the `jmods` directory. Only *java.base*, the *base module*, is explicitly known to the module system.
  - Library, framework, and application developers create *modular JARs*, which are plain JARs containing a *module descriptor* `module-info.class`. These are called *application modules*, with the one containing the `main` method being the *initial module*.
- The module descriptor is compiled from a *module declaration* `module-info.java` that developers (and tools) can edit. It lies at the heart of the work with the module system and defines a module's properties:
  - Its name, which should be globally unique due to the reverse-domain naming scheme
  - Its dependencies, which are stated with `requires` directives that refer to other modules by name
  - Its API, which is defined by exporting selected packages with `exports` directives

- Dependency declarations and the *readability edges* the module system is creating from them are the basis for *reliable configuration*. It's achieved by making sure, among other things, that all modules are present exactly once and no dependency cycles exist between them. This allows you to catch application-corrupting or crashing problems earlier.
- Readability edges and package exports together are the basis for *strong encapsulation*. Here the module system ensures that only public types in exported packages are accessible and only to modules that read the exporting one. This prevents accidental dependencies on transitive dependencies and enables you to make sure outside code can't easily depend on types you designed as being internal to a module.
- Accessibility limitations apply to reflection as well! This requires a little more work to interact with reflection-based frameworks like Spring, Guice, or Hibernate.

The module path (option `--module-path` or `-p`) consists of files or directories and makes JARs available to the module system, which will represent them as modules. Use it instead of the class path to make the compiler or JVM aware of your project's artifacts.

The application modules, specified on the module path, and the platform modules, contained in the runtime, make up the *universe of observable modules*. During resolution, the universe is searched for modules, starting with root modules, so all required modules must either be on the module path or in the runtime.

Module resolution verifies that the configuration is reliable (all dependencies present, no ambiguities, and so on, as introduced in section 3.2) and results in the module graph—a close representation within the module system of how you see artifact dependencies. Only modules that make it into the module graph are available at run time.

Building modules from
source to JAR

This chapter covers

- Project directory structures
- Compiling sources from a single module to class files
- Compiling multiple modules at the same time
- Packaging class files into a modular JAR

Being able to define modules as described in chapter 3 is a good skill to have, but what is it good for without knowing how to turn those source files into modular artifacts (JARs) that can be shipped and executed? This chapter looks into building modules, all the way from organizing sources, to compiling them to class files, and eventually packaging those into modular JARs that can be distributed and executed. Chapter 5 focuses on running and debugging modular applications.

At times we'll look at the `javac` and `jar` commands available on the command line. You may be wondering about that—aren't IDEs and other tools going to use them for you? Likely, yes, but even putting aside the argument that it's always good to know how those tools work their magic, there is a more important reason to get to know these commands: they're the most direct path into the module system's heart. We'll use them to explore its features inside and out, and when we're done, you can use any tool that gives access to these features.

The first thing we'll look at in this chapter is how a project's files should be organized on disk (section 4.1). This may seem trivial, but a new recommendation is making the rounds and it's worth looking into. With the sources laid out and the modules declared as described in chapter 3, we'll turn to compiling them. This can happen one module at a time (section 4.2) or for multiple modules at once (section 4.3). The final section discusses how to package class files into modular JARs. To see some real-life build scripts, take a look at *ServiceMonitor*'s `master` branch.

By the end of this chapter, you'll be able to organize, compile, and package your source code and module declarations. The resulting modular JARs are ready to be deployed or shipped to anyone who uses Java 9 or later and is ready to take full advantage of modules.

4.1 Organizing your project in a directory structure

A real-life project consists of myriad files of many different types. Obviously, source files are the most important, but are nonetheless only one kind of many—others are test sources, resources, build scripts or project descriptions, documentation, source control information, and many others. Any project has to choose a directory structure to organize those files, and it's important to make sure it doesn't clash with the module system's characteristics.

If you've been following the module system's development under Project Jigsaw and studied the official quick-start guide or early tutorials, you may have noticed that they use a particular directory structure. Let's look at the recommendation to check whether it should become a new convention and juxtapose it with the established default that's implicitly understood by tools like Maven and Gradle.

4.1.1 New proposal—new convention?

In early publications covering the module system, the project directory often contains a `src` directory in which each module that belongs to the project has its own subdirectory containing the project's source files. If the project needs more than just sources, the proposal suggests organizing these concerns in parallel trees with folders like `test` and `build` next to `src`. This results in a hierarchy `concern/module`, as shown in figure 4.1.

It's important to recognize this single-`src` structure for what it is: the structure of a particular project (the JDK) and a proposal used in introductory material. Due to its tendency to split a single module's files across parallel trees, I wouldn't advise following it for anything but the smallest projects or ones where a meticulous examination concludes that this structure is preferable. Otherwise, I recommend using the established default, which we'll discuss next.

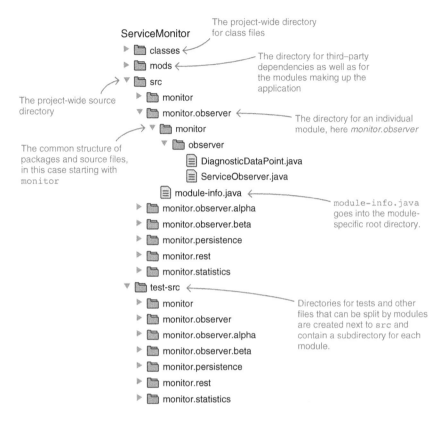

Figure 4.1 **This structure has top-level directories** `classes,` `mods,` `src,` **and** `test-` `src.` **Sources of individual modules are in directories below** `src` **or** `test-src` **that have the module's name.**

4.1.2 *Established directory structure*

Most projects that consist of several subprojects (what we now call *modules*) prefer separate root directories, where each contains a single module's sources, tests, resources, and everything else mentioned earlier. They use a hierarchy `module/concern`, and this is what established project structures provide.

The default directory structure, implicitly understood by tools like Maven and Gradle, implements that hierarchy (see figure 4.2). First and foremost, the default structure gives each module its own directory tree. In that tree, the `src` directory contains production code and resources (in `main/java` and `main/resources`, respectively) as well as test code and resources (in `test/java` and `test/resources`, respectively).

It's no requirement to structure projects this way. Putting aside the added work of configuring build tools for deviating directories and the specific case of multimodule compilation (covered in section 4.3.), all structures are equally valid and should be chosen based on their merits for the project at hand.

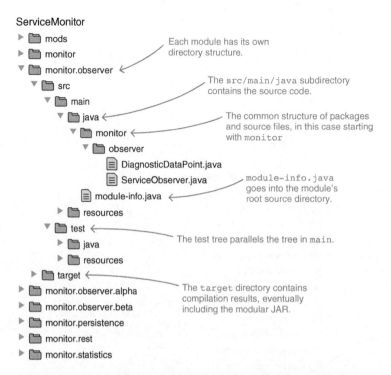

Figure 4.2   This structure has a top-level directory for each module. The modules can then organize their own files as best fits their needs. Here, *monitor.observer* uses the common directory structure used in Maven and Gradle projects.

All of that being said, the examples in this book use this default structure with one exception: using the command line is less cumbersome if all modular JARs end up in the same directory, so the *ServiceMonitor* application's tree has a top-level `mods` folder containing the created modules.

4.1.3   *The place for module declarations*

However the source files are structured, module declarations have to be named `module-info.java`. Otherwise, the compiler produces an error like this one, which tries to compile `monitor-observer-info.java`:

```
> monitor.observer/src/main/java/monitor-observer-info.java:1:
>      error: module declarations should be in a file named module-info.java
> module monitor.observer {
> ^
> 1 error
```

Although not strictly necessary, the declaration should be located in the root source directory. Otherwise, using the module source path as described in section 4.3.2

doesn't work properly because the module system can't locate the descriptor. As a consequence, it doesn't recognize the module, leading to "module not found" errors.

To try that out, move the descriptor of *monitor.observer* into a different directory and compile *monitor.* As you can see, this results in an error that the module *monitor.observer,* which is required by *monitor,* can't be found:

```
> ./monitor/src/main/java/module-info.java:2:
>     error: module not found: monitor.observer
>         requires monitor.observer;
>                          ^
> 1 error
```

4.2 Compiling a single module

Once the project files are laid out in a directory structure, some code has been written, and the module declarations are created, it's time to compile the source files. But what will it be—a collection of types or a shiny module? Because the former didn't change, we'll focus on the latter before exploring how the compiler discerns the two cases.

4.2.1 Compiling modular code

This section focuses on the compilation of a single module in a world where all dependencies are already modularized. You can only compile a module if a declaration `module-info.java` is among the source files, so let's assume this is the case.

In addition to operating on the module path and checking readability and accessibility, another addition to the compiler is its ability to process module declarations. The result of compiling a module declaration is a module descriptor, a file `module-info.class`. Like other `.class` files, it contains bytecode and can be analyzed and manipulated by tools like ASM and Apache's Byte Code Engineering Library (BCEL).

Other than using the module path instead of the class path, compilation works exactly as it did before Java 9. The compiler will compile all given files and produce a directory structure that matches the package hierarchy in the output directory specified with `-d`.

Figure 4.3 shows how the *monitor.observer* module, which uses the default directory structure, is laid out. To compile it, you create a `javac` call that's similar to what you would have done before Java 9:

- The `--module-path` option points the compiler to the directory that contains required application modules.
- The `-d` options determines the target directory for the compilation; it works the same as before Java 9.
- List or `find` all source files in `monitor.observer/src/main/java/`, including `module-info.java` (represented by `${source-files}`).

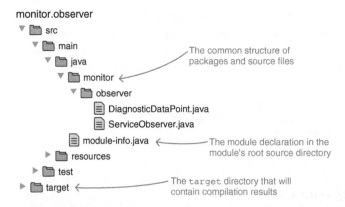

Figure 4.3   Directory structure of the monitor.observer module with the `src` directory expanded

Put together, you issue the following command in the *ServiceMonitor* application's root directory (i.e. the one containing *monitor.observer*):

```
$ javac
    --module-path mods
    -d monitor.observer/target/classes
    ${source-files}
```

Collapsing `src` and looking into `target/classes`, figure 4.4 shows the expected result.

4.2.2   *Modular or non-modular?*

The Java Platform Module System is built with the intention to create and eventually run modules, but this is by no means mandatory. It's still possible to build plain JARs, and this begs the question of how these two cases are distinguished. How does the compiler know whether to create a module or a bunch of types?

 ESSENTIAL INFO   As discussed in section 3.1.2, a modular JAR is nothing but a plain JAR with a module descriptor `module-info.class`, which is compiled from a module declaration `module-info.java`. For that reason, the compiler uses the presence or absence of `module-info.java` in the list of sources to compile that to discern whether it works on a module. That's why there is no compiler option `--create-module` or similar.

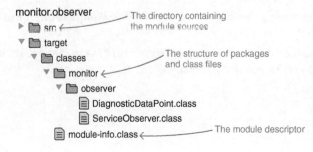

Figure 4.4   Directory structure of the *monitor.observer* module with the `target` directory expanded

What's the difference between compiling a module and compiling just types? It comes down do readability, as explained in section 3.2. If code that includes a module declaration is compiled

- It must require its dependencies to be able to access the types these dependencies export
- The required dependencies have to be present

If, on the other hand, non-modular code is compiled, no dependencies are expressed, due to the lack of a module declaration. In that case, the module system lets the code under compilation read all modules and everything it finds on the class path. Section 8.2 goes into detail on that *class-path mode*.

In contrast to readability, the accessibility rules described in section 3.3 apply to both cases. Regardless of whether the code is compiled as a module or as a bunch of sources, it's bound to the rules when accessing types in other modules. This is particularly relevant regarding JDK-internal classes, be they public classes in non-exported packages or nonpublic classes, because they're inaccessible regardless of how code is compiled. Figure 4.5 shows the difference between readability and accessibility.

A Note about compiler errors

Let's pick the *ServiceMonitor* application as an example. Its subproject *monitor* contains the source files `Main.java`, `Monitor.java`, and `module-info.java`.

If you include the module declaration in the list of files, `javac` sets out to compile a module and verifies that all dependencies on application and platform modules are declared in the descriptor. If you leave it out, the compiler falls back to only recognizing dependencies between types, as shown in figure 3.1.

But regardless of whether *monitor* is compiled as a module or not, if it uses types that the JDK modules or other application modules don't make accessible, the result will be the same: a compile error.

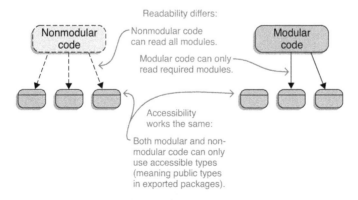

Figure 4.5 Comparing the compilation of non-modular code (left) with modular code (right). Readability rules differ slightly whereas accessibility rules are identical.

Compiling a module obviously requires clearing more hurdles than compiling just types. So why do it? Again, I come back to the comparison to writing code in a statically typed language. As Java developers, we generally believe that static typing is worth the additional upfront costs because in exchange, we get fast and reliable consistency checks. They don't prevent all errors, but they do prevent a lot of them.

The same applies here: using the module system to compile modules requires more effort than creating plain JARs, but in exchange we get checks that reduce the likelihood of runtime errors. We exchange compile-time effort for runtime safety—a deal I'll make any day of the week.

4.3   *Compiling multiple modules*

Compiling a single module as just described is straightforward, and compiling all seven *ServiceMonitor* modules is more of the same. But is it necessary to compile modules one by one? Or, to look at it another way, is there any reason *not* to do it like that? The answer to the latter is yes, a few details may make it preferable to compile multiple modules at once:

- *Effort*—Although compiling a single module is simple, the effort required for multiple modules adds up quickly. And it surely feels redundant to more or less repeat the same command over and over with only slight variations. Chances are you'll rarely do that by hand unless you're experimenting with Java 9. But the developers working on your tools should be considered as well.
- *Performance*—Compiling a single module descriptor takes about half a second on my system, and compiling all modules of the *ServiceMonitor* application takes about four. That's a little much, considering that there are less than 20 source files involved and full builds of much larger projects take less time. It stands to reason that I pay the price for launching the compiler seven times (for seven modules).
- *Weak circular dependencies*—Although the module system forbids circular dependencies with `requires` directives, there are other ways to have modules reference one another (trust me for now) that are deemed acceptable. Although the dependencies are circular, they can be considered weak because if the right one is missing, you only get a warning. Still, warning-free compilation is worth some effort, and to get there, both modules must be compiled together.

 ESSENTIAL INFO   With a few reasons to compile multiple modules at once, it's a good thing the compiler can do just that!

4.3.1   *The naive approach*

How does compiling multiple modules at once work? Can you list source files from several modules and have the compiler figure it out? Nope:

```
$ javac
    --module-path mods:libs
```

```
    -d classes
    monitor/src/main/java/module-info.java
    monitor.rest/src/main/java/module-info.java
```

```
> monitor.rest/src/main/java/module-info.java:1:
>     error: too many module declarations found
> module monitor.rest {
> ^
> 1 error
```

Clearly, the compiler prefers to work on a single module at a time. This makes sense, too, because as discussed previously, it enforces readability and accessibility based on clearly defined module boundaries. Where would they come from, with sources from many different modules mixed up in the list of files to compile? Somehow the compiler needs to know where one module ends and the next begins.

4.3.2 The module source path: Informing the compiler about the project structure

The way out of that default single-module mode is a command-line option that informs the compiler about the project's directory structure. The compiler supports *multimodule compilation*, where it can build multiple modules at once. The command-line option `--module-source-path ${path}` is used to enable this mode and to point out the directory structure containing the modules. All other compiler options work as usual.

That sounds pretty easy, but there are important details to consider. Before doing that, though, let's get a simple example to work.

Let's assume for a moment the *ServiceMonitor* application used the single-`src` structure defined in section 4.1.1 with all module source directories below `src` (see figure 4.6). Then you could use `--module-source-path src` to point the compiler toward the `src` folder, which contains all the modules' sources, and tell it to compile everything it finds at once.

As with a single-module build, the module path is used to point the compiler to the directory that contains required application modules—in this case, these are external dependencies because all *ServiceMonitor* modules are currently being compiled. The `-d` option works the same way as with a single-module build, and you still list all source files in `src`, including all module declarations.

Figure 4.6 The module source path is easiest to use if the project has a single `src` directory with each module's root source directory below it.

Put together, this is the command:

```
$ javac
    --module-path mods:libs
    --module-source-path src
    -d classes
    ${source-files}
```

A look into `classes` shows a directory per module, each containing that module's class files, including the module descriptor. Neat.

But it's not always that easy. How would this apply to a project that doesn't use the single-`src` structure? This is where a nifty detail of the module source path comes in.

4.3.3   *The asterisk as a token for the module name*

The module source path can contain an asterisk (`*`). Although it's commonly interpreted as a wildcard, which in paths usually means "anything in the directory up to the asterisk," this isn't the case here. Instead, the asterisk functions as a token that indicates where on the path the module names appear. The rest of the path after the asterisk must point to the directory containing the modules' packages.

This way, the compiler can match source file paths to the module source path and deduce which module a source file belongs to. For that to work, each source file must match the module source path.

This may seem complicated, but an example will clarify. Let's return to the *Service-Monitor* application as structured in section 4.1.2, where each module has the common `src/main/java` directories that contain the source files. Starting in the project's top-level directory, these are the relative paths to some of the sources:

- `monitor/src/main/java/monitor/Monitor.java`
- `monitor/src/main/java/monitor/Main.java`
- `monitor/src/main/java/module-info.java`
- `monitor.rest/src/main/java/monitor/rest/MonitorServer.java`
- `monitor.rest/src/main/java/module-info.java`
- `monitor.persistence/src/main/java/monitor/persistence/Statistics-Repository.java`
- `monitor.persistence/src/main/java/module-info.java`

This makes the shared structure pretty obvious: all paths follow the schema `${modules}/src/main/java/${packages}/${sources}`.

Looking back at how the module source path is to be used, you can see that `${modules}` must be replaced with `*` and that you have to omit the package directories, leaving `*/src/main/java`. Unfortunately, it doesn't work yet, because the compiler doesn't accept the asterisk as the first character—you have to pad it with `./`. Now, multimodule compilation works like a charm:

```
$ javac
    --module-path mods:libs
    --module-source-path "./*/src/main/java"
```

```
-d classes
${source-files}
```

As before, all class files end up in module-specific subdirectories of classes. With what you know about the asterisk being a token for the module name, you could summarize those paths as -d classes/*. Unfortunately, the -d option doesn't understand the token, and you can't use it to build output paths like ./*/target/classes. What a shame.

You may wonder how the asterisk relates to the use of --module-source-path src in the first example. After all, there you didn't specify where the module names would appear, and the compiler was able to deduce them. What may look like an inconsistency at first glance is an effort to make the simple case simple to use.

If the module source path contains no asterisk, the compiler will silently add it as the final path element. So you've effectively been specifying src/* as the module source path, which matches the directory structure in that example.

Being able to compile multiple modules if all use the same directory structure should cover most cases. For those with more complicated setups, we need another technique.

4.3.4 *Multiple module source path entries*

It's possible a single module source path doesn't suffice. Maybe different modules have different directory structures or some modules have sources in more than one directory. In such cases, you can specify several module source path entries to make sure every source file matches a path.

The JDK, being a complex project, has a nontrivial directory structure. Figure 4.7 shows just a tiny snippet of it—there are many more directories on all levels.

Assuming you're in the directory jdk and want to build for UNIX, what would a module source path look like that spans all modules and the correct source folders? The path to the UNIX sources is src/java.desktop/unix/classes or, more generally,

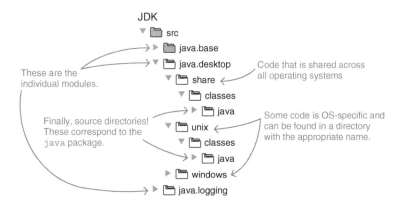

Figure 4.7 **A limited view into the JDK's source directories. Note how the module directories below** src **are further divided. It's the** classes **directories further below that are the roots for the actual source files.**

src/${module}/unix/classes. Similarly, for the shared sources, it's src/${module}/share/classes. Putting these two together, you get

```
--module-source-path "src/*/unix/classes":"src/*/share/classes"
```

To reduce redundancy, the module source path lets you define alternative paths with {dir1,dir2}. You can unify various paths if they only differ in the name of single path elements. With alternatives, you can unify the paths to source in share and unix as follows:

```
--module-source-path "src/*/{share,unix}/classes"
```

4.3.5 Setting the initial module

With everything set up for multimodule compilation, another possibility opens up: compiling a single module and its dependencies just by naming it. Why would you want to do that? Because it no longer requires you to explicitly list the source files to compile!

If the module source path is set, the option --module lets you compile a single module and its transitive dependencies *without* explicitly listing the source files. The module source path is used to determine which source files belong to the specified module, and dependencies are resolved based on its declaration.

Compiling *monitor.rest* and its dependencies is now easy. As before, you use --module-path mods:libs to specify where to find dependencies and -d classes to define the output folder. With --module-source-path "./*/src/main/java", you inform the compiler of your project's directory structure; and with --module monitor.rest, you command it to start with compiling *monitor.rest*:

```
$ javac
    --module-path mods:libs
    --module-source-path "./*/src/main/java"
    -d classes
    --module monitor.rest
```

If classes was empty before, it now contains class files for monitor.rest (specified module), monitor.statistics (direct dependency), and monitor.observer (transitive dependency).

Listings 2.3, 2.4, and 2.5 showed how to compile the ServiceMonitor application step by step. Armed with the knowledge of how to use multimodule compilation, it could instead be done as easily as the following:

```
$ javac
    --module-path mods:libs
    --module-source-path "./*/src/main/java"
    -d classes
    --module monitor
```

Because the initial module *monitor* depends on all other modules, all of them are built. Unlike with the step-by-step approach, the class files don't go in */target/classes, but in classes/* (using * as a token for the module name).

In addition to making the command easier to read, the combination of `--module-source-path` and `--module` also operates on a higher level of abstraction. As opposed to listing individual source files, it clearly states the intent of compiling a specific module. I like that.

There are two downsides, though:

- The compiled class files can't be redistributed into deeper directory structures and instead all end up below the same directory (in the recent examples, `classes`). If following stages of the build process depend on a precise location of those files, additional preparatory steps would have to be taken, which may void the advantages of using the module source path in the first place.

- If compilation is kicked off with `--module` (as opposed to listing all module's source files), the compiler will apply optimizations that can lead to unexpected results. One of them is unused code detection: classes that aren't transitively referenced from the initial module aren't compiled, and even entire modules can be missing from the output if they were decoupled via services (see chapter 10).

4.3.6   Is it worth it?

Does multimodule compilation pay off? I listed three reasons to motivate its use, so it makes sense to return to them:

- *Effort*—Once you grasp how the module source path has to be constructed, it's considerably less effort to compile multiple modules. This expressly includes building a particular module and its dependencies, which becomes easier as well. At the same time, build tools usually compile projects one by one, and configuring them to do so all at once may add complexity, particularly if further steps have to be taken to distribute the class files into module-specific directories.

- *Performance*—With multimodule compilation, the *ServiceMonitor* application builds in less than a second, which is four times faster than building seven modules step by step. But this is a pretty extreme case, because each module contains only two or three classes. Relatively speaking, there's a lot of overhead in launching the compiler seven times; but in absolute terms, it comes down to only three seconds. Given the build time of any decently sized project, shaving off a couple of seconds is hardly worth making the build more complex.

- *Weak circular dependencies*—In this case, there's no way around multimodule compilation if the build should be free of warnings.

Multimodule compilation is optional, and its benefits aren't substantial enough to recommend it as the default practice. Particularly if your tools don't support it seamlessly, setting it up may not be worth the effort. This is a classic "it depends" situation. I have to say, though, I like it for operating on a higher level of abstraction: modules instead of just types.

4.4   *Compiler options*

With the module system comes a host of new command-line options that are explained throughout this book. To make sure you can easily find them, table 4.1 lists all of those pertaining to the compiler. Have a look at https://docs.oracle.com/javase/9/tools/javac.htm for the official compiler documentation.

Table 4.1 An alphabetized table of all module-related compiler (`javac` command) options. The descriptions are based on the documentation, and the references point to the sections in this book that explain in detail how to use the options.

Option	Description	Ref.
`--add-exports`	Lets a module export additional packages	11.3.4
`--add-modules`	Defines root modules in addition to the initial module	3.4.3
`--add-reads`	Adds read edges between modules	3.4.4
`--limit-modules`	Limits the universe of observable modules	5.3.5
`--module, -m`	Sets the initial module	4.3.5
`--module-path, -p`	Specifies where to find application modules	3.4
`--module-source-path`	Conveys a project's directory structure	4.3.2
`--module-version`	Specifies the version of the modules under compilation	13.2.1
`--patch-module`	Extends an existing module with classes during the course of compilation	7.2.4
`--processor-module-path`	Specifies where to find annotation processor modules	4.2.1
`--system`	Overrides the location of system modules	
`--upgrade-module-path`	Defines the location of upgradeable modules	6.1.3

New --release option

Have you ever used the `-source` and `-target` options to compile your code to run on an older version of Java, only to see it crash at runtime because a method call failed with a seemingly inexplicable error? Maybe you forgot to specify `-bootclasspath`.

Without that option, the compiler creates bytecode that a JVM with the target version understands (good), but it links against the current version's core library API (bad). That can create calls to types or methods that didn't exist in the older JDK version and thus cause runtime errors.

From Java 9 on, the compiler prevents that common operating error with the `--release` option that sets all three options to the correct value.

4.5   *Packaging a modular JAR*

On the way from idea to running code, the next step after coding and compiling is to
take the class files and package them as a module. As section 3.1.2 explains, this should
result in a *modular JAR*, which is just like a plain JAR but contains the module's descriptor `module-info.class`. Consequently, you expect the trusted `jar` tool to be in charge
of packaging. This is how simple it is to create a modular JAR (in this case for *monitor.*
observer):

```
$ jar --create
    --file mods/monitor.observer.jar
    -C monitor.observer/target/classes .
```

Putting the new command-line aliases aside, this call works exactly the same as before
Java 9. The interesting and implicit detail is that because `monitor.observer/target/`
`classes` contains a `module-info.class`, so will the resulting `monitor.observer.jar`,
making it a modular JAR.

Although the `jar` tool works much like before, there are a couple of module-related
details and additions, like defining a module's entry point, that we should look at.

> **NOTE** JAR isn't the only format used to deliver Java bytecode. JEE also works
> with WAR and EAR files. Until the specification is updated to embrace mod-
> ules, though, it isn't possible to create modular WARs or EARs.

4.5.1   *Quick recap of jar*

To make sure we're all on the same page, let's take a quick look at how `jar` is used
to package archives. As I just pointed out, the result is a modular JAR if the list of
included files contains a module descriptor `module-info.class`.

Let's take the command that packages *monitor.observer* as an example. The result is
a `module.observer.jar` in `mods` that contains all class files from `monitor.observer/`
`target/classes` and its subdirectories. Because `classes` contains a module descriptor,
the JAR will also contain it and thus be a modular JAR without any additional effort:

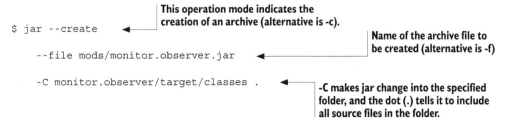

You should consider recording a module's version with `--module-version` when packaging it. Section 13.2.1 explains how to do that.

4.5.2   *Analyzing a JAR*

When working with JARs, it helps to know ways to analyze what you've created. Particularly important are the files a JAR contains and what its module descriptor has to say. Fortunately, `jar` has options for both.

LISTING A JAR'S CONTENTS

The most obvious thing to do is to look at a JAR's contents, which is possible with `--list`. The following snippet shows the content of the `monitor.observer.jar` created in the previous section. It contains a `META-INF` folder, which we don't go into because it's been around for years and doesn't pertain to the module system. There's also a module descriptor, and `DiagnosticDataPoint` and `ServiceObserver` classes in the package `monitor.observer`. Nothing spectacular or unexpected:

```
$ jar --list --file mods/monitor.observer.jar

> META-INF/
> META-INF/MANIFEST.MF
> module-info.class
> monitor/
> monitor/observer/
> monitor/observer/DiagnosticDataPoint.class
> monitor/observer/ServiceObserver.class
```

This is not a new command—it just looks different due to new aliases: `--list` is long for `-t`, and `--file` is long for `-f`. Before Java 9, `jar -t -f some.jar` would have done the same thing.

EXAMINING MODULE DESCRIPTOR

A module descriptor is a class file and thus consists of bytecode. This makes it necessary to use tools to look at its content. Fortunately, `jar` can do that with `--describe-module` (alternatively `-d`). Examining `monitor.observer.jar`, you see that it's a module named *monitor.observer* that exports a package of the same name and requires the base module:

```
$ jar --describe-module --file mods/monitor.observer.jar

> monitor.observer jar:.../monitor.observer.jar/!module-info.class
> exports monitor.observer
> requires java.base mandated
```

(If you wonder what `mandated` means, remember from section 3.1.4 that every module implicitly requires the base module, meaning the presence of *java.base* is mandated.)

4.5.3   *Defining an entry point*

To launch a Java application, it's necessary to know the entry point, which is one of the classes containing a `public static void main(String[])` method. A class containing that method can either be specified on the command line when the application launches or be recorded in the manifest file that ships with the JAR. Don't worry if you don't know exactly how one or even both of these options work, because Java 9 adds a third one that's the way to go with modules.

When `jar` is used to package class files into an archive, you can define a main class with `--main-class ${class}`, where `${class}` is the fully qualified name (meaning the package name appended with a dot and the class name) of the class with the `main` method. It will be recorded in the module descriptor and used by default as the main class when the module is the initial module for launching an application (see section 5.1 for details).

> **NOTE** If you're used to setting the manifest's `Main-Class` entry for creating executable JARs, you'll be pleased to hear that `jar --main-class` sets it as well.

The *ServiceMonitor* application has a single entry point in `monitor.Main`. You can use `--main-class monitor.Main` to record that during packaging:

```
$ jar --create
    --file mods/monitor.jar
    --main-class monitor.Main
    -C monitor/target/classes .
```

Using `--describe-module`, you can see that the main class was recorded in the descriptor:

```
$ jar --describe-module
    --file mods/monitor.jar

> monitor jar:.../monitor.jar/!module-info.class
# requires and contains truncated
> main-class monitor.Main
```

It's interesting that the `jar` tool has neither the capabilities nor the responsibility to verify your claim that there is such a class. There's no check of whether it exists or whether it contains a suitable `main` method. If things go wrong, no error will occur now, but launching the module will fail.

4.5.4 Archiver options

We just explored only the most important options `jar` has to offer. A couple of others become interesting in different contexts and are explained in the relevant chapters. To make sure you can find them easily, table 4.2 lists the options that have to do with the module system. Visit https://docs.oracle.com/javase/9/tools/jar.htm for the official `jar` documentation.

Table 4.2   An alphabetized table of all module-related archiver (`jar` command) options. The descriptions are based on the documentation, and the references point to the sections in this book that explain in detail how to use the options.

Option	Description	Ref.
`--hash-modules`	Records hashes of dependent modules	
`--describe-module, -d`	Shows the module's name, dependencies, exports, packages, and more	4.5.2
`--main-class`	Application entry point	4.5.3
`--module-path, -p`	Specifies where to find application modules for recording hashes	3.4
`--module-version`	Specifies the version of the modules under compilation	13.2.1
`--release`	Creates a multi-release JAR containing bytecode for different Java versions	Appendix E
`--update`	Updates an existing archive, for example by adding more class files	9.3.3

Summary

- Make sure to pick a directory structure that fulfills your project's requirements. If in doubt, stick to your build system's default structure.
- The `javac` command to compile all of a module's sources, including the declaration, is the same as before Java 9, except that it uses the module path instead of the class path.
- The module source path (`--module-source-path`) informs the compiler of how the project is structured. This lifts the compiler operation from processing types to processing modules, allowing you to compile a selected module and all its dependencies with a simple option (`--module` or `-m`) instead of listing source files.
- Modular JARs are just JARs with a module descriptor `module-info.class`. The `jar` tool processes them just as well as other class files, so packaging all of them into a JAR requires no new options.
- Optionally, `jar` allows the specification of a module's entry point (with `--main-class`), which is the class with the `main` method. This makes launching the module simpler.

Running and debugging
modular applications

This chapter covers

- Launching a modular application by specifying an initial module

- Loading resources from modules

- Validating modules, sets of modules, and module graphs

- Reducing and listing the universe of observable modules

- Debugging a modular application with logging

With modules defined, compiled, and packaged into modular JARs as explained in chapters 3 and 4, it's finally time to power up the JVM and run applications with the `java` command. This gives us the opportunity to discuss a runtime-related concept: how to load resources from modules (section 5.2). Sooner or later things will go wrong, though, so in section 5.3 we also look into debugging a module configuration with a variety of command-line options.

By the end of the chapter, you'll be able to launch an application made up of modules. Beyond that, you'll have a firm understanding of how the module system processes a given configuration and how that can be observed through logging and other diagnostic tools.

This also finishes part 1 of the book, which teaches everything you need to know to write, compile, and run simple modular applications. It lays the groundwork for the more advanced features that parts 2 and 3 are going to look into, chief among them those that support a gradual migration to the module system.

5.1   Launching the JVM with modules

After all the build-up—defining module dependencies and APIs, creating modular JARs, and placing them on the module path—launching the JVM with a modular application is embarrassingly easy. All you need to do is specify the initial module and maybe the main class.

The `java` command has an option `--module ${module}` that specifies the initial module `${module}`. Module resolution starts from there, and it's also the module from which a main class, meaning one with a `public static void main` method, will be launched.

The specific class is either defined by the initial module's descriptor or specified with `--module ${module}/${class}` by appending the module name with a slash and the fully qualified class name (see section 5.1.1).

For the *ServiceMonitor* application, all preparations culminate in the call you've already seen, which launches the JVM with *monitor* as the initial module:

```
$ java
    --module-path mods:libs
    --module monitor
```

As discussed in section 3.4, `--module-path mods:libs` informs the module system that the `mods` and `libs` directories contain *ServiceMonitor*'s application modules. The option `--module monitor` defines *monitor* as the initial module, as a consequence of which the module system will resolve all of *monitor*'s dependencies and build the module graph as discussed in the previous section. It will then launch the main class you set in the module descriptor during packaging in section 4.5.3: `monitor.Main`.

5.1.1   Specifying the main class

The `--module` option can also be used to define the application's main class. To this end, the initial module's name is followed by a forward slash and the fully qualified class name (package name followed by a dot and the class name).

Here, you explicitly define that the application is launched by calling the `main` method in *monitor*'s class `monitor.Main`:

```
$ java
    --module-path mods:libs
    --module monitor/monitor.Main
```

Specifying the main class on the command line overrides whatever the module descriptor defines. This means applications can still have several entry points, just like without the module system. In case one of them is a sensible default, it makes sense to bake it into the module descriptor as described in section 4.5.3.

If *monitor* defines `monitor.Main` as its main class but for some reason you don't want to use it, you can easily override it. With the following command, the application is launched by calling *monitor*'s `some.other.MainClass`, ignoring whatever is defined in *monitor*'s descriptor:

```
$ java
    --module-path mods:libs
    --module monitor/some.other.MainClass
```

For this to work, the initial module must contain the specified class. Because that isn't the case for *monitor* and `some.other.MainClass`, executing the command you just saw results in an error:

```
> Error: Could not find or load main class
>     some.other.MainClass in module monitor
```

5.1.2   *If the initial module and main module aren't the same*

What can you do if the module you'd like to use as the initial one doesn't contain the application's main class? First, this seems to be a weird problem; but hey, software development is full of those, so that doesn't mean it won't occur.

As an example, imagine a desktop application that can be launched in several modes (data entry, evaluation, administration) and that a mode is selected on launch by picking the correct main class. Being complex, the app consists of many modules, and each mode has its own module (*data.entry*, *data.evaluation*, *administration*). Each mode's module also contains the respective entry point. On top comes *app*, which depends on all the application's modules. (Figure 5.1 shows the module graph.)

To launch this application, you'd like to use `--module app` and then specify a main class from one of the other modules—but is that possible? To solve this, we need some terminology for the two involved modules:

- There's the module that (transitively) depends on all modules the application needs—I'll call it *all*.
- Then there's the module containing the main class you want to launch—I'll call it *main*.

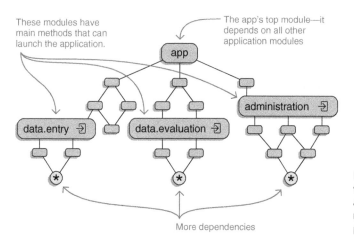

Figure 5.1   The module graph for a desktop application, with *app* at the top and the three modules containing entry points further down

Up to now, these two modules were always the same, so you passed the module name to `--module`, making it the initial module. What do you do if these are two separate modules?

The crux of the matter is that the module system is adamant about the origin of the main class. There's no way to trick it into searching any module but the initial one for it. You hence have to pick *main* as the initial module, passing it to `--module`.

By assumption, this doesn't resolve all dependencies correctly, so how do you ensure that *all*'s dependencies are taken into account? At this point, the `--add-modules` option introduced in section 3.4.3 comes in handy. With it, you can define *all* as an additional root module and make the module system resolve its dependencies as well:

```
$ java
    --module-path mods
    --add-modules all
    --module main
```

For the desktop application, that means you always use the `--add-modules app` option to make sure the graph contains all required modules and then select the module for the desired mode as the main module. For example:

```
$ java
    --module-path mods
    --add-modules app
    --module data.entry
```

By the way, if you're wondering why the modules for the various modes wouldn't depend on all required modules, there are at least three answers:

- The application may be decoupled via services, as shown in chapter 10, and *app* is the consumer.
- The mode modules may have some optional dependencies, as explained in section 11.2, and *app* makes sure they're all present.
- I did say it was a weird case, remember?

5.1.3   *Passing parameters to the application*

Passing parameters to the application is just as easy as before. The JVM puts everything after the initial module into an array of strings (split on space) and passes it to the main method.

Assume you call *ServiceMonitor* as follows. What do you think will be passed to `Main::main`? (Careful, it's a trick question!)

```
$ java
    --module-path mods:libs
    --module monitor
    --add-modules monitor.rest
    opt arg
```

It's a trick question because `--add-modules monitor.rest` looks like something the module system should be in charge of. And it would be, if the option were in the right place, which is *before* --module. As it stands, the option comes after --module, making the JVM interpret it as an option for the application and passing it along.

To demonstrate, let's extend Main::main to print the parameters:

```
public static void main(String[] args) {
    for (String arg : args) {
        System.out.print(arg + " / ");
    }

    // [...]

}
```

And indeed, you get the output --add-modules / monitor.rest / opt / arg.

Be careful to make --module the last option you want the JVM to process and to put all application options behind it.

5.2   *Loading resources from modules*

Section 3.3 extensively covers how the module system's accessibility rules provide strong encapsulation across module boundaries. It only discusses types, though, and at runtime you usually need to access resources, too. Whether those are configurations, translations, media files, or in some instances even raw .class files, it's common for code to load these from JARs that ship with the project. Because the JPMS turns modular JARs into modules, which claim to strongly encapsulate their internals, we need to explore how that affects resource loading. Before we go into that, in the following sections I'll give a short recap of how resources were loaded in the past and point out the changes Java 9+ incurs. We'll then take a closer look at loading package resources across module boundaries.

> **TIP** The topic of resource access surfaces a few more times throughout the book: section 6.3 explains how to access JDK resources and section 8.2.1 goes into access of non-modular resources. For a practical demonstration of how to load resources, check out *ServiceMonitor*'s feature-resources branch.

5.2.1   *Resource loading before Java 9*

Without any boundaries between JARs, Java versions before 9 give every class access to all resources on the class path. That's even worse than for types, because at least they can use package visibility to hide themselves in a package. No such thing exists for resources.

> **ESSENTIAL INFO** To load a resource, you call getResource or getResource-AsStream on either Class or ClassLoader. Conceptually, these methods are almost identical: you hand them the name of a resource file as a String, and they return a URL or InputStream if they find it; otherwise you get null back. To not make things more complicated than they have to be, we'll stick to using Class::getResource.

Listing 5.1 shows how to load various resources. As long as all classes and resources are on the class path, it doesn't matter which JAR they're in. Figure 5.2 shows a single JAR that contains all the loaded resources—if it's on the class path, each call to `Class::getResource` returns a `URL` instance.

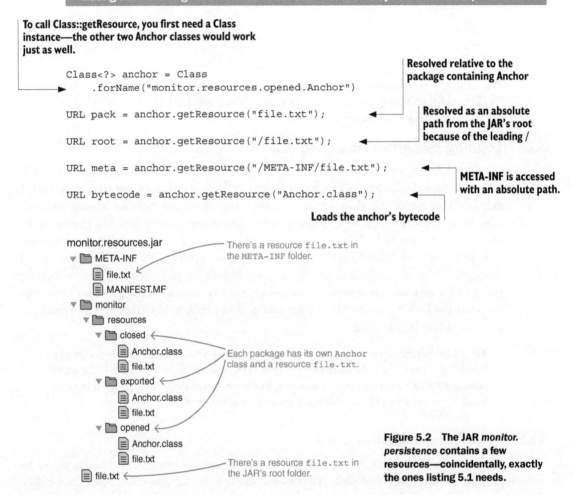

Listing 5.1   Loading resources: all successful because they're on the class path

To call Class::getResource, you first need a Class instance—the other two Anchor classes would work just as well.

```
Class<?> anchor = Class
    .forName("monitor.resources.opened.Anchor")

URL pack = anchor.getResource("file.txt");

URL root = anchor.getResource("/file.txt");

URL meta = anchor.getResource("/META-INF/file.txt");

URL bytecode = anchor.getResource("Anchor.class");
```

Resolved relative to the package containing Anchor

Resolved as an absolute path from the JAR's root because of the leading /

META-INF is accessed with an absolute path.

Loads the anchor's bytecode

monitor.resources.jar
- META-INF
  - file.txt
  - MANIFEST.MF
- monitor
  - resources
    - closed
      - Anchor.class
      - file.txt
    - exported
      - Anchor.class
      - file.txt
    - opened
      - Anchor.class
      - file.txt
  - file.txt

There's a resource file.txt in the META-INF folder.

Each package has its own Anchor class and a resource file.txt.

There's a resource file.txt in the JAR's root folder.

Figure 5.2   The JAR *monitor. persistence* contains a few resources—coincidentally, exactly the ones listing 5.1 needs.

5.2.2   *Resource loading on Java 9 and later*

You may wonder why listing 5.1 gives so many different examples. Some work with modules, but others don't, and I want to discuss each of them in turn. Before we come to that, though, let's consider the various resource APIs in Java 9:

- The methods on `Class` are a good way to load resources from modules—we'll explore their behavior momentarily.

- The methods on `ClassLoader` have a different and generally less-useful behavior when it comes to modules, and we won't discuss them. If you want to use them, have a look at their Javadoc.
- A new class, `java.lang.Module`, which we'll explore in depth in section 12.3.3, also has methods `getResource` and `getResourceAsStream`. They behave pretty much like the ones on `Class`.

With that settled, we can turn to using the workhorse `Class::getResource` to load the various kinds of resources in listing 5.1 from modules. The first important observation is that within the same module, each call returns a `URL` instance, meaning all resources are found. This is true regardless of which packages the module encapsulates. When it comes to loading resources across module boundaries, things are a little different:

- Resources from a package are by default encapsulated (see section 5.2.3 for details).
- Resources from the JAR's root or from folders whose names can't be mapped to packages (like `META-INF` because of the dash) are never encapsulated.
- `.class` files are never encapsulated.
- If resources are encapsulated, the `getResource` call returns `null`.

The reason most forms of access aren't encapsulated comes down to ease of migration. Many critical and widely used tools and frameworks in the Java ecosystem rely on configurations in the JAR root or `META-INF` folder (for example, JPA implementations) or scan `.class` files (for example, to locate annotated classes). If all resources were encapsulated by default, these tools could, by default, not work with modules.

At the same time, the benefits of strong encapsulation of resources are much less significant than of types, so the decision was made to only encapsulate resources in packages. Let's see how to get around that.

5.2.3　*Loading package resources across module boundaries*

Whenever `Class::getResource` or any of its equivalents is tasked to load a resource, it checks whether the path conforms to a package name. In simplified terms, if removing the file name from the path and then replacing all `/` with `.` yields a valid package name, the resource is loaded from a package.

Let's pick some lines from listing 5.1 as examples. The call `anchor.getResource("file.txt")` tells the JVM to load the resource `file.txt` relative to the `anchor` class. Because the class is in a package—`monitor.resources.opened` in this example—the resource is loaded from that package.

A counterexample is `anchor.getResource("/META-INF/file.txt")`. The leading slash indicates an absolute path (so it doesn't matter which package `anchor` is in), and trying to transform that to a package name would yield `META-INF`. That's not valid in Java, and hence the resource isn't loaded from a package.

Opening a package

It's important to understand how the JVM determines whether a resource is in a package, because if it's in a package, it's strongly encapsulated. Furthermore, `exports` clauses *don't* give access to resources. Because `getResource` is bound to the reflection API, a different mechanism is needed.

We haven't discussed it so far, but what you're looking for when wanting to give access to a resource is the `opens` clause. Syntactically it works exactly like `exports`, but it only gives reflective access to a package, which makes it a great fit for this use case.

There's much more to learn about `opens`, and section 12.2 discusses it in detail, but all you need to know here is that it gives access to resources in otherwise encapsulated packages. Let's try it and build a module *monitor.resources* around the resources loaded in listing 5.1. Here's the module declaration:

```
module monitor.resources {
    exports monitor.resources.exported;
    opens monitor.resources.opened;
}
```

Comparing it to figure 5.2, you can see that out of its three packages, one is encapsulated, one is exported, and one is opened. What can you expect if you run the code in listing 5.2?

That depends on the module that runs the code. If it's *monitor.resources*, the calls go through because encapsulation only operates across module boundaries. If any other module runs the code, only the package `monitor.resources.opened` is made accessible to it for reflection. Hence, `getResource` will only return a non-`null` URL for `opened`, whereas it will return `null` for loading resources from `closed` and `exported`.

The other calls from listing 5.1—`getResource("Anchor.class")`, `getResource ("/file.txt")`, and `getResource("/META-INF/file.txt")`—will go through, because they load either bytecode or resources that aren't in packages. As discussed in section 5.2.2, those aren't encapsulated.

Listing 5.2   Loading resources from packages with varying accessibility

```
URL closed = Class
    .forName("monitor.resources.closed.Anchor")       Fails to load a resource from
    .getResource("file.txt");                         the encapsulated package
URL exported = Class
    .forName("monitor.resources.exported.Anchor")     Fails to load a resource from
    .getResource("file.txt");                         the exported package
URL opened = Class
    .forName("monitor.resources.opened.Anchor")       Succeeds in loading a resource
    .getResource("file.txt");                         from the opened package
```

In summary, if you want to give access to resources in a module's package, you have to open it.

Opening packages to give access to resources invites other code to depend on your module's internal structure. To avoid that, consider exposing a type in your public API that can be tasked with loading resources. You're then free to rearrange resource internally as you see fit without breaking other modules.

> **TIP** If you'd like to avoid dependencies on the module containing the resources, you can create a service instead. Chapter 10 introduces services, and using them to access resources would be straightforward, were it not for the name-wrangling required. Fortunately, there's excellent documentation for that laborious process, so I won't repeat it here. Check out the Javadoc for `ResourceBundle-Provider`, but make sure you're reading at least the Java 10 version—it works the same as on Java 9, but the docs are clearer: http://mng.bz/G28M.

5.3   *Debugging modules and modular applications*

The module system tackles a complex problem and has ambitious goals. I think it does a good job of making the simple cases simple to use, but let's not kid ourselves: it's intricate machinery, and things will go wrong—particularly when you get into the following two parts of this book, which explore migrations to the module system and its more advanced features. In such cases, it can be helpful to peek into the module system's inner workings. Fortunately, it provides a couple of ways to do just that:

- Analyzing and validating modules
- Test-building a module graph
- Examining the universe of observable modules
- Excluding modules during resolution
- Logging module system behavior

In the following sections, I introduce each of them in turn.

5.3.1   *Analyzing individual modules*

You've seen that `jmod describe` shows a JMOD's modular properties (section 3.1.1) and that `jar --describe-module` does a similar job for JARs (section 4.5.2). These are great ways to examine individual artifacts. A slightly different path to the same destination takes `java --describe-module`. Followed by a module name, this option prints the path to the corresponding artifact as well as the module's descriptor. The module system does nothing else and neither resolves modules nor launches the application.

So whereas `jmod describe` and `jar --describe-module` operate on artifacts, `java --describe` operates on modules. Depending on the situation, one or the other may be handier, but in the end their output is similar.

Once again turning to *ServiceMonitor*, you can use `--describe-module` to peek into descriptors of its modules as well as of platform modules:

```
$ java
    --module-path mods
    --describe-module monitor.observer

> monitor.observer file:...monitor.observer.jar
> exports monitor.observer
> requires java.base mandated
```

```
$ java
    --module-path mods
    --describe-module java.sql

> java.sql@9.0.4
> exports java.sql
> exports javax.sql
> exports javax.transaction.xa
> requires java.base mandated
> requires java.logging transitive
> requires java.xml transitive
> uses java.sql.Driver
```

5.3.2   Validating sets of modules

Looking into individual modules comes in handy for analyzing known problems. But what about unknown issues? Is the module path free of duplicate modules? Do any modules split packages?

The java option `--validate-modules` scans the module path for errors. It reports duplicate modules and split packages but builds no module graph, so it can't discover missing modules or dependency cycles. After executing the checks, java exits.

For this example, I created a module *monitor.rest* that contains the package monitor .observer just like the module *monitor.observer* does. This is the result of validating those modules:

```
$ java
    --module-path mods
    --validate-modules

# truncated standardized Java modules
# truncated non-standardized JDK modules
> file:.../monitor.rest.jar monitor.rest
> file:.../monitor.observer.beta.jar monitor.observer.beta
> file:.../spark.core.jar spark.core
> file:.../monitor.statistics.jar monitor.statistics
> file:.../monitor.jar monitor
> file:.../monitor.observer.jar monitor.observer
>     contains monitor.observer conflicts with module monitor.rest
> file:.../monitor.persistence.jar monitor.persistence
> file:.../monitor.observer.alpha.jar monitor.observer.alpha
> file:.../hibernate.jpa.jar hibernate.jpa
```

The output first lists all JDK modules, which are error-free, and then proceeds with the application modules. It lists the scanned JAR files and the modules discovered therein as well as the split package between *monitor.rest* and *monitor.observer*.

5.3.3   Validating a module graph

With the `--dry-run` option, the JVM executes the full module resolution, including building a module graph and asserting a reliable configuration, but then stops right before executing the main method. That may not sound particularly useful, but I find it is. Using `--dry-run` in a command that contains errors and thus prevents an application launch doesn't change anything. But when you finally get it right, the command exits, and you're back on the command line. This enables you to quickly experiment with command-line options until you get them right without continuously launching and aborting the application.

As an example of a faulty command, let's try to launch *ServiceMonitor* without a module path. As expected, it fails, because without a place to search for application modules the module system can't find the initial module *monitor*:

```
$ java --module monitor

> Error occurred during initialization of boot layer
> java.lang.module.FindException:
>     Module monitor not found
```

Adding `--dry-run` to the mix changes nothing:

```
$ java --dry-run --module monitor

> Error occurred during initialization of boot layer
> java.lang.module.FindException:
>     Module monitor not found
```

Now for a command that's supposed to work:

```
$ java
    --module-path mods:libs
    --dry-run
    --module monitor
```

This results in—nothing. The command is correct, and the module system is content, so it exits after module resolution without any messages.

Remember from section 5.1.2 that `--dry-run` must come before `--module` even if that looks sequentially displeasing. And a note for experts: if you're using a custom class loader, custom security manager, or agents, they will be initiated even with `--dry-run`.

5.3.4   *Listing observable modules and dependencies*

You used the option `--list-modules` in section 3.1.1, where it listed all platform modules in the current runtime with `java --list-modules`. With a better comprehension of how the module system works, I can let you in on the fact that it does more than that.

LISTING THE UNIVERSE OF OBSERVABLE MODULES

The option `--list-modules` lists the universe of observable modules. The module system does nothing else and neither resolves modules nor launches the application.

As introduced in section 3.1.4, the universe of observable modules consists of the platform modules (the ones in the runtime) and the application modules (the ones on the module path). During resolution, modules are picked from this set to build the module graph. The application can never contain modules that aren't listed with `--list-modules`. (But note that it's possible and pretty likely that many observable modules won't make it into the graph because they aren't required by any of the root modules—not even transitively.)

When calling `java --list-modules`, you tasked the JVM with listing all observable modules. Because you didn't specify a module path, only the runtime's platform modules would be printed.

Let's look at a less trivial example and list the modules in the *ServiceMonitor* application's `mods` and `libs` folders:

```
$ java
    --module-path mods:libs
    --list-modules

> spark.core
# truncated Spark dependencies
# truncated standardized Java modules
# truncated non-standardized JDK modules
> monitor
> monitor.observer
> monitor.observer.alpha
> monitor.observer.beta
> monitor.persistence
> monitor.rest
> monitor.statistics
> hibernate.jpa
# truncated Hibernate dependencies
```

If executed on a regular JDK install, the output is overwhelming, because it lists the roughly 100 platform modules. It also always contains all modules on the module path. Together, these are useful to see which modules the module graph can be built from, but they also make it hard to see the forest for the trees. There's a way to limit the output to a sensible subset, though, and we'll look into that next.

LISTING TRANSITIVE DEPENDENCIES

One interesting subset of that long list of observable modules is the transitive dependencies of an initial module. Luckily you can cut the list down to just that with the option `--limit-modules`. I'll explain in a minute how exactly it works—for now, trust me when I say that combined with `--list-modules`, you can use it to print the list of all transitive dependencies of any given module.

Here are a few experiments with some platform modules:

```
$ java --limit-modules java.xml --list-modules

> java.base
> java.xml
$ java --limit-modules java.sql --list-modules

> java.base
> java.logging
> java.sql
> java.xml
$ java --limit-modules java.desktop --list-modules

> java.base
> java.datatransfer
> java.desktop
```

```
> java.prefs
> java.xml
```

You can see that *java.xml* only depends on *java.base*, that the SQL module uses logging and XML capabilities, and that even *java.desktop*, which encompasses all of AWT, Swing, some media APIs, and the JavaBeans API has surprisingly few dependencies (although the reason isn't flattering—it's a humongous module containing *a lot* of functionality).

You can also use this approach to examine application modules. This becomes particularly useful once an application grows beyond a handful of modules, because then it quickly becomes difficult to keep all of them in mind.

Let's once again look at *ServiceMonitor* and examine the dependencies of some of its modules:

```
$ java
    --module-path mods:libs
    --limit-modules monitor.statistics
    --list-modules

> java.base
> monitor.observer
> monitor.statistics
$ java
    --module-path mods:libs
    --limit-modules monitor.rest
    --list-modules

> spark.core
# truncated Spark dependencies
> java.base
> monitor.observer
> monitor.rest
> monitor.statistics
```

The combination of --limit-modules and --list-modules shows that *monitor.statistics* only depends on *monitor.observer* (and on the omnipresent base module) and that *monitor.rest* pulls in all of Spark's dependencies.

Now it's time to look at how --limit-modules works.

5.3.5 *Excluding modules during resolution*

You just used --limit-modules to cut down the output of --list-modules. How does that work? Given that --list-modules prints the universe of observable modules, --limit-modules obviously limits it. And because you could use it to see all transitive dependencies of a module, these must get evaluated. Taken together, these two observations pretty much define the option.

The option --limit-modules ${modules} accepts a list of comma-separated module names. It limits the universe of observable modules to the specified ones and their transitive dependencies. If the option --add-modules (see section 3.4.3) or--module (see section 5.1) is used together with --limit-modules, the modules specified for those two options become observable *but their dependencies don't!*

Step by step, this is how the module system evaluates the option:

1 Starting from the modules specified to --limit-modules, the JPMS determines all their transitive dependencies. This is subject to the requirements for reliable configuration described in section 3.2.1.

2 If --add-modules or --module was used, the JPMS adds the specified modules (but not their dependencies).

3 The JPMS uses the resulting set as the universe of observable modules for any further steps (like listing modules or launching the application).

Some experimentation with --limit-modules should make it clear how exactly that works. Let's start by listing all transitive dependencies of *monitor.rest*:

```
$ java
    --module-path mods:libs
    --limit-modules monitor.rest
    --list-modules

> java.base
# to unclutter the output
# I'm leaving out the file paths
> monitor.observer
> monitor.rest
> monitor.statistics
> spark.core
```

You can flip back to figure 2.4 to verify that these are the right dependencies. Now, what do you think happens if you try to launch the application? To do that, you have to replace --list-modules with --module monitor:

```
$ java
    --module-path mods:libs
    --limit-modules monitor.rest
    --module monitor

> Error occurred during initialization of boot layer
> java.lang.module.FindException:
>     Module monitor.persistence not found,
>     required by monitor
```

This result demonstrates two aspects of how --limit-modules works:

- The initial module specified with --module becomes observable (otherwise the exception would complain about *monitor* not being found).
- None of the initial module's dependencies become observable (otherwise the application would launch).

The same is supposed to be true for --add-modules, so what can you expect to see when you add add-modules monitor.persistence?

- Because *monitor.persistence* is now observable, that particular error should disappear.
- Because its dependency *hibernate.jpa* isn't observable, you can expect an error about that.

Let's try it:

```
$ java
    --module-path mods:libs
    --limit-modules monitor.rest
    --add-modules monitor.persistence
    --module monitor

> Error occurred during initialization of boot layer
> java.lang.module.FindException:
>     Module monitor.observer.alpha not found,
>     required by monitor
```

This specific case is shown in figure 5.3.

Darn—the observer implementations are missing as well, so you never find out about Hibernate. Fortunately, this is nothing you can't solve with more --add-modules:

```
$ java
    --module-path mods:libs
    --limit-modules monitor.rest
    --add-modules monitor.persistence,
        monitor.observer.alpha,monitor.observer.beta
    --module monitor

> Error occurred during initialization of boot layer
> java.lang.module.FindException:
>     Module hibernate.jpa not found,
>     required by monitor.persistence
```

There you go!

In the previous section, you used the computed universe to list all modules referenced, thus effectively printing all transitive dependencies of some module. That isn't the only use case for --limit-modules, though. More will come up when we discuss services in chapter 10 (see section 10.1.2 on limiting service providers).

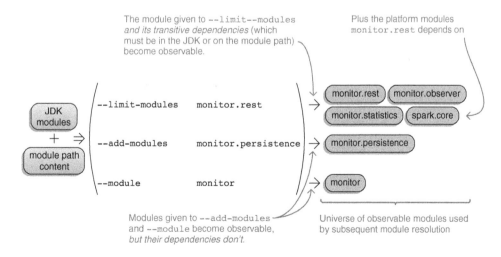

Figure 5.3 The --limit-modules option is evaluated before module resolution.

5.3.6   *Observing the module system with log messages*

Last but not least, we come to the magic bullet of debugging: log messages. Whenever a system misbehaves, and looking for problems in the obvious places (wherever those are for the particular misbehavior) doesn't turn up anything actionable, it's time to turn to the log.

Once you arrive here, chances are you're dealing with a relatively rare problem. For those cases, it's good to know how to extract log messages and related information as well as what the log is supposed to look like in the best-case scenario, where everything works. This section doesn't show how to fix a concrete problem—instead, it gives you tools to do those things yourself.

The module system logs messages into two different mechanisms (because, hey, why not?), one simpler and one more complex to configure:

- Diagnostic messages from the resolver
- Unified JVM logging

We'll look at both, starting with the simpler variant.

DIAGNOSTIC MESSAGES DURING MODULE RESOLUTION

With the option `--show-module-resolution`, the module system prints messages during module resolution. The following is the output from launching the *ServiceMonitor* application with that option. It identifies the root modules (one, in this case), modules that were loaded as a dependency, and which dependency that was:

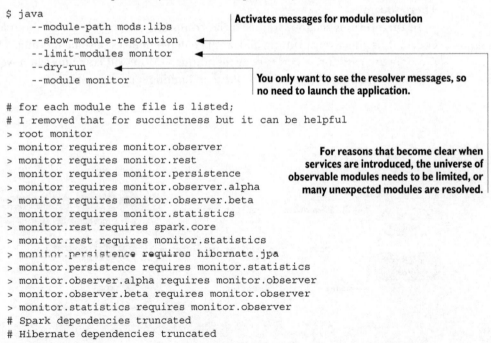

```
$ java
    --module-path mods:libs
    --show-module-resolution       ◄─── Activates messages for module resolution
    --limit-modules monitor        ◄───┐
    --dry-run          ◄───┐           │
    --module monitor       │           │
                           │   You only want to see the resolver messages, so
                           │   no need to launch the application.

# for each module the file is listed;
# I removed that for succinctness but it can be helpful
> root monitor
> monitor requires monitor.observer            For reasons that become clear when
> monitor requires monitor.rest                services are introduced, the universe of
> monitor requires monitor.persistence         observable modules needs to be limited, or
> monitor requires monitor.observer.alpha      many unexpected modules are resolved.
> monitor requires monitor.observer.beta
> monitor requires monitor.statistics
> monitor.rest requires spark.core
> monitor.rest requires monitor.statistics
> monitor.persistence requires hibernate.jpa
> monitor.persistence requires monitor.statistics
> monitor.observer.alpha requires monitor.observer
> monitor.observer.beta requires monitor.observer
> monitor.statistics requires monitor.observer
# Spark dependencies truncated
# Hibernate dependencies truncated
```

Teasing the resolver's diagnostic messages out of the module system is fairly simple but not customizable. Time to turn toward a more complex and powerful mechanism.

Java 9 brought a unified logging architecture that pipes a lot of messages the JVM generates through the same mechanism. Appendix C introduces it and explains how to configure it. If you never did that before, you should take a look now. I'll wait here.

Great—you're back. Armed with an understanding of the logging mechanism and configuration, you can have a closer look at how the module system works. The following experiments all launch the *ServiceMonitor* application with the known command, using --dry-run to prevent actual execution:

```
$ java
    --module-path mods:libs
    --dry-run
    --module monitor
```

The snippets will only show the -Xlog configuration used in addition to that command to define the output. To reduce the noise and keep your eye on the ball, I removed all tags and manually edited the messages to only show the most important parts—the real log contains much more information.

Following my own advice from appendix C, I looked into -Xlog:help and saw the tag module, which looks promising. I used it as module* to get all messages tagged with it:

```
# -Xlog:module*

# truncated many modules
> java.base location: jrt:/java.base
> jdk.compiler location: jrt:/jdk.compiler
> spark.core location: file://...
> monitor.persistence location: file://...
> monitor.observer location: file://...
> monitor location: file://...
> monitor.rest location: file://...
> Phase2 initialization, 0.0977682 secs
```

Here, the module system tells about the modules it loaded. These are all the involved platform modules as well as the *monitor.** modules and their dependencies. To get more details, let's include debug messages:

```
# -Xlog:module*=debug

# Argh! About 1500 lines of log messages
```

That output is a little overwhelming, but when you go through it step by step, it isn't complicated. Also, you have the chance to see in action some of the details of how the module system works. So let's do it!

The first thing the module system deals with is, interestingly enough, the unnamed module. That's still largely a mystery—see section 8.2. Next comes the base module—as described in section 3.1.4, all other modules depend on it, so it makes sense to define it early on:

```
> recording unnamed module for boot loader
> java.base location: jrt:/java.base
> Definition of module: java.base
```

Then starts the creation of all observable modules:

```
> jdk.compiler location: jrt:/jdk.compiler
> creation of module: jdk.compiler
> jdk.localedata location: jrt:/jdk.localedata
> creation of module: jdk.localedata
> monitor.observer.alpha location: file://...
> creation of module: monitor.observer.alpha
# many other modules get created
```

After all modules are created, the module system processes their descriptors, adding reads edges and package exports as defined therein:

```
> Adding read from module java.xml to module java.base
> package com/sun/org/apache/xpath/internal/functions in module java.xml
>       is exported to module java.xml.crypto
> package javax/xml/datatype in module java.xml
>       is exported to all unnamed modules
> package org/w3c/dom in module java.xml
>       is exported to all unnamed modules
> Adding read from module monitor.statistics to module monitor.observer
> Adding read from module monitor.statistics to module java.base
> package monitor/statistics in module monitor.statistics
>       is exported to all unnamed modules
```

You can see that it phrases package exports as "to module ..." and sometimes the value isn't even all unnamed modules. What's going on? Section 11.3 goes into that—here it suffices to recognize that package exports are processed.

And that's it! The last message is one you've seen before, which comes shortly before aborting the dry run:

```
> Phase2 initialization, 0.1048592 secs
```

If you take one step further into the Matrix and turn the log level to trace, you're confronted with a few thousand messages, but no spectacular revelations await you. You just see that as each class is loaded, the module system records which package and module it belongs to before eventually defining the packages. Once that's done, the corresponding module is created.

If you remove --dry-run and execute the application, you don't get much more information. On debug, no new messages are created; and on trace, you just see how a bunch of nested classes are assigned to the existing packages.

> **NOTE** In case you wondered, all of this happens in a single thread. You can verify that by printing the thread ID with -Xlog:module*=debug:stdout:tid, which shows the same ID for all module related operations.

Now you know how to configure logging and what the log is supposed to look like. That knowledge can be a great diagnostic tool. It comes in handy when a modular application doesn't work the way it's supposed to and other approaches failed to yield an analysis that helped solve the problem.

5.4 Java Virtual Machine options

Just like compiler and archiver, the virtual machine gets a number of new command-line options that interact with the module system. For your convenience, table 5.1 lists them. You can find the official documentation at https://docs.oracle.com/javase/9/tools/java.htm.

Table 5.1 Alphabetized list of all module-related VM (`java` command) options. The descriptions are based on the documentation, and the references point to the sections in this book that explain in detail how to use the options.

Option	Description	Ref.
`--add-exports`	Lets a module export additional packages	11.3.4
`--add-modules`	Defines root modules in addition to the initial module	3.4.3
`--add-opens`	Makes a module open additional packages	12.2.2
`--add-reads`	Adds read edges between modules	3.4.4
`--describe-module, -d`	Shows the module's name, dependencies, exports, packages, and more	5.3.1
`--dry-run`	Launches the VM but exits before calling the `main` method	5.3.3
`--illegal-access`	Configures how access from the class path to JDK-internal APIs is handled	7.1.4
`--limit-modules`	Limits the universe of observable modules	5.3.5
`--list-modules`	Lists all observable modules	5.3.4
`--module, -m`	Sets the initial module and launches its main class	5.1
`--module-path, -p`	Specifies where to find application modules	3.4
`--patch-module`	Extends an existing module with classes during the course of the compilation	7.2.4
`--show-module-resolution`	Prints messages during module resolution	5.3.6
`--upgrade-module-path`	Defines the location of upgradeable modules	6.1.3
`--validate-modules`	Scans the module path for errors	5.3.2

Beyond being able to use these options on the command line, you can also specify some of them in an executable JAR's manifest, define them in a specific environment variable the `java` command picks up, or put them into an argument file you hand to the launching JVM. Section 9.1.4 explains them all.

You've reached the second milestone and the conclusion of part 1. You're now well versed in the module system's fundamentals. If you have a chance, spend some time working with what you learned—maybe create your own demo or play around with *ServiceMonitor* (https://github.com/CodeFX-org/demo-jpms-monitor). What to read next depends on whether you have a project you'd like to migrate to Java 9+ and maybe even modularize (see part 2) or are more interested in learning what else the module system can do for you (see part 3).

Summary

- The initial module is defined with `--module`. If it defines a main class, no more is needed to launch the application; otherwise, the fully qualified class name is appended to the module name after a forward slash.
- Make sure to list all JVM options before `–module`, or they will be treated as application options and won't affect the module system.
- Observable modules can be listed with `--list-modules`. This comes in handy if you need to debug problems and want to see which modules were available for resolution.
- If `--limit-modules` is used, the universe of observable modules only consists of the specified modules and their transitive dependencies, thus reducing the modules that are available during resolution. Together with `--list-modules`, it's a great way to determine a module's transitive dependencies.
- The option `--add-modules` can be used to define additional root modules beyond the initial module. If a module isn't required (for example, because it's only accessed via reflection), `--add-modules` must be used to make sure it becomes part of the module graph.
- The option `--dry-run` launches the JVM and lets the module system process the configuration (module path, initial module, and so on) and build a module graph, but it exits just before the main method is called. This lets you verify a configuration without launching the application.
- The module system logs a variety of messages, which can be printed with either the simple `--show-module-resolution` or the more complex `-Xlog:module*`. They let you analyze how the module system puts together the module graph, which can help with troubleshooting.
- Loading resources from modules works much like loading them from JARs. The only exceptions are resources that aren't `.class` files and are in a different module's package (as opposed to, for example, the JAR's root or `META-INF` folder). These are by default encapsulated and therefore not accessible.
- A module can use `opens` directives to give reflective access to packages, which exposes resources located therein and allows other modules to load them. Unfortunately, this solution invites other code to depend on the module's internal structure.
- When loading resources, default to the methods `getResource` and `getResource-AsStream` on `Class` or their counterparts on the new type `java.lang.Module`. Those on `ClassLoader` generally have less-useful behavior

Adapting real-world projects

Part 1 of this book explored the module system's basics and how to compile, package, and run modular applications. In addition to teaching the relevant mechanisms, it showed how future Java projects will be organized and developed.

But what about existing projects? I'm sure you'd like to see them running on Java 9 or later, maybe even as modules. This part covers how to make that happen.

The first step, getting a project to compile and run on Java 9+, is obligatory for any code base that doesn't want to stay on Java 8 past its end of life or pay for support. The second step, turning the project's artifacts into modular JARs, is optional and can be done over time.

Chapters 6 and 7 are dedicated to the migration to Java 9. They're all about making your non-modular, class path-based project work on the newest release (without creating any modules). Chapter 8 then covers the features that allow you to incrementally modularize your project. Chapter 9 gives some strategic advice on how to migrate and modularize your project by using what you learned in chapters 6–8.

I recommend reading the chapters in that order, but if you prefer studying the technical details only when you need them, you could start with chapter 9. Alternatively, you could read up on the challenges you'll most likely encounter first: dependencies on JEE modules (section 6.1) and on JDK internals (section 7.1).

There are no specific examples for everything shown in this part of the book. The repository at https://github.com/CodeFX-org/demo-java-9-migration contains a variant of the *ServiceMonitor* application with a bunch of problems that need fixing to work on Java 9+. Give it a try!

Compatibility challenges when moving to Java 9 or later

This chapter covers

- Why JEE modules are deprecated and not resolved by default

- Compiling and running code that depends on JEE modules

- Why casts to `URLClassLoader` fail

- Understanding the new JDK run-time image layout

- Replacing the removed extension mechanism, endorsed standards override mechanism, and boot class path option

This chapter and chapter 7 discuss compatibility challenges when migrating an existing code base to Java 9 and beyond. You won't be creating any modules yet; these chapters are about building and running an existing project on the newest release.

Why does moving to Java 9+ require two entire chapters? Can't you install the newest JDK and expect everything to just work? Isn't Java meant to be backward-compatible? Yes—if your project, including its dependencies, only relies on nondeprecated, standardized, documented behavior. But that's a big *if*, and it turns out that in the absence of any enforcement, the wider Java community has strayed from that path.

As you'll see in this chapter, the module system deprecated some Java features, removed others, and changed some internals:

- Modules containing JEE APIs are deprecated and need to be resolved manually (section 6.1).
- The application class loader (also called the system class loader) is no longer a URLClassLoader, which breaks some casts (section 6.2).
- The directory layout of the Java run-time image (JRE and JDK) was overhauled (section 6.3)
- A number of mechanisms like compact profiles and the endorsed-standards override mechanisms were removed (section 6.4).
- A few smaller things were changed, too, like no longer allowing the single underscore as an identifier (section 6.5).

That's not all, though. Chapter 7 discusses two more challenges (internal APIs and split packages). They got their own chapter because chances are you'll encounter them again with non-JDK modules after you've migrated your project.

Taken together, these changes break some libraries, frameworks, tools, techniques, and maybe your code, too, so unfortunately updating to Java 9+ isn't always an easy task. Generally speaking, the larger and older the project, the higher the chances it will take some work. Then again, it's usually well-invested time, because it's an opportunity to pay back some technical debt and get the code base into better shape.

By the end of this chapter and the next, you'll know the challenges of updating to Java 9, 10, and 11 or even later. Given an application, you'll be able to make informed guesses about what needs to be done; and assuming all your dependencies play along, you'll be able to make it work on the newest release. You'll also be well prepared for chapter 9, which discusses strategies for migrating to Java 9 and later.

About the class path

Chapter 8 has a lot to say about how non-modular code runs on the modularized JDK. For now you only need to know the following:

- The class path is still fully functional. During a migration to Java 9+, you'll continue to use it instead of the module path.
- Even then, the module system is still in play: for example, regarding module resolution.
- Code on the class path will automatically read most modules (but not all: check section 6.1), so they're available at compile time or run time without additional configuration.

6.1 Working with JEE modules

A lot of code in Java SE is related to Java EE / Jakarta EE (which I abbreviate as JEE): CORBA comes to mind, and so do Java Architecture for XML Binding (JAXB) and Java API for XML Web Services (JAX-WS). These and other APIs ended up in the six modules shown in table 6.1. This could be nothing more than a small side note and the end of the story, but unfortunately it's not. When you try to compile or run code that depends on a class from these modules, the module system will claim the modules are missing from the graph.

Here's a compile error on Java 9 for a class using JAXBException from the *java.xml. bind* module:

```
> error: package javax.xml.bind is not visible
> import javax.xml.bind.JAXBException;
>                       ^
>     (package javax.xml.bind is declared in module java.xml.bind,
>       which is not in the module graph)
> 1 error
```

If you get it past the compiler but forget to massage the runtime, you'll get a NoClassDefFoundError:

```
> Exception in thread "main" java.lang.NoClassDefFoundError:
>         javax/xml/bind/JAXBException
>     at monitor.Main.main(Main.java:27)
> Caused by: ClassNotFoundException:
>         javax.xml.bind.JAXBException
>     at java.base/BuiltinClassLoader.loadClass
>         (BuiltinClassLoader.java:582)
>     at java.base/ClassLoaders$AppClassLoader.loadClass
>         (ClassLoaders.java:185)
>     at java.base/ClassLoader.loadClass
>         (ClassLoader.java:496)
>     ... 1 more
```

What's going on? Why are properly standardized Java APIs not present for code on the class path, and what can be done about that?

Table 6.1 The six JEE modules. The descriptions cite the documentation.

Module name	Description	Packages
java.activation	Defines the JavaBeans Activation Framework (JAF) API	`javax.activation`
java.corba	Defines the Java binding of the Open Management Group (OMG) CORBA APIs, and the RMI-IIOP API	`javax.activity,` `javax.rmi,` `javax.rmi.CORBA,` `org.omg.*`

Table 6.1   The six JEE modules. The descriptions cite the documentation. *(continued)*

Module name	Description	Packages
java.transaction	Defines a subset of the Java Transaction API (JTA) to support CORBA interop	`javax.transaction`
java.xml.bind	Defines the JAXB API	`javax.xml.bind.*`
java.xml.ws	Defines the JAX-WS and Web Services Metadata APIs	`javax.jws,` `javax.jws.soap,` `javax.xml.soap,` `javax.xml.ws.*`
java.xml.ws.annotation	Defines a subset of the Common Annotations API to support programs running on the Java SE platform	`javax.annotation`

6.1.1   *Why are the JEE modules special?*

Java SE contains a few packages that consist of *endorsed standards* and *standalone technologies*. These technologies are developed outside the Java Community Process (JCP), often because they rely on standards governed by other bodies. Examples are the Document Object Model (DOM), developed by the World Wide Web Consortium (W3C) and the Web Hypertext Application Technology Working Group (WHATWG), and Simple API for XML (SAX). If you're interested, you can find a list of them and the packages they're in at http://mng.bz/8Ek7. Disproportionately many of them fall into the JEE modules listed in table 6.1: *java.corba*, *java.xml.bind*, and *java.xml.ws*.

Historically, the Java Runtime Environment (JRE) shipped with implementations of these technologies but was ready to let users upgrade them independently of the JRE. This could be done with the *endorsed standards override mechanism* (see section 6.5.3).

Similarly, application servers often extend or upgrade the CORBA, JAXB, or JAX-WS APIs as well as the JavaBeans Activation Framework (in *java.activation*) or the JTA (in *java.transaction*) by providing their own implementations. Finally, *java.xml.ws.annotation* contains the `javax.annotation` package. It's often extended by the various JSR 305 implementations, which are most famous for their `null`-related annotations.

In all these cases of extending or replacing APIs that ship with Java, the trick is to use the exact same package and class names, so the classes are loaded from an external JAR instead of the built-in ones. In the parlance of the module system, this is called a *split package*: the same package is split across different modules or a module and the class path.

> ### The end of split packages
>
> Splitting packages no longer works in Java 9+ and later. We'll look into that in detail in section 7.2—for now it suffices to know that classes on the class path in a package that's distributed with Java are effectively invisible:
>
> - If Java contains a class with the same fully qualified name, that one will be loaded.
> - If the Java built-in version of the package doesn't contain the required class, the result is the compile error or `NoClassDefFoundError` that I showed earlier. And that happens regardless of whether the class is present on the class path.

This is a general mechanism for all packages of all modules: splitting them between a module and the class path makes the class-path portion invisible. What makes the six JEE modules special is that unlike other modules, it's customary to extend or upgrade them with the split-package approach.

To keep application servers and libraries like the JSR 305 implementations working without extensive configuration, a trade-off was made: for code on the class path, Java 9 and 10 by default don't resolve the JEE modules, meaning they don't make it into the module graph and hence aren't available (see section 3.4.3 for unresolved modules and section 8.2.2 for details of the class path scenario).

That works well for applications that come with their own implementations of these JEE APIs, but not so much for those that relied on the JDK variants. Without further configuration, code on the class path using types from those six modules will fail to compile and run.

To get rid of this complexity and to properly separate Java SE from JEE, these modules are deprecated in Java 9 and removed in Java 11. With their removal, command-line tools like wsgen and xjc are also no longer shipped with the JDK.

6.1.2 *Manually resolving JEE modules*

What do you do if you get a compile or run-time error due to missing JEE APIs, or if a JDeps analysis (see appendix D) shows that you depend on JEE modules? There are three answers:

- If your application runs in an application server, it may provide an implementation of those APIs, in which case you shouldn't encounter run-time errors. Depending on your setup, you may have to fix build errors, though—either of the other two solutions should do that.
- Pick a third-party implementation of that API, and add it as a dependency to your project. Because JEE modules aren't resolved by default, that implementation is used during compilation and at run time without problems.
- On Java 9 and 10, add the platform module with --add-modules as described in section 3.4.3. Because the JEE modules are removed in Java 11, this won't work there.

The example at the beginning of the section tried to use JAXBException from the *java.xml.bind* module. Here's how to make that module available for compilation with --add-modules:

```
$ javac
    --class-path ${jars}
    --add-modules java.xml.bind
    -d ${output-dir}
    ${source-files}
```

When the code is compiled and packaged, you need to add the module again for execution:

```
$ java
    --class-path ${jars}
    --add-modules java.xml.bind
    ${main-class}
```

If you depend on a few of the JEE APIs, it may be easier to add the *java.se.ee* module instead of each individual module. It makes all six EE modules available, which simplifies things a bit. (How does it make them available? Read about aggregator modules in section 11.1.5.)

 ESSENTIAL INFO   Instead of --add-modules, I recommend seriously considering adding third-party implementations of the required APIs as regular project dependencies. Section 9.1.4 discusses the drawbacks of using command-line options, so make sure to give it a read before going down that road. And because the JEE modules are removed in Java 11, sooner or later you'll need a third-party implementation anyway.

The effort of manually adding JEE modules is only required for unmodularized code. Once it's modularized, the EE modules stop being special: you can require them like any other module, and they will be resolved like any other module—at least, until they're removed.

> **Third-party JEE implementations**
>
> Comparing and discussing third-party implementations of the various JEE APIs would lead far away from the module system, so I won't do it here. For a list of alternatives, see JEP 320 (http://openjdk.java.net/jeps/320) or Stack Overflow (http://mng.bz/0p29).

6.1.3 *Dropping in third-party implementations of JEE modules*

Maybe you've been using the endorsed standards override mechanism to update standards and standalone technologies. In that case, you may wonder what happened to it in a time of modules. As you may have guessed, it was removed and replaced by something new.

Both the compiler and runtime offer the --upgrade-module-path option, which accepts a list of directories, formatted like the ones for the module path. When the module system creates the module graph, it searches those directories for artifacts and uses them to replace upgradeable modules. The six JEE modules are always upgradeable:

- *java.activation*
- *java.corba*
- *java.transaction*
- *java.xml.bind*
- *java.xml.ws*
- *java.xml.ws.annotation*

JDK vendors may make more modules upgradeable. On Oracle JDK, for example, this applies to *java.jnlp*. Furthermore, application modules that were linked into an image with jlink are always upgradeable—see section 14.2.1 for more on that.

JARs on the upgrade module path don't have to be modular. If they lack a module descriptor, they'll be turned into automatic modules (see section 8.3) and can still replace Java modules.

6.2 Casting to URLClassLoader

Running a project on Java 9 or later, you may encounter a class-cast exception like the one shown in the following example. Here, the JVM complains that it couldn't cast an instance of jdk.internal.loader.ClassLoaders.AppClassLoader to URLClassLoader:

```
> Exception in thread "main" java.lang.ClassCastException:
>     java.base/jdk.internal.loader.ClassLoaders$AppClassLoader
>     cannot be cast to java.base/java.net.URLClassLoader
>         at monitor.Main.getClassPathContent(Main.java:46)
>         at monitor.Main.main(Main.java:28)
```

The class loader returned by getClass is an AppClassLoader.

AppClassLoader doesn't extend URLClassLoader, so the cast fails.

What's this new type, and why does it break the code? Let's find out! In the process, you'll learn how Java 9 changes class-loading behavior to improve launch performance. So even if your project doesn't suffer from this particular problem, it's still a great opportunity to deepen your Java knowledge.

6.2.1 Application class loaders, then and now

In all Java versions, the *application class loader* (often called the *system class loader*) is one of three class loaders the JVM uses to run an application. It loads JDK classes that don't need any special privileges as well as all application classes (unless the app uses its own class loaders, in which case none of the following applies).

You can access the application class loader by calling ClassLoader.getSystemClass-Loader() or by calling getClass().getClassLoader() on an instance of one of your classes. Both methods promise to give you an instance of type ClassLoader. On Java 8 and before, the application class loader is a URLClassLoader, a subtype of ClassLoader;

and because `URLClassLoader` offers some methods that can come in handy, it's common to cast the instance to it. You can see an example of that in listing 6.1.

Without modules as a run-time representation of JARs, `URLClassLoader` has no idea in which artifact to find a class; as a consequence, whenever a class needs to be loaded, `URLClassLoader` scans every artifact on the class path until it finds what it's looking for (see figure 6.1). That's obviously pretty ineffective.

Listing 6.1   Casting the application class loader to `URLClassLoader`

```
                                              Gets the application class loader and
private String getClassPathContent() {              casts it to URLClassLoader
    URLClassLoader loader =
        (URLClassLoader) this.getClass().getClassLoader(); ◄
    return Arrays.stream(loader.getURLs())  ◄
            .map(URL::toString)                 getURLs doesn't exist on ClassLoader,
            .collect(joining(", "));            which is the reason for the cast.
}
```

Now let's turn to Java 9+. With JARs getting a proper representation at run time, the class-loading behavior could be improved: when a class needs to be loaded, the package it belongs to is identified and used to determine a specific modular JAR. Only that JAR is scanned for the class (see figure 6.1). This relies on the assumption that no two

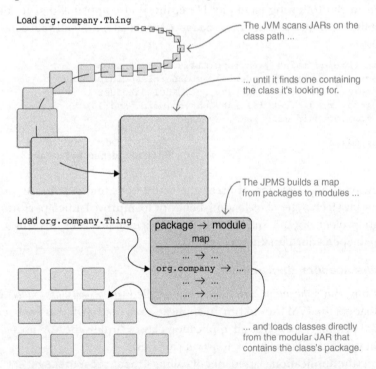

Figure 6.1   Without modules (top), a particular class is loaded by scanning all artifacts on the class path. With modules (bottom), the class loader knows which modular JAR a package comes from and loads it directly from there.

modular JARs contain types in the same package—if they do, it's called a *split package*, and the module system throws an error as section 7.2 explains.

The new type `AppClassLoader` and its equally new supertype `BuiltinClassLoader` implement the new behavior, and from Java 9 on, the application class loader is an `AppClassLoader`. That means the occasional `(URLClassLoader) getClass().getClass-Loader()` sequence will no longer execute successfully. If you want to learn more about the structure and relationships of class loaders in Java 9+, take a look at section 12.4.1.

6.2.2 *Getting by without URLClassLoader*

If you encounter a cast to `URLClassLoader` in a project you depend on and there's no Java 9+-compatible version to update to, you can't do much except one of the following:

- Open an issue with the project, or contribute a fix.
- Fork or patch the project locally.
- Wait.

If push came to shove, you could switch to another library or framework if it had versions that run fine on Java 9+.

If your own code does the casting, you can (and have to) do something about it. Unfortunately, chances are you may have to give up a feature or two. It's likely you cast to `URLClassLoader` to use its specific API, and although there have been additions to `ClassLoader`, it can't fully replace `URLClassLoader`. Still, have a look—it may do the thing you want.

If you just need to see the class path an application was launched with, check the system property `java.class.path`. If you've used `URLClassLoader` to dynamically load user-provided code (for example, as part of a plugin infrastructure) by appending JARs to the class path, then you have to find a new way to do that, because it can't be done with the application class loader used by Java 9 and later versions.

Instead, consider creating a new class loader—which has the added advantage that you'll be able to get rid of the new classes, because they aren't loaded into the application class loader. If you're compiling at least against Java 9, layers could be an even better solution (see section 12.4).

You may be tempted to investigate `AppClassLoader` and use its abilities if it does what you need. Generally speaking, don't! Relying on `AppClassLoader` is ugly because it's a private inner class, so you have to use reflection to call it. Relying on its public supertype `BuiltinClassLoader` isn't recommended, either.

As the package name `jdk.internal.loader` suggests, it's an *internal* API; and because the package was added in Java 9, it isn't available by default, so you'd have to use `--add-exports` or even `--add-opens` (see section 7.1 for details). This not only complicates the code and build process, it also exposes you to possible compatibility problems on future Java updates—for example, when these classes are refactored. So don't do it unless it's absolutely necessary to implement a mission-critical feature.

6.2.3 Finding troublesome casts

Examining the code for these casts is simple: a full-text search for "(URLClassLoader)" should do it and contain few false positives (include the parentheses to only find casts). As for finding them in your dependencies, I don't know of any tool that make that process comfortable. I guess a combination of build-tool magic (to get all your dependencies' source JARs in one place), command-line sorcery (to access all their .java files and *their* file content), and yet another full-text search could do the trick.

6.3 Updated run-time image directory layout

The JDK's and JRE's directory structures evolved incrementally, and it shouldn't be surprising that over the course of more than 20 years, they collected dust. One reason for not reorganizing them over time was, of course, backward compatibility. As is true for seemingly every detail, some code depends on their specific layout. Two examples:

- Some tools, particularly IDEs, depend on the exact location of rt.jar (the classes making up the core Java runtime), tools.jar (support classes for tools and utilities), and src.zip (the JDK source code).
- There exists code that searches for Java commands like javac, jar, or javadoc by speculating that the running JRE has a sibling directory bin containing them—which is true if the JRE is part of a JDK install, because that contains a bin folder with those commands and a jre folder next to each other.

Then came the module system, which broke with the basic assumptions that made these two examples possible:

- The JDK code is now modularized and should hence be delivered in individual modules instead of monolithic JARs like rt.jar and tools.jar.
- With a modularized Java code base and a tool like jlink, run-time images can be created from any set of modules.

Starting with Java 11, there is no longer a standalone JRE package. Running a program requires either a JDK or a package created by jlink.

As it became clear the module system would incur some breaking changes, the decision was made to go all the way and completely reorganize the run-time image directory structure. You can see the resulting changes in figure 6.2. Overall, the new layout is much simpler:

- A single bin directory and no duplicate binaries
- A single lib directory
- A single directory, conf, to contain all files meant for configuration

The most immediate consequence of these changes is that you need to update your development tools, because old versions likely won't work with JDK installs of version 9 and later. Depending on the project, it may make sense to search it for code that rummages around in the JDK/JRE folder to look up binaries, property files, or anything else.

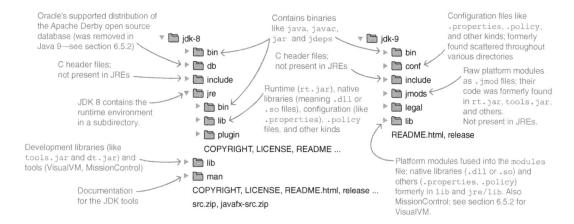

Figure 6.2 Comparison of the directory structure of JDK 8 and 9. The new one is much cleaner.

The URL you get for system resources, for example from `ClasLoader::getSystem-Resource`, has also changed. It used to be of the following form, where `${path}` is something like `java/lang/String.class`:

```
jar:file:${java-home}/lib/rt.jar!${path}
```

It now looks like this:

```
jrt:/${module}/${path}
```

All JDK APIs that create or consume such URLs operate on the new schema, but non-JDK code handcrafting these URLs must be updated for Java 9+.

Furthermore, the `Class::getResource*` and `ClassLoader::getResource*` methods no longer read JDK-internal resources. Instead, to access module-internal resources, use `Module::getResourceAsStream` or create a JRT file system as follows:

```
FileSystem fs = FileSystems.getFileSystem(URI.create("jrt:/"));
fs.getPath("java.base", "java/lang/String.class"));
```

For more details on how to access resources, see section 5.2.

6.4 *Selecting, replacing, and extending the platform*

When compiling code or launching the JVM, there used to be various ways to specify which classes constitute the JDK platform. You could select a subset of the JDK, replace a specific technology (like JAXB) with another, add a few classes, or pick an entirely different platform version to compile against or launch with. The module system made some of these features obsolete and reimplemented others with a more modern approach; and regardless of the JPMS, the Java 9 release removes a few more.

If you're relying on one or more of the features discussed in this section, you'll have to put in some work to keep your project running. Nobody likes to be forced into reworking something that doesn't cause any apparent problems, but looking over these features (most of which I never used), I can only imagine how much simpler the JDK internals became without them.

6.4.1   *No more compact profiles*

As section 1.5.5 explains, one goal of the module system was to allow users to create a run-time image with only the modules they need. This is particularly interesting for small devices with limited storage and for virtualizing environments, because both are interested in small run-time images. When it became apparent the module system wouldn't be released with Java 8, which was the plan for a while, compact profiles were created as an interim solution.

The three compact profiles define subsets of the Java SE 8 API and JREs with just the required classes to support those API subsets. After picking a profile that matches your application's requirements, you'd use the `javac` option `-profile` to compile against it (to make sure you stay within the selected subset) and then run the bytecode on the matching variant.

With the module system in play, much more flexible run-time images can be created with `jlink` (see section 14.1), and compact profiles are no longer needed. The Java 9+ compiler will hence only accept `-profile` if compiling for Java 8. To compile against a specific selection of modules, you can use the `--limit-modules` option, as explained in section 5.3.5.

These are the modules you need to get the same APIs as the three compact profiles:

- *For the compact1 profile—java.base, java.logging,* and *java.scripting*
- *For the compact2 profile—*Those for compact1 plus *java.rmi, java.sql,* and *java.xml*
- *For the compact3 profile—*Those for compact2 plus *java.compiler, java.instrument, java.management, java.naming, java.prefs, java.security.jgss, java.security.sasl, java.sql. rowset,* and *java.xml.crypto*

Instead of relying on a fixed selection, I recommend a different approach. Use `jlink` to create an image with only the platform modules you need (see section 14.1); if your application and its dependencies are fully modularized, you can even include your application modules (see section 14.2).

6.4.2   *Extension mechanism removed*

Before Java 9, the extension mechanism let us add classes to the JDK without having to place them on the class path. It loaded them from various directories: from directories named by the system property `java.ext.dirs`, from `lib/ext` in the JRE, or from a platform-specific system-wide directory. Java 9 removes this feature, and the compiler and runtime will exit with an error if the JRE directory exists or the system property is set.

Alternatives are as follows:

- The `java` and `javac` option `--patch-module` injects content into modules (see section 7.2.4).
- The `java` and `javac` option `--upgrade-module-path` replaces an upgradeable platform module with another one (see section 6.1.3).
- The extending artifacts can be placed on the class path.

6.4.3   *Endorsed standards override mechanism removed*

Before Java 9, the endorsed standards override mechanism let us replace certain APIs with custom implementations. It loaded them from the directories named by the system property `java.endorsed.dirs` or the `lib/endorsed` directory in the JRE. Java 9 removes this feature, and the compiler and runtime will exit with an error if the JRE directory exists or the system property is set. The alternatives are the same as for the extension mechanism (section 6.4.2).

6.4.4   *Some boot class path options removed*

The `-Xbootclasspath` and `-Xbootclasspath/p` options were removed. Use the following options instead:

- The `javac` option `--system` specifies an alternate source of system modules.
- The `javac` option `--release` specifies an alternate platform version.
- The `java` and `javac` option `--patch-module` injects content into modules in the initial module graph.

6.4.5   *No compilation for Java 5*

The Java compiler can process sources from various Java language versions (for example, Java 7, specified with `-source`) and can likewise produce bytecode for various JVM versions (for example, for Java 8, specified with `-target`). Java used to follow a "one plus three back" policy, which means `javac` 9 supports Java 9 (obviously) as well as 8, 7, and 6.

Setting `-source 5` or `-target 5` on `javac` 8 leads to a deprecation warning and is no longer supported by `javac` 9. Similarly, setting `-source 6` or `-target 6` on Java 9 results in the same warning. Now that there are releases every six months, this policy no longer applies. Java 10, 11, and 12 can compile for Java 6 just fine.

> **NOTE**   The compiler can *recognize and process* bytecode of all previous JDKs—it just no longer *produces* bytecode for versions before 6.

6.4.6   *JRE version selection removed*

Before Java 9, you could use the `-version:N` option on `java` (or the corresponding manifest entry) to launch the application with a JRE of version N. In Java 9, the feature was removed: the Java launcher quits with an error for the command-line option and prints a warning for the manifest entry while otherwise ignoring it. If you've been relying on that feature, here's what the Java documentation has to say about that:

> *Modern applications are typically deployed via Java Web Start (JNLP), native OS packaging systems, or active installers. These technologies have their own methods to manage the JREs needed, by finding or downloading and updating the required JRE, as needed. This makes the launcher's launch-time JRE version selection obsolete.*

Looks like the docs think applications using `-version:N` aren't modern—what a rude thing to say. Joking aside, if your application depended on that feature, you have no other option but to make it work without `-version:N`; for example, by bundling it with the JRE it works best on.

6.5   *Little things that make big things fail*

In addition to the larger challenges posed by the module system, there are a few changes, often not related to the JPMS, that are smaller but will cause trouble all the same:

- New format for version strings
- Removal of a number of JDK and JRE tools
- Single underscore no longer a valid identifier
- Java Network Launch Protocol (JNLP) syntax update
- Removal of JVM options

I don't want to keep you too long, but I also don't want to leave out something that stops your migration dead in its tracks. So I'll address each of these but be quick about it.

6.5.1   *New version strings*

After more than 20 years, Java has finally and officially accepted that it's no longer on version 1.x. About time. From now on, the system property `java.version` and its siblings `java.runtime.version`, `java.vm.version`, `java.specification.version`, and `java.vm.specification.version` no longer start with `1.x` but with `x`. Similarly, `java -version` returns x, so on Java 9 you get `9.something`.

> **Version string format**
>
> The exact format of the new version-string is still in flux. On Java 9, you get `9.${MINOR}.${SECURITY}.${PATCH}`, where `${SECURITY}` has the peculiarity that it doesn't reset to zero when a new minor version is released—you'll always be able to tell which version contains more security patches by looking at that number.
>
> On Java 10 and later, you get `${FEATURE}.${INTERIM}.${UPDATE}.${PATCH}`, where `${FEATURE}` starts with `10` and increases every six months with each feature release. `${INTERIM}` acts as you'd expect from `${MINOR}`, but because no minor releases are planned in the new schedule, it's assumed to always stay `0`.

An unfortunate side effect is that version-sniffing code may suddenly stop reporting the correct results, which could lead to weird program behavior. A full-text search for the involved system properties should find such code.

As for updating it, if you're willing to raise a project's requirements to Java 9+, you can eschew the system property prodding and parsing and instead use the new `Runtime.Version` type, which is much easier:

```
Version version = Runtime.version();
// on Java 10 and later, use `version.feature()`
switch (version.major()) {
```

```
    case 9:
        System.out.println("Modularity");
        break;
    case 10:
        System.out.println("Local-Variable Type Inference");
        break;
    case 11:
        System.out.println("Pattern Matching (we hope)");
        break;
}
```

6.5.2   Tool exodus

The JDK accrued a lot of tools, and over time some became superfluous or were superseded by others. Some were included in Java 9's spring cleaning:

- JavaDB is no longer included. It was an Apache Derby DB, which you can download from https://db.apache.org.
- VisualVM is no longer bundled with the JDK and became a standalone project at https://github.com/oracle/visualvm.
- The `hprof` agent library has been removed. Tools replacing its features are `jcmd`, `jmap`, and the Java Flight Recorder.
- The `jhat` heap visualizer was removed.
- The `java-rmi.exe` and `java-rmi.cgi` launchers were removed. As an alternative, use a servlet to proxy RMI over HTTP.
- The `native2ascii` tool was used to convert UTF-8–based property resource bundles to ISO-8859-1. Java 9+ supports UTF-8 based bundles, though, so the tool became superfluous and was removed.

Furthermore, all JEE-related command-line tools like `wsgen` and `xjc` are no longer available on Java 11 because they were removed together with the modules containing them (see section 6.1 for details on JEE modules).

6.5.3   The littlest things

Here comes probably the littlest thing that can make your Java 9 build fail: Java 8 deprecated the single underscore _ as an identifier, and on Java 9 you get a compile error when using it as one. This was done to reclaim the underscore as a possible keyword; future Java versions will give it special meaning.

Another issue: `Thread.stop(Throwable)` now throws an `UnsupportedOperation-Exception`. The other `stop` overloads continue to work, but using them is highly discouraged.

The JNLP syntax has been updated to conform with the XML specification and "to remove inconsistencies, make code maintenance easier, and enhance security." I won't list the changes—you can find them at http://mng.bz/dnfM.

Each Java version removes some deprecated JVM options, and Java 9 is no different. It has a particular focus on garbage collection, where a few combinations are no longer supported (`DefNew + CMS, ParNew + SerialOld, Incremental CMS`) and some configurations were removed (`-Xincgc, -XX:+CMSIncrementalMode, -XX:+UseCMS-CompactAtFullCollection, -XX:+CMSFullGCsBeforeCompaction, -XX:+UseCMS-CollectionPassing`) or deprecated (`-XX:+UseParNewGC`). Java 10, in turn, removes `-Xoss, -Xsqnopause, -Xoptimize, -Xboundthreads,` and `-Xusealtsigs`.

6.5.4   *New deprecations in Java 9, 10, and 11*

Finally, here's a non-exhaustive list of things that are deprecated in Java 9, 10, and 11:

- The Applet API in the `java.applet` package, together with the `appletviewer` tool and the Java browser plugin
- Java Web Start, JNLP, and the `javaws` tool
- The Concurrent Mark Sweep (CMS) garbage collector
- The HotSpot FlatProfiler, activated with `-Xprof`
- The `policytool` security tool

Java 10 and 11 already followed through on some of the deprecations:

- Java 10 removes FlatProfiler and `policytool`.
- Java 11 removes the Applet API and Web Start.

For more, as well as for details and suggested alternatives, check the release notes (Java 9: http://mng.bz/GLkN; Java 10: http://mng.bz/zLeV) and the list of deprecated code that's marked for removal (Java 9: http://mng.bz/YX9e; Java 10: http://mng.bz/qRoU).

Summary

- JEE modules are deprecated in Java 9 and removed in Java 11. You need to find a third-party dependency that fulfills your requirements sooner rather than later.
- In Java 9 and 10, these modules aren't resolved by default, which can lead to compile-time and run-time errors. To fix this, either use a third-party dependency that implements the same API or make the JEE module available with `--add-modules`.
- The application class loader is no longer of type `URLClassLoader`, so code like `(URLClassLoader) getClass().getClassLoader()` fails. Solutions are to only rely on the `ClassLoader` API, even if that means a feature must be removed (recommended); create a layer to dynamically load new code (recommended); or hack into the class-loader internals and use `BuiltinClassLoader` or even `AppClassLoader` (not recommended)
- The directory structure of the run-time image changed, and you likely have to update your tools, particularly IDEs, to work with Java 9 and later. Code rattling around in JDK/JRE directories or handcrafting URLs for system resources needs to be updated, too.
- Several mechanisms that modified the set of classes constituting the platform were removed. For most of them, the module system offers alternatives:

- – Instead of using compact profiles, create run-time images with `jlink` and configure compilation with `--limit-modules`.
- – Instead of the extension mechanism or the endorsed standards mechanism, use `--patch-module`, `--upgrade-module-path`, or the class path.
- – Instead of the `-Xbootclasspath` option, use `--system`, `--release`, or `--patch-module`.

- It's no longer possible to compile for Java 5 or to use the `-version:N` option to launch an application with Java version N.
- Java's command-line tools and the system property `java.version` report their version as `9.${MINOR}.${SECURITY}.${PATCH}` (in Java 9) or as `${FEATURE}.${INTERIM}.${UPDATE}.${PATCH}` (in Java 10 and later), meaning on Java X they start with X instead of `1.x`. A new API `Runtime.Version` makes parsing that property unnecessary.
- The following tools were removed:
  - – In Java 9: JavaDB, VisualVM, `hprof`, `jhat`, `java-rmi.exe`, `java-rmi.cgi`, and `native2ascii`
  - – In Java 10: `policytool`
  - – In Java 11: `idlj`, `orbd`, `schemagen`, `servertool`, `tnameserv`, `wsgen`, `wsimport`, and `xjc`
- The single underscore is no longer a valid identifier.
- The JNLP syntax has been updated to conform with the XML specification, so you may have to update your JNLP files.
- Each Java version removes deprecated JVM command-line options, which may break some of your scripts.
- Java 9 deprecates the Applet technology and Java Web Start, and Java 11 removes them.

Recurring challenges when running on Java 9 or later

This chapter covers

- Distinguishing standardized, supported, and internal JDK APIs

- Finding dependencies on JDK-internal APIs with JDeps

- Compiling and running code that depends on internal APIs

- Why a split package can make classes invisible

- Mending split packages

Chapter 6 discusses some problems you may come up against when migrating a project to Java 9+. Once you're done with that, though, you aren't going to encounter those issues again unless you pick up pre-Java 9 dependencies. This chapter explores two challenges you might still need to deal with:

- Relying on internal APIs leads to compile errors (section 7.1). This is true for JDK-internal APIs, such as classes from sun.* packages, but also for code internal to the libraries or frameworks you depend on.

- Splitting packages across artifacts causes compile-time and run-time errors (section 7.2). Again, this can happen between your code and JDK modules as well as between any other two artifacts: for example, your code and a third-party dependency.

Just like the problems we've discussed so far, you'll also have to work through these two issues when getting your project to work on Java 9+, but it doesn't stop there: you'll occasionally encounter them, even after migration, when working on code or pulling in new dependencies. Dependencies on module internals and split packages cause trouble regardless of the kinds of modules involved. You're just as likely to encounter them with class-path code and platform modules (the migration scenario) as with application modules (a scenario in which you're already running on Java 9 or later and are using modules).

This chapter shows how to break a module's encapsulation and how to mend package splits, regardless of the context in which these situations occur. Together with chapter 6, this prepares you for most things that could go wrong during a migration.

About the class path

In case you didn't read the note in chapter 6, I want to repeat it here:

- The class path is still fully functional, and during a migration to Java 9+ you'll continue to use it instead of the module path.
- Even then, the module system is still in play, particularly regarding strong encapsulation.
- Code on the class path will automatically read most modules (but not all; check section 6.1), so they're available at compile time or run time without additional configuration.

7.1 Encapsulation of internal APIs

One of the module system's biggest selling points is strong encapsulation. As section 3.3 explains in depth, we can finally make sure only supported APIs are accessible to outside code while keeping implementation details hidden.

The inaccessibility of internal APIs applies to the platform modules shipped with the JDK, where only `java.*` and `javax.*` packages are fully supported. As an example, this happens when you try to compile a class with a static dependency (meaning an import or a fully qualified class name, as opposed to reflective access) on `NimbusLookAndFeel` in the now-encapsulated package `com.sun.java.swing.plaf.nimbus`:

```
> error: package com.sun.java.swing.plaf.nimbus is not visible
> import com.sun.java.swing.plaf.nimbus.NimbusLookAndFeel;
>                                ^
>     (package com.sun.java.swing.plaf.nimbus is declared
>      in module java.desktop, which does not export it)
> 1 error
```

Surprisingly, many libraries and frameworks, but also application code (often the more important parts), use classes from `sun.*` or `com.sun.*` packages, most of which are inaccessible from Java 9 on. In this section, I'll show you how to find such dependencies and what to do about them.

But why discuss that? If internal APIs are inaccessible, there's nothing to talk about, right? Well, it's time to let you in on something: they're not *totally* inaccessible. At run time, everything will continue to work until the next major Java release (although you may get some undesired warning messages); and with control over the command line, any package can be made accessible at compile time. (I think I just heard a sigh of relief—was that you?)

Section 9.1.4 discusses the broader implications of using command-line options to configure the module system; here we focus on solving the immediate problem. We'll distinguish between static and reflective and between compile-time and run-time access (sections 7.1.3 and 7.1.4) because there are some critical differences. But before we get to that, you need to know exactly what constitutes an internal API and how the Java Dependency Analysis Tool (JDeps) can help find problematic code in your project and your dependencies.

> **TIP** If you're not sure how exactly reflection works, have a look at appendix B, which gives a brief introduction. Also, in this section we focus on reflective access into the JDK; for a more general view of reflection in a modular world, see chapter 12.

When you're done with this section, it will be an easy task for you to break open modules to benefit from APIs their maintainers didn't want you to use. More important, you'll be able to evaluate the benefits and drawbacks of that strategy, so you can make an informed decision about whether it's worth going down that road.

7.1.1 *Internal APIs under the microscope*

Which APIs are internal? In general, every class that's not public or not in an exported package—and this rule fully applies to application modules. Regarding the JDK, the answer isn't that simple, though. On top of the already historically complicated situation with standardized, supported, and internal APIs, Java 9+ adds a layer of complexity by making a special case for some APIs and removing others. Let's unravel the situation step by step.

THREE KINDS OF JDK APIs: STANDARDIZED, SUPPORTED, AND INTERNAL

Historically speaking, the Java Runtime Environment (JRE) has three kinds of APIs:

- The public classes found in `java.*` and `javax.*` packages are *standardized* and fully supported across all JREs. Using only these makes for the most portable code.
- Some `com.sun.*` and `jdk.*` packages and some classes they contain are marked with the `jdk.Exported` annotation, in which case they're *supported* by Oracle but not necessarily present in non-Oracle JREs. Depending on these binds code to specific JREs.
- Most `com.sun.*` packages and all `sun.*` packages as well as all non-public classes are *internal* and can change between different versions and JREs. Depending on these is the most unstable, because such code could theoretically stop working on any minor update.

With Java 9+ and the module system in play, these three kinds of APIs—standardized, supported, and internal—still exist. Whether a module exports a package is a key indicator but obviously doesn't suffice to demarcate three categories. The other indicator is the module's name. As you may recall from section 3.1.4, platform modules are split into those defined by the Java specification (prefixed with *java.**) and JDK-specific ones (prefixed with *jdk.**):

- The public classes found in packages exported by *java.** modules (these can be java.* and javax.* packages) are *standardized*.
- The public classes found in packages exported by *jdk.** modules aren't standardized but are *supported* on Oracle's and OpenJDK's JDK.
- All other classes are *internal* APIs.

Which specific classes are standardized, supported, or internal is largely unchanged from Java 8 to Java 9+. As a consequence, many classes in com.sun.* and all classes in sun.* are internal APIs just as they were before. The difference is that the module system turns this convention into an actively enforced distinction. Figure 7.1 shows the split where internal APIs are not exported.

That the *jdk.** modules aren't standardized is only a convention, and the module system is unaware of it. So although it may not be wise to depend on their exported APIs, the JPMS won't encapsulate them, and none of the command-line options we'll discuss are necessary. Here, when I talk about internal APIs, I mean those the module system makes inaccessible because classes aren't public or packages aren't exported.

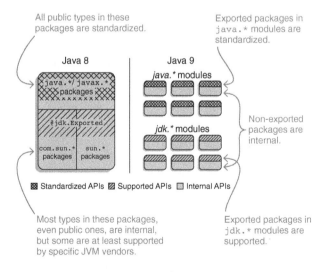

Figure 7.1 In Java 8 (left), package names and the rarely seen @jdk.Exported annotation decided whether an API was standardized, supported, or internal. From Java 9 on (right), module names and export directives fill this role.

A SPECIAL CASE FOR THE INFAMOUS SUN.MISC.UNSAFE

As you might imagine, the original idea was to encapsulate every API that was internal prior to Java 9. That caused a ruckus when the larger Java community realized it in 2015. Although the average Java developer may only occasionally use internal APIs, many of the best-known libraries and frameworks do so frequently, and some of their most-critical features depend on it.

The poster child for this situation is `sun.misc.Unsafe`, a class that, given its package name, is obviously internal. It offers functionality that's uncommon for Java and, as the class name suggests, unsafe. (Talk about expressive names!) Maybe the best example is direct memory access, which the JDK has to perform occasionally.

But it went beyond the JDK. With `Unsafe` readily available, some libraries, particularly those focused on high performance, started using it; over time, large parts of the ecosystem ended up directly or indirectly depending on it. The prospect of that class and others like it getting encapsulated led to the community uproar.

Following that, the team working on Project Jigsaw decided to allow a smoother migration path. A survey of the existing internal APIs and their use outside the JDK yielded this result:

- Most affected APIs are rarely or never used.
- Some affected APIs are occasionally used, but standardized alternatives existed before Java 9. A prime example is the `BASE64Encoder`/`BASE64Decoder` pair in `sun.misc`, which can be replaced with `java.util.Base64`.
- Some affected APIs are used occasionally but deliver critical functionality, for which no alternatives exist. This is where `sun.misc.Unsafe` can be found.

The decision was made to encapsulate the first two kinds but leave the third accessible for at least another major Java version. Exporting them from their respective modules would be confusing, though, because it would make them look like supported or even standardized APIs, which they're most definitely not. How better to make that point than by creating a suitably named module?

The critical APIs, for which no replacements existed before Java 9, are exported by the module *jdk.unsupported*. As the name suggests, it's JDK-specific (only guaranteed to be present on Oracle JDK and OpenJDK) and unsupported (content may change in the next release). In Java 9 to 11, it contains the following classes:

- From `sun.misc`: `Signal`, `SignalHandler`, and `Unsafe`
- From `sun.reflect`: `Reflection` and `ReflectionFactory`
- From `com.sun.nio.file`: `ExtendedCopyOption`, `ExtendedOpenOption`, `Extended-WatchEventModifier`, and `SensitivityWatchEventModifier`

If your code or dependencies depend on these classes (section 7.1.2 shows how to find out), then even though they were internal API before Java 9, you don't need to do anything to keep using them. For now. As standardized alternatives for their functionality are released (like variable handles, which replace parts of `Unsafe`), they will be encapsulated. I strongly recommend you have a close look at your use of these classes and prepare for their eventual disappearance.

REMOVED APIS

Although some internal APIs remain available for a few more years and most have been encapsulated, a few met an even harsher fate and were removed or renamed. This breaks code that uses them beyond the reach of any transition period and command-line option. Here they are:

- Everything in `sun.misc` and `sun.reflect` that isn't part of *jdk.unsupported*: for example, `sun.misc.BASE64Encoder`, `sun.misc.BASE64Decoder`, `sun.misc.Cleaner`, and `sun.misc.Service`
- `com.sun.image.codec.jpeg` and `sun.awt.image.codec`
- `com.apple.concurrent`
- `com.sun.security.auth.callback.DialogCallbackHandler`
- Methods `addPropertyChangeListener` and `removePropertyChangeListener` on `java.util.logging.LogManager`, `java.util.jar.Pack200.Packer`, and `java.util.jar.Pack200.Unpacker` (deprecated in Java 8)
- Methods with parameters or return types from `java.awt.peer` and `java.awt.dnd.peer` (these packages were never standardized and are internal in Java 9 and later)

Most of these classes and packages have alternatives, and you can use JDeps to learn about them.

7.1.2 Analyzing dependencies with JDeps

Now that we've discussed the distinction between standardized, supported, and internal APIs and the special case of *jdk.unsupported*, it's time to apply that knowledge to a real-life project. For it to be compatible with Java 9+, you need to figure out which internal APIs it depends on.

Just going through the project's code base won't cut it—you're in trouble if the libraries and frameworks it depends on cause problems, so you need to analyze them as well. This sounds like horrible manual work, sifting through a lot of code in the search for references to such APIs. Fortunately, there's no need to do that.

Since Java 8, the JDK ships with the command-line *Java Dependency Analysis Tool* (JDeps). It analyses Java bytecode, meaning `.class` files and JARs, and records all statically declared dependencies between classes, which can then be filtered or aggregated. It's a neat tool for visualizing and exploring the various dependency graphs I've been talking about. Appendix D provides a JDeps primer; you may want to read it if you've never used JDeps. It isn't strictly necessary to understand this section, though.

One feature is particularly interesting in the context of internal APIs: the option `--jdk-internals` makes JDeps list all internal APIs that the referenced JARs depend on, including those exported by *jdk.unsupported*. The output contains the following:

- The analyzed JAR and the module containing the problematic API
- The specific classes involved
- The reason that dependency is problematic

I'm going to use JDeps on Scaffold Hunter, "a Java-based open source tool for the visual analysis of data sets." The following command analyzes internal dependencies:

```
$ jdeps --jdk-internals        ◀—————  Tells JDeps to analyze use of internal APIs

    -R --class-path 'libs/*'   ◀—————  Recursively analyzes all dependencies

    scaffold-hunter-2.6.3.jar  ◀—————  Starts with the application JAR
```

The output begins with mentions of split packages, which we'll look at in section 7.2. It then reports on problematic dependencies, of which a few are shown next. The output is detailed and gives all the information you need to examine the code in question or open issues in the respective projects:

JPEGImageWriter (I truncated the package) depends on a few different classes.   **batik-codec depends on the removed API.**   **States what the problem is**

```
> batik-codec.jar -> JDK removed internal API        ◀———
>       JPEGImageWriter -> com.sun.image.codec.jpeg.JPEGCodec
>           JDK internal API (JDK removed internal API)   ◀———
>       JPEGImageWriter -> com.sun.image.codec.jpeg.JPEGEncodeParam
>           JDK internal API (JDK removed internal API)
>       JPEGImageWriter -> com.sun.image.codec.jpeg.JPEGImageEncoder
>           JDK internal API (JDK removed internal API)
# [...]
> guava-18.0.jar -> jdk.unsupported        ◀———
>       Striped64 -> sun.misc.Unsafe        ◀———
>           JDK internal API (jdk.unsupported)
>       Striped64$1 -> sun.misc.Unsafe
>           JDK internal API (jdk.unsupported)
>       Striped64$Cell -> sun.misc.Unsafe
>           JDK internal API (jdk.unsupported)
# [...]
> scaffold-hunter-2.6.3.jar -> java.desktop        ◀———
>       SteppedComboBox -> com.sun.java.swing.plaf.windows.WindowsComboBoxUI
>           JDK internal API (java.desktop)
>       SteppedComboBox$1 -> com.sun.java.swing.plaf.windows.WindowsComboBoxUI
>           JDK internal API (java.desktop)
```

Guava depends on jdk.unsupported.

Striped64 depends on sun.misc.Unsafe, and so do two of its internal classes.

Scaffold Hunter depends on classes internal to java.desktop.

JDeps ends with the following note, which gives useful background information and suggestions for some of the discovered problems.

```
> Warning: JDK internal APIs are unsupported and private to JDK
> implementation that are subject to be removed or changed incompatibly
> and could break your application. Please modify your code to eliminate
> dependence on any JDK internal APIs. For the most recent update on JDK
> internal API replacements, please check:
> https://wiki.openjdk.java.net/display/JDK8/Java+Dependency+Analysis+Tool
>
```

```
> JDK Internal API                        Suggested Replacement
> ---------------                         --------------------
> com.sun.image.codec.jpeg.JPEGCodec      Use javax.imageio @since 1.4
> com.sun.image.codec.jpeg.JPEGDecodeParam Use javax.imageio @since 1.4
> com.sun.image.codec.jpeg.JPEGEncodeParam Use javax.imageio @since 1.4
> com.sun.image.codec.jpeg.JPEGImageDecoder Use javax.imageio @since 1.4
> com.sun.image.codec.jpeg.JPEGImageEncoder Use javax.imageio @since 1.4
> com.sun.image.codec.jpeg.JPEGQTable     Use javax.imageio @since 1.4
> com.sun.image.codec.jpeg.TruncatedFileException
>                                         Use javax.imageio @since 1.4
> sun.misc.Unsafe                         See JEP 260
> sun.reflect.ReflectionFactory           See JEP 260
```

7.1.3 Compiling against internal APIs

The purpose of strong encapsulation is that the module system by default doesn't let you use internal APIs. This affects the compilation *and* run-time behavior of any Java version starting with 9. Here we discuss compilation—section 7.1.4 addresses run-time behavior. In the beginning, strong encapsulation will mostly be relevant for platform modules, but as your dependencies are modularized, you'll see the same barrier around their code.

Sometimes, though, you may be in a situation where you absolutely *have* to use a public class in a non-exported package to solve the problem at hand. Fortunately, that's possible even with the module system in place. (I'm stating the obvious, but I want to point out that this is only a problem for *your* code, because your dependencies are already compiled—they will still be impacted by strong encapsulation, but only at run time.)

> **Exporting to a module**
>
> The option `--add-exports ${module}/${package}=${reading-module}`, available for the `java` and `javac` commands, exports `${package}` of `${module}` to `${reading-module}`. Code in `${reading-module}` can hence access all public types in `${package}`, but other modules can't.
>
> When setting *${reading-module}* to `ALL-UNNAMED`, all code from the class path can access that package. When migrating to Java 9+, you'll always use that placeholder—only once your own code runs in modules can you limit exports to specific modules.

Until now, exports were always untargeted, so being able to export *to* specific modules is a new aspect. This feature is available for module descriptors as well, as section 11.3 explains. Also, I'm being a little handwavy about what `ALL-UNNAMED` means. It's connected to the unnamed module, which section 8.2 discusses in detail, but for now "all code from the class path" is a good approximation.

Let's return to the code that caused the following compile error:

```
> error: package com.sun.java.swing.plaf.nimbus is not visible
> import com.sun.java.swing.plaf.nimbus.NimbusLookAndFeel;
>                            ^
```

```
>      (package com.sun.java.swing.plaf.nimbus is declared
>       in module java.desktop, which does not export it)
> 1 error
```

Here, some class (which I omitted from the output because it's irrelevant) imports NimbusLookAndFeel from the encapsulated package com.sun.java.swing.plaf.nimbus. Note how the error message points out the specific problem, including the module that contains the class.

This clearly doesn't work out of the box on Java 9, but what if you want to keep using it? Then you'd likely be making a mistake, because there's a standardized alternative in javax.swing.plaf.nimbus; on Java 10, only that version remains, because the internal version is removed. But for the sake of this example, let's say you still want to use the internal version—maybe to interact with legacy code that can't be changed.

All you have to do to successfully compile against com.sun.java.swing.plaf.nimbus.NimbusLookAndFeel is to add --add-exports java.desktop/com.sun.java.swing.plaf.nimbus=ALL-UNNAMED to the compiler command. If you do that manually, it will look similar to the following (all placeholders would have to be replaced with concrete values):

```
$ javac
    --add-exports java.desktop/com.sun.java.swing.plaf.nimbus=ALL-UNNAMED
    --class-path ${dependencies}
    -d ${target-folder}
    ${source-files}
```

With a build tool, you'll have to put the option somewhere in the build descriptor. Check your tool's documentation to find out how to add command-line options for the compiler.

This way, code happily compiles against encapsulated classes. But it's important to realize that you've only pushed the problem to run time! Adding this export on the command line only changes the one compilation—no information is put into the resulting bytecode that would allow that class to access the package during execution. You still have to figure out how to make it work at run time.

7.1.4   *Executing against internal APIs*

I mentioned that, at least in Java 9, 10, and 11, JDK-internal dependencies are still available at run time. With everything else I've been telling you, that should be a little surprising. Throughout the book, I've been touting the benefits of strong encapsulation and said it's as important as visibility modifiers—so why isn't it enforced at run time?

Like many other Java quirks, this one was born from a dedication to backward compatibility: strong encapsulation of JDK internals will break a lot of applications. Even if it's just the outdated use of the Nimbus look and feel, the application will crash. How many end users or IT departments would install Java 9+ if legacy apps stopped working? How many teams would develop against Java 9+ if few users had it available?

To make sure the module system doesn't split the ecosystem in "pre Java 9" and "post Java 9," the decision was made to grant code on the class path illegal access to JDK-internal APIs until at least Java 11. Each of those aspects was chosen deliberately:

- *Code on the class path* … —Running code from the module path expresses that it has been prepared for the module system, in which case there's no need to make an exception. It's hence limited to class-path code.
- … to *JDK-internal APIs*—From a compatibility perspective, there's no reason to grant access to application modules, because they didn't exist before Java 9. So the exception is limited to platform modules.
- … *at* least Java 11—If the exception were permanent, the incentive to update troublesome code would be much lower.

As you saw in chapter 6, this doesn't solve all problems an application may run into when being executed on Java 9, 10, or 11, but it will be more likely to run successfully.

MANAGING BLANKET ILLEGAL ACCESS TO JDK-INTERNAL APIs

For a successful migration, it's important to understand the details behind the blanket illegal access to JDK-internal APIs; but exploring it will make your mental model of the module system more complicated. It helps to keep the big picture in mind: strong encapsulation disallows access to all internal APIs at compile time and run time. On top of that, a big exception was built, whose specific design was driven by compatibility concerns. It will disappear over time, though, bringing us back to the much more clear-cut behavior.

When allowing class-path code to access JDK-internal APIs, a distinction is made between code that statically depends on them and code that accesses them reflectively:

- *Reflective access results in warnings.* Because it's impossible to exactly identify all such calls by static analysis, execution is the only time to reliably report them.
- *Static access results in no warning.* It can easily be discovered during compilation or with JDeps. Due to the omnipresence of static access, it's also a performance-sensitive area, where checking for and occasionally emitting log messages is problematic.

The exact behavior can be configured with a command-line option. The `java` option `--illegal-access=${value}` manages how illegal access to JDK-internal APIs is handled, where `${value}` is one of the following:

- `permit`—Access to all JDK-internal APIs is permitted to code on the class path. For reflective access, a single warning is issued for the *first* access to each package.
- `warn`—Behaves like `permit`, but a warning is issued for *each* reflective access.
- `debug`—Behaves like `warn`, but a stack trace is included in each warning.
- `deny`—The option for those who believe in strong encapsulation: all illegal access is forbidden by default.

On Java 9 to 11, `permit` is the default value. In some future Java version, `deny` will become the default; and at some point the entire option may disappear, but I'm sure that will take a few more years.

It looks like once you get troubling code past the compiler, either by using the Java 8 version or by adding the required options to the Java 9+ version, the Java 9+ runtime will begrudgingly execute it. To see `--illegal-access` in action, it's time to finally look at the class that plays around with the internal Nimbus look and feel:

```
import com.sun.java.swing.plaf.nimbus.NimbusLookAndFeel;

public class Nimbus {

    public static void main(String[] args) throws Exception {
        NimbusLookAndFeel nimbus = new NimbusLookAndFeel();
        System.out.println("Static access to " + nimbus);

        Object nimbusByReflection = Class
                .forName("com.sun.java.swing.plaf.nimbus.NimbusLookAndFeel")
                .getConstructor()
                .newInstance();
        System.out.println("Reflective access to " + nimbusByReflection);
    }

}
```

It doesn't do anything particularly useful, but it clearly tries to access `NimbusLookAnd-Feel` both statically and reflectively. To compile it, you need to use `--add-exports`, as described in the previous section. Running it is simpler:

```
$ java --class-path ${class} j9ms.internal.Nimbus

> Static access to "Nimbus Look and Feel"
> WARNING: An illegal reflective access operation has occurred
> WARNING: Illegal reflective access by j9ms.internal.Nimbus
>     (file:...) to constructor NimbusLookAndFeel()
> WARNING: Please consider reporting this to the maintainers
>     of j9ms.internal.Nimbus
> WARNING: Use --illegal-access=warn to enable warnings of
>     further illegal reflective access operations
> WARNING: All illegal access operations will be denied in a
>     future release
> Reflective access to "Nimbus Look and Feel"
```

You can observe the behavior defined by the default option `--illegal-access=permit`: static access succeeds without comments, but reflective access results in a lengthy warning. Setting the option to `warn` would change nothing, because there's only one access, and `debug` adds the stack trace for the troublesome call. With `deny`, you get the same messages you saw in section 3.3.3 when you tested the accessibility requirements:

```
$ java
    --class-path ${class}
    --illegal-access=deny
    j9ms.internal.Nimbus
```

```
> Exception in thread "main" java.lang.IllegalAccessError:
>     class j9ms.internal.Nimbus (in unnamed module @0x6bc168e5) cannot
>     access class com.sun.java.swing.plaf.nimbus.NimbusLookAndFeel (in
>     module java.desktop) because module java.desktop does not export
>     com.sun.java.swing.plaf.nimbus to unnamed module @0x6bc168e5
```

There's one more detail to discuss: what happens with illegal access to JDK internals introduced in Java 9? Because the `--illegal-access` option was introduced to ease migration, it would be a shame if it made the eventual transition *harder* by giving you a few years to start depending on *new* internal APIs. That's indeed a risk!

 ESSENTIAL INFO   To minimize the risk of depending on new JDK-internal APIs, `--illegal-access` doesn't apply to packages introduced in Java 9. This shrinks the set of new APIs that projects may accidentally depend on to classes added to packages that existed before Java 9.

The things that are done for compatibility—I told you it would get more complex. And I'm not done yet, because we can also manage illegal access more specifically (see the next section). Table 7.1 in section 7.1.5 then compares the different variants.

MANAGING SPECIFIC ILLEGAL ACCESS TO SELECTED APIS

The `illegal-access` option is characterized by three central properties:

- It manages illegal access in a wholesale manner.
- It's a transitional option that will eventually disappear.
- It bugs you with warnings.

What happens when it's gone? Will strong encapsulation be insurmountable? The answer is no, it won't be. There will always be edge cases that require access to internal APIs (of platform and application modules), and hence some mechanism (maybe not an overly comfortable one) should exist to make that possible. Once again, we turn to command-line options.

 ESSENTIAL INFO   As I mentioned in section 7.1.3 when discussing internal APIs during compilation, `--add-exports` is also available for the `java` command. It works just the same and makes the specified package accessible to either the specified module or all running code. That means such code can use public members of public types in these packages, which covers all static access.

The class `NimbusLookAndFeel` is public, so all you need to do to properly access it is export the package that contains it. To make sure you observe the effect of `--add-exports`, deactivate the default permission of illegal access with `--illegal-access=deny`:

```
$ java
    --class-path ${class}
    --illegal-access=deny
    --add-exports java.desktop/com.sun.java.swing.plaf.nimbus=ALL-UNNAMED
    j9ms.internal.Nimbus

> Static access to ${Nimbus Look and Feel}
> Reflective access to ${Nimbus Look and Feel}
```

The reflective access goes through. Also notice that you don't get a warning—more on that in a minute.

This covers access to public members of public types, but reflection can do more than that: with the generous use of setAccessible(true), it allows interaction with nonpublic classes as well as nonpublic fields, constructors, and methods. Even in an exported package, these members are encapsulated, though, so to successfully reflect over them, you need something else.

The option --add-opens uses the same syntax as --add-exports and opens the package to deep reflection, meaning all of its types and their members are accessible regardless of their visibility modifiers. Because of its primary relation to reflection, the option is more formally introduced in section 12.2.2.

Still, its use case is to access internal APIs, so it makes sense to look at an example here. A fairly common one is provided by tools generating instances of classes from other representations, for example JAXB creating a Customer instance from an XML file. Many such libraries rely on internals of the class-loading mechanism, for which they reflectively accessed nonpublic members of the JDK class ClassLoader. Note that there are plans to remove the -illegal-access option in a future version of Java, but Oracle has not yet decided which version.

If you run such code with --illegal-access=deny, you'll get an error:

```
> Caused by: java.lang.reflect.InaccessibleObjectException:
>   Unable to make ClassLoader.defineClass accessible:
>   module java.base does not "opens java.lang" to unnamed module
```

The message is pretty clear—the solution is to use --add-opens when launching the application:

```
$ java
    --class-path ${jars}
    --illegal-access=deny
    --add-opens java.base/java.lang=ALL-UNNAMED
    ${main-class}
```

Unlike --illegal-access and its current default value permit, the options --add-exports and --add-opens can be seen as "the proper way" (or rather, "the least shady way") to access internal APIs. Developers deliberately formulate them based on their project requirements, and the JDK supports them in the long term. Accordingly, the module system emits no warnings for access permitted by these options.

More than that, they keep illegal-access from emitting warnings for packages that are made accessible by them. If these warnings bug you but you can't solve the underlying problem, exporting and opening packages this way makes the warnings go away. If even that won't work for you (maybe you don't have access to the command line), take a look at this on Stack Overflow: http://mng.bz/Bx6s. But don't tell anyone where you got that link.

NOTE As I explain in section 7.1.2, JDeps is a great tool to find static access to JDK-internal APIs. But what about reflective access? There's no foolproof way to find uses of APIs called via reflection, but a call hierarchy on java.lang.reflect.AccessibleObject::setAccessible or a full-text search for *setAccessible* will uncover most of them in your code. To verify your project as a whole, run the test suite or the entire application with `--illegal-access=debug` or `deny` to ferret out all illegal access via reflection.

7.1.5   Compiler and JVM options for accessing internal APIs

After working through this section, you've earned a pat on the back. The whole problem of internal APIs may look simple on the surface, but once you factor in the ecosystem's legacy and compatibility concerns, it gets a little complicated. Table 7.1 gives an overview of the options and how they behave.

Table 7.1   A comparison of the different mechanisms allowing run-time access to internal APIs; split between static access (code compiled against such classes or members) and reflective access (using the reflection API)

Static access				
Class or member	**Public**		**Nonpublic**	
Package	**Exported**	**Non-exported**	**Exported**	**non-exported**
Strong encapsulation	✔	✗	✗	✗
Default in Java 9 due to `--illegal-access=permit`	✔	✔	✗	✗
`--illegal-access=warn`	✔	✔	✗	✗
`--illegal-access=debug`	✔	✔	✗	✗
`--illegal-access=deny`	✔	✗	✗	✗
`--add-exports`	✔	✔	✗	✗
`--add-opens`	✔	✔	✗	✗

Reflective access				
Class or member	**Public**		**Nonpublic**	
Package	**Exported**	**Non-exported**	**Exported**	**Non-exported**
Strong encapsulation	✔	✗	✗	✗
Default in Java 9 due to `--illegal-access=permit`	✔	✗	Pre Java 9: ⚠ on first / else ✗	✗
`--illegal-access=warn`	✔	✗	Pre Java 9: ⚠ on all / else ✗	✗
`--illegal-access=debug`	✔	✗	Pre Java 9: ⚠ on all, and stack trace / else ✗	✗
`--illegal-access=deny`	✔	✗	✗	✗
`--add-exports`	✔	✔	✗	✗
`--add-opens`	✔	✔	✔	✔

Beyond technical details, it's important to look at possible strategies that bind these and other options together in a path to Java 9 compatibility. That's what section 9.1 does. If you're not looking forward to specifying options on the command line (for example, because you're building an executable JAR), take an especially close look at section 9.1.4—it shows three alternatives to that approach.

7.2 Mending split packages

Problems with illegal access to internal APIs, with unresolved JEE modules, or with most of the other changes discussed so far, as annoying as they may be, have something going for them: the underlying concepts are fairly easy to grasp; and thanks to precise error messages, the problems are easy to recognize. Neither can be said about split packages. In the worst case, the only symptom you'll see is the compiler or JVM throwing errors because a class that's clearly in a JAR on the class path can't be found.

As an example, let's take the class `MonitorServer`, which, among other annotations, uses JSR 305's `@Nonnull`. (Don't worry if you've never seen it—I explain in a minute.) Here's what happens when I try to compile it:

```
> error: cannot find symbol
>       symbol:    class javax.annotation.Nonnull
>       location: class monitor.MonitorServer
```

That's even though `jsr305-3.0.2.jar` is on the class path.

What's happening? Why are some types not loaded even though the class path contains them? The critical observation is that those types are in a package that's also contained in a module. Now let's see why that makes a difference and leads to classes not being loaded.

When different artifacts contain classes in the same package (exported or not), they're said to *split* the package. If at least one of the modular JARs doesn't export the package, this is also called a *concealed package conflict*. The artifacts may contain classes with the same fully qualified name, in which case the splits overlap; or the classes may have different names and only share the package name prefix. Regardless of whether split packages are concealed and whether they overlap, the effects discussed in this section are the same. Figure 7.2 shows a split and concealed package.

Split packages and unit tests

The split-package problem is one of two reasons unit tests, which are usually placed in a different source tree but in the same package as the production code, don't make up their own module. (The other reason is strong encapsulation, because unit tests often test classes and methods that aren't public or aren't in an exported package.)

Abundant sources for split-package examples are application servers, which typically run various JDK technologies. Take, for example, the JBoss application server and the artifact *jboss-jaxb-api_2.2_spec*. It contains classes like `javax.xml.bind.Marshaller`, `javax.xml.bind.JAXB`, and `javax.xml.bind.JAXBException`. This clearly overlaps

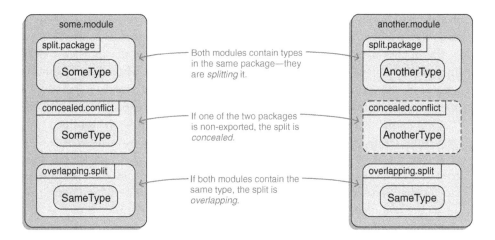

Figure 7.2 When two modules contain types in the same package, they split the package.

with and thus splits the `javax.xml.bind` package, contained in the *java.xml.bind* module. (By the way, JBoss is doing nothing wrong—JAXB is a standalone JEE technology, as explained in section 6.1.1 and the artifact contains a full implementation of it.)

An example for a non-overlapping and generally more questionable split package comes from JSR 305. The Java Specification Request (JSR) 305 wanted to bring "annotations for software defect detection" into the JDK. It decided on a few annotations like `@Nonnull` and `@Nullable` that it wanted to add to the `javax.annotation` package, created a reference implementation, was successfully reviewed according to the Java Community Process (JCP), and then—went silent. That was 2006.

The community, on the other hand, liked the annotations, so static analysis tools like FindBugs supported them and many projects adopted them. Although not exactly standard practice, they're commonly used throughout the Java ecosystem. Even in Java 9, they aren't part of the JDK, and unfortunately the reference implementation places most of the annotations in the `javax.annotation` package. This creates a non-overlapping split with the *java.xml.ws.annotation* module.

7.2.1 What's the problem with split packages?

What's wrong with split packages? Why would they lead to classes not being found even though they're obviously present? The answer isn't straightforward.

A strictly technical aspect of split packages is that Java's entire class-loading mechanism was implemented on the assumption that any fully qualified class name is unique—at least, within the same class loader, but because there's by default only one class loader for the entire application code, this is no meaningful way to relax this requirement. Unless Java's class loading is redesigned and reimplemented from the ground up, this forbids overlapping package splits. (Section 13.3 shows how to tackle that problem by creating multiple class loaders.)

Another technical aspect is that the JDK team wanted to use the module system to improve class-loading performance. Section 6.2.1 describes the details, but the gist is that it relies on knowing for each package which module it belongs to. This is simpler and more performant if every package only belongs to a single module.

Then, split packages collide with an important goal of the module system: strong encapsulation across module boundaries. What happens when different modules split a package? Shouldn't they be able to access each other's package-visible classes and members? Allowing that would seriously undermine encapsulation—but disallowing that would collide head-on with your understanding of visibility modifiers. Not a design decision I'd want to make.

Maybe the most important aspect is conceptual, though. A package is supposed to contain a coherent set of classes with a single purpose, and a module is supposed to contain a coherent set of packages with a single, although somewhat larger, purpose. In that sense, two modules containing the same package have overlapping purposes. Maybe they should be one module, then … ?

Although there's no single killer argument against split packages, they have a lot of properties that are undesired and would foster inconsistencies and ambiguity. The module system hence views them with suspicion and wants to prevent them.

7.2.2   *The effects of split packages*

Given the inconsistencies and ambiguities split packages can incur, the module system practically forbids them:

- A module isn't allowed to read the same package from two different modules.
- No two modules in the same layer are allowed to contain the same package (exported or not).

What's a *layer*? As section 12.4 explains, it's a container bundling a class loader with an entire graph of modules. So far, you've always implicitly been in the single-layer case, in which the second bullet wholly includes the first one. So unless different layers are involved, split packages are forbidden.

As you'll see next, the module system behaves differently, though, depending on where the split occurs. After we've covered that, we can finally turn to mending the split.

SPLITS BETWEEN MODULES

When two modules, such as a platform module and an application module, split a package, the module system will detect that and throw an error. This can happen at compile time or run time.

As an example, let's fiddle with the *ServiceMonitor* application. As you may recall, the *monitor.statistics* module contains a package monitor.statistics. Let's create a package with the same name (and the class SimpleStatistician) in *monitor*. When compiling that module, I get the following error:

```
> monitor/src/main/java/monitor/statistics/SimpleStatistician.java:1:
>     error: package exists in another module: monitor.statistics
>         package monitor.statistics;
>         ^
> 1 error
```

When trying to compile a module with a package that's also exported from a required module, the compiler notices the error. But what happens when the package isn't exported, meaning you have a concealed package conflict?

To find out, I added a class monitor.Utils to *monitor.statistics*, which means I split the monitor package between *monitor* and *monitor.statistics*. The split is concealed, because *monitor.statistics* doesn't export monitor.

In that situation—and I found this a little surprising—compiling *monitor* works. It's up to the runtime to report the error, which it dutifully does, immediately when launching the application:

```
> Error occurred during initialization of boot layer
> java.lang.reflect.LayerInstantiationException:
>     Package monitor in both module monitor.statistics and module monitor
```

The same is true if two modules (where neither requires the other) contain the same package: not the compiler but the runtime will find the error.

SPLITS BETWEEN A MODULE AND THE CLASS PATH

This chapter is focused on compiling and running a class-path application on Java 9 or later, so let's turn back to that use case. Interestingly, the module system's behavior is different. All code from the class path ends up in the *unnamed module* (more on that in section 8.2); to maximize compatibility, it is, generally speaking, not scrutinized, and no module-related checks are applied to it. As a consequence, the module system won't discover split packages and lets you compile and launch the application.

At first that may sound great: one less thing to worry about. Alas, the problem is still there, it just got less obvious. And arguably worse.

The module system knows for each named module (as opposed to the unnamed module), which packages it contains and that each package belongs to only one module. As I explained in section 6.2.1, the new class-loading strategy benefits from that knowledge; whenever it loads a class, it looks up the module containing the package and tries to load from there. If it contains the class, great; if it doesn't, the result is a NoClassDefFoundError.

If a package is split between a module and the class path, the class loader will always *and only* look into the module when loading classes from that package (see figure 7.3).

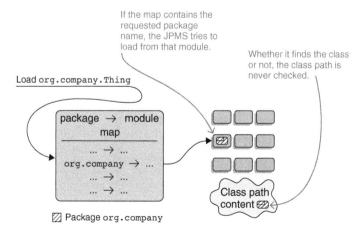

If the map contains the requested package name, the JPMS tries to load from that module.

Whether it finds the class or not, the class path is never checked.

Load org.company.Thing

package → module map

... → ...
org.company → ...
... → ...
... → ...

Class path content ▨

▨ Package org.company

Figure 7.3 Class-path content isn't exposed to module checks, and its packages aren't indexed. If it splits a package with a module, the class loader will only know about the module and look there for classes. Here it looks for org.company and checks the corresponding module, ignoring the class-path portion of the package.

Classes in the class-path portion of the package are effectively invisible! This is true for splits between platform modules and the class path and just the same for application modules (meaning JARs loaded from the module path) and the class path.

Yes, you got that right. If some code contains a class from, say, the `javax.annotation` package, then the class loader will look into the only module that contains that package: *java.xml.ws.annotation*. If the class isn't found there, you get a `NoClassDefFoundError`, *even if the class is present on the class path!*

As you may imagine, arbitrarily missing classes can lead to some head-scratching. This is the precise reason JEE modules, which foster package splits, aren't resolved by default, as section 6.1 explains. Still, these modules can make for the weirdest split-package case.

Consider a project that uses the annotations `@Generated` and `@Nonnull`. The first is present in Java 8, and the second comes from a JSR 305 implementation the project has on its class path. Both are in the `javax.annotation` package. What happens when you compile that on Java 9 or later?

```
> error: cannot find symbol
>     symbol:   class Generated
>     location: package javax.annotation
```

So *the Java class* is missing? Yes, because it comes from the JEE module *java.xml.ws .annotation*, which isn't resolved by default. But the error message is different here: it doesn't hint toward the solution. Fortunately, you paid attention earlier and know that you can fix this by adding the containing module with `--add-modules java.xml.ws .annotation`. Then you get the following:

```
> error: cannot find symbol
>     symbol:   class Nonnull
>     location: class MonitorServer
```

The compiler found that class a minute ago—why doesn't it now? Because now there's a module containing the `javax.annotation` package, so the class-path portion becomes invisible.

To repeat (you can also see this in figure 7.4):

- The first error was caused by JEE modules not being resolved by default.
- The second error was caused by the module system ignoring the class-path part of a split package.

Makes perfect sense (right?). Now that you thoroughly understand what's going on, let's turn toward fixing the situation.

7.2.3   *Many ways to handle split packages*

There are quite a few ways to make a split package work. Here they are, in the general order I recommend considering them:

- Rename one of the packages.
- Move all parts of the split package into the same artifact.
- Merge the artifacts.

- Leave both artifacts on the class path.
- Upgrade the JDK module with the artifact.
- Patch a module with the artifact's content.

NOTE Only the last two apply to the typical split-package scenario during a migration, where the package is split between a platform module and an artifact on the class path.

The first approach works when the package-name collision was accidental—it should be the most obvious choice and be used whenever possible. When the split was made on purpose, this is unlikely to work, though. In that case, you could try to mend the split by moving a few classes or by merging the artifacts. These first three options are proper, long-term solutions to the problem, but obviously they only work when you have control over the splitting artifacts.

If the splitting code doesn't belong to you, or the solutions aren't applicable, you need other options that make the module system work even though the package remains split. A straightforward fix is to leave both artifacts on the class path, where they will be bundled into the same unnamed module and behave as they did before Java 9. This is a valid intermediate strategy while you wait for the project(s) to hash out the collision and fix it.

Unfortunately, none of the solutions discussed so far apply when part of the split belongs to a JDK module, because you have no direct control over it—to overcome that

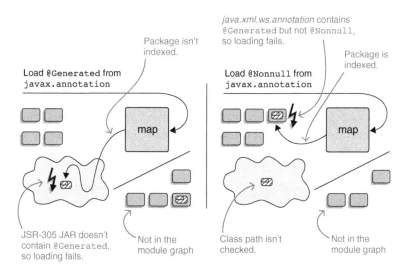

Figure 7.4 Loading from the same package can fail for different reasons. At left, the JEE module *java.xml.ws.annotation* wasn't added, so loading @Generated fails because the JSR 305 artifact on the class path doesn't contain it. At right, the module was added, so class loading tries to load all javax.annotation classes from there—even @Nonnull, which only JSR 305 contains. In the end, both approaches fail to load all required annotations.

split, you need bigger guns. If you're lucky, the splitting artifact consists of more than just a few classes that go into a random JDK package and a replacement for an entire, upgradeable JDK module is provided. In that case, see section 6.1.3, which explains how to use `--upgrade-module-path`.

If none of that helped, you're stuck with the final and most hacky approach: patching modules.

7.2.4   *Patching modules: Last resort for handling split packages*

One technique can fix pretty much every split package but should always be the last resort: making the module system pretend the troublesome classes on the class path belonged into the split package's module. The compiler and run-time option `--patch-module ${module}=${artifact}` merges all classes from `${artifact}` into `${module}`. There are a few things to look out for, but let's see an example before we get to them.

Earlier, we looked at the example of a project that uses the annotations `@Generated` (from the *java.xml.ws.annotation* module) and `@Nonnull` (from a JSR 305 implementation). We discovered three things:

- Both annotations are in the `javax.annotation` package, thus creating a split.
- You need to add the module manually, because it's a JEE module.
- Doing so makes the JSR 305 portion of the split package invisible.

Now you know that you can use `--patch-module` to mend the split:

```
javac
    --add-modules java.xml.ws.annotation
    --patch-module java.xml.ws.annotation=jsr305-3.0.2.jar
    --class-path 'libs/*'
    -d classes/monitor.rest
    ${source-files}
```

This way, all classes in `jsr305-3.0.2.jar` become part of the module *java.xml.ws.annotation* and can be loaded for a successful compilation (or, on `java`, execution). Yay!

There are a few things to look out for. First, patching a module doesn't automatically add it to the module graph. If it isn't required explicitly, it may still need to be added with `--add-modules` (see section 3.4.3).

Next, classes added to a module with `--patch-module` are subject to normal accessibility rules (see section 3.3 and figure 7.5):

- Code that depends on such classes needs to read the patched module, which must export the necessary packages.
- Likewise, these classes' dependencies need to be in exported packages in modules read by the patched one.

This may require manipulating the module graph with command-line options like `--add-reads` (see section 3.4.4) and `--add-exports` (see section 11.3.4). Because named modules can't access code from the class path, it may also be necessary to create some automatic modules (see section 8.3).

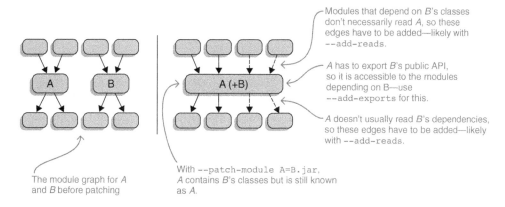

Modules that depend on *B*'s classes don't necessarily read *A*, so these edges have to be added—likely with --add-reads.

A has to export *B*'s public API, so it is accessible to the modules depending on *B*—use --add-exports for this.

A doesn't usually read *B*'s dependencies, so these edges have to be added—likely with --add-reads.

The module graph for *A* and *B* before patching

With --patch-module A=B.jar, *A* contains *B*'s classes but is still known as *A*.

Figure 7.5   If a module's classes are patched into another module (here *B* into *A*), the patched module's incoming and outgoing dependencies as well as package exports must be manually edited for the included classes to work properly.

7.2.5   *Finding split packages with JDeps*

Finding split packages by trial and error is unnerving. Fortunately, JDeps reports them. Appendix D gives a general introduction to the tool; you don't need to know much more than that, because split packages are included in pretty much any output.

Let's see what JDeps reports for the application that uses javax.annotation .Generated from *java.xml.ws.annotation* and javax.annotation.Nonnull from JSR 305. After copying all dependencies into the lib folder, you can execute JDeps as follows:

```
$ jdeps -summary
    -recursive --class-path 'libs/*' project.jar

> split package: javax.annotation
>     [jrt:/java.xml.ws.annotation, libs/jsr305-3.0.2.jar]
>
# lots of project dependencies truncated
```

That's unambiguous, right? If you're curious what depends on the split package, you can use --package and -verbose:class:

```
$ jdeps -verbose:class
    --package javax.annotation
    -recursive --class-path 'libs/*' project.jar

# split packages truncated
# dependencies *from* javax.annotation truncated

> rest-1.0-SNAPSHOT.jar -> libs/jsr305-3.0.2.jar
>     monitor.rest.MonitorServer -> Nonnull jsr305-3.0.2.jar
```

7.2.6   *A note on dependency version conflicts*

You saw in section 1.3.3 how Java 8 has no out-of-the-box support for running multiple versions of the same JAR—for example, if an application transitively depends on both

Guava 19 and 20. Just a few pages later, in section 1.5.6, you learned that, unfortunately, the module system won't change that. With what we just discussed about split packages, it should be clear why that's the case.

The Java module system changed the class-loading strategy (looking into specific modules instead of scanning the class path) but didn't change underlying assumptions and mechanisms. For each class loader, there can still be only one class with the same fully qualified name, which makes multiple versions of the same artifact impossible. For more details on the module system's support for versions, check out chapter 13.

> **TIP** You've learned about all the common and a few of the uncommon migration challenges. If you're eager to put your knowledge into practice and upgrade a project to Java 9+, skip to chapter 9—it discusses how to best approach that. Once your application runs on Java 9+, you can use `jlink` to create run-time images with just the modules it needs—see section 14.1. If you're interested in the next step, turning an existing code base into modules, read on in chapter 8.

Summary

- To know how the classes your project may depend on can be accessed under the module system, it's important to understand how they're categorized in the era of the module system:
  - All public classes in `java.*` or `javax.*` packages are standardized. These packages are exported by *java.** modules and are safe to depend on, so no changes are required.
  - Public classes in some `com.sun.*` packages are supported by Oracle. Such packages are exported by *jdk.** modules, and depending on them limits the code base to specific JDK vendors.
  - A few select classes in `sun.*` packages are temporarily supported by Oracle until replacements are introduced in future Java versions. They're exported by *jdk-unsupported*.
  - All other classes are unsupported and inaccessible. Using them is possible with command-line flags, but code that does so can break on JVMs with different minor versions or from different vendors; thus it's generally inadvisable.
- Some internal APIs have been removed, so there's no way to continue using them even with command-line options.
- Although strong encapsulation generally forbids access to internal APIs, an exception is made for code on the class path accessing JDK-internal APIs. This will ease migration considerably but also complicates the module system's behavior:
  - During compilation, strong encapsulation is fully active and prevents access to JDK-internal APIs. If some APIs are required nevertheless, it's possible to grant access with `--add-exports`.

- At run time, static access to public classes in non-exported JDK packages is allowed by default on Java 9 to 11. This makes it more likely that existing applications will work out of the box, but that will change with future releases.

- Reflective access to all JDK-internal APIs is permitted by default but will result in a warning either on first access to a package (default) or on each access (with `--illegal-access=warn`). The best way to analyze this is `--illegal-access=debug`, which includes a stack trace in each warning.

- Stricter behavior for static and reflective access is possible with `--illegal-access=deny`, using `--add-exports` and `--add-opens` where necessary to access critically required packages. Working toward that target early on makes migration to future Java updates easier.

- The module system forbids two modules (in the same layer) to contain the same package—exported or not. This isn't checked for code on the class path, though, so an undiscovered package split between a platform module and class-path code is possible.

- If a package is split between a module and the class path, the class-path portion is essentially invisible, leading to surprising compile-time and run-time errors. The best fix is to remove the split, but if that isn't possible, the platform module in question can either be replaced with the splitting artifact with `--upgrade-module-path` (if it's an upgradeable module) or patched with its content with `--patch-module`.

Incremental modularization of existing projects

This chapter covers
- Working with the unnamed
- Helping modularization with automatic modules
- Incrementally modularizing a code base
- Mixing class path and module path

Depending on how smoothly your migration to Java 9+ went (see chapters 6 and 7), you may have encountered a few of the more unpleasant effects of introducing a module system to an ecosystem that's old enough to order its own beer. The good news is it was worth it! As I briefly showed in section 1.7.1, Java 9+ has a lot to offer beyond the module system. If you're in a position to raise your project's Java requirements to 9, you can start using them right away.

You can also finally start modularizing your project. By turning artifacts into modular JARs, you and your users can benefit from reliable configuration (see section 3.2.1), strong encapsulation (section 3.3.1), decoupling via services (see chapter 10), run-time images including entire applications (see 14.2), and more module-related goodness. As section 9.3.4 shows, you can even modularize projects that run on Java 8 and before.

There are two ways to make JARs modular:

- Wait until all your dependencies are modularized, and then create module descriptors for all artifacts in one fell swoop.
- Start early by modularizing only artifacts, possibly just a few at a time.

Given everything discussed in chapters 3, 4, and 5, implementing the first option should be straightforward. You may need some of the more-advanced module system features that chapters 10 and 11 present, but other than that, you're good to go: create a module declaration for each artifact you're building, and model their relationships as you learned earlier.

Maybe your project sits atop a deep dependency tree, though, and you're not one to wait until all the dependencies are finished modularizing. Or perhaps your project is too big to turn all artifacts into modules in one go. In those cases, you may be curious about the second option, which allows you to incrementally modularize artifacts regardless of whether their dependencies are modular or plain JARs.

Being able to use modular and mon-modular artifacts side by side not only is important for individual projects, but also means the ecosystem as a whole can embrace modules independently of one another. Without that, the ecosystem's modularization might have taken several decades—this way, everyone should be able to do it within one decade.

This chapter is dedicated to features that enable incrementally modularizing existing projects: we start by discussing the combination of class path and module path, then examine the unnamed module, and wrap up by looking at automatic modules. When you're done, your project or parts of it will benefit from the module system despite potentially unmodularized dependencies. You'll also be well prepared for chapter 9, which discusses strategies for modularizing applications.

8.1 *Why incremental modularization is an option*

Before we get into how to incrementally modularize a project, I want to contemplate why that is even an option. Module systems usually require everything to be a module. But if they're late to the game (like the JPMS) or are only used by a small share of their ecosystem (like OSGi or JBoss Modules), they can hardly expect that to be the case. They have to find a way to interact with mon-modular artifacts.

In this section, we first ponder what would happen if every JAR had to be modular to run on Java 9+, leading to the conclusion that it must be possible to mix plain JARs and modules (section 8.1.2). I then show how using the class path and the module path side by side allows this mix-and-match approach (section 8.1.3).

8.1.1 *If every JAR had to be modular ...*

If the JPMS was strict and demanded that everything be a module, you could only use it if all JARs contained a module descriptor. And because the module system is an integral part of Java 9+, by extension you couldn't even update to it without having modularized all your code and dependencies. Imagine the consequences if that were the case.

Some projects might update to Java 9+ early, forcing all their users to modularize their code bases or stop using the project. Others might not want to force that decision or have other reasons not to make the jump, thus holding their users back. I wouldn't want my project to have dependencies that made opposing decisions. What could I do?

Then again, some projects would ship separate variants with and without module descriptors, for which they would have to use two entirely disjoint sets of dependencies (one with and one without module descriptors). Furthermore, unless they were back-porting across old major and minor versions, users would be forced to perform a lot of (possibly time-consuming) updates all at once to be able to make the jump to Java 9+. And that doesn't even consider projects that are no longer maintained, which would swiftly become unusable on Java 9+ even if they didn't have any dependencies themselves.

The only way to avoid wasted effort and a deep split would be for the entire ecosystem to have a day on which *every project* updated to Java 9+ and started to release modular JARs. But there's no way that would work. And whichever way we sliced it, anyone executing a JAR would have to know which Java version it was created for, because it wouldn't work on 8 *and* 9. In summary: we'd be in big trouble!

8.1.2   Mixing and matching plain JARs with modules

To bypass that trouble, the module system must offer a way to run mon-modularized code on top of the modularized JVM. In the introduction to chapter 6, I explain that this is indeed the case and that plain JARs on the class path work just as they did before Java 9+. (As chapters 6 and 7 explain, the code they contain may not function, but that's a different matter.) Section 8.2 explains how *class-path mode* works.

Just the fact *that* it works is already an important revelation: the module system can handle mon-modularized artifacts and knows how to navigate the boundary between them and explicit modules. That's good news—and there's more: that boundary isn't set in stone. It doesn't have to separate application JARs from JVM modules. As figure 8.1 shows and the rest of this chapter explores, the module system allows you to move that boundary and to mix and match modularized and mon-modularized application JARs with platform modules as your projects require.

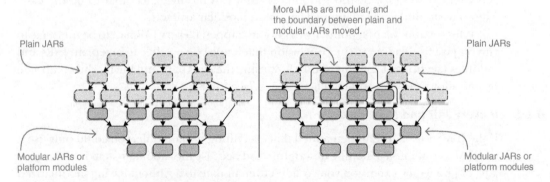

Figure 8.1   The module system allows non-modular code to run on a modular JDK (left). More important, it gives you the tools to move that boundary (right).

8.1.3 Technical underpinnings of incremental modularization

The basic principle that makes incremental modularization possible is that the class path and module path can be used side by side. There is no need to move all application JARs from the class to the module path in one go. Instead, existing projects are encouraged to start on the class path and then slowly move their artifacts to the module path as modularization efforts progress.

Using both paths at the same time with plain as well as modular JARs requires a clear understanding of how these concepts relate. You may be thinking that JARs lacking a module descriptor go onto the class path and that modular JARs go onto the module path. Although I never said it like that, you'd be excused for having read between the lines. Nevertheless, that theory is wrong, and now is the time to let go of it.

Two mechanisms invalidate that theory and make incremental modularization possible:

- The *unnamed module* is implicitly created by the module system with all the content loaded from the class path. In it, the chaos of the class path lives on. (Section 8.2 explains in detail.)
- *An automatic module* is created by the module system for each plain JAR it finds on the module path. (Section 8.3 is dedicated to this concept.)

The class path makes no distinction between plain and modular JARs: if it's on the class path, it ends up in the unnamed module. Similarly, the module path makes little distinction between plain and modular JARs: if it's on the module path, it ends up as its own named module. (For plain JARs, the module system creates an automatic module; for modular JARs, it creates an explicit module according to the description.)

To understand the rest of this chapter as well as to perform a modularization, it's important to fully internalize that behavior. Table 8.1 shows a two-dimensional recast. Not the type of JAR (plain or modular) but the path it's placed on (class path or module path) determines whether it becomes part of the unnamed module or a named module.

Table 8.1   It isn't the type of the JAR but the path it's placed on that determines whether a class ends up as a named module or in the unnamed module.

	Class path	Module path
Plain JAR	Unnamed module (section 8.2)	Automatic module (section 8.3)
Modular JAR		Explicit module (section 3.1.4)

When deciding whether to place a JAR on the class path or the module path, it's not about *where the code comes from* (is the JAR modular?); it's about *where you need the code to be* (in the unnamed or a named module). The class path is for code you want to go into the ball of mud, and the module path is for code you want to be a module.

But how do you decide where code needs to go? As a general guideline, the unnamed module is about *compatibility*, enabling projects using the class path to work on Java 9+; whereas automatic modules are about *modularization*, allowing projects to use the module system even if dependencies aren't yet modularized.

For a more detailed answer, it's time to look more closely at the unnamed and automatic modules. Chapter 9 then defines larger modularization strategies. If you're wondering whether modularizing an existing project is worth the hassle, take a look at section 15.2.1.

> **NOTE** Your build tool may make a lot of these decisions for you. You're still likely to end up in situations where something went wrong, though, in which case you can apply what we explore in this chapter to correctly configure your build.

8.2   *The unnamed module, aka the class path*

There's one aspect I haven't yet explained in detail: how do the module system and the class path work together? The first part of the book gives a clear view of how modular applications place everything on the module path and run on the modularized JDK. Then came chapters 6 and 7, which are big on compiling non-modular code and running applications from the class path. But how does the class-path content interact with the module system? Which modules are resolved, and how? Why can the class-path content access all platform modules? The unnamed module answers these questions.

Exploring them has more than academic value. Unless an application is fairly small, it probably can't be modularized all at once; but incremental modularization involves mixing JARs and modules, class path and module path. This makes it important to understand the underlying details of how the module system's class-path mode works.

> **NOTE** The mechanisms surrounding the unnamed module generally apply at compile time and run time, but always mentioning both needlessly bloats the text. Instead, I describe run-time behavior and only mention compile time if the behavior isn't exactly the same.

The *unnamed module* contains all mon-modular classes, which are

- At compile time, the classes being compiled, if they don't include a module descriptor
- At compile time and run time, all classes loaded from the class path

As section 3.1.3 describes, all modules have three central properties, and this is also true for the unnamed module:

- *Name*—The unnamed module has none (makes sense, right?), which means no other module can mention it in their declarations (for example, to require it).
- *Dependencies*—The unnamed module reads all other modules that make it into the graph.
- *Exports*—The unnamed module exports all its packages and also opens them for reflection (see section 12.2 for details on open packages and modules).

In contrast to the unnamed module, all other modules are said to be *named*. Services provided in META-INF/services are made available to the ServiceLoader. See chapter 10 for an introduction to services and particularly section 10.2.6 for their interaction with the unnamed module.

Although it isn't exactly straightforward, the concept of the unnamed module makes sense. Here you have the orderly module graph, and over there, a little to the side, you have the chaos of the class path, lumped into its own free-for-all module with some special properties (see figure 8.2). (To not make matters more complicated than they have to be, I didn't tell you at the time, but the unnamed module underlies all of chapters 6 and 7, where you could replace every occurrence of *class-path content* with *unnamed module*.)

Let's get back to the *ServiceMonitor* application and assume it was written before Java 9. The code and its organization are identical to what we discussed in previous chapters, but it lacks module declarations, so you create plain JARs instead of modular JARs.

Assuming the jars folder contains all application JARs and libs contains all dependencies, you can launch the application as follows:

```
$ java --class-path 'jars/*':'libs/*' monitor.Main
```

This works on Java 9+, and, aside from the alternative form of the --class-path option, it does the same on Java 8 and earlier. Figure 8.2 shows the module graph the module system creates for this launch configuration.

Armed with that understanding, you're well prepared to run simple, mon-modular applications from the class path. Beyond that basic use case, and particularly when slowly modularizing an application, the subtleties of the unnamed module become relevant, so we look at them next.

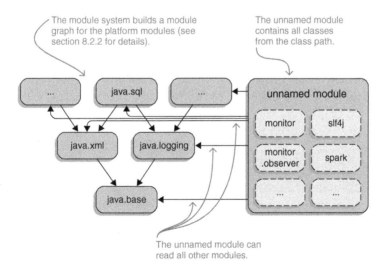

Figure 8.2   Launched with all application JARs on the class path, the module system builds a module graph from the platform modules (left) and assigns all classes on the class path to the unnamed module (right), which can read all other modules

8.2.1 *The chaos of the class path, captured by the unnamed module*

The unnamed module's main goal is to capture class-path content and make it work in the module system. Because there were never any boundaries between JARs on the class path, it makes no sense to establish them now; so having a single unnamed module for the entire class path is a reasonable decision. Within it, just like on the class path, all public classes are accessible and the concept of split packages doesn't exist.

The unnamed module's distinct role and its focus on backward compatibility give it a few special properties. You saw in section 7.1 that at run time, strong encapsulation of platform modules is mostly disabled for code in the unnamed module (at least on Java 9, 10, and 11). When we discussed split packages in section 7.2, you discovered that the unnamed module isn't scanned, so package splits between it and other modules aren't discovered and the class path portion isn't available.

One detail that's a little counterintuitive and easy to get wrong is what constitutes the unnamed module. It seems obvious that modular JARs become modules and hence plain JARs go into the unnamed module, right? As explained in section 8.1.3, this is wrong: the unnamed module is in charge of *all JARs on the class path*, modular or not.

As a consequence, modular JARs aren't bound to be loaded as modules! If a library starts delivering modular JARs, its users are by no means forced to use them as modules. Users can instead leave them on the class path, where their code is bundled into the unnamed module. As section 9.2 explains in more detail, this allows the ecosystem to modularize almost independently of one another.

As an example, let's launch the fully modularized version of *ServiceMonitor*, once from the class path and once from the module path:

```
$ java --class-path 'mods/*':'libs/*' -jar monitor
$ java --module-path mods:libs --module monitor
```

Both work fine and without any obvious differences.

One way to see how the module system treats both cases is to use an API that we take a closer look at in section 12.3.3. You can call `getModule` on a class to get the module it belongs to and then call `getName` on that module to see what it's called. For the unnamed module, `getName` returns `null`.

Let's include the following lines of code in `Main`:

```
String moduleName = Main.class.getModule().getName();
System.out.println("Module name: " + moduleName);
```

When launched from the class path, the output is `Module name: null`, indicating that the `Main` class ended up in the unnamed module. When launched from the module path, you get the expected `Module name: monitor`.

Section 5.2.3 discusses how the module system encapsulates resources in packages. This only partly applies to the unnamed module: within a module, there are no access restrictions (so all JARs on the class path can access resources from one another), and the unnamed module opens all packages to reflection (so all modules can access resources from JARs on the class path). Strong encapsulation does apply to access from the unnamed to a named module, though.

8.2.2   Module resolution for the unnamed module

An important aspect of the unnamed module's relation to the rest of the module graph is which other modules it can read. As described, it can read all modules that make it into the graph. But which modules are those?

Remember from section 3.4.1 that module resolution builds a module graph by starting with the root modules (particularly the initial module) and then iteratively adding all their direct and transitive dependencies. How would that work if the code under compilation or the application's main method is in the unnamed module, as is the case when launching an application from the class path? After all, plain JARs don't express any dependencies.

If the initial module is the unnamed one, module resolution starts in a predefined set of root modules. As a rule of thumb, these are the system modules (see section 3.1.4) that don't contain JEE APIs, but the actual rule is a little more detailed:

- The precise set of *java.** modules that become root depends on the presence of the *java.se* module (the module representing the entire Java SE API—it's present in full Java images but may be absent from custom run-time images created with `jlink`):
  - If *java.se* is observable, it becomes root.
  - If it isn't, every *java.** system module and *java.** module from the upgrade module path that exports at least one package without qualification (meaning without limitation to who can access the package—see section 11.3) becomes root.
- Beyond *java.** modules, every other system module and module on the upgrade module path that isn't an incubating module and exports at least one package without qualification becomes a root module. This is particularly relevant to *jdk.** and *javafx.** modules.
- Modules defined with `--add-modules` (see section 3.4.3) are always root modules.

This is a little complicated (see figure 8.3 for a visualization), but it may become important in edge cases. The rule of thumb that all system modules except the JEE and incubating ones are resolved should cover at least 90% of cases.

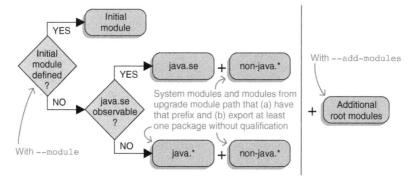

Figure 8.3   Which modules become the root for module resolution (see section 3.4.1) depends on whether the initial module was defined with `--module` (if not, the unnamed module is the initial one) and whether *java.se* is observable. In any case, modules defined with `--add-modules` are always root modules.

As an example, you can run java --show-module-resolution and observe the first few lines of output:

```
> root java.se jrt:/java.se
> root jdk.xml.dom jrt:/jdk.xml.dom
> root javafx.web jrt:/javafx.web
> root jdk.httpserver jrt:/jdk.httpserver
> root javafx.base jrt:/javafx.base
> root jdk.net jrt:/jdk.net
> root javafx.controls jrt:/javafx.controls
> root jdk.compiler jrt:/jdk.compiler
> root oracle.desktop jrt:/oracle.desktop
> root jdk.unsupported jrt:/jdk.unsupported
```

This isn't the entire output, and the order could be different on your system. But starting at the top, you can see that *java.se* is the only *java.** module. Then there are a bunch of *jdk.** and *javafx.** modules (spot *jdk.unsupported* from section 7.1.1) as well as an *oracle.** module (no idea what that one does).

 ESSENTIAL INFO   Note that with the unnamed module as the initial one, the set of root modules is always a subset of the system modules contained in the runtime image. Modules present on the module path will never be resolved unless added explicitly with --add-modules. If you handcrafted the module path to contain exactly the modules you need, you may want to add all of them with --add-modules ALL-MODULE-PATH, as explained in section 3.4.3.

You can easily observe that behavior by launching *ServiceMonitor* from the module path without defining an initial module:

```
$ java --module-path mods:libs monitor.Main

> Error: Could not find or load main class monitor.Main
> Caused by: java.lang.ClassNotFoundException: monitor.Main
```

Running the same command with --show-module-resolution confirms that no *monitor.** modules are resolved. To fix that, you can either use --add-modules monitor, in which case *monitor* is added to the list of root modules, or --module monitor/monitor.Main, in which case *monitor* becomes the only root module (the initial module).

8.2.3   *Depending on the unnamed module*

One of the module system's primary goals is reliable configuration: a module must express its dependencies, and the module system must be able to guarantee their presence. We settled that in section 3.2 for explicit modules with a module descriptor. What would happen if you tried to expand reliable configuration to the class path?

Let's make a thought experiment. Imagine modules could depend on the class-path content, maybe with something like requires class-path in their descriptor. What guarantees could the module system make for such a dependency? As it turns out, almost none. As long as there is at least one class on the class path, the module system would have to assume the dependency is fulfilled. That wouldn't be helpful (see figure 8.4).

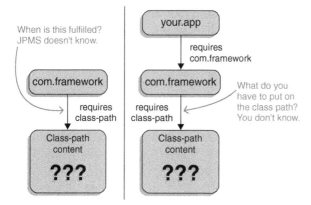

Figure 8.4 If *com.framework* depended on some class-path content with the hypothetical `requires class-path`, the module system couldn't determine whether that requirement was fulfilled (left). If you build your application on that framework, you wouldn't know what to do to fulfill that dependency (right).

Even worse, it would seriously undermine reliable configuration, because you might end up depending on a module that `requires class-path`. Well, that contains next to no information—what *exactly* needs to go on the class path (again, see figure 8.4)?

Spinning this hypothetical even further, imagine two modules, *com.framework* and *org. library*, depended on the same third module, say SLF4J. One declared the dependency before SLF4J was modularized and hence `requires class-path`; the other declared its dependency on a modularized SLF4J and hence `requires org.slf4j` (assuming that's the module name). Now, on which path would anybody depending on *com.framework* and *org.library* place the SLF4J JAR? Whichever they chose: the module system had to determine that one of the two transitive dependencies wasn't fulfilled. Figure 8.5 shows this hypothetical situation.

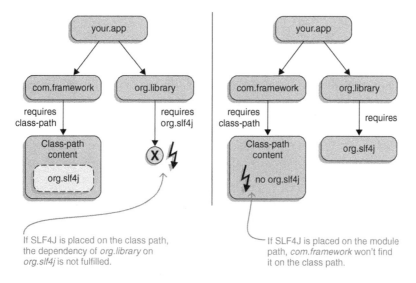

Figure 8.5 If *com.framework* depended on SLF4J with the hypothetical `requires class-path` and *org.library* required it as a module with `requires org.slf4j`, there would be no way to satisfy both requirements. Whether SLF4J was placed on the class path (left) or the module path (right), one of the two dependencies would be considered unfulfilled.

Thinking this through leads to the conclusion that depending on arbitrary class-path content isn't a good idea if you want reliable modules. And for that reason, there's no `requires class-path`.

How do we best express that the module that ends up holding the class-path content can't be depended on? In a module system that uses names to reference other modules? Not giving that module a name—making it *unnamed*, so to speak—sounds reasonable.

And there you have it: the unnamed module has no name because no module is supposed to ever reference it in a `requires` directive—or any other directive, for that matter. Without `requires`, there's no readability edge, and without that edge, code in the unnamed module is inaccessible to modules.

In summary, for an explicit module to depend on an artifact, that artifact has to be on the module path. As mentioned in section 8.1.3, this may mean you place plain JARs on the module path, which turns them into automatic modules—a concept we explore next.

8.3   *Automatic modules: Plain JARs on the module path*

The long-term goal of any modularization effort is to upgrade plain JARs to modular JARs and to move them from the class path to the module path. One way to get there is to wait until all your dependencies come to you as modules and then modularize your own project—this is a bottom-up approach. That could be a long wait, though, so the module system also allows top-down modularization.

Section 9.2 explains both approaches in detail, but for the top-down approach to work you first need a new ingredient. Think about it: how can you declare a module if your dependencies come in plain JARs? As you saw in section 8.2.3, if you place them on the class path, they end up in the unnamed module, and your module can't access that. But you paid attention in section 8.1.3, so you know that plain JARs can also go onto the module path, where the module system automatically creates modules for them.

> **NOTE** The mechanisms surrounding automatic modules generally apply at compile time and run time. As I said earlier, always mentioning both adds little information and makes the text harder to read.

For every JAR on the module path that has no module descriptor, the module system creates an *automatic module*. Like any other named module, it has three central properties (see section 3.1.3):

- *Name*—An automatic module's name can be defined in the JAR's manifest with the `Automatic-Module-Name` header. If it's missing, the module system generates a name from the filename.
- *Dependencies*—An automatic module reads all other modules that make it into the graph, including the unnamed module (as you'll see soon, this is important).
- *Exports*—An automatic module exports all its packages and also opens them for reflection (see section 12.2 for details on open packages and modules).

In addition, executable JARs result in *executable modules*, which have their main class marked as described in section 4.5.3. Services provided in META-INF/services are made available to the ServiceLoader—see chapter 10 for an introduction to services and particularly section 10.2.6 for their interaction with automatic modules.

Once again assuming *ServiceMonitor* wasn't yet modularized, you can nonetheless place its artifacts on the module path. If the directory jars-mp contains monitor.jar, monitor.observer.jar, and monitor.statistics.jar, and jars-cp contains all other application and dependency JARs, you could launch *ServiceMonitor* as follows:

```
$ java
    --module-path jars-mp
    --class-path 'jars-cp/*'
    --module monitor/monitor.Main
```

You can see the resulting module graph in figure 8.6. Some details may be unclear (like, why did all three automatic modules make it into the graph even though only *monitor* was referenced on the command line?). Don't worry; I explain in the next sections.

Automatic modules are full-fledged named modules, which means

- They can be referenced by name in other modules' declarations: for example, to require them.
- Strong encapsulation keeps them from using platform module internals (unlike for the unnamed module).
- They're subject to split-package checks.

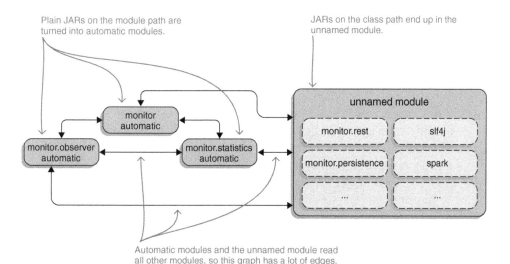

Figure 8.6 With the plain JARs monitor.jar, monitor.observer.jar, **and** monitor.statistics.jar **on the module path, the JPMS creates three automatic modules for them. The class-path content ends up in the unnamed module as before. Note how automatic modules read each other and the unnamed module, creating lots of cycles in the graph.**

On the other hand, they do have a few peculiarities. I want to discuss those before you start using automatic modules in earnest in section 9.2.

8.3.1 Automatic module names: Small detail, big impact

The main point of turning plain JARs into modules is to be able to require them in module declarations. For this they need a name, but lacking module descriptors, where does it come from?

FIRST MANIFEST ENTRIES, THEN FILENAME

One way to determine a plain JAR's module name relies on its manifest, which is a file `MANIFEST.MF` in a JAR's `META-INF` folder. The manifest contains all kinds of information in the form of header-value pairs. One of the most prominent headers is `Main-Class`, which defines a mon-modular application's entry point by naming the class containing the main method—this makes it possible to launch the application with `java -jar app.jar`.

If a JAR on the module path contains no descriptor, the module system follows a two-step process to determine the automatic module's name:

1. It looks for the `Automatic-Module-Name` header in the manifest. If it finds it, it uses the corresponding value as the module's name.
2. If the header isn't present in the manifest, the module system infers a module name from the filename.

Being able to infer the module's name from the manifest is preferable by a wide margin because it's much more stable—see section 8.3.4 for details.

The exact rules for inferring a module name from the filename are a little complicated, but the details aren't overly important. Here's the gist:

- JAR filenames often end with a version string (like `-2.0.5`). These are recognized and ignored.
- Every character apart from letters and digits is turned into a dot.

This process can lead to unfortunate results, where the resulting module name is invalid. An example is the bytecode manipulation tool Byte Buddy: it's published in Maven Central as `byte-buddy-${version}.jar`, which leads to the automatic module name `byte.buddy`. Unfortunately, this is illegal, because `byte` is a Java keyword. (Section 9.3.3 gives advice for how to fix such problems.)

To not leave you guessing which name the module system chooses for a given JAR, you can use the `jar` tool to find out:

```
$ jar --describe-module --file=${jarfile}
```

If the JAR lacks a module descriptor, the output starts as follows:

```
> No module descriptor found. Derived automatic module.
>
> ${module-name}@${module-version} automatic
> requires java.base mandated
```

${module-name} is a placeholder for the actual name—which is what you're looking for. Unfortunately, this doesn't tell you whether the name was picked from the manifest entry or the filename. To find that out, you have several options:

- Extract the manifest with `jar --file ${jarfile} --extract META-INF/ MANIFEST.MF`, and look at it manually.
- On Linux, `unzip -p ${jarfile} META-INF/MANIFEST.MF` prints the manifest to the terminal and thus saves you opening the file.
- Rename the file, and run `jar --describe-module` again.

Let's pick Guava 20.0 as an example:

```
$ jar --describe-module --file guava-20.0.jar

> No module descriptor found. Derived automatic module.
>
> guava@20.0 automatic
> requires java.base mandated
# truncated contained packages
```

Used as an automatic module, Guava 20.0 is known as *guava*. But is that universal or due to the module name? Using `unzip`, I looked at the manifest:

```
Manifest-Version: 1.0
Build-Jdk: 1.7.0-google-v5
Built-By: cgdecker
Created-By: Apache Maven Bundle Plugin
[... truncated OSGi-related entries ...]
```

As you can see, `Automatic-Module-Name` isn't set. Renaming the file to `com.google. guava-20.0.jar` yields the module name *com.google.guava*.

If you used a less outdated version of Guava—23.6, for example—you'd get the following output:

```
$ jar --describe-module --file guava-23.6-jre.jar

> No module descriptor found. Derived automatic module.
>
> com.google.common@23.6-jre automatic
> requires java.base mandated
# truncated contained packages
```

As you can see from the fact that the chosen name and the filename aren't the same, Google chose *com.google.common* as Guava's module name. Let's check with `unzip`:

```
Manifest-Version: 1.0
Automatic-Module-Name: com.google.common
Build-Jdk: 1.8.0_112-google-v7
```

There you go: `Automatic-Module-Name` is set.

WHEN TO SET AUTOMATIC-MODULE-NAME

If you're maintaining a project that's publicly released, meaning its artifacts are available via Maven Central or another public repository, you should carefully consider when to set `Automatic-Module-Name` in the manifest. As I'll explain in section 8.3.4, it makes using a project as an automatic module much more reliable, but it also comes with the promise that future, explicit modules will be drop-in replacements for the current JARs. You're essentially saying, "This is what the modules will look like; I just didn't get around to releasing them yet."

The fact that defining an automatic module name invites users to start relying on your project artifacts as modules has a few important implications:

- The names of the future modules must be exactly those that you declare now. (Otherwise, reliable configuration will bite your users because modules are missing.)
- The artifact structure must remain the same, so you can't move supported classes or packages from one JAR to another. (Even without modules, this isn't recommended practice. But with the class path, it doesn't matter which JAR contains a class, so you could get away with it. With the module system in play, on the other hand, a class's origin is relevant because accessibility forces users to require the correct module.)
- The project runs reasonably well on Java 9+. If it needs command-line options or other workarounds, these are well documented. (Otherwise, you can't be sure there aren't problems hidden in your code that make the other promises moot.)

Software development is, of course … let's say, "not entirely predictable," so these can't be guarantees. But you should have good reasons to believe you can hold to these promises. If you don't have the bandwidth to test on Java 9+, or you discovered problems that make a modularization unpredictable, be honest about it and don't set `Automatic-Module-Name` yet. If you set it and have to make such changes anyway, a major version bump is in order. Figure 8.7 shows an example of setting `Automatic-Module-Name`.

Your project doesn't need to target Java 9+ for you to be able to set `Automatic-Module-Name`. The JAR may contain bytecode compiled for older JVM versions, but defining the module name still helps users who are using the module system. The same is even true for module descriptors, as section 9.3.4 explains.

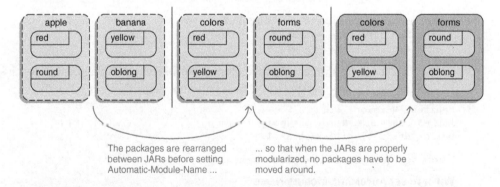

The packages are rearranged between JARs before setting Automatic-Module-Name …

… so that when the JARs are properly modularized, no packages have to be moved around.

Figure 8.7   If you're planning to move classes between packages or packages between JARs before modularizing your project, wait to set `Automatic-Module-Name` until you're finished. Here, the project's JARs (left) were refactored before being published with an automatic module name (middle), so when they're modularized (right), the structure doesn't change.

8.3.2   *Module resolution for automatic modules*

A critical ingredient to comprehending and predicting the module system's behavior is to understand how it builds the module graph during module resolution. For explicit modules, this is straightforward (it follows requires directives; see section 3.4.1); but for the unnamed modules, it's more complicated (see section 7.2.2) because plain JARs can't express dependencies.

Automatic modules are also created from plain JARs, so they have no explicit dependencies either, which begs the question how they behave during resolution. We'll answer that question momentarily, but as you'll see, that leads to a new one: Should you place an automatic module's dependencies on the class or the module path? When you're done with this section, you'll know.

RESOLVING AUTOMATIC MODULE DEPENDENCIES

The first question to answer is what happens during module resolution if the JPMS encounters an automatic module. Automatic modules were created for modularization in the face of mon-modular dependencies, so they're used in situations where developers are actively working on a modular representation of their project. In that scenario, it would be detrimental if automatic modules pulled in nearly every platform module (like the unnamed module does), so they don't do that. (To be clear, they also don't pull in any explicit application modules.)

Still, JARs have the tendency to depend on one another; and if the module system only resolved automatic modules that were explicitly required, all other automatic modules would have to be added to the graph with `--add-modules`. Imagine doing that for a large project with hundreds of dependencies you decided to place on the module path. To prevent such excessive and fragile manual module-adding, the JPMS pulls in all automatic modules *once it encounters the first one.*

As soon as one automatic module is resolved, so are all others. You get either all plain JARs as automatic modules (if at least one is required or added) or none (otherwise). That explains why figure 8.6 shows three *monitor.** modules even though only *monitor,* which can't express dependencies, was explicitly resolved by making it the root module.

Note that automatic modules imply readability (see section 9.1) on other automatic modules, which means any module that reads *one,* reads *all* of them. Keep this in mind when determining dependencies on automatic modules—going with trial and error can lead to fewer `requires` directives than are needed.

In the *ServiceMonitor* application, the *monitor.rest* module depends on the Spark web framework and, for the sake of this example, on Guava. Both dependencies are plain JARs, so *monitor.rest* needs to require them as automatic modules:

```
module monitor.rest {
    requires spark.core;
    requires com.google.common;
    requires monitor.statistics;

    exports monitor.rest;
}
```

The thing is, one of the `requires` directives on *spark.core* or *com.google.common* could be missing, and everything would still work. As soon as the module system resolves the first automatic module, it resolves all others, and any module reading one of them reads all of them.

So even without `requires com.google.common`, `guava.jar` would be picked up as an automatic module together with `spark.core.jar`; and because *monitor.rest* reads *spark. core*, it would also read *guava*. Be sure to properly determine dependencies (for example, with JDeps—see appendix D)!

Cycles in the module graph

There's a detail hidden in "automatic modules read all other modules" that's worth pointing out: this approach creates cycles in module graphs. Apparently at least one module depends on the automatic module (why else would it be there?) and thus reads it, and likewise the automatic module reads it back.

Although this has no practical consequence, I bring it up to clarify that it isn't in violation of the rule stated in section 3.2.1 that there can't be static dependency cycles. The cycles due to automatic modules aren't statically declared—they're introduced dynamically by the module system.

If automatic modules could only read other named modules, you'd be done. Once you placed a plain JAR on the module path, all of its direct dependencies would have to go onto the module path as well, and then their dependencies, and so on, until all transitive dependencies were treated as modules, explicit or automatic.

Turning all plain JARs into automatic modules has downsides, though (more on that in section 8.3.3), so it would be nice to be able to leave them on the class path and have them loaded into the unnamed module. And the module system allows just that by letting automatic modules read the unnamed module, which means their dependencies can be on the class path *or* the module path.

CHOOSING A PATH FOR TRANSITIVE DEPENDENCIES

You generally have two options for automatic modules' dependencies (remember, you can use JDeps to list them, too): the class path or the module path. Unfortunately, not all circumstances allow you to choose freely, and in some cases, you need to do more than just decide on the path.

Table 8.2 presents the options to bring those dependencies into the module graph, based on whether they're required by another module and whether they're platform modules, plain JARs, or modular JARs. The following figures shine a spotlight on specific situations:

- Figure 8.8 shows how platform modules that are only required by an automatic module aren't resolved by default.

- Figure 8.9 covers the different cases for plain JARs that are needed by an automatic module.
- Figure 8.10 shows the module graph's evolution if a transitive dependency is turned from a plain into a modular JAR.

Table 8.2   How to add an automatic module's dependencies to the module graph

Dependency required by another, explicit module		
	Class path	**Module path**
Platform module		✔
Plain JAR	✘ (dependency unfulfilled)	✔
Modular JAR	✘ (dependency unfulfilled)	✔

Dependency *not* required by an explicit module		
	Class path	**Module path**
Platform module		! (resolve manually)
Plain JAR	✔	✔ (automatically resolved)
Modular JAR	✔	! (resolve manually)

Focusing on platform modules for a moment, we see that an automatic module can't express dependencies on them. As a consequence, the module graph may or may not contain them; and if it doesn't, the automatic module is likely to fail at run time with an exception due to missing classes.

The only way around this is for the project's maintainers to publicly document which modules they need, so their users can make sure the required modules are present. Users can do that by requiring them either explicitly, for example in the module that depends on the automatic module, or with `--add-modules`.

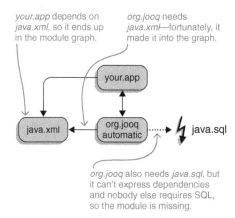

your.app depends on *java.xml*, so it ends up in the module graph.

org.jooq needs *java.xml*—fortunately, it made it into the graph.

org.jooq also needs *java.sql*, but it can't express dependencies and nobody else requires SQL, so the module is missing.

Figure 8.8   If a project (`your.app` in this case) uses an automatic module (*org.jooq*), you can't be sure the module graph works out of the box. Automatic modules don't express dependencies, so platform modules they need may not make it into the graph (here, that happened with *java.sql*) and have to be added manually with `--add-modules`.

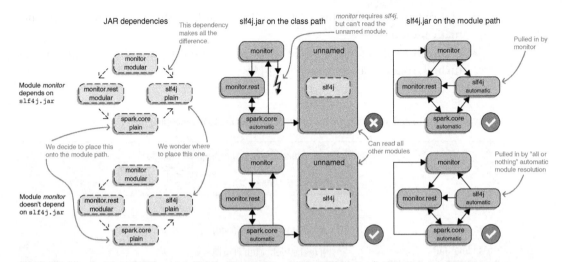

Figure 8.9   Starting with the dependency of *monitor.rest* (a modular JAR) on *spark.core* (a plain JAR), the latter needs to be placed on the module path. But what about its dependency *slf4j* (another plain JAR)? Here you see the resulting module graphs depending on whether *slf4j* is required by another modular JAR (top versus bottom row) or which path it's placed on (middle versus right column). Looks like a clear win for the module path, but take a look at figure 8.10.

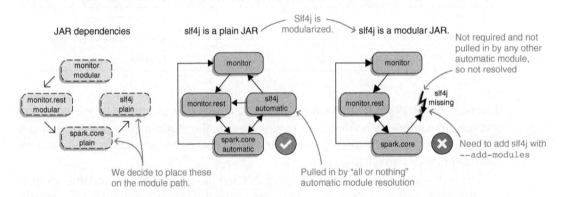

Figure 8.10   In the same situation as figure 8.9's bottom right corner, what happens if an automatic module's transitive dependency (slf4j) that's placed on the module path gets modularized? It's no longer resolved by default and needs to be added manually with --add-modules.

With dependencies on platform modules checked off, let's look at application modules. If an automatic module's dependencies are required by an explicit module, they have to be placed on the module path and are then resolved by the module system—nothing else needs to be done. If no explicit module requires them, JARs can either be placed on the class path, where they're rolled into the unnamed module and are hence always accessible, or be placed on the module path, where some other mechanism needs to pull them into the graph:

- Plain JARs are pulled in by the all-or-nothing approach to automatic module loading.
- Platform and explicit application modules aren't resolved by default. You either have to require them from some other module or add them manually with --add-modules (see section 3.4.3).

Combined with the fact that most or even all dependencies will at some point go from plain to modular JARs, these two observations attract attention: they imply that transitive dependencies on the module path work fine as long as they're plain JARs, but disappear from the module graph as soon as they're modularized.

Let's focus on the second bullet point and consider modules that mon-modular dependencies need to access. If neither you nor other modules require them, they won't make it into the module graph, and dependencies won't be able to access them. In that case, you can either require them in your module descriptors (don't forget to add a comment why you do that) or add them with command-line flags during compilation and at launch time. Sections 9.2.2 and 9.2.3 briefly discuss the trade-offs involved in that decision, depending on the specific scenario.

An additional bump in the road can be the types an automatic module exposes in its public API. Assume a project (a modular JAR) depends on a library (a plain JAR) with a method that returns an `ImmutableList` from Guava (also a plain JAR):

```
public ImmutableList<String> getAllTheStrings() {
    // ...
}
```

If you place the project and the library on the module path and Guava on the class path, you'll get the module graph shown in figure 8.11: the project (explicit module) reads the library (automatic module), which reads the unnamed module (containing Guava). If the code now calls the method that returns an `ImmutableList`, the accessibility check for that type won't end in your favor, because your module doesn't read the unnamed one.

This isn't entirely new. If `ImmutableList` were a nonpublic type of the library, you also wouldn't be able to call that method due to lacking visibility. And just as in that case, this hinges on the declared return type. If the method instead declared to return

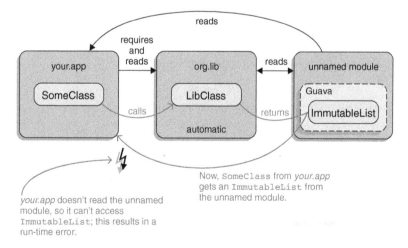

Figure 8.11 If a method in an automatic module (*org.lib* in this case) returns a type from the unnamed module (`ImmutableList`), named modules (*your. app*) can't access it, because they don't read the unnamed module. This crashes the application if the method declares that it returns the inaccessible type (`ImmutableList`). Declaring a supertype (here, most likely `List`) would work.

a List and then chose an ImmutableList as the concrete type to return, everything would be fine. This is about which type the API declares, not which type it returns.

Consequently, if an automatic module exposes types from another JAR, that JAR needs to go onto the module path as well. Otherwise, its types would end up in the unnamed module, where they're inaccessible to explicit modules. This would result in an IllegalAccessError due to a lacking read edges, as described in section 3.3.3.

If, despite your best efforts, you end up in a situation where a named module needs to access the unnamed module, you're left with one option—literally. The command-line option --add-reads, introduced in section 3.4.4, can be used to add a readability edge from a named module to the unnamed module by using ALL-UNNAMED as the target value. This couples your modular code to the unpredictable class-path content, though, so it should be a last resort.

By using --add-reads, the example with Guava on the class path and an automatic module returning an ImmutableList can work out after all. If the explicit module that gets the instance of ImmutableList (and subsequently fails the accessibility check) was named *app*, then adding --add-reads app=ALL-UNNAMED to both compiler and runtime would make the application work.

All that said, when do you choose which path? Should you go all in on automatic modules or prefer leaving as many dependencies as possible on the class path? Read on to find out.

8.3.3   *All in on automatic modules?*

With the ability to place plain JARs on the module path to turn them into automatic modules, do you still need the class path? Can't you place every JAR on the module path, turning them all into explicit or automatic modules (depending on whether they contain a descriptor)? The technical answer to that question is, yes, you could do that. Nevertheless, I don't recommend it—let me explain why.

PLAIN JARS DON'T MAKE GOOD MODULES

Generally speaking, plain JARs don't make good modules:

- They may access JDK-internal APIs (see section 7.1).
- They may split packages between themselves and JEE modules (see section 7.2).
- They don't express their dependencies.

If they're turned into automatic modules, the module system will impose its rules on them, and you may have to spend some time fixing the resulting issues. On top of that, once a plain JAR is upgraded to a modular JAR, it's no longer resolved by default (see table 8.2 and figure 8.10), so for every such upgrade somewhere in your project's dependency tree, you have to go in and add it manually. The only upside of automatic modules is that they can be required by explicit modules, but if you don't need that, you get little in return for your troubles making everything automatic.

If left on the class path, on the other hand, the JARs are rolled into the unnamed module, where

- Illegal access is by default allowed for at least one more Java release.

- Splits between JARs don't matter, although they still do between JARs and platform modules.
- They can read all Java SE platform modules if they contain the application entry point.
- Nothing needs to be done when a plain JAR is upgraded to a modular JAR

This makes life much easier.

 ESSENTIAL INFO   Despite the thrill of having everything as a module, I recommend that you place only the minimum number of plain JARs on the module path that are needed to make a project work, and put the rest on the class path.

An automatic module's modularized dependencies, on the other hand, should generally go onto the module path. Because they come as modular JARs, they shouldn't need the module system to treat them as leniently as the unnamed module; if loaded as modules, they benefit from reliable configuration and strong encapsulation.

AUTOMATIC MODULES AS A BRIDGE TO THE CLASS PATH

There's a philosophical point to be made for working with fewer automatic modules: this turns them into a bridge between the modular world and the chaotic class path (figure 8.12). Modules can sit on one side and require their direct dependencies as automatic modules, and indirect dependencies can remain on the other side. Every time one of your dependencies turns into an explicit module, it leaves the bridge on the modular side and draws its direct dependencies as automatic modules onto the bridge. This is the top-down approach I mentioned earlier; we'll look at it more closely when discussing modularization strategies in section 9.2.

Figure 8.12   Long Biên Bridge in Hanoi 1939. Photo by manhhai. Used under Creative Commons CC BY 2.0.

8.3.4 Depending on automatic modules

The sole purpose of automatic modules is to depend on plain JARs, so it becomes possible to create explicit modules without having to wait until all dependencies are modularized. There's an important caveat, though: if the JAR's manifest doesn't contain the `Automatic-Module-Name` entry, the dependency is inherently fragile.

As section 8.3.1 explains, without that entry, the automatic module name is inferred from the filename. But depending on their setup, different projects may use different names for the same JARs. Furthermore, most projects use a Maven-backed local repository, where the JAR files are named `${artifactID}-${version}`, from which the module system will likely infer *${artifactID}* as the automatic module's name. That's problematic because artifact IDs generally don't follow the reverse-domain naming schema defined in section 3.1.3: once the project is modularized, the module name will likely change.

Because it's so commonly used, Google's Guava continues to be a great example. As you saw earlier, for `guava-20.0.jar`, the module system derives the automatic module name *guava*. That's the name the file has in Maven's local repository, but other projects may have a different setup.

Let's say one names JARs `${groupID}-${artifactID}-${version}`, in which case the file would be called `com.google.guava-guava-20.0.jar` and the automatic module name would be *com.google.guava.guava*. A modularized Guava, on the other hand, will be called *com.google.common*, so none of the automatic module names were correct.

In summary, the same JAR may get different module names in different projects (depending on their setup) and at different times (before and after modularization). This has the potential to cause havoc downstream.

Think about your favorite project, and imagine that one of your dependencies referenced one of *its* dependencies as an automatic module with a name that doesn't match the project's setup (see figure 8.13). Maybe the dependency named files `${groupID}-${artifactID}-${version}`, whereas you use Maven and name them `${artifactID}-${version}`. Now the dependency requires an automatic module `${groupID}.${artifactID}`, but the module system will infer `${artifactID}` in your project. That would break the build—and although there are ways to fix it (see section 9.3.3), none of them are pleasant.

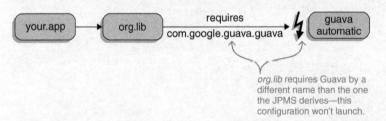

org.lib requires Guava by a different name than the one the JPMS derives—this configuration won't launch.

Figure 8.13 The dependency *org.lib* requires Guava by the automatic module name it got in the build, which is *com.google.guava.guava*. Unfortunately, on the system, the artifact is called `guava.jar`, so the module name *guava* is derived. Without further work, the module system will complain about missing dependencies.

And it's getting worse! Stick with that same project, and mentally add another dependency that requires the same automatic module but with a different name (see figure 8.14). This is the modular diamond of death described in section 3.2.2: a single JAR can't fulfill requirements for modules with different names, and multiple JARs with the same content won't work due to the rule against split packages. This situation needs to be avoided at all costs!

In both cases, it may look as if the critical mistake was to require a plain JAR by a module name that's based on its filename. But that's not the case—using this approach is fine for applications and in other scenarios where the developer has full control over the module descriptors requiring such automatic modules.

The straw that broke the camel's back was *publishing* modules with such dependencies to a public repository. Only then could users be into a situation where a module implicitly depends on details they have no control over, and that can lead to additional work or even unresolvable divergences.

The conclusion is that you should *never* publish (to an openly accessible repository) modules that require a plain JAR without an `Automatic-Module-Name` entry in its manifest. Only with that entry are automatic module names sufficiently stable to rely on.

Yes, that may mean you can't yet publish a modularized version of your library or framework and must wait for your dependencies to add that entry. That's unfortunate, but doing it anyway would be a great disservice to your users.

TIP Migration and modularization—we've covered all the challenges and mechanisms that apply to existing code bases. Continue to chapter 9 to find out how to best apply them. After that, part 3 teaches the module system's more advanced features.

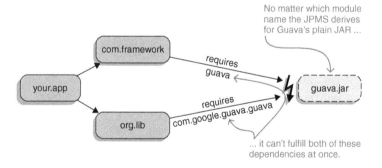

Figure 8.14 Compared to figure 8.12, the situation has gotten worse. Another dependency, *com.framework*, also depends on Guava, but it requires it with a different name (*guava*). Now the same JAR needs to appear as two differently named modules—that ain't gonna work.

Summary

- An incremental modularization will often use the class path *and* the module path. It's important to understand that any JAR on the class path, plain or modular, ends up in the unnamed module and that any JAR on the module path ends up as a named module—either as an automatic module (for a plain JAR) or an explicit module (for a modular JAR). This allows the user of a JAR (instead of its creator) to determine whether it becomes a named module.
- The unnamed module is a compatibility feature that makes the module system work with the class path:
  - It captures class-path content, has no name, reads every other module, and exports and opens all packages.
  - Because it has no name, explicit modules can't refer to it in their module declarations. One consequence is that they can't read the unnamed module and can hence never use types that are defined on the class path.
  - If the unnamed module is the initial one, a specific set of rules is used to ensure that the right set of modules is resolved. By and large these are the non-JEE modules and their dependencies. This lets code from the class path read all Java SE APIs without further configuration, thus maximizing compatibility.
- Automatic modules are a migration feature that allows modules to depend on plain JARs:
  - An automatic module is created for each JAR on the module path. Its name is defined by the `Automatic-Module-Name` header in the JAR's manifest (if present) or derived from its filename otherwise. It reads every other module, including the unnamed one, and exports and opens all packages.
  - It's a regular named module and as such can be referenced in module declarations, for example to require it. This allows projects that are being modularized to depend on others that haven't been yet.
  - An automatic module's dependency can be placed on the class path or the module path. Which path to use depends on circumstances, but placing modular dependencies on the module path and plain ones on the class path is a sensible default.
  - As soon as the first automatic module is resolved, so are all others. Furthermore, any module that reads one automatic module reads all of them due to implied readability. Take this into account when testing out dependencies on automatic modules.

Migration and
modularization strategies

This chapter covers

- Preparing a migration to Java 9 and beyond
- Continually integrating changes
- Incrementally modularizing projects
- Generating module declarations with JDeps
- Hacking third-party JARs with the `jar` tool
- Publishing modular JARs for Java 8 and older

Chapters 6, 7, and 8 discuss the technical details behind migrating to Java 9+ and turning an existing code base into a modular one. This chapter takes a broader view and looks at how to best compose these details into successful migration and modularization efforts. We'll first discuss how to perform a gradual migration that cooperates well with the development process, particularly build tools and continuous integration. Next, we'll look at how to use the unnamed module and automatic modules as building blocks for specific modularization strategies. And finally, we'll cover options for making JARs modular—yours or your dependencies'. When you're done with this chapter, you'll not only understand the mechanisms behind migration challenges and modularization features—you'll also know how to best employ them in your efforts.

9.1   Migration strategies

With all the knowledge you've gathered in chapters 6 and 7, you're prepared for every fight Java 9+ may pick with you. Now it's time to broaden your view and develop a larger strategy. How can you arrange the bits and pieces to make the migration as thorough and predictable as possible? This section gives advice on preparing for a migration, estimating migration efforts, setting up a continuous build on Java 9+, and drawbacks of command-line options.

> **NOTE**   Many topics in this section are connected to build tools, but they're kept generic enough that they don't require you to know any *specific* tool. At the same time, I wanted to share my experience with Maven (the only build tool I've used on Java 9+ so far), so I occasionally point out the Maven feature I used to fulfill a specific requirement. I won't go into any detail, though, so you'll have to figure out for yourself how those features help.

9.1.1   Preparatory updates

First, if you're not on Java 8 yet, you should make that update! Do yourself a favor and don't jump two or more Java versions at once. Make an update, get all your tools and processes working, run it in production for a while, and then tackle the next update. The same is true if you want to update from Java 8 to 11—take it one step at a time. If you have any problems, you'll *really* want to know which Java version or dependency update caused them.

Speaking of dependencies, another thing you can do without even looking at Java 9+ is to start updating them as well as your tools. Besides the general benefit of being up to date, you may inadvertently update from a version that has problems with Java 9+ to one that works fine with it. You won't even notice you *had* a problem. If there's no version compatible with Java 9+ yet, being on the most recent release of your dependency or tool still makes it easier to update once a compatible version is published.

> **AdoptOpenJDK quality outreach**
>
> AdoptOpenJDK, "a community of Java user group members, Java developers and vendors who are advocates of OpenJDK," has a list of various open source projects and how well they're doing on the latest and next version of Java: http://mng.bz/90HA.

9.1.2   Estimating the effort

There are a few things you can do to get an idea of what lies ahead, and we'll look at those first. The next step is to evaluate and categorize the problems you found. I end this section with a small note on estimating concrete numbers.

LOOKING FOR TROUBLE

These are the most obvious choices to gather a list of problems:

- Configure your build to compile and test on Java 9+ (Maven: toolchain), ideally in a way that lets you gather all errors instead of stopping at the first (Maven: `--fail-never`).
- Run your entire build on Java 9+ (Maven: `~/.mavenrc`), again gathering all errors.
- If you're developing an application, build it as you do normally (meaning not yet on Java 9+), and then run it on Java 9+. Use `--illegal-access=debug` or `deny` to get more information on illegal access.

Carefully analyze the output, take note of new warnings and errors, and try to link them to what previous chapters discussed. Look out for the removed command-line options described in section 6.5.3.

It's a good idea to apply some quick fixes like adding exports or JEE modules. This allows you to see the tougher problems that may be hiding behind benign ones. In this phase, no fix is too quick or too dirty—anything that gets the build to throw a new error is a victory. If you get too many compile errors, you could compile with Java 8 and just run the tests on Java 9+ (Maven: `mvn surefire:test`).

Then run JDeps on your project *and your dependencies.* Analyze dependencies on JDK-internal APIs (section 7.1.2), and note any JEE modules (section 6.1). Also look for split packages between platform modules and application JARs (section 7.2.5).

Finally, search your code base for calls to `AccessibleObject::setAccessible` (section 7.1.4), casts to `URLClassLoader` (section 6.2), parsing of `java.version` system properties (section 6.5.1), or handcrafting resource URLs (section 6.3). Put everything you found on one big list—now it's time to analyze it.

HOW BAD IS IT?

The problems you've found should fall into two categories: "I've seen it in this book" and "What the *&*!#* is going on?" For the former, split the issue further into "Has at least a temporary fix" and "Is a hard problem." Particularly difficult problems are removed APIs and package splits between platform modules and JARs that don't implement an endorsed standard or a standalone technology.

It's important not to confuse prevalence with importance! You may get about a thousand errors because a JEE module is missing, but fixing that is trivial. You're in big trouble, on the other hand, if your core feature depends on one cast of the application class loader to `URLClassLoader`. Or you may have a critical dependency on a removed API but because you've designed your system well, it just causes a few compile errors in one subproject.

A good approach is to ask yourself for each specific problem for which you don't know a solution off the top of your head, "How bad would it be if I cut out the troublesome code and everything that depends on it?" How much would that hurt your project? In that vein, would it be possible to temporarily deactivate the troublesome code?

Tests can be ignored, and features can be toggled with flags. Get a sense for the how feasible it is to delay a fix and run the build and the application without it.

When you're finished, you should have a list of issues in these three categories:

- A known problem with an easy fix
- A known, hard problem
- An unknown problem that needs investigation

For problems in the last two categories, you should know how dangerous they are for your project and how easily you could get by without fixing them right now.

ON ESTIMATING NUMBERS

Chances are that somebody wants you to make an estimate that involves some hard numbers—maybe in hours, maybe in currency. That's tough in general, but here it's particularly problematic.

A Java 9+ migration makes you face the music of decisions long past. Your project may be tightly coupled to an outdated version of a web framework you wanted to update for years, or it may have accrued a lot of technical debt around an unmaintained library. And unfortunately, both stop working on Java 9+. What you have to do now is pay back some technical debt—and everybody knows the fees and interest can be difficult to estimate. Finally, just like a good boss battle, the critical problem—the one that costs the most to fix—may be hidden behind a few other troublemakers, so you can't see it until you're in too deep. I'm not saying these scenarios are *likely*, just that they're *possible*, so be careful about guessing how long it may take you to migrate to Java 9.

9.1.3 *Continuously build on Java 9+*

Assuming you're continuously building your project, the next step is to set up a successful Java 9+ build. There are many decisions to make:

- Which branch should you build?
- Should there be a separate version?
- How should you slice the build if it can't fully run on Java 9+ from day one?
- How do you keep Java 8 and Java 9+ builds running side by side?

In the end, it's up to you to find answers that fit your project and continuous integration (CI) setup. Let me share some ideas that worked well in my migrations, and you can combine them any way you like.

WHICH BRANCH TO BUILD?

You may be tempted to set up your own branch for the migration effort and let your CI server build that one with Java 9+ while the others are built with Java 8 as before. But the migration can take time, so it's likely to result in a long-lived branch—and I generally try not to have those for various reasons:

- You're on your own, and your changes aren't continuously scrutinized by a team that bases their work on them.

- Both branches may accrue a lot of changes, which increases the chance of conflicts when updating or merging the Java 9+ branch.
- If it takes a while for changes on the main development branch to find their way into the Java 9+ branch, the rest of the team is free to add code that creates new problems on Java 9+ without getting immediate feedback.

Although it can make sense to do the initial investigation into the migration on a separate branch, I recommend switching to the main development branch early and setting up CI there. That does require a little more fiddling with your build tool, though, because you need to separate some parts of the configuration (for example, command-line options for the compiler) by Java version (the Java compiler doesn't like unknown options).

WHICH VERSION TO BUILD?

Should the Java 9+ build create a separate version of your artifacts—something like `-JAVA-LATEST-SNAPSHOT`? If you've decided to create a separate Java 9+ branch, you're likely forced to create a separate version, too. Otherwise, it's easy to mix snapshot artifacts from different branches, which is bound to break the build, the more the branches deviate. If you've decided to build from the main development branch, creating a separate version may not be easy; but I never tried, because I found no good reason to do it.

Regardless of how you handle versions, when trying to get something to work on Java 9+, you'll probably occasionally build the same subproject with the same version with Java 8. One thing I do again and again, even though I resolve not to, is install the artifacts I build with Java 9+ in my local repository. You know, the knee-jerk `mvn clean install`? That's not a good idea: then you can't use those artifacts in a Java 8 build, because it doesn't support Java 9+ bytecode.

When building locally with Java 9+, try to remember not to install the artifacts! I use `mvn clean verify` for that.

WHAT TO BUILD WITH JAVA 9+?

The end goal is to have the build tool run on Java 9+ and build all projects across all phases/tasks. Depending on how many items on that list you created earlier, it's possible you only need to change a few things to get there. In that case, go for it—there's no reason to complicate the process. On the other hand, if your list is more daunting, there are several ways to slice the Java 9 build:

- You may run the build on Java 8 and only compile and test against Java 9+. I'll discuss that in a minute.
- You may make the migration per goal/task, meaning you first try to compile your entire project against Java 9+ before starting to make the tests work.
- You may migrate by subproject, meaning you first try to compile, test, and package an entire subproject before moving to the next.

Generally speaking, I prefer the "by goal/task" approach for large, monolithic projects and the "by subproject" approach if the project is split into parts small enough to be tackled in one go.

If you go by subproject, but one of them can't be built on Java 9+ for whatever reason, you can't easily build the subprojects depending on it. I was in that situation once, and we decided to set up the Java 9 build in two runs:

1 Build everything with Java 8.
2 Build everything with Java 9+ except the troublesome subprojects (subprojects depending on them were then built against the Java 8 artifacts).

YOUR BUILD TOOL ON JAVA 9+

Until your project is fully migrated to Java 9+, you may need to switch often between building it with 8 and 9+. See how you can configure the version of Java for your build tool of choice without having to set the default Java version for your entire machine (Maven: `~/.mavenrc` or the toolchain). Then consider automating the switch. I ended up writing a little script that set `$JAVA_HOME` to either JDK 8 or JDK 9+, so I could quickly pick the one I need.

Then, and this is a little meta, the build tool may not work properly on Java 9+. Maybe the tool needs a JEE module, or maybe a plugin uses removed APIs. (I had that problem with a JAXB plugin for Maven, which needs *java.xml.bind* and relies on its internals.)

In that case, you could consider running the build on Java 8 and only compiling or testing against Java 9+, but that won't work if the build does something with the created bytecode (for Java 9+) in its own process (which is Java 8). (I ran into that problem with the Java Remote Method Invocation Compiler (`rmic`); it forced us to run the entire build on Java 9+ even though we would have preferred not to.)

If you decide to run the build on Java 9+ even though it doesn't play nicely, you'll have to configure the build process with some of the new command-line options. Doing this so it's easy on your fellow team members (nobody wants to add options manually) while keeping it working on Java 8 (which doesn't know the new options) can be nontrivial (Maven: `jvm.config`). I found no way to make it work on both versions without requiring a file rename, so I ended up including that in my "Switch Java version" script.

HOW TO CONFIGURE THE JAVA 9+ BUILD

How do you keep a Java 8 build *and* a Java 9+ build running when you have to add version-specific configuration options to compiler, test runtime, or other build tasks? Your build tool should help. It likely has a feature that allows you to adapt the overall configuration to various circumstances (Maven: profiles). Familiarize yourself with it, because you may end up using it a lot.

When working with version-specific command-line options for the JVM, there's an alternative to letting your build tool sort them out: with the nonstandard JVM option `-XX:+IgnoreUnrecognizedVMOptions`, you can instruct the launching VM to ignore unknown command-line options. (This option isn't available on the compiler.) Although this allows you to use the same options for both Java 8 and Java 9+, I recommend not making it your first choice because it disables checks that can help you find mistakes. Instead, I prefer separating the options by version if at all possible.

TESTING ON BOTH PATHS

If you're working on a library or framework, you have no control over the path, class path, or module path on which users place your JAR. Depending on the project, that may make a difference, in which case it becomes necessary to test both variants.

Unfortunately, I can't give any tips here. At the time of writing, neither Maven nor Gradle has good support for running the tests once on each path, and you may end up having to create a second build configuration. Let's hope tool support improves over time.

FIX FIRST, SOLVE LATER

Typically, most items on the list of Java 9+ problems are straightforward to fix with a command-line flag. Exporting an internal API, for example, is easy. That doesn't solve the underlying problem, though. Sometimes the solution is easy as well, like replacing the internal `sun.reflect.generics.reflectiveObjects.NotImplementedException` with an `UnsupportedOperationException` (no kidding: I've had to do that more than once), but often it isn't.

Should you aim for quick and dirty or for proper solutions that take a little longer? In the phase of trying to get a full build working, I recommend making the quick fix:

- Add command-line flags where necessary.
- Deactivate tests, preferably just on Java 9+ (on JUnit 4 it's easy to use assumptions for that; on JUnit 5 I recommend conditions).
- Switch a subproject back to compiling or testing against Java 8 if it uses a removed API.
- If all else fails, skip the project entirely.

A working build that gives the entire team immediate feedback on their project's Java 9+ compatibility is worth a lot, including taking shortcuts to get there. To be able to improve on these temporary fixes later, I recommend coming up with a system that helps identify them.

I mark temporary fixes with a comment like `// [JAVA LATEST, <PROBLEM>]:` `<explanation>` so a full-text search for `JAVA LATEST, GEOTOOLS` leads me to all tests I had to deactivate because the GeoTools version wasn't Java 9-compatible.

It's common to find new problems that were originally hidden behind an earlier build error. If that happens, make sure to add them to your list of Java 9+ problems. Likewise, scratch off those that you solve.

KEEPING IT GREEN

Once you've set up a successful build, you should have a complete picture of all the Java 9+ challenges you face. It's now time to solve them one by one.

Some of the issues may be tough or time-intensive to solve; you may even determine they can't be addressed until a later point—maybe once an important release is made or the budget has a little wiggle room. Don't worry if it takes some time. With a build that every developer on the team can break and fix, you can never take a step in the wrong direction; even if you have a lot of work ahead of you, you'll eventually get there in little steps.

9.1.4 *Thoughts on command-line options*

With Java 9+, you may end up applying more command-line options than ever before—it sure has been like that for me. I have a few insights I want to share about the following:

- Four ways to apply command-line options
- Relying on weak encapsulation
- Pitfalls of command-line options

Let's go through them one by one.

FOUR WAYS TO APPLY COMMAND-LINE OPTIONS

The most obvious way to apply command-line options is to use the command line and append the options after `java` or `javac`. But did you know there are three more possibilities?

If your application is delivered as an executable JAR, using the command line isn't an option. In that case, you can use the new manifest entries `Add-Exports` and `Add-Opens`, which take a comma-separated list of `${module}/${package}` pairs and export or open that package to code on the class path. The JVM only scans the application's executable JAR, meaning the one specified with the runtime's `-jar` option, for these manifest entries, so there's no point in adding them to library JARs.

Another way to permanently set command-line options, at least for the JVM, is the environment variable `JDK_JAVA_OPTIONS`. It was introduced in Java 9+, so Java 8 won't pick it up. You're hence free to include any command-line options specific to Java 9+ that each execution of `java` on your machine will apply. This will hardly be a long-term solution, but it may make some experiments easier.

Finally, command-line options don't have to be entered directly on the command line. An alternative is so-called *argument files* (or *@-files*), which are plain-text files that can be referenced on the command line with `@${file-name}`. Compiler and runtime will then act as if the file content had been added to the command.

Section 7.2.4 shows how to compile code that uses annotations from JEE and JSR 305:

```
$ javac
    --add-modules java.xml.ws.annotation
    --patch-module java.xml.ws.annotation=jsr305-3.0.2.jar
    --class-path 'libs/*'
    -d classes/monitor.rest
    ${source-files}
```

Here, `--add-modules` and `--patch-module` are added to make the compilation work on Java 9+. You could put these two lines in a file called `java-LATEST-args` and then compile as follows:

```
$ javac
    @java-LATEST-args
```

```
--class-path 'libs/*'
-d classes/monitor.rest
${source-files}
```

What's new in Java 9+ is that the JVM also recognizes argument files, so they can be shared between compilation and execution.

> ## Maven and argument files
>
> Unfortunately, argument files don't work with Maven. The compiler plugin already creates a file for all its own options, and Java doesn't supported nested argument files.

RELYING ON WEAK ENCAPSULATION

As section 7.1 explains in detail, the Java 9–11 (or more) runtimes allow illegal access by default with nothing more than a warning. That's great for running unprepared applications, but I advise against relying on it during a proper build because it allows new illegal accesses to slip by unnoticed. Instead, I collect all the `--add-exports` and `--add-opens` I need and then activate strong encapsulation at run time with `--illegal-access=deny`.

THE PITFALLS OF COMMAND-LINE OPTIONS

Using command-line options has a few pitfalls:

- These options are infectious in the sense that if a JAR needs them, all of its dependencies need them as well.
- Developers of libraries and frameworks that require specific options will hopefully document that their clients need to apply them, but nobody reads the documentation until it's too late.
- Application developers must maintain a list of options that merge the requirements of several libraries and frameworks they use.
- It isn't easy to maintain the options in a way that allows sharing them between different build phases and execution.
- It isn't easy to determine which options can be removed due to an update to a Java 9–compatible version.
- It can be tricky to apply the options to the right Java processes: for example, for a build-tool plugin that doesn't run in the same process as the build tool.

These pitfalls make one thing clear: command-line options are a fix, not a proper solution, and they have their own long-term costs. This is no accident—they were designed to make the undesired possible. Not easy, though, or there would be no incentive to solve the underlying problem.

Do your best to only rely on public and supported APIs, not to split packages, and to generally avoid the trouble this chapter describes. And, importantly, reward libraries and frameworks that do the same! But the road to hell is paved with good intentions, so if everything else fails, use every command-line flag at your disposal.

9.2   *Modularization strategies*

In chapter 8, you learned all about the unnamed module, automatic modules, and mixing plain JARs, modular JARs, class path, and module path. But how do you put that into practice? What are the best strategies to incrementally modularize a code base? To answer these questions, imagine the entire Java ecosystem as a huge layered graph of artifacts (see figure 9.1).

At the bottom is the JDK, which used to be a single node but, thanks to the module system, is now made up of about a hundred nodes with *java.base* as the foundation. On top of them sit libraries that have no run-time dependencies outside the JDK (like SLF4J, Vavr, and AssertJ), followed by those with just a few (for example, Guava, JOOQ, and JUnit 5). Somewhere in the middle are the frameworks with their deeper stacks (for example, Spring and Hibernate), and at the very top sit the applications.

Except for the JDK, all these artifacts were plain JARs when Java 9 came out, and it will take a few years before most of them contain a module descriptor. But how will that happen? How can the ecosystem undergo such a massive change without breaking apart? The modularization strategies enabled by the unnamed module (section 8.2) and automatic modules (section 8.3) are the answer. They make it possible for the Java community to modularize the ecosystem almost independently of one another.

The developers who have it easiest maintain a project that has no dependencies outside the JDK or whose dependencies were already modularized—they can implement the *bottom-up* strategy (section 9.2.1). For applications, the *top-down* approach (section 9.2.2) offers a way forward. Maintainers of libraries and frameworks with unmodularized dependencies have it a little harder and need to do things *inside-out* (section 9.2.3).

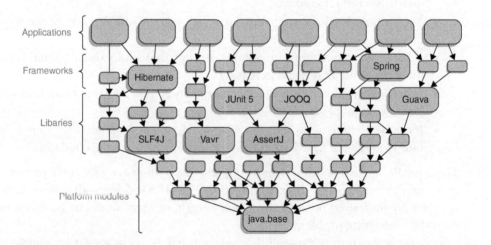

Figure 9.1   Artistic interpretation of the Java ecosystem's global dependency graph: *java.base* with the rest of the JDK at the bottom; then libraries without third-party dependencies; further above more complex libraries and frameworks; and applications on top. (Don't pay attention to any individual dependencies.)

Looking at the ecosystem as a whole, your project's place in it determines which strategy you must use. Figure 9.2 will help you pick the right one. But as section 9.2.4 explains, these approaches also work *within* individual projects, in which case you can choose any of the three. Before we come to that, though, learning the strategies is easier when we assume you modularize all artifacts at once.

By including a module descriptor in your JARs, you advertise that the project is ready to be used as a module on Java 9+. You should do that only if you've taken all possible steps to ensure it works smoothly—chapters 6 and 7 explains most challenges, but if your code uses reflection, you should also read chapter 12.

If users have to do anything to make your modules work, like adding command-line flags to their application, this should be well documented. Note that you can create modular JARs that still work seamlessly on Java 8 and older versions—section 9.3.4 has you covered.

As I've often mentioned, a module has three basic properties: a name, a clearly defined API, and explicit dependencies. When creating a module, you obviously have to pick the name. The exports can be quibbled over, but are mostly predetermined by which classes need to be accessible. The real challenges, and where the rest of the ecosystem comes into play, are the dependencies. This section focuses on that aspect.

> **Know your dependencies**
>
> You have to know quite a bit about your dependencies, direct and indirect, to modularize a project. Remember that you can use JDeps to determine dependencies (particularly on platform modules; see appendix D) and `jar --describe-module` to check a JAR's modularization status (see sections 4.5.2 and 8.3.1).

With all of that said, it's time to see how the three modularization strategies work.

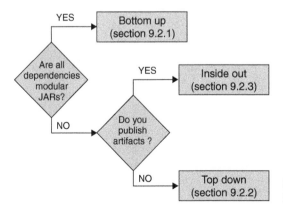

Figure 9.2 How to decide which modularization strategy fits your project

9.2.1   *Bottom-up modularization: If all project dependencies are modular*

This is the easiest case for turning a project's JARs into modules: the assumption is that the code only depends on explicit modules (directly and indirectly). It doesn't matter whether those are platform or application modules; you can go straight ahead:

1   Create module declarations that require all your direct dependencies.
2   Place the JARs with your non-JDK dependencies on the module path.

You've now fully modularized your project—congratulations! If you're maintaining a library or framework and users place your JARs on the module path, they will become explicit modules, and users can start benefiting from the module system. See Figure 9.3 for an example of a bottom-up modularization.

Almost as important but less obvious, thanks to the fact that all JARs on the class path end up in the unnamed module (see section 8.2), no one is forced to use it as a module. If someone sticks with the class path a while longer, your project will work just as if the module descriptor weren't there. If you'd like to modularize your library but your dependencies aren't modules yet, see section 9.2.3.

9.2.2   *Top-down modularization: If an application can't wait for its dependencies*

If you're an application developer and want to modularize any time soon, it's unlikely that all your dependencies already ship modular JARs. If they do, you're lucky and can take the bottom-up approach I just described. Otherwise, you have to use automatic modules and start mixing module path and class path as follows:

1   Create module declarations that require all your direct dependencies.
2   Place all modular JARs, the ones you build *and* your dependencies, on the module path.
3   Place all plain JARs that are directly required by modular JARs on the module path, where they're turned into automatic modules.
4   Ponder what to do with the remaining plain JARs (see section 8.3.3).

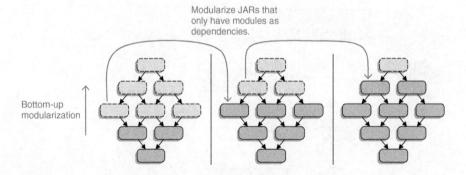

Figure 9.3   Artifacts depending on modular JARs can be modularized straight away, leading to a bottom-up migration

It may be easiest to place all remaining JARs on the module path in your build tool or IDE and give it a try. Although I don't think that's generally the best approach, it may work for you. In that case, go for it.

If you have problems with package splits or access to JDK-internal APIs, you may try placing those JARs on the class path. Because only automatic modules need them, and they can read the unnamed module, that works fine.

In the future, once a formerly automatic module is modularized, that setup may fail because it's now a modular JAR on the module path and hence can't access code from the class path. I consider that to be a good thing, because it gives better insight into which dependencies are modules and which aren't—it's also a good opportunity to check out its module descriptor and learn about the project. To fix the problem, move that module's dependencies onto the module path. See Figure 9.4 for an example of a top-down modularization.

Note that you don't have to worry about where automatic module names come from (see section 8.3.4). True, if they're based on the filename, you have to change some `requires` directives once they get an explicit module name; but because you control all module declarations, that's not a big deal.

What about making sure modules that non-modular dependencies require make it into the graph? An application could either require them in a module declaration or use `--add-modules` to add them manually at compile and launch time. The latter is an option only if you have control over the launch command. The build tool may be able to make these decisions, but you still need to be aware of the options and how to configure them, so you can fix problems should they arise.

9.2.3 *Inside-out modularization: If a project is in the middle of the stack*

Most libraries and, particularly, frameworks are neither at the bottom nor at the top of the stack—what are they to do? They modularize inside-out. This process has a bit of bottom-up (section 9.2.1) in it because releasing modular JARs doesn't force users to use them as modules. Other than that, it works like top-down (section 9.2.2), with one important difference: you're planning to *publish* the modular JARs you built. See figure 9.5 for an example of an inside-out modularization.

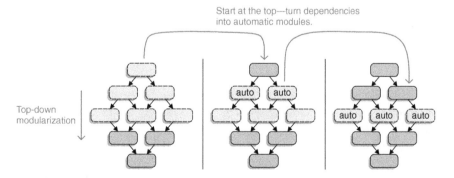

Figure 9.4 **Thanks to automatic modules it's possible to modularize artifacts that depend on plain JARs. Applications can use this to modularize from the top down.**

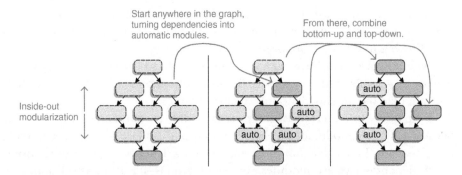

Figure 9.5   If automatic modules are used carefully, libraries and frameworks in the middle of the stack can publish modular JARs even though their dependencies and their users may still be plain JARs, thus modularizing the ecosystem from the inside out.

As I discussed at length in section 8.3.4, you should only ever publish modules with dependencies on automatic modules if those plain JARs define the `Automatic-Module` `-Name` entry in their manifest. Otherwise, the risk of causing problems down the road when the module name changes is too high.

This may mean you can't yet modularize your project. If you're in this situation, please resist the temptation to do it anyway, or you're likely to cause users difficult problems.

I want to take this one step further: examine your direct and indirect dependencies, and make sure none depend on an automatic module whose name is derived from the JAR filename. You're looking for any dependency that isn't a modular JAR and doesn't define the `Automatic-Module-Name` entry. I wouldn't publish an artifact with a module descriptor that pulls in *any* such JAR—whether it's my dependency or somebody else's.

There's also a subtle difference when it comes to platform modules your non-modular dependencies need but you don't. Whereas applications can easily use command-line options, libraries or frameworks can't. They can only document for users that they need to be added, but that's bound to be overlooked by some users. I hence advise explicitly requiring all platform modules that non-modular dependencies need.

9.2.4   *Applying these strategies within a project*

Which of the three strategies to use is determined by a project's place in the gigantic, ecosystem-wide dependency graph. But if a project is rather large, you may not be able to modularize it all at once and may wonder how to instead do that incrementally. Good news: you can apply similar strategies on a smaller scale.

It's often easiest to apply a bottom-up strategy to a project, first modularizing subprojects that only depend on code outside your code base. This works particularly well if your dependencies are already modularized, but it isn't limited to that scenario. If they aren't, you need to apply top-down logic to the lowest rung of your subprojects, making them use automatic modules to depend on plain JARs, and then build up from there.

Applied to a single project, the top-down approach works the same as when applied to the ecosystem as a whole. Modularize an artifact at the top of the graph, place it on the module path, and turn its dependencies into automatic modules. Then slowly progress down the dependency tree.

You may even do it inside-out. Chapter 10 introduces services: a great way to use the module system to decouple dependencies internal to your project but also across different projects. They're a good reason to start modularizing somewhere in the middle of a project's dependency graph and move upward or downward from there.

 ESSENTIAL INFO Note that whatever approach you chose internally, you still mustn't publish explicit modules that depend on automatic modules whose names aren't defined by the JAR filename as opposed to the `Automatic-Module-Name` manifest entry.

Although all that's possible, you shouldn't needlessly complicate matters. Once you've settled on an approach, try to quickly and methodically modularize your project. Drawing out this process and creating modules here and there means you'll have a hard time understanding the project's dependency graph—and that's the antithesis of one of the module system's important goals: reliable configuration.

9.3 Making JARs modular

All you need to do to turn a plain JAR into a modular JAR is add a module declaration to the source. Easy, right? Yes (wait for it), but (there you go!) there's more to say about that step than immediately meets the eye:

- You may want to consider creating open modules (see section 9.3.1 for a quick explanation).
- You may be overwhelmed by creating dozens or even hundreds of module declarations and wish for a tool that does it for you (section 9.3.2).
- You may want to modularize a JAR you didn't build yourself, or maybe a dependency fouled up their module descriptor and you need to fix it (section 9.3.3).
- You may wonder about module descriptors in JARs built for Java 8 or earlier—is that even possible (section 9.3.4)?

This section tackles these topics to make sure you're getting the most bang for your buck.

9.3.1 Open modules as an intermediate step

A concept that can be useful during incremental modularization of an application is that of *open modules*. Section 12.2.4 goes into details, but the gist is that an open module opts out of strong encapsulation: all its packages are exported and opened to reflection, which means all its public types are accessible during compilation and all other types and members are accessible via reflection. It's created by beginning its module declaration with `open module`.

Open modules come in handy when you aren't happy with a JAR's package layout. Maybe there are lots of packages, or maybe many packages contain public types that you'd rather not have accessible—in both cases, a refactoring may take too much time in the moment. Or maybe the module is used heavily under reflection, and you don't want to go through determining all the packages you need to open.

In such cases, opening the entire module is a good way to push those problems into the future. Caveats about technical debt apply—these modules opt out of strong encapsulation, which denies them the benefits that come with it.

 ESSENTIAL INFO   Because turning an open module into a regular, encapsulated module is an incompatible change, libraries and frameworks should never take the route of starting out with an open module with the goal to close it down later. It's hard to come up with any reason why such a project should ever publish an open module. Better to only use it for applications.

9.3.2   *Generating module declarations with JDeps*

If you have a big project, you may have to create dozens or even hundreds of module declarations, which is a daunting task. Fortunately, you can use JDeps for most of it, because large parts of that work are mechanical:

- The module name can often be derived from the JAR name.
- A project's dependencies can be analyzed by scanning bytecode across JAR boundaries.
- Exports are the inverse of that analysis, meaning all packages that other JARs depend on that need to be exported.

Beyond those basic properties, some fine-tuning may be involved to make sure all dependencies are recorded and to configure the use of services (see chapter 10) or more detailed dependencies and APIs (see chapter 11), but everything up to that point can be generated by JDeps.

Launched with `--generate-module-info ${target-dir} ${jar-dir}`, JDeps analyzes all JARs in `${jar-dir}` and generates `module-info.java` for each one in `${target-dir}/${module-name}`:

- The module name is derived from the JAR filename as it has been for automatic modules (including heeding the `Automatic-Module-Name` header; see section 8.3.1).
- Dependencies are derived based on JDeps' dependency analysis. Exposed dependencies are marked with the `transitive` keyword (see section 11.1).
- All packages that contain types used by other JARs in the analysis are exported.

When JDeps generates the `module-info.java` files, it's up to you to inspect and adapt them and move them into the correct source folders, so your next build can compile and package them.

Once again assuming *ServiceMonitor* wasn't yet modularized, you could use JDeps to generate module declarations. To that end, you build *ServiceMonitor* and place its JARs together with its dependencies in a directory `jars`. Then you call `jdeps --generate -module-info declarations jars`, and JDeps generates module declarations, which it writes into the directory structure shown in figure 9.6.

declarations
- ▼ 📁 monitor
  - 📄 module-info.java
- ▼ 📁 monitor.observer
  - 📄 module-info.java
- ▼ 📁 monitor.observer.alpha
  - 📄 module-info.java
- ▼ 📁 monitor.observer.beta
  - 📄 module-info.java
- ▼ 📁 monitor.persistence
  - 📄 module-info.java
- ▼ 📁 monitor.rest
  - 📄 module-info.java
- ▼ 📁 monitor.statistics
  - 📄 module-info.java

Figure 9.6 After you call `jdeps --generate-module-info` `declarations jars`**, JDeps analyzes the dependencies among all JARs in the** `jars` **directory (not shown) and creates module declarations for them in the** `declarations` **directory (non-*ServiceMonitor* projects aren't shown).**

JDeps creates a folder for each module and places in them module declarations that look similar to the ones you wrote by hand earlier. (To jog your memory, you can find them in listing 2.2, but the details aren't important here.)

JDeps can also generate module declarations for open modules (see section 12.2.4) with `--generate-open-module`. Module names and `requires` directives are determined as before; but because open modules can't encapsulate anything, no exports are required, and hence none are generated.

INSPECTING GENERATED DECLARATIONS

JDeps does a good job of generating module declarations, but you should still manually check them. Are the module names to your liking? (Probably not, because JAR names rarely follow the inverse-domain naming scheme; see section 3.1.3.) Are dependencies properly modeled? (See sections 11.1 and 11.2 for more options.) Are those the packages you want your public API to consist of? Maybe you need to add some services. (See chapter 10.)

If you develop an application that has too many JARs to manually inspect all declarations, and you're fine with some hiccups, there's a more lenient option: you may get away with trusting your tests, your CI pipeline, and your fellow developers and testers with finding the little problems. In that case, make sure you have some time before the next release, so you can be confident you've fixed everything.

If you're publishing artifacts, though, you absolutely have to check declarations with great care! These are the most public parts of your API, and changing them is often incompatible—work hard to prevent that from happening without good reason.

BEWARE OF MISSING DEPENDENCIES

For JDeps to properly generate `requires` directives for a set of JARs, all of these JARs as well as all their direct dependencies must be present in the scanned directory. If dependencies are missing, JDeps will report them as follows:

```
> Missing dependence: .../module-info.java not generated
> Error: missing dependencies
```

```
>     depending.type -> missing.type    not found
>     ...
```

To avoid erroneous module declarations, none are generated for modules where not all dependencies are present.

When generating module declarations for *ServiceMonitor*, I glossed over these messages. Some indirect dependencies were missing, presumably because Maven regarded them as optional, but that didn't hinder the correct creation of *ServiceMonitor*'s declarations:

```
> Missing dependence:
>     declarations/jetty.servlet/module-info.java not generated
# truncated further log messages
> Missing dependence:
>     declarations/utils/module-info.java not generated
# truncated further log messages
> Missing dependence:
>     declarations/jetty.server/module-info.java not generated
# truncated further log messages
> Missing dependence:
>     declarations/slf4j.api/module-info.java not generated
# truncated further log messages
> Error: missing dependencies
>     org.eclipse.jetty.servlet.jmx.FilterMappingMBean
>         -> org.eclipse.jetty.jmx.ObjectMBean        not found
>     org.eclipse.jetty.servlet.jmx.HolderMBean
>         -> org.eclipse.jetty.jmx.ObjectMBean        not found
>     org.eclipse.jetty.servlet.jmx.ServletMappingMBean
>         -> org.eclipse.jetty.jmx.ObjectMBean        not found
>     org.eclipse.jetty.server.handler.jmx.AbstractHandlerMBean
>         -> org.eclipse.jetty.jmx.ObjectMBean        not found
>     org.eclipse.jetty.server.jmx.AbstractConnectorMBean
>         -> org.eclipse.jetty.jmx.ObjectMBean        not found
>     org.eclipse.jetty.server.jmx.ServerMBean
>         -> org.eclipse.jetty.jmx.ObjectMBean        not found
>     org.slf4j.LoggerFactory
>         -> org.slf4j.impl.StaticLoggerBinder        not found
>     org.slf4j.MDC
>         -> org.slf4j.impl.StaticMDCBinder        not found
>     org.slf4j.MarkerFactory
>         -> org.slf4j.impl.StaticMarkerBinder        not found
```

CAREFULLY ANALYZE EXPORTS

Export directives are solely based on the analysis of which types are needed by other JARs. This almost guarantees that library JARs will see way too few exports. Keep this in mind when checking JDeps' output.

As a library or framework developer, you may not feel comfortable publishing artifacts that export packages you consider internal to a project just because several of your modules need them. Have a look at qualified exports in section 11.3 to address that problem.

9.3.3 *Hacking third-party JARs*

It can sometimes be necessary to update third-party JARs. Maybe you need ones to be an explicit module or at least an automatic module with a specific name. Maybe it's already a module, but the module descriptor is faulty or causes problems with dependencies you'd prefer not to draw in. In such cases, the time has come to pull out the sharp tools and get to work. (Be careful not to cut yourself.)

A good example for the weird edge cases that are bound to exist in an ecosystem as large as Java's is the bytecode-manipulation tool Byte Buddy. It's published in Maven Central as `byte-buddy-${version}.jar`, and when you try to use it as an automatic module, you get this reply from the module system:

```
> byte.buddy: Invalid module name: 'byte' is not a Java identifier
```

Oops: `byte` isn't a valid Java identifier because it clashes with the primitive type of the same name. This particular case is solved in Byte Buddy version 1.7.3 and later (with the `Automatic-Module-Name` entry), but you may run into similar edge cases and need to be prepared.

In general, it's not advisable to locally modify published JARs, because it's hard to do that reliably and in a self-documenting fashion. It gets a little easier if your development process includes a local artifact repository like Sonatype's Nexus that all developers connect to. In that case, somebody can create a modified variant, change the version to make the modification obvious (for example, by adding `-patched`), and then upload it to the internal repository.

It may also be possible to execute the modification during the build, in which case standard JARs can be used and edited on the fly as needed. The modification then becomes part of the build script.

Note that you should never publish artifacts that depend on modified JARs! Users won't be able to easily reproduce the modifications and will be left with a broken dependency. This largely limits the following advice to applications.

With the caveats out of the way, let's see how to manipulate third-party JARs if they don't work well with your project. I show you how to add or edit an automatic module name, add or edit a module descriptor, and add classes to modules.

ADDING AND EDITING AN AUTOMATIC MODULE NAME

A good reason to add an automatic module name to a JAR, other than the scenario where the JPMS otherwise can't derive a name, is if the project already defined one in newer versions but you can't yet update to it for whatever reason. In that case, editing the JAR allows you to use a future-proof name in your module declarations.

The `jar` tool has an option `--update` (alternative is `-u`) that allows modification of an existing Java archive. Together with the `--manifest=${manifest-file}` option, you can append anything to the existing manifest—the `Automatic-Module-Name` entry, for example.

Let's take an older version of Byte Buddy, version 1.6.5, and make sure it works fine as an automatic module. First create a plain text file, say `manifest.txt` (you can choose any name you want), that contains a single line:

```
Automatic-Module-Name: net.bytebuddy
```

Then use `jar` to append that line to the existing manifest:

```
$ jar --update --file byte-buddy-1.6.5.jar --manifest=manifest.txt
```

Now let's check whether it worked:

```
$ jar --describe-module --file byte-buddy-1.6.5.jar

> No module descriptor found. Derived automatic module.
>
> net.bytebuddy@1.6.5 automatic
> requires java.base mandated
```

Neat: no error, and the module name is as desired.

The same approach can be used to edit an existing automatic module name. The `jar` tool will complain about `Duplicate name in Manifest`, but the new value nevertheless replaces the old one.

ADDING AND EDITING MODULE DESCRIPTORS

If turning a third-party JAR into a properly named automatic module isn't enough, or you have trouble with an explicit module, you can use `jar --update` to add or override a module descriptor. An important use case for the latter is to resolve the modular diamond of death described in section 8.3.4:

```
$ jar --update --file ${jar} module-info.class
```

This adds the file `module-info.class` to `${jar}`. Note that `--update` doesn't perform any checks. This makes it easy to, accidentally or on purpose, create JARs whose module descriptor and class files don't agree, for example on required dependencies. Use with care!

The more complicated task is to come up with a module descriptor. For the compiler to create one, you need not only a module declaration, but also all dependencies (their presence is checked as part of reliable configuration) and some representation of the JAR's code (as sources or bytecode; otherwise the compiler complains of nonexistent packages).

Your build tool should be able to help you with the dependencies (Maven: copy-dependencies). For the code, it's important that the compiler sees the entire module, not just the declaration. This can best be achieved by compiling the declaration while the module's bytecode is added from its JAR with `--patch-module`. Section 7.2.4 introduces that option, and the following example shows how to use it:

Generates module declarations for all JARs (although only the one for ${jar} is of interest)

```
$ jdeps --generate-module-info . jars

# edit ${module-name}/module-info.java
```

Edit the declaration as you see fit.

```
$ javac
    --module-path jars
    --patch-module ${module-name}=jars/${jar}
    ${module-name}/module-info.java
$ mv ${module-name}/module-info.java .

$ jar --update --file jars/${jar} module-info.class

$ jar --describe-module --file jars/${jar}
```

Moves the module descriptor for ${jar} to the root folder (otherwise, updating the JAR won't work properly)

Adds the module descriptor to ${jar}

Compiles the declaration by using jars as module path and patching the module's bytecode into the module with --patch-module

Verifies that everything worked—the module should now have the desired properties

ADDING CLASSES TO MODULES

If you already need to add some classes to a dependency's packages, you may have placed them on the class path. Once that dependency moves to the module path, the rule against split packages forbids that approach, though. Section 7.2.4 shows how to handle that situation on the fly with the --patch-module option. If you're looking for a more lasting solution to your problem, you can once again use jar --update, in this case to add class files.

9.3.4 *Publishing modular JARs for Java 8 and older*

Whether you maintain an application, a library, or a framework, it's possible you target more than one Java version. Does that mean you have to skip the module system? Fortunately, no! There are two ways to deliver modular artifacts that work fine on Java versions older than 9.

Whichever you chose, you first need to build your project for the target version. You can use either the compiler from the corresponding JDK or a newer one by setting -source and -target. If you pick the Java 9+ compiler, check out the new flag --release in section 4.4. Finish this step by creating a JAR as you normally would. Note that this JAR runs perfectly on your desired Java release but doesn't yet contain a module descriptor.

The next step is to compile the module declarations with Java 9+. The best and most reliable way is to build the entire project with the Java 9+ compiler. Now you have two options for how to get the module descriptor into your JAR, described next.

USING JAR –UPDATE

You can use jar --update as described in section 9.3.3 to add the module descriptor to the JAR. That works because JVMs before version 9 ignore the module descriptor. They only see other class files; and because you build them for the correct version, everything just works.

Although that's true for the JVM, it can't necessarily be said for all tools that process bytecode. Some trip over module-info.class and thus become useless for modular JARs. If you want to prevent that, you have to create a multi-release JAR.

CREATING A MULTI-RELEASE JAR

From Java 9 on, `jar` allows the creation of *multi-release JARs* (MR-JARs), which contain bytecode for different Java versions. Appendix E gives a thorough introduction to this new feature; to make the most out of this section, you should give it a read. Here, I'm focusing on how to use MR-JARs so the module descriptor doesn't end up in the JAR's root.

Let's say you have a regular JAR and want to turn it into a multi-release JAR, where a module descriptor is loaded on Java 9 (and later). Here's how to do that with `--update` and `--release`:

```
$ jar --update
    --file ${jar}
    --release 9
    module-info.class
```

You can also create a multi-release JAR in one go:

```
$ jar --create
    --file mr.jar
    -C classes .
    --release 9
    classes-9/module-info.class
```

The first three lines are the regular way to create a JAR from class files in `classes`. Then comes `--release 9`, followed by the additional sources to be loaded by JVMs version 9 and higher. Figure 9.7 show the resulting JAR—as you can see, the root directory doesn't contain `module-info.class`.

This feature goes far beyond adding module descriptors. So, if you haven't already, I recommend reading appendix E.

Now that we've covered the basics for green-field projects as well for existing code bases, read on to learn about the module system's advanced features in part 3.

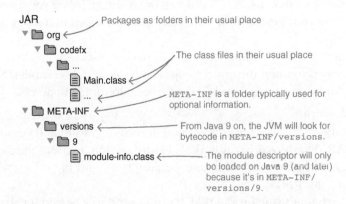

Figure 9.7   By creating a multi-release JAR, you can place the module descriptor in `META-INF/versions/9` instead of the artifact's root.

Summary

- If you're not yet on Java 8, make that update first. If a preliminary analysis shows that some of your dependencies cause problems on Java 9+, update them next. This ensures that you take one step at a time, thus keeping complexity to a minimum.
- You can do several things to analyze migration problems:
  - Build on Java 9+, and apply quick fixes (`--add-modules`, `--add-exports`, `--add-opens`, `--patch-module`, and others) to get more information.
  - Use JDeps to find split packages and dependencies on internal APIs.
  - Search for specific patterns that cause problems, like casts to `URLClassLoader` and the use of removed JVM mechanisms.
- After gathering this information, it's important to properly evaluate it. What are the risks of the quick fixes? How hard is it to solve them properly? How important is the affected code for your project?
- When you start your migration, make an effort to continuously build your changes, ideally from the same branch the rest of the team uses. This makes sure the Java 9+ efforts and regular development are well integrated.
- Command-line options give you the ability to quickly fix the challenges you face when getting a build to work on Java 9+, but be wary of keeping them around too long. They make it easy to ignore problems until future Java releases exacerbate them. Instead, work toward a long-term solution.
- Three modularization strategies exist. Which one applies to a project as a whole depends on its type and dependencies:
  - *Bottom-up* is for projects that only depend on modules. Create module declarations, and place all dependencies on the module path.
  - *Top-down* is for applications whose dependencies aren't yet all modularized. They can create module declarations and place all direct dependencies on the module path—plain JARs are turned into automatic modules that can be depended on.
  - *Inside-out* is for libraries and frameworks whose dependencies aren't yet all modularized. It works like top-down but has the limitation that only automatic modules that define an `Automatic-Module-Name` manifest entry can be used. Otherwise, the automatic module name is unstable across build setups and over time, which can lead to significant problems for users.
  - Within a project, you can choose any strategy that fits its specific structure.
- JDeps allows the automatic generation of module declarations with `jdeps --generate-module-info`. This is particularly relevant to large projects, where hand-writing module declarations would take a lot of time.
- With the `jar` tool's `--update` option, you can modify existing JARs: for example, to set `Automatic-Module-Name` or to add or overwrite a module descriptor. If a

dependency's JAR makes problems that aren't otherwise fixable, this is the sharpest tool to resolve them.

- By compiling and packaging source code for an older Java version and then adding the module descriptor (either in the JARs root directory or with `jar --version` to a Java 9+ specific subdirectory), you can create modular JARs that work on various Java versions *and* as a module if placed on a Java 9 module path.

Part 3

Advanced module system features

Whereas parts 1 and 2 were akin to four-course dinners, this part of the book is more like a buffet. It covers the module system's advanced features, and you're free to pick whatever interests you the most in whatever order you prefer.

Chapter 10 introduces services, a great mechanism to decouple users and implementations of an API. If you're more interested in refining `requires` and `exports`—for example, to model optional dependencies—check out chapter 11. Look into chapter 12 to prepare your modules for reflective access by your favorite framework and to learn how to update your own reflecting code.

The module system doesn't process module version information, but you can record it when building modules and to evaluate them at run time. Chapter 13 explores that as well as the reasons why there is no further support for versions, for example to run multiple versions of the same module.

Chapter 14 takes a step back from developing modules and instead sees them as input for creating custom run-time images that contain just the modules you need to run your project. Going one step further, you can include your entire application and create a single deployable unit to ship to your customers or servers.

Finally, chapter 15 puts all the pieces together. It shows you a variant of the *ServiceMonitor* application that uses most of the advanced features and then gives some tips for designing and maintaining modular applications before daring to portray Java's future: a modular ecosystem.

By the way, these features aren't *advanced* in the sense that they're more complicated than the basic mechanisms. It's that they build on top of those mechanisms and thus require a little more background knowledge of the module system. If you've read part 1, particularly chapter 3, you're good to go.

(I know, I've said it a couple of times already, but remember that the module names I've chosen were cut short to make them more amenable. Use the reverse-domain naming scheme as described in section 3.1.3.)

Using services to decouple modules

This chapter covers

- Improving project designs with services
- Creating services, consumers, and providers in the JPMS
- Using the `ServiceLoader` to consume services
- Developing well-designed services
- Deploying services in plain and modular JARs across different Java versions

Up to now, we represented relationships between modules with `requires` directives where the depending module has to reference each specific dependency by name. As section 3.2 explains in depth, this lies at the heart of reliable configuration. But sometimes you want a higher level of abstraction.

This chapter explores services in the module system and how to use them to decouple modules by removing direct dependencies between them. The first step to solving any problems with services is to get the basics down. Following that, we look at the details, particularly how to properly design services (section 10.3) and how to use the JDK's API to consume them (section 10.4). (To see services in practice, check out the `feature-services` branch in *ServiceMonitor*'s repository.)

217

By the end of this chapter, you'll know how to design services well, how to write declarations for modules that use or provide services, and how to load services at run time. You can use these skills to connect with services in the JDK or third-party dependencies as well as to remove direct dependencies in your own project.

10.1 Exploring the need for services

If we were talking about classes instead of modules, would you be happy with always depending on concrete types? Or with having to instantiate each dependency in the class that needs it? If you like design patterns like inversion of control and dependency injection, you should be vigorously shaking your head at this point. Compare listings 10.1 and 10.2—doesn't the second one look better? It allows the caller to pick the stream that gets to be awesome and even gives the caller the freedom to choose any InputStream implementation.

Listing 10.1 Depends on a concrete type and establishes the dependency

```
public class InputStreamAwesomizer {

    private final ByteArrayInputStream stream;        ◄──┐ Depends on a concrete type

    public AwesomeInputStream(byte[] buffer) {
        stream = new ByteArrayInputStream(buffer);    ◄──
    }
                                                         Establishes the
    // [... awesome methods ...]                         dependency directly

}
```

Listing 10.2 Depends on an abstract type; caller establishes the dependency

```
public class InputStreamAwesomizer {
                                                  Depends on an abstract type
    private final InputStream stream;         ◄──┘

    public AwesomeInputStream(InputStream stream) {
        this.stream = stream;         ◄──┐
    }                                     Dependency established
                                          by the caller
    // [... awesome methods ...]

}
```

Another important benefit of depending on interfaces or abstract classes and letting someone else pick the concrete instance is that doing so inverts the direction of dependencies. Instead of high-level concepts (let's say Department) depending on low-level details (`Secretary`, `Clerk`, and `Manager`), both can depend on an abstraction (`Employee`). As figure 10.1 shows, this breaks the dependency between high- and low-level concepts and thus decouples them.

Turning back to modules, `requires` directives are much like the code in listing 10.1, just on a different level of abstraction:

- Modules depend on other concrete modules.
- There is no way for the user to exchange dependencies.
- There is no way to invert the direction of dependencies.

Fortunately, the module system doesn't leave it at that. It offers *services*, a way for modules to express that they depend on an abstract type or provide a concrete type that fulfills such a dependency, with the module system in the middle, negotiating between them. (If you're now thinking about the service locator pattern, you're spot on!) As you'll see, services don't perfectly solve all the mentioned issues, but they go a long way. Figure 10.4 shows two types of dependencies.

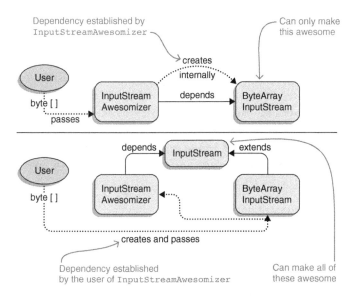

Figure 10.1 **If a type establishes its own dependencies (top), users can't influence them. If a type's dependencies are passed during construction (bottom), users can pick the implementation that best fits their use case.**

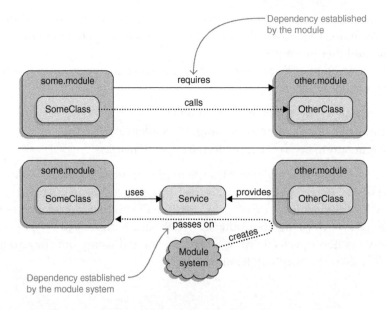

Figure 10.2   If a module requires another (top), the dependency is fixed; it can't be changed from the outside. On the other hand, if a module uses a service (bottom), the concrete implementation is chosen at run time.

10.2   *Services in the Java Platform Module System*

When we talk about a service in the context of the JPMS, it comes down to a specific type, usually an interface, that we want to use, but for which we don't instantiate implementations. Instead, the module system pulls in implementations from other modules that said they would provide them and instantiates those implementations. This section shows in detail how that process works so you know what to put into module descriptors and how to get instances at run time as well as how that impacts module resolutions).

10.2.1   *Using, providing, and consuming services*

A *service* is an accessible type that one module wants to use and another module provides an instance of:

- The module *consuming* the service expresses its requirement with a uses ${service} *directive* in its module descriptor, where ${service} is the fully qualified name of the service type.
- The module *providing* the service expresses its offer with a provides ${service} with ${provider} *directive*, where ${service} is the same type as in the uses directive and ${provider} the fully qualified name of another class, which is one or the other of the following:

- A concrete class that extends or implements ${service} and has a public, parameterless constructor (called a *provider constructor*)
- An arbitrary type with a public, static, parameterless method provide that returns a type that extends or implements ${service} (called a *provider method*)

At run time, the depending module can use the ServiceLoader class to get all provided implementations of a service by calling ServiceLoader.load(${service}.class). The module system then returns a Provider<${service}> for each provider any module in the module graph declares. Figure 10.3 illustrates implementing a Provider.

There are a lot of details to consider around services; but generally speaking, they're a good abstraction and straightforward to use in practice, so let's start with that. Settle in; going through the motions takes longer than typing out a requires or exports directive.

The *ServiceMonitor* application provides a perfect example for a good use of services. The Monitor class from the monitor module needs a List<ServiceObserver> to contact the services it's supposed to monitor. So far, Main has done this as follows:

```
private static Optional<ServiceObserver> createObserver(String serviceName) {
    return AlphaServiceObserver.createIfAlphaService(serviceName)
        .or(() -> BetaServiceObserver.createIfBetaService(serviceName));
}
```

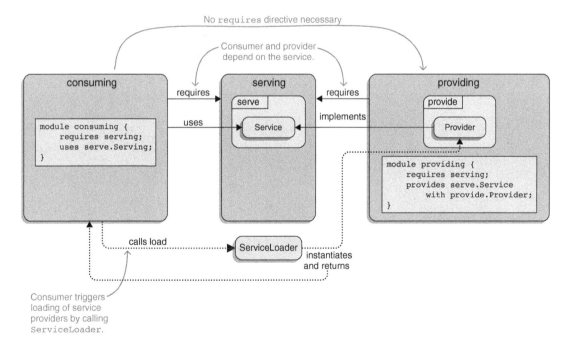

Figure 10.3 At the center of using services is a specific type, here called Service. **The class** Provider **implements it, and the module containing it declares that with a** provides −with **directive. Modules consuming services need to declare that with a** uses **directive. At run time, they can then use the** ServiceLoader **to get instances of all providers for a given service.**

It isn't overly important how exactly the code works. What's relevant is that it uses the concrete types `AlphaServiceObserver` from *monitor.observer.alpha* and `BetaService-Observer` from *monitor.observer.beta*. Hence *monitor* needs to depend on those modules, and they need to export the corresponding packages—figure 10.4 shows the matching section of the module graph.

Now let's turn this into services. First, the module creating those observers needs to declare that it plans to use a service. Start by using `ServiceObserver` for that, so *monitor*'s module declaration looks like this:

```
module monitor {
    // [... truncated requires directives ...]
    // removed dependencies on monitor.observer.alpha and beta - yay!
    uses monitor.observer.ServiceObserver;
}
```

The second step is to declare the `provides` directives in the provider modules *monitor. observer.alpha* and *monitor.observer.beta*:

```
module monitor.observer.alpha {
    requires monitor.observer;
    // removed export of monitor.observer.alpha - yay!
    provides monitor.observer.ServiceObserver
        with monitor.observer.alpha.AlphaServiceObserver;
}
```

This doesn't work, though—the compiler throws an error:

```
> The service implementation does not have
> a public default constructor:
>       AlphaServiceObserver
```

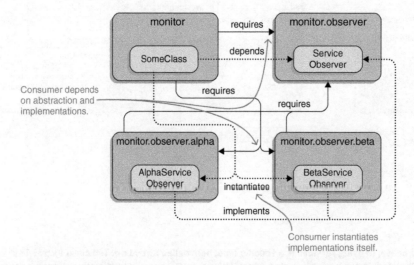

Figure 10.4   Without services, the monitor module needs to depend on all other involved modules: *observer*, *alpha*, **and** *beta*, **as shown in this partial module graph.**

Provider constructors and provider methods need to be parameterless, but `Alpha-ServiceObserver` expects the URL of the service it's supposed to observe. What to do? You could set the URL after creation, but that would make the class mutable, and raises the question of what to do if the service isn't *alpha*. No, it's cleaner to create a factory for observers that returns an instance only if the URL is correct and make that factory the service.

So, create a new interface, `ServiceObserverFactory`, in *monitor.observer*. It has a single method, `createIfMatchingService`, that expects the service URL and returns an `Optional<ServiceObserver>`. In *monitor.observer.alpha* and *monitor.observer.beta*, create implementations that do what the static factory methods on `AlphaServiceObserver` and `BetaServiceObserver` used to do. Figure 10.5 shows the corresponding portion of the module graph.

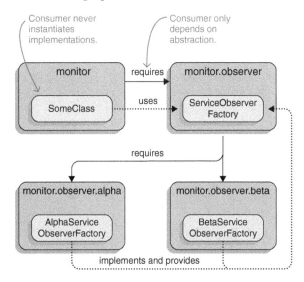

Figure 10.5 With services, *monitor* only depends on the module defining the service: *observer*. The providing modules, *alpha* and *beta*, are no longer directly required.

With those classes, you can provide and consume the `ServiceObserverFactory` as a service. The following listing shows the module declarations for *monitor, monitor. observer, monitor.observer.alpha,* and *monitor.observer.beta.*

Listing 10.3   Four modules that work with `ServiceObserverFactory`

The consuming module monitor requires monitor.observer because it contains ServiceObserverFactory. Thanks to services, it requires neither alpha nor beta.

Nothing changed for monitor.observer: it's unaware that it's used as a service. All that's needed is the usual export of the package containing ServiceObserver and ServiceObserverFactory.

```
module monitor {
    requires monitor.observer;
    // [... truncated other requires directives ...]
    uses monitor.observer.ServiceObserverFactory;
}

module monitor.observer {
    exports monitor.observer;
}
```

The consuming module monitor uses the service interface ServiceObserverFactory.

```
module monitor.observer.alpha {
    requires monitor.observer;
    provides monitor.observer.ServiceObserverFactory
        with monitor.observer.alpha.AlphaServiceObserverFactory;
}

module monitor.observer.beta {
    requires monitor.observer;
    provides monitor.observer.ServiceObserverFactory
        with monitor.observer.beta.BetaServiceObserverFactory;
}
```

> **Both provider modules require monitor.observer because they implement the interfaces it contains—services changed nothing.**

> **Each provider module provides the service ServiceObserverFactory with its concrete class.**

The final step is to get the observer factories in *monitor*. To that end, call `Service-Loader.load(ServiceObserverFactory.class)`, stream over the returned providers, and get the service implementations:

```
List<ServiceObserverFactory> observerFactories = ServiceLoader
    .load(ServiceObserverFactory.class).stream()
    .map(Provider::get)
    .collect(toList());
```

> **Provider::get instantiates a provider (see section 10.4.2).**

And there you go: you have a bunch of service providers, and neither the consuming nor the providing modules know each other. Their only connection is that all have a dependency on the API module.

The platform modules also declare and use a lot of services. A particularly interesting one is `java.sql.Driver`, declared and used by *java.sql*:

```
$ java --describe-module java.sql

> java.sql
# truncated exports
# truncated requires
> uses java.sql.Driver
```

This way, *java.sql* can access all `Driver` implementations provided by other modules.

Another exemplary use of services in the platform is `java.lang.System.Logger-Finder`. This is part of a new API added in Java 9 and allows users to pipe the JDK's log messages (not the JVM's!) into the logging framework of their choice (say, Log4J or Logback). Instead of writing to standard out, the JDK uses `LoggerFinder` to create `Logger` instances and then logs all messages with them.

For Java 9 and later, logging frameworks can implement factories for loggers that use the framework's infrastructure:

```
public class ForesterFinder extends LoggerFinder {

    @Override
    public Logger getLogger(String name, Module module) {
        return new Forester(name, module);
    }

}
```

> **Belongs to the fictitious Forester logging framework**

But how can logging frameworks inform *java.base* of their `LoggerFinder` implementation? Easy: they provide the `LoggerFinder` service with their own implementation:

```
module org.forester {
    provides java.lang.System.LoggerFinder
        with org.forester.ForesterFinder;
}
```

This works because the base module uses `LoggerFinder` and then calls the `Service-Loader` to locate `LoggerFinder` implementations. It gets a framework-specific finder, asks it to create `Logger` implementations, and then uses them to log messages.

This should give you a good idea of how to create and use services. On to the details!

10.2.2 *Module resolution for services*

If you've ever started a simple modular application and observed what the module system is doing (for example, with `--show-module-resolution`, as explained in section 5.3.6), you may have been surprised by the number of platform modules that are resolved. With a simple application like *ServiceMonitor*, the only platform modules should be *java.base* and maybe one or two more, so why are there so many others? Services are the answer.

 ESSENTIAL INFO Remember from section 3.4.3 that only modules that make it into the graph during module resolution are available at run time. To make sure that's the case for all observable providers of a service, the resolution process takes into account `uses` and `provides` directives. Beyond the resolution behavior described in section 3.4.1, once it resolves a module consuming a service, it adds all observable modules to the graph that provides that service. This is called *binding*.

Launching *ServiceMonitor* with `--show-module-resolution` shows a lot of service bindings:

```
$ java
    --show-module-resolution
    --module-path mods:libs
    --module monitor

> root monitor
> monitor requires monitor.observer
# truncated many resolutions
> monitor binds monitor.observer.beta
> monitor binds monitor.observer.alpha
> java.base binds jdk.charsets jrt:/jdk.charsets
> java.base binds jdk.localedata jrt:/jdk.localedata
# truncated lots of more bindings for java.base
# truncated rest of resolution
```

The module *monitor* binds the modules *monitor.observer.alpha* and *monitor.observer.beta* even though it doesn't depend on either of them. The same happens to *jdk.charsets*, *jdk.localedata*, and many more due to *java.base* and other platform modules. Figure 10.6 shows the module graph.

EXCLUDING SERVICES WITH –LIMIT-MODULES

Services and the `--limit-modules` option have an interesting interaction. As section 5.3.5 describes, `--limit-modules` limits the universe of observable modules to the specified ones and their transitive dependencies. This doesn't include services! Unless modules providing services are transitively required by the modules listed after `--limit-modules`, they aren't observable and won't make it into the module graph. In that case, calls to `ServiceLoader::load` will often return empty-handed.

If you launch *ServiceMonitor* as when examining module resolution but limit the observable universe to modules depending on *monitor*, the output is much simpler:

```
$ java
    --show-module-resolution
    --module-path mods:libs
    --limit-modules monitor
    --module monitor
root monitor
# truncated monitor's transitive dependencies
```

That's it: no services—neither observer factories nor the many services platform modules usually bind. Figure 10.7 shows this simplified module graph.

Particularly powerful is the combination of `--limit-modules` and `--add-modules`: the former can be used to exclude all services and the latter to add back the desired ones. This allows you to try out different service configurations at launch without having to manipulate the module path.

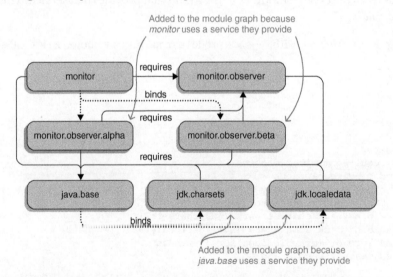

Figure 10.6   Service binding is part of module resolution: Once a module is resolved (like *monitor* or *java.base*), its uses directives are analyzed, and all modules that provide matching services (*alpha* and *beta* as well as *charsets* and *localedata*) are added to the module graph.

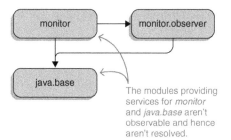

The modules providing services for *monitor* and *java.base* aren't observable and hence aren't resolved.

Figure 10.7 **With `--limit-modules monitor`, the universe of observable modules is limited to *monitor*'s transitive dependencies, which excludes the service providers resolved in figure 10.6.**

Why are uses directives necessary?

In a small aside, I want to answer a question some developers have about the `uses` directive: Why is it necessary? Couldn't the module system look for providers once `Service-Loader::load` is called?

If modules are properly decoupled via services, there's a good chance the providing modules aren't transitive dependencies of any root module. Without further efforts, service-provider modules routinely wouldn't make it into the module graph and thus wouldn't be available at run time when a module tries to use a service.

For services to properly work, provider modules must make it into the module graph even if they aren't transitively required from any root module. But how can the module system identify which modules provide services? Does that mean all modules that have a `provides` directive? That would be too many. No, only providers of needed services should be resolved.

This makes it necessary to identify service *uses*. Analyzing the bytecode that calls `ServiceLoader::load` is both slow and unreliable, so a more explicit mechanism is required to guarantee efficiency and correctness: `uses` directives. By requiring you to declare which services a module uses, the module system can reliably and efficiently make all service provider modules available.

10.3 Designing services well

As you saw in section 10.2, services are a play with four actors:

- *Service*—In the JPMS, a class or an interface.
- *Consumer*—Any piece of code that wants to use services.
- *Provider*—A concrete implementation of the service.
- *Locator*—The puppet master that, triggered by the consumer's request, locates providers and returns them. In Java, this is the `ServiceLoader`.

The `ServiceLoader` is provided by the JDK (we take a closer look at it in section 10.4), but when you're creating services, the other three classes are your responsibility. Which types do you choose for services (see section 10.3.1), and how do you best design them (section 10.3.2)? Isn't it weird that consumers depend on ugly global state (section 10.3.3)? How should the modules containing services, consumers, and providers be related to one another (section 10.3.4)? To design well-crafted services, you need to be able to answer these questions.

We'll also look into using services to break cyclic dependencies between modules (section 10.3.5). Last but not least—and this is particularly interesting for those who plan to use services on different Java versions—we discuss how services work across plain and modular JARs (section 10.3.6).

10.3.1 Types that can be services

A service can be a concrete class (even a final one), an abstract class, or an interface. Although only enums are excluded, using a concrete class (particularly a final one) as a service is unconventional—the entire point is that the module is supposed to depend on something abstract. Unless a specific use case requires it, a service should always be an abstract class or an interface.

> **On abstract classes**
>
> Personally, I'm not a fan of deep class hierarchies and thus have a natural aversion to abstract classes. With Java 8's ability to implement methods in interfaces, a big use case for abstract classes fell away: providing basic implementations of interface methods for which a good default behavior exists.
>
> Now I mainly use them as local support (usually package-scoped or inner classes) for implementing complex interfaces, but I make a point to not let them seep into a public API unless absolutely necessary. In that vein, I've never created a service—which is necessarily part of a module's public API—that wasn't an interface.

10.3.2 Using factories as services

Let's go back to the first try at refactoring the service observer architecture to use JPMS services in section 10.2.1. That didn't go well. Using the `ServiceObserver` interface as the service and its implementations `AlphaServiceObserver` and `BetaService-Observer` as providers had a number of problems:

- Providers need parameterless provider methods or constructors, but the classes we wanted to use needed to be initialized with a concrete state that wasn't meant to be mutated.
- It would have been awkward for observer instances, which can handle either the alpha or beta API, to decide whether they're suitable for a specific network service. I prefer creating instances in their correct state.
- The service loader caches providers (more on that in section 10.4), so depending on how you use the API, there may be only one instance per provider: in this case, one `AlphaServiceObserver` and one `BetaServiceObserver`.

This made it impractical to directly create the instance we needed, so we used a factory instead. As it turns out, that wasn't a special case.

Whether it's the URL to connect to or the name of the logger, it's common for a consumer to want to configure the services it uses. The consumer might also like to create more than one instance of any specific service provider. Taken together with the service loader's requirement for parameterless construction and its freedom to cache instances, this makes it impractical to make the used type, `ServiceObserver` or `Logger`, the service.

Instead, it's common to create a factory for the desired type, like `ServiceObserver-Factory` or `LoggerFinder`, and make *it* the service. According to the factory pattern, factories have the sole responsibility to create instances in the correct state. As such, it's often straightforward to design them so they have no state of their own and you don't particularly care how many of them there are. This makes factories a great fit for the peculiarities of the `ServiceLoader`.

And they have at least two further bonuses:

- If instantiating the desired type is expensive, having a factory for it as the service makes it easiest for consumers to control when instances are created.
- If it's necessary to check whether a provider can handle a certain input or configuration, the factory can have a method indicating that. Alternatively, its methods can return a type indicating that creating an object wasn't possible (for example, an `Optional`).

I want to show you two examples for selecting services depending on their applicability to a certain situation. The first comes from *ServiceMonitor*, where `ServiceObserver-Factory` doesn't have a method `create(String)` returning a `ServiceObserver`, but does have a `createIfMatchingService(String)` method returning an `Optional<ServiceObserver>`. This way, you can throw any URL at any factory and the return value informs you whether it could handle it.

The other example doesn't use the `ServiceLoader`, but rather uses a similar API deep in the JDK, the `ServiceRegistry`. It was created exclusively for Java's ImageIO API, which uses it to locate an `ImageReader` for a given image depending on its codec, for example, JPEG or PNG.

Image IO locates readers by requesting implementations of the abstract class `ImageReaderSpi` from the registry, which returns instances of classes like `JPEGImage-ReaderSpi` and `PNGImageReaderSpi`. It then calls `canDecodeInput(Object)` on each `ImageReaderSpi` implementation, which returns `true` if the image uses the right codec as indicated by the file header. Only when an implementation returns `true` will Image IO call `createReaderInstance(Object)` to create an actual reader for the image. Figure 10.8 shows using a factory.

`ImageReaderSpi` acts as a factory service, where `canDecodeInput` is used to select the correct provider and `createReaderInstance` is used to create the needed type: an `ImageReader`. As section 10.4.2 shows, there's an alternative approach to selecting a suitable provider.

In summary, you should routinely consider not picking the type you want to use as a service, but instead choosing another type, a factory, that returns instances of what you want to use. That factory should require no state of its own to function correctly. (This also makes it much easier to implement it in a thread-safe manner if that's relevant for your use case.) See factories as a way to separate the original requirements for the type you want to use from the service infrastructure's specific requirements instead of mixing them in one type.

10.3.3 *Isolating consumers from global state*

Code calling `ServiceLoader::load` is inherently hard to test because it depends on the global application state: the modules with which the program was launched. That can easily become a problem when the module using a service doesn't depend on the module providing it (as should be the case), because then the build tool won't include the providing module in the test's module path.

Manually preparing the `ServiceLoader` for a unit test so that it returns a specific list of service providers requires some heavy lifting. That's anathema to unit tests, which are supposed to run in isolation and on small units of code.

Beyond that, the call to `ServiceLoader::load` doesn't usually solve any problem the application's user cares about. It's just a necessary and technical step *toward* such a solution. This puts it on a different level of abstraction than the code that uses the received service providers. Friends of the single responsibility principle would say such code has two responsibilities (requesting providers and implementing a business requirement), which seems to be one too many.

These properties suggest that code handling service loading shouldn't be mixed with code implementing the application's business requirements. Fortunately, keeping them separate isn't too complicated. Somewhere the instance that ends up using the providers is created, and that's usually a good place to call `ServiceLoader` and then pass the providers. *ServiceMonitor* follows the same structure: it creates all instances required

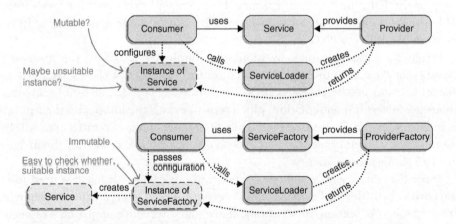

Figure 10.8   Making the desired type the service often doesn't go well with the JDK's peculiarities. Instead, consider designing a factory that creates instances in the correct configuration, and make it the service.

to run the app in the Main class (including loadingServiceObserver implementations) and then hands off to Monitor, which does the actual work of monitoring services.

Listings 10.4 and 10.5 show a comparison. In listing 10.4, IntegerStore does the heavy service lifting itself, which mixes responsibilities. This also makes code using IntegerStore hard to test, because tests have to be aware of the ServiceLoader call and then make sure it returns the desired integer makers.

In listing 10.5, IntegerStore is refactored and now expects the code constructing it to deliver a List<IntegerMaker>. This makes its code focus on the business problem at hand (making integers) and removes any dependency on the ServiceLoader and thus the global application state. Testing it is a breeze. Somebody still has to deal with loading services, but a create... method that's called during application setup is a much better place for that.

Listing 10.4 Hard to test due to too many responsibilities

```
public class Integers {

    public static void main(String[] args) {
        IntegerStore store = new IntegerStore();
        List<Integer> ints = store.makeIntegers(args[0]);
        System.out.println(ints);
    }

}

public class IntegerStore {

    public List<Integer> makeIntegers(String config) {
        return ServiceLoader
            .load(IntegerMaker.class).stream()
            .map(Provider::get)
            .map(maker -> maker.make(config))
            .distinct()
            .sorted()
            .collect(toList());
    }

}

public interface IntegerMaker {

    int make(String config);

}
```

The results of this call directly depend on the module path content, which makes it hard to unit test.

Solves the technical requirement to load integer makers

Solves the business problem: making unique integers and sorting them

Listing 10.5 Rewritten to improve its design and testability

```
public class Integers {

    public static void main(String[] args) {
        IntegerStore store = createIntegerStore();
```

```
        List<Integer> ints = store.makeIntegers(args[0]);
        System.out.println(ints);
    }

    private static IntegerStore createIntegerStore() {
        List<IntegerMaker> makers = ServiceLoader
            .load(IntegerMaker.class).stream()
            .map(Provider::get)
            .collect(toList());
        return new IntegerStore(makers);
    }

}


public class IntegerStore {

    private final List<IntegerMaker> makers;

    public IntegerStore(List<IntegerMaker> makers) {
        this.makers = makers;
    }

    public List<Integer> makeIntegers(String config) {
        return makers.stream()
            .map(maker -> maker.make(config))
            .distinct()
            .sorted()
            .collect(toList());
    }

}

public interface IntegerMaker {

    int make(String config);

}
```

Solves the technical requirement to load integer makers during setup

IntegerStore gets makers during construction and has no dependency on ServiceLoader.

The makeIntegers method can focus on its business requirement.

Depending on the particular project and requirements, you may have to pass providers more than one method or constructor call, wrap it into another object that defers loading until the last moment, or configure your dependency-injection framework, but it should be doable. And it's worth the effort—your unit tests and colleagues will thank you.

10.3.4 *Organizing services, consumers, and providers into modules*

With the service's type, design, and consumption settled, the question emerges: how can you organize the service and the other two actors, consumers and providers, into modules? Services obviously need to be implemented, and to provide value, code in modules other than the one containing the service should be able implement the service. That means the service type must be public and in an exported package.

The consumer doesn't have to be public or exported and hence may be internal to its module. It must access the service's type, though, so it needs to require the module containing the service (*the service*, not the classes implementing it). It isn't uncommon for the consumer and service to end up in the same module, as is the case with *java.sql* and Driver as well as *java.base* and LoggerFinder.

Finally, we come to providers. Because they implement the service, they have to read the module defining it—that much is obvious. The interesting question is whether the providing type should become part of the module's public API beyond being named in a provides directive.

A service provider must be public, but there's no technical requirement for exporting its package—the service loader is fine with instantiating inaccessible classes. Thus, exporting the package containing a provider needlessly enlarges a module's API surface. It also invites consumers to do things they're not supposed to, like casting a service to its real type to access additional features (analogous to what happened with URLClassLoader; see section 6.2.1). I hence advise you to not make service providers accessible.

In summary (see also figure 10.9)

- Services need to be public and in an exported package.
- Consumers can be internal. They need to read the module defining the service or may even be part of it.
- Providers must be public but shouldn't be in an exported package, to minimize misuse and API surface. They need to read the module defining the service.

NOTE In case you're wondering, a module can only provide a service with a type it owns. The service implementation named in the provides directive must be in the same module as the declaration.

10.3.5 *Using services to break cyclic dependencies*

When working with a code base that's split into subprojects, there always comes a point where one of them becomes too large and we want to split it into smaller projects. Doing so requires some work, but given enough time to disentangle classes, we can usually accomplish the goal. Sometimes, though, the code clings together so tightly that we can't find a way to cut it apart.

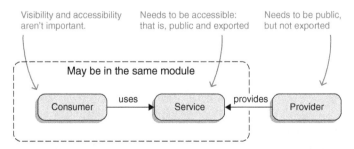

Figure 10.9 Visibility and accessibility requirements for consumers, services, and providers

A common reason is cyclic dependencies between classes. There could be two classes importing each other, or a longer cycle involving a number of classes where each imports the next. However you ended up with such a cycle, if you'd prefer to have some of its constituting classes in one project and some in another, it's a problem. This is true even without the module system, because build tools usually don't like cyclic dependencies either; but the JPMS voices its own strong disagreement.

> **NOTE**   Due to the accessibility rules, dependencies between classes that live in separate modules require dependencies between those modules (see section 3.3). If the class dependencies are circular, so are the module dependencies, and the readability rules don't allow that (see section 3.2).

What can you do? Because you're reading the chapter about services, it may not surprise you to learn that services can help. The idea is to invert one of the dependencies in the cycle by creating a service that lives in the depending module. Here's how to do it, step by step (see also figure 10.10):

1 Look at the cycle of module dependencies, and identify which dependency you'd like to invert. I'll call the two involved modules *depending* (the one that will have the `requires` directive) and *depended*. Ideally, *depending* uses a single type from *depended*. I'll focus on that special case—if there are more types, repeat the following steps for each of them.

2 In *depending*, create a service type, and extend the module declaration with a `uses` directive for that type.

3 In *depending*, remove the dependency on *depended*. Take note of the resulting compile errors, because *depended*'s type is no longer accessible. Replace all references to it with the service type:
   - Update imports and class names.
   - Method calls should require no changes.
   - Constructor calls won't work out of the box because you need the instances from *depended*. This is where the `ServiceLoader` comes in: use it to replace constructions of *depended*'s type by loading the service type you just created.

4 In *depended*, add a dependency to *depending* so the service type becomes accessible. Provide that service with the type that originally caused the trouble.

Success! You just inverted the dependency between *depending* and *depended* (now the latter depends on the former) and thus broke the cycle. Here are a few further details to keep in mind:

- The type in *depended* that *depending* used may not be a good candidate for a service. If that's so, consider creating a factory for it, as explained in section 10.3.2, or look for another dependency you can replace.
- Section 10.3.3 explores the problem with sprinkling `ServiceLoader` calls all over a module; that issue applies here. Maybe you need to refactor *depending*'s code to minimize the number of loads.

- The service type doesn't have to be in *depending*. As section 10.3.4 explains, it can live in any module. Or, rather, in almost any module—you don't want to put it in one that recreates the cycle, for example in *depended*.
- Most important, try to create a service that stands on its own and is more than just a cycle breaker. There may be more providers and consumers than just the two modules involved so far.

10.3.6 Declaring services across different Java versions

Services aren't new. They were introduced in Java 6, and the mechanisms designed back then still work today. It makes sense to look at how they operate without modules and particularly how they work across plain and modular JARs.

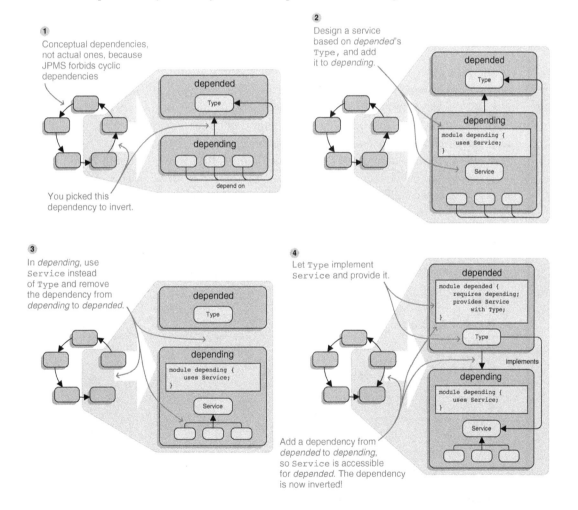

Figure 10.10 Using services to break dependency cycles in four steps: ❶ Pick a dependency, ❷ introduce a service on the depending end, ❸ use that service on the depending end, and ❹ provide the service on the depended end.

DECLARING SERVICES IN META-INF/SERVICES

Before the module system entered the picture, services worked much the same as they do now. The only difference is that there were no module declarations to declare that a JAR uses or provides a service. On the using side, that's fine—all code could use every service it wanted. On the providing side, though, JARs had to declare their intentions, and they did so in a dedicated directory in the JAR.

To have a plain JAR declare a service, follow these simple steps:

1 Place a file with the service's fully qualified name as the filename in META-INF/ services.

2 In the file, list all fully qualified names of classes that implement the service.

As an example, let's create a third `ServiceObserverFactory` provider in the newly envisioned plain JAR *monitor.observer.zero*. To do so, you first need a concrete class `ZeroServiceObserverFactory` that implements `ServiceObserverFactory` and has a parameterless constructor. That's analogous to the *alpha* and *beta* variants, so I don't need to discuss it in detail.

A plain JAR has no module descriptor to declare the services it provides, but you can use the META-INF/services directory for that: put a simple text file `monitor.observer.ServiceObserverFactory` (the fully qualified name of the *service type*) in the directory, with the single line `monitor.observer.zero.ZeroServiceObserverFactory` (the fully qualified name of the *provider type*). Figure 10.11 shows what that looks like.

I promise you this works, and the `ZeroServiceObserverFactory` is properly resolved when `Main` streams all observer factories. But you'll have to take my word for it until we've discussed how plain and modular JARs' services interact. That's next.

NOTE There's a small difference between declaring services in META-INF/ services and declaring them in module declarations. Only the latter can use provider methods—the former need to stick to public, parameterless constructors.

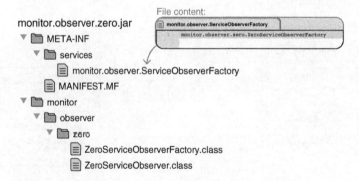

Figure 10.11   To declare service providers without module declarations, the folder META-INF/services **needs to contain a plain text file with the name of the service and a single line per provider.**

COMPATIBILITY ACROSS JARS AND PATHS

Because the service loader API was around before the module system arrived in Java 9, there are compatibility concerns. Can consumers in plain and modular JARs use services the same way? And what happens with providers across different kinds of JARs and paths?

For service consumers, the picture is simple: explicit modules can use the services they declare with uses directives; automatic modules (see section 8.3) and the unnamed module (section 8.2) can use all existing services. In summary, on the consumer side, it just works.

For service providers, it's a little more complicated. There are two axes with two expressions each, leading to four combinations:

- Kind of JAR: plain (service declaration in `META-INF/services`) or modular (service declaration in module descriptor)
- Kind of path: class or module

No matter which path a plain JAR ends up on, the service loader will identify and bind services in `META-INF/services`. If the JAR is on the class path, its content is already part of the unnamed module. If it's on the module path, service binding results in the creation of an automatic module. This triggers the resolution of all other automatic modules, as described in section 8.3.2.

Now you know why you could try out *monitor.observer.zero*, a plain JAR providing its service in `META-INF/services`, with the modularized *ServiceMonitor* application. And it doesn't matter which path I choose; it works from both without further ado.

 ESSENTIAL INFO Modular JARs on the module path are the sweet spot for services in the module system, so they work without limitations. On the class path, modular JARs can cause problems, though. They're treated like plain JARs, so they need entries in the `META-INF/services` folder. As a developer whose project relies on services and whose modular artifacts are supposed to work on both paths, you need to declare services in the module descriptor *and* `META-INF/services`.

Launching *ServiceMonitor* from the class path leads to no useful output, because no observer factory can be found—unless you add *monitor.observer.zero* to the mix. With its provider definition in `META-INF/services`, it's well suited to work from the unnamed module, and indeed it does—unlike the *alpha* and *beta* providers.

10.4 *Accessing services with the ServiceLoader API*

Despite the fact that the `ServiceLoader` has been around since Java 6, it hasn't seen wide adoption, but I expect that with its prominent integration into the module system, its use will increase considerably. To make sure you know your way around its API, we explore it in this section.

As usual, the first step is to get to know the basics, which in this case won't take long. The service loader does have some idiosyncrasies, though, and to make sure they won't trip you up, we'll discuss them too.

10.4.1 Loading and accessing services

Using the `ServiceLoader` is always a two-step process:

1. Create a `ServiceLoader` instance for the correct service.
2. Use that instance to access service providers.

Let's have a quick look at each step so you know the options. Also check table 10.1 for an overview of all the `ServiceLoader` methods.

Table 10.1 `ServiceLoader` **API at a glance**

Return type	Method name	Description
Methods to create a new service loader for the given type		
ServiceLoader<S>	load(Class<S>)	Loads providers starting from the current thread's context class loader
ServiceLoader<S>	load(Class<S>, ClassLoader)	Loads providers starting from the specified class loader
ServiceLoader<S>	load(ModuleLayer, Class<S>)	Loads providers starting from modules in the given module layer
ServiceLoader<S>	loadInstalled(Class<S>)	Loads providers from the platform class loader
Methods to access service providers		
Optional<S>	findFirst()	Loads the first available provider
Iterator<S>	iterator()	Returns an iterator to lazily load and instantiate available providers
Stream<Provider<S>>	stream()	Returns a stream to lazily load available providers
void	reload()	Clears this loader's provider cache so all providers will be reloaded

WAYS TO CREATE A SERVICELOADER

The first step, creating a `ServiceLoader` instance, is covered by its several static `load` methods. The simplest one just needs an instance of `Class<S>` for the service you want to load (this is called a *type token*, in this case for type S):

```
ServiceLoader<TheService> loader = ServiceLoader.load(TheService.class);
```

You only need the other `load` methods if you're juggling several class loaders or module layers (see section 12.4); that's not a common case, so I won't go into it. The API docs for the corresponding overloads have you covered.

One other method gets a service loader: `loadInstalled`. It's interesting here because it has a specific behavior: it ignores the module path and class path and only loads services from platform modules, meaning only providers found in JDK modules will be returned.

ACCESSING SERVICE PROVIDERS

With a `ServiceLoader` instance for the desired service in hand, it's time to start using those providers. There are two and a half methods for doing that:

- `Iterator<S> iterator()` lets you iterate over the instantiated service providers.
- `Optional<S> findFirst()` uses `iterator` to *return the first provider* if any were found (this is a convenience method, so I only count it as a half).
- `Stream<Provider<S>> stream()` lets you *stream over service providers*, which are wrapped into a `Provider` instance. (What's up with that? Section 10.4.2 explains.)

If you have specific laziness/caching needs (see section 10.4.2 for more), you may want to keep the `ServiceLoader` instance around. But in most cases that isn't necessary and you can immediately start iterating over or streaming the providers:

```
ServiceLoader
    .load(TheService.class)
    .iterator()
    .forEachRemaining(TheService::doTheServiceThing);
```

In case you're wondering about the inconsistency between `iterator` listing `S` and `stream` listing `Provider<S>`, it has historic reasons: although `iterator` has been around since Java 6, `stream` and `Provider` were only added in Java 9.

One detail that's obvious when you think about it but still easily overlooked is that there may not be a provider for a given service. `Iterator` and `stream` may be empty, and `findFirst` may return an empty `Optional`. If you filter by capabilities, as described in sections 10.3.2 and 10.4.2, ending with zero suitable providers is even more likely.

Make sure your code either handles that case gracefully and can operate without the absent service or fails fast. It's annoying if an application ignores an easily detectable error and keeps running in an undesired and unexpected state.

10.4.2 *Idiosyncrasies of loading services*

The `ServiceLoader` API is pretty simple, but don't be fooled. A few important things are going on behind the curtains, and you need to be aware of them when using the API for anything beyond a basic "Hello, services!" example. This concerns the service loader's laziness, its concurrency capabilities (or lack thereof), and proper error handling. Let's go through these one by one.

LAZINESS AND PICKING THE RIGHT PROVIDER

The service loader is as lazy as possible. Called on a `ServiceLoader<S>` (where `S` is the service type with which `ServiceLoader::load` was called), its `iterator` method returns an `Iterator<S>` that finds and instantiates the next provider only when `hasNext` or `next` is called.

The `stream` method is even lazier. It returns a `Stream<Provider<S>>` that not only lazily finds providers (like `iterator`) but also returns `Provider` instances, which further defer service instantiation until their `get` method is called. Their `type` method gives access to a `Class<? extends S>` instance for their specific provider (meaning the type *implementing* the service, *not* the type that *is* the service).

Accessing the provider's type is useful to scan annotations without having an actual instance of the class. Similar to what we discussed toward the end of section 10.3.2, this gives you a tool to pick the right service provider for a given configuration but without the possible performance impact of instantiating it first. That's if the class is annotated to give you some indication of the provider's suitability.

Continuing the *ServiceMonitor* example of `ServiceObserver` factories being applicable to specific REST service generations, the factories can be annotated with `@Alpha` or `@Beta` to indicate the generation they were created for:

```
Optional<ServiceObserverFactory> alphaFactory = ServiceLoader
    .load(ServiceObserverFactory.class).stream()
    .filter(provider -> provider.type().isAnnotationPresent(Alpha.class))
    .map(Provider::get)
    .findFirst();
```

Here, `Provider::type` is used to access `Class<? extends ServiceObserver>`, which you then ask with `isAnnotationPresent` whether it was annotated with `@Alpha`. Only when `Provider::get` is called is a factory instantiated.

To top off the laziness, a `ServiceLoader` instance caches the providers loaded so far and always returns the same ones. It does have a `reload` method, though, which empties the cache and will trigger new instantiations on the next call to `iterate`, `stream`, or `findFirst`.

USING CONCURRENT SERVICELOADERS

`ServiceLoader` instances aren't thread-safe. If several threads need to operate concurrently on a set of service providers, either each of them needs to make the same `ServiceLoader::load` call, thus getting its own `ServiceLoader` instance, or you must make one call for all of them and store the results in a thread-safe collection.

HANDLING ERRORS WHEN LOADING SERVICES

All kinds of things can go wrong when the `ServiceLoader` tries to locate or instantiate service providers:

- A provider may not fulfill all requirements. Maybe it doesn't implement the service type or doesn't have a suitable provider method or constructor.
- A provider constructor or method can throw an exception or (in case of a method) return `null`.
- A file in `META-INF/services` may violate the required format or not be processed for other reasons.

And those are just the obvious problems.

Because loading is done lazily, `load` can't throw any exception. Instead, the iterator's `hasNext` and `next` methods, as well as the stream processing and the `Provider` methods, can throw errors. These will all be of type `ServiceConfigurationError`, so catching that error lets you handle all problems that can occur.

Summary

- The service architecture is made up of four parts:
  - The *service* is a class or an interface.
  - The *provider* is a concrete implementation of the service.
  - The *consumer* is any piece of code that wants to use a service.
  - The `ServiceLoader` creates and returns an instance of each provider of a given service to consumers.
- Requirements and recommendations for the service type are as follows:
  - Any class or interface can be a service, but because the goal is to provide maximum flexibility to consumers and providers, it's recommended to use interfaces (or, at the least, abstract classes).
  - Service types need to be public and in an exported package. This makes them part of their module's public API, and they should be designed and maintained appropriately.
  - The declaration of the module defining a service contains no entry to mark a type as a service. A type becomes a service by consumers and providers using it as one.
  - Services rarely emerge randomly, but are specifically designed for their purpose. Always consider making the used type not the service but a factory for it. This makes it easier to search for a suitable implementation as well as to control when instances are created and in which state.
- Requirements and recommendations for providers are as follows:
  - Modules providing services need to access the service type, so they must require the module containing it.
  - There are two ways to create a service provider: a concrete class that implements the service type and has a provider constructor (a public, parameterless constructor), or a type with a provider method (a public, static, parameterless method called `provide`) that returns an instance implementing the service type. Either way, the type must be public, but there's no need to export the package containing it. On the contrary, it's advisable not to make the providing type part of a module's public API.
  - Modules providing services declare that by adding a `provides ${service} with ${provider}` directive to their descriptor.
  - If a modular JAR is supposed to provide services even if placed on the class path, it also needs entries in the `META-INF/services` directory. For each `provides ${service} with ${provider}` directive, create a plain file called

${service} that contains one line per ${provider} (all names must be fully qualified).

- Requirements and recommendations for consumers are as follows:
  - Modules consuming services need to access the service type, so they must require the module containing it. They shouldn't require the modules providing that service, though—on the contrary, that would be against the main reason to use services in the first place: to decouple consumers and providers.
  - There's nothing wrong with service types and the service's consumers living in the same module.
  - Any code can consume services regardless of its own accessibility, but the module containing it needs to declare which services it uses with a `uses` directive. This allows the module system to perform service binding efficiently and makes module declarations more explicit and readable.
  - Modules are consumed by calling `ServiceLoader::load` and then iterating or streaming over the returned instances by calling either `iterate` or `stream`. It's possible that will be providers are found, and consumers must handle that case gracefully.
  - The behavior of code that consumes services depends on global state: which provider modules are present in the module graph. This gives such code undesirable properties like making it hard to test. Try to push service loading into setup code that creates objects in their correct configuration (for example, your dependency injection framework), and always allow regular provider code to pass service providers to consuming classes (for example, during construction).
  - The service loader instantiates providers as late as possible. Its `stream` method even returns a `Stream<Provider<S>>`, where `Provider::type` can be used to access the `Class` instance for the provider. This allows searching for a suitable provider by checking class-level annotations without instantiating the provider yet.
  - Service-loader instances aren't thread-safe. If you use them concurrently, you have to provide synchronization.
  - All problems during loading and instantiating providers are thrown as `Service-ConfigurationError`. Due to the loader's laziness, this doesn't happen during `load`, but later in `iterate` or `stream` when problematic providers are encountered. Always be sure to put the entire interaction with `ServiceLoader` into a `try` block if you want to handle errors.
- Here are some points about module resolution and more:
  - When module resolution processes a module that declares the use of a service, all modules providing that service are resolved and thus included in the application's module graph. This is called *service binding*, and together with the use

of services in the JDK, it explains why by default even small apps use a lot of platform modules.

– The command-line option `--limit-modules`, on the other hand, does no service binding. As a consequence, providers that aren't transitive dependencies of the modules given to this option don't make it into the module graph and aren't available at run time. The option can be used to exclude services, optionally together with `--add-modules` to add some of them back.

Refining dependencies and APIs

Chapter 3 explains how `requires` and `exports` directives are the basis for readability and accessibility. But these mechanisms are strict: *every* module has to be explicitly required, *all* required modules have to be present for the application to compile and launch, and exported packages are accessible to *all* other modules. This suffices for the majority of use cases, but there's still a significant portion in which these solutions are too broad.

The most obvious use case is optional dependencies, which a module wants to compile against but which aren't necessarily present at run time. Spring, for example, does this with the Jackson databind library. If you run a Spring application and want to use JSON as a data-transfer format, you can get support for that by dropping in the Jackson artifact. If, on the other hand, that artifact is absent, Spring is still happy—it doesn't support JSON then. Spring *uses* Jackson but doesn't *require* it.

Regular `requires` directives don't cover this use case, though, because the modules would have to be present for the application to launch. Services can be the solution in some such cases, but using them for all optional dependencies would lead to many awkward and complex implementations. Hence, plainly expressing that a dependency isn't required at run time is an important feature; section 11.2 shows how the JPMS implements it.

Another use case where the module system's strictness can become a hindrance is refactoring modules over time. In any decently sized project, the architecture evolves as time goes by, and developers will want to merge or split modules. But then what happens to code that depends on the old modules? Wouldn't it be missing functionality (if it was split off into a new module) or even entire modules (if they were merged)? Fortunately the module system offers a feature, called *implied readability*, that can be of use here.

Although the `requires` and `exports` mechanisms we know so far make for a comparatively simple mental model, they offer no elegant solutions for use cases that don't fit into their one-size-fits-all approaches. In this chapter, we look into such specific use cases and explore the solutions the module system offers.

By the time you've worked through it, you'll be able to use more refined mechanisms to access dependencies and export functionality. This will allow you to, among other things, express optional dependencies (section 11.2), refactor modules (section 11.1), and share code between a defined set of modules while keeping it private from other code (section 11.3).

11.1 *Implied readability: Passing on dependencies*

In section 3.2, we explored in depth how `requires` directives establish dependencies between modules and how the module system uses them to create reads edges (eventually resulting in the module graph, as sections 3.4.1 and 3.4.2 show). In section 3.3, you saw that accessibility is based on these edges, and to access a type, the accessing module must read the module containing the type (the type must also be public and the package exported, but that isn't relevant here).

In this section, we'll look at another way to give modules access to other modules. We'll start by discussing a motivating use case before I introduce the new mechanism and develop some guidelines for how best to use it. Toward the end, you'll see how powerful it is and how it can help with much more than the initial examples.

Check out *ServiceMonitor*'s `feature-implied-readability` branch for the code accompanying this section.

11.1.1 *Exposing a module's dependencies*

When it comes to the interplay between `requires` directives and accessibility, there's a fine detail to observe: The `requires` *directives* create reads edges but the *edges* are a prerequisite for accessibility. Doesn't that beg the question of which other mechanisms can establish readability and thus unlock access to types? This is more than theoretical pondering—approaching the situation from a practical angle, we end up in the same place.

Let's turn back to the *ServiceMonitor* application, particularly the modules *monitor. observer* and *monitor.observer.alpha*. Assume that a new module, let's call it *monitor.peek*, wants to use *monitor.observer.alpha* directly. It has no need for *monitor.observer* or the service architecture you created in the previous chapter. Can *monitor.peek* just require *monitor.observer.alpha* and start using it?

```
ServiceObserver observer = new AlphaServiceObserver("some://service/url");
DiagnosticDataPoint data = observer.gatherDataFromService();
```

It looks like it needs the types `ServiceObserver` and `DiagnosticDataPoint`. Both are in *monitor.observer*, so what happens if *monitor.peek* doesn't require *monitor.observer*? It can't access its types, resulting in compile errors. As you saw when we discussed the encapsulation of transitive dependencies in section 3.3.2, this is a feature of the module system.

Here it's an impediment, though. Without the types from *monitor.observer*, *monitor. observer.alpha* is effectively useless; and every module that wants to use it *has to* read *monitor.observer* as well. (This is shown in figure 11.1.) Does every module using *monitor. observer.alpha* have to require *monitor.observer*, too?

That's not a comfortable solution. If only there was another mechanism to establish readability and thus unlock access to types.

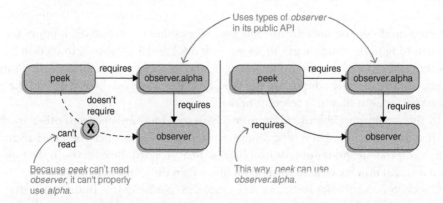

Figure 11.1   The module *peek* uses *observer.alpha*, which uses types from *observer* in its public API. If *peek* doesn't require *observer* (left), it can't read its types, making *observer.alpha* useless. With regular `requires` directives, the only way around that is to have *peek* also require *observer* (right), which becomes cumbersome when more modules are involved.

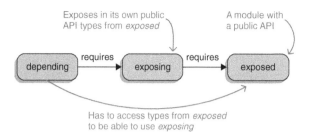

Figure 11.2 Three modules are involved in the problem of exposed dependencies: the innocent one that provides some types (*exposed*; right), the guilty one using those types in its public API (*exposing*; middle), and the impacted one having to accesses the innocent's types (*depending*; left).

What happens in the previous example is common. A module *exposing* depends on some module *exposed*, but uses types from *exposed* in its own public API (as defined in section 3.3). In such cases, *exposing* is said to *expose its dependency* on *exposed* to its clients because they also need to depend on *exposed* in order to use *exposing*.

To make talking about this situation a little less confusing, make sure you understand these definitions in figure 11.2. I'll stick to these terms when describing the involved modules:

- The module exposing its dependency is called the *exposing* module.
- The module that is exposed as a dependency is the *exposed* module.
- The module depending on that mess is called the *depending* module.

Many examples can be found in the JDK. The *java.sql* module, for example, contains a type java.sql.SQLXML (used by java.sql.Connection, among others), which uses types from the *java.xml* module in its public methods. The type java.sql.SQLXML is public and in an exported package, so it's part of the API of *java.sql*. That means in order for any depending module to properly use the exposing *java.sql*, it must read the exposed *java.xml* as well.

11.1.2 *The transitive modifier: Implying readability on a dependency*

Looking at the situation, it's clear that the developers of the *exposing* module are the ones who need to solve this problem. After all, they decide to use the *exposed* module's types in their own API, forcing the modules depending on them to read the exposed modules.

The solution for these situations is to use a requires transitive directive in the *exposing* module's declaration. If *exposing* declares requires transitive exposed, then any module reading *exposing* will implicitly also read *exposed*. The effect is called *implied readability*: reading *exposing* implies reading *exposed*. Figure 11.3 shows this directive.

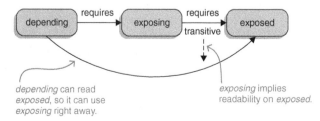

Figure 11.3 When *exposing* uses a requires transitive directive to depend on *exposed*, reading *exposing* implies readability of *exposed*. As a consequence, modules like *depending* (left) can read *exposed* even if they only require *exposing*.

The use of implied readability is obvious when looking at a module declaration or descriptor. With the skills you learned in section 5.3.1, you can look into *java.sql*. The following listing shows that the dependency on *java.xml* is marked with `transitive`.

Listing 11.1   *java.sql* module descriptor: implies readability of *java.xml* and *java.logging*

```
$ java --describe-module java.sql

> java.sql@9.0.4
> exports java.sql
> exports javax.sql
> exports javax.transaction.xa
> requires java.base mandate
> requires java.logging transitive
> requires java.xml transitive
> uses java.sql.Driver
```

These directives indicate that modules reading java.sql can also read java.xml and java.logging.

Likewise, the dependency on *java.logging* is marked `transitive`. The reason is the public interface `java.sql.Driver` and its method `Logger getParentLogger()`. It exposes the type `java.util.logging.Logger` from *java.logging* in the public API of *java.sql*, so *java.sql* implies readability of *java.logging*. Note that although `java --describe-module` puts `transitive` last, the module declaration expects the modifier to come between `requires` and the module name (`requires transitive ${module}`).

Going back to the motivating example of how to make *monitor.observer.alpha* usable without depending modules also having to require *monitor.observer*, the solution is now obvious—use `requires transitive` to declare the dependency of *monitor.observer.alpha* on *monitor.observer*:

```
module monitor.observer.alpha {
    requires transitive monitor.observer;
    exports monitor.observer.alpha;
}
```

When exploring reliable configuration and missing dependencies in section 3.2.2, you discovered that although the run time requires all dependencies (direct and indirect) to be observable, the compiler only mandates that for direct ones. This means you can compile your module against *exposing* without its dependencies being present. Now, how does implied readability fit into this?

 ESSENTIAL INFO   Modules whose readability is implied to the module under compilation go into the "must be observable" bucket. That means every dependency that *exposing* requires transitively, like *exposed* in the earlier examples, must be observable when you compile your module against *exposing*.

That's regardless of whether you use types from *exposed*, which might at first seem overly strict. But remember from section 3.4.1 that modules are resolved and the module graph is built *before* the code is compiled. The module graph is the basis for compilation, not the other way around, and mutating it based on the encountered types would go against the goal of reliable configuration. The module graph must hence always contain transitive dependencies.

Chains of dependencies

You may wonder what happens in a chain of dependencies, where each `requires` directive uses `transitive`. Will readability be implied along longer paths? The answer is yes. It doesn't matter whether an exposing module is read because of an explicit dependency or implied readability—it will imply readability of its dependencies just the same. The following figure illustrates the transitivity of `transitive`.

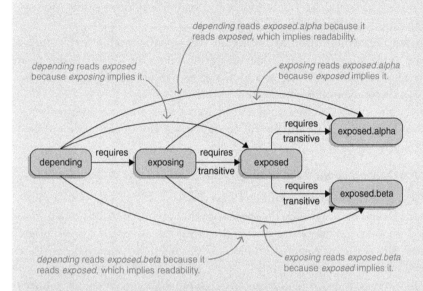

The *depending* module requires *exposing*, which implies readability of *exposed*, which in turn implies readability of *exposed.alpha* and *exposed.beta*. Implied readability is transitive, so *depending* can read all other four modules even though it only depends on one of them.

11.1.3 *When to use implied readability*

As you've seen, implied readability reduces the need for explicit `requires` directives in depending modules. This can be a good thing, but I want to return to something I only mentioned in passing before. Implied readability goes against a feature of the module system: the encapsulation of transitive dependencies discussed in section 3.2.2. With two opposing requirements (strictness versus convenience) and two features to fulfill them (`requires` versus `requires transitive`), it's important to carefully consider the trade-offs.

The situation is similar to visibility modifiers. For convenience's sake, it would be easy to make every class, every field, and every method public. We don't do that, though, because we know that exposing less reduces the contact surface between different parts of the code and makes modification, replacement, and reuse easier. And like making a type or member public, exposing a dependency becomes part of that module's public API, and clients may rely on the fact that readability is implied. This can make evolving the module and its dependencies more difficult, so it shouldn't be undertaken lightly.

ESSENTIAL INFO Following this line of thought, using `transitive` should be the exception and only be done under very specific circumstances. The most prominent is what I've described so far: if a module uses types from a second module in its own public API (as defined in section 3.3), it should imply readability of that second module by using a `requires transitive` directive.

Other use cases are aggregation, decomposition, and merging of modules, all of which we'll discuss in section 11.1.5. Before that, I want to explore a similar use case that may warrant another solution.

So far, the assumption has been that the *exposing* module can't operate without *exposed*. Interestingly enough, that isn't always the case. The *exposing* module could implement utility functions based on the *exposed* module that only code that's already using the *exposed* module would call.

Say a library *uber.lib* offers utility functions based on *com.google.common*. Then only users of Guava had a use for *uber.lib*. In such cases, optional dependencies may be the way to go; see section 11.2.

11.1.4 *When to rely on implied readability*

You've seen how implied readability allows a module to "pass on" readability of exposed dependencies. We discussed considerations that go into deciding when to use that feature. That was from the perspective of the developer writing the *exposing module*.

Now, let's switch perspective and look at this from the point of view of the *depending module*: the one to which readability of the exposed module is passed on. To what extent should it rely on implied readability? At what point should it instead require the *exposed* module?

As you saw when we first explored implied readability, *java.sql* exposes its dependency on *java.logging*. That begs the question, should modules using *java.sql* also require *java.logging*? Technically, such a declaration isn't needed and may seem redundant.

That's also true for the motivating example of *monitor.peek, monitor.observer*, and *monitor.observer.alpha*: in the final solution, *monitor.peek* uses types from both other modules but only requires *monitor.observer.alpha*, which implies readability of *monitor.observer*. Should it also explicitly require *monitor.observer*? And if not, just not in that specific example, or never?

To decide when to rely on a dependency implying readability on a module or when to require that module directly, it makes sense to turn back to one of the core promises of the module system: reliable configuration (see section 3.2.1). Using `requires` directives makes code more reliable by making dependencies explicit, and you can apply that principle here to make a decision by asking a different question.

ESSENTIAL INFO Does the *depending* module depend on the *exposed* module regardless of the *exposing* one? Or, in other words, if the *depending* module is modified to no longer use the *exposing* module, might it still need the *exposed* one?

- If the answer is negative, removing the code that uses the *exposing* module also removes the dependency on the *exposed* module. We could say that the *exposed* module was only used on the *boundary* between the *depending* and the *exposing* modules. In that case, there's no need to explicitly requiring it, and relying on implied readability is fine.
- If, on the other hand, the answer is positive, then the *exposed* module is used on more than just the boundary to the *exposing* module. Accordingly, it should be explicitly depended on with a `requires` directive.

Figure 11.4 illustrates visualizes these two options.

Looking back on the example of *java.sql*, you can answer the question based on how the depending module, let's say it's *monitor.persistence*, uses *java.logging*:

- It may only need to read *java.logging*, so it's able to call `java.sql.Driver.getParentLogger()`, change the logger's log level, and be done with it. In this case, its interaction with *java.logging* is limited to the boundary between *monitor.persistence* and *java.sql*, and you're in the sweet spot for implied readability.
- Alternatively, *monitor.persistence* may use logging throughout its own code. Then, types from *java.logging* appear in many places, independently of `Driver`, and can no longer be considered limited to the boundary. In that case, *monitor.persistence* should explicitly require *java.logging*.

A similar juxtaposition can be made for the example from the *ServiceMonitor* application. Does *monitor.peek*, which requires *monitor.observer.alpha*, only use types from *monitor.observer* to create a `ServiceObserver`? Or does it have a use for the types from the *monitor.observer* module independently of its interaction with *monitor.observer.alpha*?

11.1.5 *Refactoring modules with implied readability*

At first glance, implied readability looks like a small feature that solves a specific use case. Interestingly, though, it isn't limited to that case! On the contrary, it unlocks some useful techniques that help with refactoring modules.

The motivation for using these techniques is often to prevent changes in modules that depend on the one(s) that are being refactored. If you have total control over all

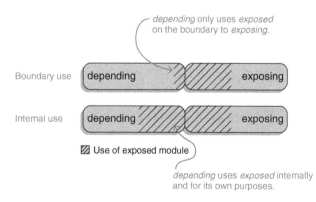

Figure 11.4 Two cases of implied readability, involving *depending*, *exposing*, and *exposed* modules. Where the two boxes touch, the *depending* module uses *exposing*, on which it explicitly depends. Both use the *exposed* module (striped area). But the degree of use can differ: The *depending* module may only use it on the boundary to *exposed* (top), or it may use the types internally to implements its own features (bottom).

clients of a module and compile and deploy them all at once, then you can change their module declarations instead of doing something more complicated. But often you can't—for example, when developing a library—so you need a way to refactor modules without breaking backward compatibility.

REPRESENTING MODULE FAMILIES WITH AGGREGATOR MODULES

Let's say your application has a couple of core modules that almost any other module must depend on. You could, of course, copy-paste the necessary `requires` directives into every module declaration, but that's rather tedious. Instead, you can use implied readability to create a so-called aggregator module.

An *aggregator module* contains no code and implies readability with `requires transitive` on all of its dependencies. It's used to create a coherent set of modules that other modules can easily depend on by just requiring the aggregator module.

The *ServiceMonitor* application is a little small to justify creating an aggregator module; but for the sake of an example, let's decide that *monitor.observer* and *monitor.statistics* are its core API. In that case, you can create *monitor.core* as follows:

```
module monitor.core {
    requires transitive monitor.observer;
    requires transitive monitor.statistics;
}
```

Now, all other modules can depend on *monitor.core* and get readability of *monitor.observer* and *monitor.statistics* for free. Figure 11.5 visualizes this example.

There is, of course, no reason to limit aggregation to core functionality. Every family of modules that cooperate to implement a feature is a candidate to get an aggregator module that represents it.

But wait: don't aggregator modules bring clients into a situation where they internally use APIs of modules they don't explicitly depend on? This can be seen as conflicting with what I said when discussing when to rely on implied readability: that it should be used on the boundary to other modules. But I think the situation is subtly different here.

Aggregator modules have a specific responsibility: to bundle the functionality of related modules into a single unit. Modifying the bundle's content is a pivotal conceptual change. "Regular" implied readability, on the other hand, often manifests between

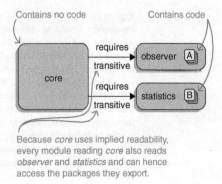

Because *core* uses implied readability, every module reading *core* also reads *observer* and *statistics* and can hence access the packages they export.

Figure 11.5 The aggregator module *core* (left) contains no code and uses `requires transitive` directives to refer to the aggregated modules *observer* and *statistics* (right), which contain the functionality. Thanks to implied readability, clients of the aggregator module can use the APIs of the aggregated modules.

modules that aren't immediately related (as with *java.sql* and *java.logging*), where the implied module is used more incidentally (although it's still API-breaking to change it; see section 15.2.4).

If you're into object-oriented programming terminology, you can compare this to association, aggregation, and composition (the comparison is far from perfect, and the terms don't neatly align, but if you know the terminology, it should give you some intuition):

- Regular `requires` directives create an uncomplicated association between the two involved modules.
- Using `requires transitive` turns this into an aggregation where one module makes the other part of its API.
- Aggregator modules are then similar to composition in the sense that the involved modules' lifecycles are coupled—the aggregator module has no raison d'être of its own. This doesn't quite hit the nail on the head, though, because in a true aggregation, the referenced modules have no purpose of their own—with aggregator modules, on the other hand, they typically do.

Given these categories, I'd say that requiring an aggregation's exposed dependencies is governed by the guideline introduced in section 11.1.4, whereas depending on a composition's exposed dependencies is always okay. To not make matters more complicated than they need to be, I won't use the terms *aggregation* and *composition* in the rest of the book; I'll stick to *implied readability* and *aggregator modules*.

ESSENTIAL INFO　Finally, a word of warning: aggregator modules are a leaky abstraction! In this case, they leak services and qualified exports and opens. The latter are introduced in sections 11.3 and 12.2.2, so I won't go into full detail. Suffice it to say that they work by naming specific modules, so only they can access a package. Although an aggregator module invites developers to use it instead of its composing modules, exporting or opening a package *to* an aggregator module is pointless because it contains no code of its own, and the composing modules will still see a strongly encapsulated package.

Service binding, as explained in section 10.1.2, also tarnishes the illusion of aggregator modules being perfect placeholders. Here, the problem is that if a composing module provides a service, binding will pull it into the module graph but, of course, not the aggregator module (because it doesn't declare to provide that service), and hence not the other composing modules. Think these cases through before creating aggregator modules.

REFACTORING MODULES BY SPLITTING THEM UP

I'm sure you've been in a situation where you realized that what you once thought of as a simple feature has grown into a more complex subsystem. You've improved and extended it again and again, and it's a little tangled; so, to clean up the code base, you refactor it into smaller parts that interact in a better-defined way while keeping its public API stable.

 ESSENTIAL INFO   Taking the *ServiceMonitor* application as an example, its statistics operations may have collected so much code that it makes sense to split it into a few smaller subprojects, such as *Averages*, *Medians*, and *Percentiles*. So far, so good; now, let's consider how this interacts with modules.

Suppose the simple feature had its own module to begin with, and the new solution would use several modules. What happens with code that depends on the original module? If that disappears, the module system will complain about missing dependencies.

With what we just discussed, why not keep the original module and turn it into an aggregator? This is possible as long as *all* of the original module's exported packages are now exported by the new modules. (Otherwise, depending on the new aggregator module doesn't grant accessibility to all types of its former API.)

 ESSENTIAL INFO   To keep dependencies on *monitor.statistics* intact, it can be turned into an aggregator module. Move all code into the new modules, and edit the module declaration of *monitor.statistics* to require the new ones with the `transitive` keyword:

```
module monitor.statistics {
    requires transitive monitor.statistics.averages;
    requires transitive monitor.statistics.medians;
    requires transitive monitor.statistics.percentiles;
}
```

See figure 11.6 to picture this decomposition. This is a good opportunity to reiterate the transitive nature of implied readability: all modules depending on the hypothetical *monitor.core* module created in the previous example will read the new *statistics* modules as well, because *monitor.core* requires `transitive` *monitor.statistics*, and *monitor.statistics* requires `transitive` the new modules.

If you want clients to replace their dependency on the old module with more specific `requires` directives on the new ones, consider deprecating the aggregator:

```
@Deprecated
module my.shiny.aggregator {
    // ...
}
```

 ESSENTIAL INFO   The earlier warning about aggregator modules being a leaky abstraction fully applies. If users use a qualified export or open on the aggregator module, the new modules won't benefit from it.

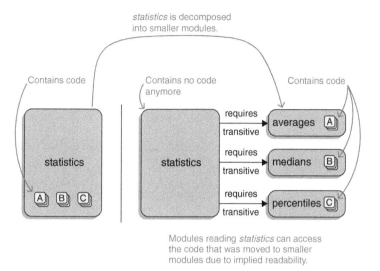

Figure 11.6 Before refactoring, the **statistics** module contains a lot of functionality (left). It's then decomposed into three smaller modules that contain all the code (right). To not mandate changes in modules depending on **statistics**, it isn't removed, but is instead turned into an aggregator module that implies readability of the modules it was split into.

11.1.6 *Refactoring modules by merging them*

Although probably less often than splitting up a module that has outgrown its roots, you may occasionally want to merge several modules into one. As before, removing the now-technically useless modules may break clients; and as before, you can use implied readability to fix that problem: keep the empty old modules around, and make sure the old module declaration has as its only line a `requires transitive` on the new module.

 ESSENTIAL INFO Working on the *ServiceMonitor* application, you may realize that having a module per observer implementation is overkill, and you'd like to merge all the modules into *monitor.observer*. Moving the code from *monitor. observer.alpha* and *monitor.observer.beta* into *monitor.observer* is simple. To keep the parts of the application that directly require the implementation modules working without changes, you make them imply readability on the larger module:

```
@Deprecated
module monitor.observer.alpha {
    requires transitive monitor.observer;
}

@Deprecated
module monitor.observer.beta {
    requires transitive monitor.observer;
}
```

You can see these modules in figure 11.7. You also deprecate them to push users toward updating their dependencies.

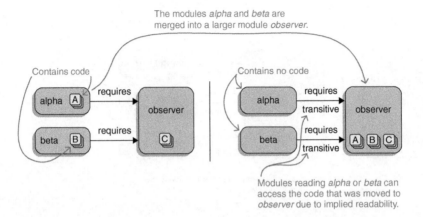

Figure 11.7   **Before refactoring, the observation code is shared between the three modules *alpha*, *beta*, and *observer* (left). Afterward, all functionality is in *observer*, and the hollowed modules *alpha* and *beta* imply readability on it in order to not require their clients to change (right).**

 ESSENTIAL INFO   Carefully consider this approach, though. It makes the smaller modules' clients suddenly depend on something much larger than they originally bargained for. On top of that, keep the earlier warning in mind that aggregator modules are a leaky abstraction.

11.2   *Optional dependencies*

In section 3.2, you saw that the module system uses `requires` directives to implement reliable configuration by making sure dependencies are present at compile and run time. But as we discussed at the end of section 2.3, after looking at the *ServiceMonitor* application for the first time, this approach can be too inflexible.

There are cases where code ends up using types that don't have to be present at run time—they *may* be, but they don't *have* to be. As it stands, the module system either requires them to be present at launch time (when you use a `requires` directive) or doesn't allow access at all (when you don't use it).

In this section, I'll show you a couple of examples in which this strictness leads to problems. Then I'll introduce the module system's solution: optional dependencies. Coding against them isn't trivial, though, so we'll take a close look at that as well. By the end of this section, you'll be able to code against modules that aren't required to be present at run time. The branch `feature-optional-dependencies` in *ServiceMonitor*'s repository demonstrates how to use optional dependencies.

11.2.1 *The conundrum of reliable configuration*

Assume that there's an advanced statistics library containing a *stats.fancy* module that can't be present on the module path for each deployment of the *ServiceMonitor* application. (The reason is irrelevant, but let's say it's a licensing issue.)

You want to write code in *monitor.statistics* that uses types from the *fancy* module, but for that to work, you need to depend on it with a `requires` directive. But if you do that, the module system wouldn't let the application launch if *stats.fancy* isn't present. Figure 11.8 shows this deadlock. (If this case seems familiar, it's because we looked at it before from another angle. I'll tell you where when we come full circle in a few minutes.)

Another example would be a utility library—let's call it `uber.lib`—that integrates with a handful of other libraries. Its API offers functionality that builds on them and thus exposes their types. So far, that may make it look like an open-and-shut case for implied readability, as discussed in section 11.1, but things can be seen in another light.

Let's play this through with the example of `com.google.common`, which `uber.lib` integrates with. The maintainers of `uber.lib` may assume that nobody who isn't already using Guava is ever going to call the Guava portion of their library. This makes sense in certain cases. Why would you call a method in `uber.lib` that creates a nice report for a `com.google.common.graph.Graph` instance if you don't have such a graph?

For `uber.lib`, that means it can function perfectly without `com.google.common`. If Guava makes it into the module graph, clients may call into that portion of the `uber.lib` API. If it doesn't, they won't, and the library will be fine as well. You can say that `uber.lib` never needs the dependency for its own sake.

With the features we've explored so far, such an optional relationship can't be implemented. According to the readability and accessibility rules from chapter 3, `uber.lib` has to require `com.google.common` to compile against its types and thus force all clients to always have Guava on the module path when launching their application.

If `uber.lib` integrates with a handful of libraries, it would make clients depend on all of them even though they may never use more than one. That's not a nice move from `uber.lib`, so its maintainers will be looking for a way to mark their dependencies as being optional at run time. As the next section shows, the module system has them covered.

> **NOTE** Build tools also know such optional dependencies. In Maven, you set a dependency's `<optional>` tag to `true`; in Gradle, you list them under `compileOnly`.

Figure 11.8 The conundrum of reliable configuration: either the module system doesn't grant *statistics* access to *stats.fancy* because *statistics* doesn't require the access (left), or *statistics* does require access, which means *stats.fancy* must always be present for the application to launch (right).

11.2.2 *The static modifier: Marking dependencies as optional*

When a module needs to be compiled against types from another module but doesn't want to depend on it at run time, you can use *a* requires static directive to establish this *optional dependency*. For two modules *depending* and *optional,* where *depending*'s declaration contains the line requires static optional, the module system behaves differently at compile and launch time:

- At compile time, *optional* must be present or there will be an error. During compilation, *optional* is readable by *depending.*
- At launch time, *optional* may be absent, and that will cause neither an error nor a warning. If it's present, it's readable by *depending.*

Table 11.1 compares this behavior with a regular requires directive. Note that although the module system doesn't issue an error, the runtime still may. Optional dependencies make run-time errors like NoClassDefFoundError much more likely because classes that a module was compiled against can be missing. In section 11.2.4, you'll see code that prepares for that eventuality.

Table 11.1   A comparison of how requires **and** requires static **behave at compile and launch time for present and missing dependencies. The only difference lies in how they treat missing dependencies at launch time (far-right column).**

	Dependency present		Dependency missing	
	Compile time	Launch time	Compile time	Launch time
requires	Reads	Reads	Error	Error
requires static	Reads	Reads	Error	Ignores

As an example, let's create an optional dependency from *monitor.statistics* to *stats.fancy.* For that, you use a requires static directive:

```
module monitor.statistics {
    requires monitor.observer;
    requires static stats.fancy;
    exports monitor.statistics;
}
```

If *stats.fancy* is missing during compilation, you get an error when the module declaration is compiled:

```
> monitor.statistics/src/main/java/module-info.java:3:
>     error: module not found: stats.fancy
>         requires static stats.fancy;
>                         ^
>
> 1 error
```

At launch time, on the other hand, the module system doesn't care whether *stats.fancy* is present.

The module descriptor for *uber.lib* declares all dependencies as optional:

```
module uber.lib {
    requires static com.google.common;
    requires static org.apache.commons.lang;
    requires static org.apache.commons.io;
    requires static io.vavr;
    requires static com.aol.cyclops;
}
```

Now that you know how to declare optional dependencies, two questions remain to be answered:

- Under what circumstances will the dependency be present?
- How can you code against an optional dependency?

We'll answer both questions next, and when we're finished, you're all set to use this handy feature.

11.2.3 *Module resolution of optional dependencies*

As discussed in section 3.4.1, module resolution is the process that, given an initial module and a universe of observable modules, builds a module graph by resolving `requires` directives. When a module is being resolved, all modules it requires must be observable. If they are, they're added to the module graph; otherwise, an error occurs. A little later I wrote this about the graph:

> *It's important to note that modules that did not make it into the module graph during resolution aren't available later during compilation or execution, either.*

 ESSENTIAL INFO At compile time, module resolution handles optional dependencies like regular dependencies. At launch time, on the other hand, `requires static` directives are mostly ignored. When the module system encounters one, it doesn't try to fulfill it, meaning it doesn't even check whether the named module is observable.

As a consequence, even if a module is present on the module path (or in the JDK, for that matter), it won't be added to the module graph because of an optional dependency. It will only make it into the graph if it's also a regular dependency of some other module that's being resolved or because it was added explicitly with the command-line option `--add-modules`, as described in section 3.4.3. Figure 11.9 illustrates both behaviors, using the option to ensure the presence of the optional dependency.

This is where we come full circle. The first time I mentioned a *fancy* statistics library was in the section when I explained why it may sometimes be necessary to explicitly add a module to the module graph. I didn't talk about optional dependencies in particular (and this isn't the only use case for that option), but the general idea was the same as now: the *fancy* statistics module isn't strictly required and hence isn't automatically added to the module graph. If you want to have it in there, you must use the `--add-modules` option—either naming the specific module or using `ALL-MODULE-PATH`.

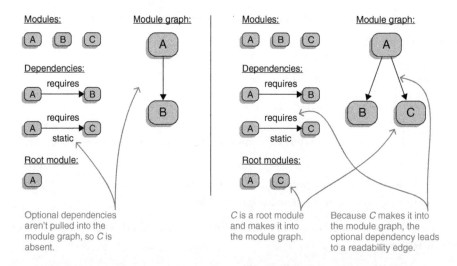

Figure 11.9   Both sides show similar situations. Both cases involve three modules A, B, and C, where A strictly depends on B and optionally depends on C. At left, A is the initial module, leading to a module graph without C because optional dependencies aren't resolved. At right, C was forced into the graph with the use of the command-line option `--add-modules`, making it the second root module. It's hence resolved and readable by A.

Maybe you tripped over the phrase that during module resolution, optional dependencies "are mostly ignored." Why *mostly*? Well, if an optional dependency makes it into a graph, the module systems adds a reads edge. So if the *fancy* statistics module is in the graph (maybe due to a regular `requires`, maybe due to an `--add-modules`), any module optionally depending on it can read it. This ensures that its types can be accessed straight away.

11.2.4   *Coding against optional dependencies*

Optional dependencies require a little more thought when you're writing code against them, because this is what happens when *monitor.statistics* uses types in *stats.fancy* but the module isn't present at run time:

```
Exception in thread "main" java.lang.NoClassDefFoundError:
    stats/fancy/FancyStats
        at monitor.statistics/monitor.statistics.Statistician
            .<init>(Statistician.java:15)
        at monitor/monitor.Main.createMonitor(Main.java:42)
        at monitor/monitor.Main.main(Main.java:22)
Caused by: java.lang.ClassNotFoundException: stats.fancy.FancyStats
        ... many more
```

Oops. You usually don't want your code to do that.

Generally speaking, when the code that's currently being executed references a type, the JVM checks whether it's already loaded. If not, it tells the class loader to do that; and if that fails, the result is a `NoClassDefFoundError`, which usually crashes the application or at least fails out of the chunk of logic that was being executed.

This is something JAR hell was famous for (see section 1.3.1). The module system wants to overcome that problem by checking declared dependencies when launching an application. But with `requires static`, you opt out of that check, which means you can end up with a `NoClassDefFoundError` after all. What can you do against that?

Before looking into solutions, you need to see whether you really have a problem. In the case of `uber.lib`, you expect to use types from an optional dependency only if the code calling into the library already uses them, meaning class loading already succeeded. In other words, when `uber.lib` is called, all required dependencies must be present or the call wouldn't have been possible. So you don't have a problem after all, and you don't need to do anything. Figure 11.10 illustrates this case.

The general case is different, though, as shown in figure 11.11. It may well be the module with the optional dependency that first tries to load classes from a dependency that might not be present so the risk of a `NoClassDefFoundError` is very real.

 ESSENTIAL INFO One solution for this is to make sure all possible calls into the module with the optional dependency have to go through a checkpoint before accessing the dependency. As shown in figure 11.12, that checkpoint has to evaluate whether the dependency is present and send all code that arrives at it down a different execution path if it isn't.

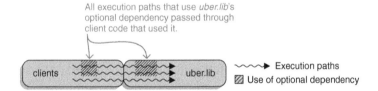

Figure 11.10 By assumption, calling `uber.lib` only makes sense when clients already use types from the optional dependency. As a consequence, all execution paths (squiggly lines) that rely on the optional dependency being available for `uber.lib` (top two) have already passed through client code that also relied on that dependency (striped areas). If that didn't fail, `uber.lib` won't fail, either.

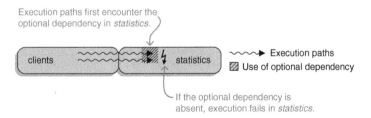

Figure 11.11 In the general case, it isn't guaranteed that the client code calling a module like *statistics* has already established the optional dependency. In that case, execution paths (squiggly lines) may first encounter the dependency in the *statistics* module (striped area) and will fail if the optional dependency is absent.

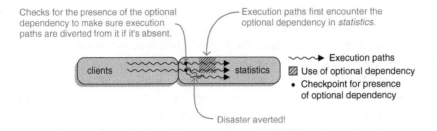

Figure 11.12   To ensure that a module like *statistics*, which has an optional dependency, is stable regardless of that dependency's presence, checkpoints are required. Based on whether the dependency is present, the code branches execution paths (squiggly lines) either into code that uses that dependency (striped area) or into other code that doesn't.

The module system offers an API to check whether a module is present. I won't go into details of how it works yet, because you lack some of the prerequisites that you need to understand the code. So you'll have to wait for (or skip ahead to) section 12.4.2 to see for yourself that a utility method like the following can be implemented:

```
public static boolean isModulePresent(String moduleName) {
    // ...
}
```

Calling this method with an argument like `"stats.fancy"` will return whether that module is present. If called with the name of a regular dependency (simple `requires` directive), the result will always be `true` because otherwise the module system wouldn't have let the application launch.

If called with the name of an optional dependency (`requires static` directive), the result will be either `true` or `false`. If an optional dependency is present, the module system established readability, so it's safe to go down an execution path that uses types from the module. If an optional dependency is absent, choosing such a path will lead to a `NoClassDefFoundError`, so a different one has to be found.

11.3   Qualified exports: Limiting accessibility to specific modules

Whereas the previous two sections show how to refine dependencies, this one introduces a mechanism that allows a finer API design. As discussed in section 3.3, a module's public API is defined by exporting packages with `exports` directives, in which case every module reading the exporting one can access all public types in those packages at compile and at run time. This lies at the heart of strong encapsulation, which section 3.3.1 explains in depth.

With what we've discussed so far, you have to choose between strongly encapsulating a package or making it accessible to everybody all the time. To handle use cases that don't easily fit into that dichotomy, the module system offers two less-candid ways to export a package: qualified exports, which we'll look at now; and open packages, which section 12.2 introduces, because they're related to reflection. As before, I'll start with examples before introducing the mechanism. By the end of this section, you'll be able to more precisely expose APIs than is possible with regular `exports` directives. Look at the branch `feature-qualified-exports` in *ServiceMonitor*'s repository to see how qualified exports pan out.

11.3.1 Exposing internal APIs

The best examples showing that `exports` directives can be too general come from the JDK. As you saw in section 7.1, only one platform module exports a `sun.*` package and few export `com.sun.*` packages. But does that mean all other packages are only used within the module they're declared in?

Far from it! Many packages are shared among modules. Here are some examples:

- Internals of the base module *java.base* are used all over the place. For example, *java.sql* (providing the Java Database Connectivity API [JDBC]) uses `jdk.internal .misc`, `jdk.internal.reflect`, and `sun.reflect.misc`. Security-relevant packages like `sun.security.provider` and `sun.security.action` are used by *java.rmi* (Remote Method Invocation API [RMI]) or *java.desktop* (AWT and Swing user interface toolkits, plus accessibility, multimedia, and JavaBeans APIs).

- The *java.xml* module defines the Java API for XML Processing (JAXP), which includes the Streaming API for XML (StAX), the Simple API for XML (SAX), and the W3C Document Object Model (DOM) API. Six of its internal packages (mostly prefixed with `com.sun.org.apache.xml` and `com.sun.org.apache. xpath`) are used by *java.xml.crypto* (API for XML cryptography).

- Many JavaFX modules access internal packages of *javafx.graphics* (mostly `com .sun.javafx.*`), which in turn uses `com.sun.javafx.embed.swing` from *javafx. swing* (integrating JavaFX and Swing), which in turn uses seven internal packages from *java.desktop* (like `sun.awt` and `sun.swing`), which ...

I could go on, but I'm sure you get my point. This poses a question, though: how does the JDK share these packages among its modules without exporting them to everybody else?

Although the JDK surely has the strongest use case for a more targeted export mechanism, it isn't the only one. This situation occurs every time a set of modules wants to share functionality between them without exposing it. This can be the case for a library, a framework, or even a subset of modules from a larger application.

This is symmetrical to the problem of hiding utility classes before the module system was introduced. As soon as a utility class has to be available across packages, it has to be public; but before Java 9, that meant all code running in the same JVM could access it. Now you're up against the case that you want to hide a utility package, but as soon as it has to be available across modules, it must be exported and can thus be accessed by all modules running in the same JVM—at least with the mechanisms you've used so far. Figure 11.13 illustrates this symmetry.

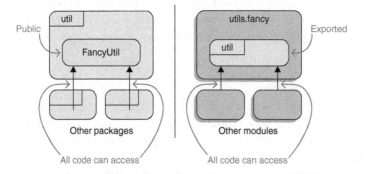

Figure 11.13   (Left) The situation before Java 9, where as soon as a type is public (like `FancyUtil` in package `util`), it can be accessed by all other code. (Right) A similar situation with modules, but on a higher level, where as soon as a package is exported (like `util` in `utils.fancy`), it's accessible to all other modules.

11.3.2 *Exporting packages to modules*

The exports directive can be qualified by following it up with to ${modules}, where ${modules} is a comma-separated list of module names (no placeholders are allowed). To the modules named in an exports to directive, the package will be exactly as accessible as with a regular exports directive. To all other modules, the package will be as strongly encapsulated as if there were no exports at all. This situation is shown in figure 11.14.

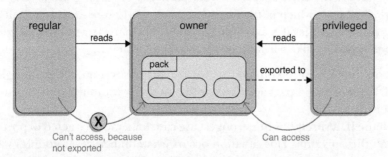

Figure 11.14   The module owner uses a qualified export to make the package `pack` accessible only to the *privileged* module. To *privileged*, it's just as accessible as if a regular export were used; but other modules, like *regular*, can't access it.

As a hypothetical example, let's say all observer implementations in the *Service-Monitor* application need to share some utility code. The first question is where to put those types. All observers already depend on *monitor.observer* because it contains the

`ServiceObserver` interface they implement, so why not put it there? Okay, they end up in the package `monitor.observer.utils`.

Now comes the interesting part. Here's the module declaration of *monitor.observer* that exports the new package only to the implementation modules:

```
module monitor.observer {
    exports monitor.observer;
    exports monitor.observer.utils
        to monitor.observer.alpha, monitor.observer.beta;
}
```

Whereas `monitor.observer` is exported to everybody, `monitor.observer.utils` will be accessible only by the modules *monitor.observer.alpha* and *monitor.observer.beta*.

This example demonstrates two interesting details:

- The modules to which a package is exported can depend on the exporting module, creating a cycle. Thinking about it, unless implied readability is used, this *must* be the case: how else would the module to which a package is exported read the exporting one?
- Whenever a new implementation wants to use the utilities, the API module needs to be changed, so it gives access to this new module. Although letting the exporting module control what can access the packages is kind of the whole point of qualified exports, it can still be cumbersome.

As a real-world example, I'd like to show you the qualified exports that *java.base* declares—but there are 65 of them, so that would be a little overwhelming. Instead, let's look at the module descriptor of *java.xml* with `java --describe-module java.xml` (as described in section 5.3.1):

```
> module java.xml@9.0.4
# everything but qualified exports are truncated
> qualified exports com.sun.org.apache.xml.internal.utils
>     to java.xml.crypto
> qualified exports com.sun.org.apache.xpath.internal.compiler
>     to java.xml.crypto
> qualified exports com.sun.xml.internal.stream.writers
>     to java.xml.ws
> qualified exports com.sun.org.apache.xpath.internal
>     to java.xml.crypto
> qualified exports com.sun.org.apache.xpath.internal.res
>     to java.xml.crypto
> qualified exports com.sun.org.apache.xml.internal.dtm
>     to java.xml.crypto
> qualified exports com.sun.org.apache.xpath.internal.functions
>     to java.xml.crypto
> qualified exports com.sun.org.apache.xpath.internal.objects
>     to java.xml.crypto
```

This shows that *java.xml* lets *java.xml.crypto* and *java.xml.ws* use some of its internal APIs.

Now that you know about qualified exports, I can clear up a small mystery that we left behind in section 5.3.6 when we analyzed the module system's logs. There you saw messages like these:

```
> Adding read from module java.xml to module java.base
> package com/sun/org/apache/xpath/internal/functions in module java.xml
>     is exported to module java.xml.crypto
> package javax/xml/datatype in module java.xml
>     is exported to all unnamed modules
```

I didn't explain why the log talks about exporting *to* a module, but with what we just discussed, that should be clear now. As you saw in the recent example, *java.xml* exports com.sun.org.apache.xpath.internal.functions to *java.xml.crypto*, which is exactly what the second message says. The third message exports javax.xml.datatype to "all unnamed modules," which looks a little weird but is the module system's way of saying that the package is exported without further qualification and hence is accessible to every module reading *java.xml,* including the unnamed module.

 ESSENTIAL INFO   Finally, two small notes on compilation:

- If a module that declares a qualified export is compiled and the target module isn't present in the universe of observable modules, the compiler will issue a warning. It's not an error because the target module is mentioned but not required.
- It isn't allowed to use a package in an exports *and* in an exports to directive. If both directives were present, the latter would be effectively useless, so this situation is interpreted as an implementation error and thus results in a compile error.

11.3.3 *When to use qualified exports*

A qualified export allows modules to share a package between them without making it available to all other modules in the same JVM. This makes qualified exports useful for libraries and frameworks that consist of several modules and want to share code without clients being able to use it. They will also come in handy for large applications that want to restrict dependencies on specific APIs.

Qualified exports can be seen as lifting strong encapsulation from guarding types in artifacts to guarding packages in sets of modules. This is illustrated by figure 11.15.

Say you're designing a module. When should you favor qualified over unqualified exports? To answer that, we have to focus on the core benefit of qualifying exports: controlling who uses an API. Generally speaking, this becomes more important the further the package in question is from its clients.

Suppose you have a small to medium-sized application made out of a handful of modules (not counting dependencies) that's maintained by a small team and compiled and deployed all at once. In that case, it's comparatively easy to control which module uses which API; and if something goes wrong, it's easy to fix it because everything is under your control. In this scenario, the benefits of qualified exports have little impact.

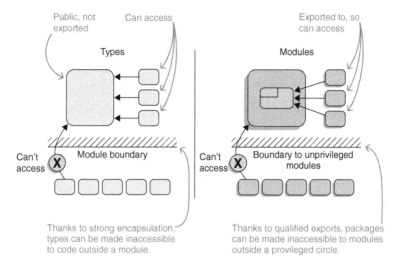

Figure 11.15 (Left) How a public type in a non-exported package can be accessed by other types in the same module but not by types from other modules. (Right) A similar situation, but on a higher level, where qualified exports are used to make a package in one module available to a defined set of modules while keeping it inaccessible to unprivileged ones.

At the other end of the spectrum is the JDK, which is used by literally every Java project in the world and has an extreme focus on backward compatibility. Having code "out there" depend on an internal API can be problematic and is hard to fix, so the need to control who accesses what is great.

The most obvious line separating these two extremes is whether you can freely change the package's clients. If you can, because you're developing the module and all its client modules, regular exports are a good way to go. If you can't, because you maintain a library or framework, only the API that you want clients to use and that you're willing to maintain should be exported without qualification. Everything short of that, particularly internal utilities, should only be exported to your modules.

The line gets blurred in larger projects. If a big code base is maintained over years by a large team, you may *technically* be able to change all clients when doing so becomes necessary due to an API change, but it can be painful. In such cases, using qualified exports not only prevents accidental dependencies on internal packages, but also documents which clients an API was designed for.

11.3.4 Exporting packages on the command line

What if the use of internal APIs wasn't foreseen (or, more likely, wasn't intended) at the time of writing? What if code absolutely *has to* access types the containing module doesn't export, qualified or not? If the module system were adamant about these rules, many applications wouldn't compile or launch on Java 9+; but if it were an easy way to circumvent strong encapsulation, it would hardly be "strong," thus losing its benefits. Middle ground was found by defining command-line options that can be used as an escape hatch but are too cumbersome to become a ubiquitous fix.

In addition to the `exports to` directive, there's a command-line option with the exact same effect that can be applied to the compiler and run-time commands: with `--add-exports   ${module}/${package}=${accessing-modules}`, the module system exports `${package}` of *$module* to all modules named in the comma-separated list `${accessing-modules}>`. If `ALL-UNNAMED` is among them, code from the unnamed module can also read that package.

Normal accessibility rules as presented in section 3.3 apply—for a module to access a type this due to an `--add-exports` option, the following conditions must be fulfilled:

- The type has to be public.
- The type has to be in `${package}`.
- The module addressed in `${accessing-modules}` must read *${module}*.

For `--add-exports` examples, flip back to sections 7.1.3 and 7.1.4, where you used it to gain access to internal APIs of platform modules at compile and run time. Like other command-line options, requiring `--add-exports` to be present for more than experiments is a maintainability problem; see section 9.1 for details.

Summary

- Implied readability:
  - With a `requires transitive` directive, a module makes its client read the thus-required module even though the module doesn't explicitly depend on it. This allows the module to use types from dependencies in its API without putting the burden to manually require those dependencies on the client modules. As a consequence, the module becomes instantly usable.
  - A module should only rely on a transitive dependency being implicitly readable if it only uses it on the boundary to the respective direct dependency. As soon as the module starts using the transitive dependency to implement its own functionality, it should make it a direct dependency. This ensures that the module declaration reflects the true set of dependencies and makes the module more robust for refactorings that may remove the transitive dependency.
  - Implied readability can be used when moving code between modules by having the modules that used to contain the code imply readability on the ones that do now. This lets clients access the code they depend on without requiring them to change their module descriptors, because they still end up reading the module that contains the code. Keeping compatibility like this is particularly interesting for libraries and frameworks.
- Optional dependencies:
  - With a `requires static` directive, a module marks a dependency that the module system will ensure is present at compile time but can be absent at run time. This allows coding against modules without forcing clients to always have those modules in their application.

– At launch time, modules required *only* by `requires static` directives aren't added to the module graph even if they're observable. Instead, you have to add them manually with `--add-modules`.

– Coding against optional dependencies should involve making sure no execution path can fail due to the dependency missing, because this would severely undermine the module's usability.

- Qualified exports:

  – With an `exports to` directive, a module makes a package accessible only to the named modules. This is a third and more targeted option between encapsulating a package and making it accessible for everybody.

  – Exporting to specific modules allows sharing code within a set of privileged modules without making it a public API. This reduces the API surface of a library or framework, thus improving maintainability.

  – With the `--add-exports` command-line option, you can export packages at compile and run time that the module's developers intended as internal APIs. On the one hand, this keeps code running that depends on those internals; on the other hand, it introduces its own maintainability problems.

Reflection in a modular world

12

This chapter covers

- Opening packages and modules to reflection
- Combining modules and reflection
- Alternatives to the reflection API
- Analyzing and modifying module properties

If you're working on a Java application, chances are good that you rely on Spring, Hibernate, JAXP, GSON, or the like. What are "the like"? Frameworks that use Java's reflection API to inspect your code, search for annotations, instantiate objects, or call methods. Thanks to reflection, they can do all that without having to compile against your code.

Moreover, the reflection API allows frameworks to access nonpublic classes and nonpublic members. It has superpowers beyond what's possible with compiled code, which bounces off of package boundaries if classes or members aren't public. The thing is that with modules, reflection no longer works out of the box.

Quite the opposite: reflection lost its superpowers and is bound to the exact same accessibility rules as compiled code. It can only access public members of public classes in exported packages. These frameworks, on the other hand, use reflection over fields and methods that often aren't public and on classes that you may not want to export because they aren't part of a module's API. What do you do then? That's what this chapter is all about!

To get the most out of this chapter, you should

- Have a basic understanding of how reflection works (otherwise, appendix B will bring you up to speed).
- Know that every time you put an annotation somewhere, you're marking that class for a framework to reflect over it (see listing 12.1 for a few examples).
- Understand the accessibility rules (as presented in section 3.3).

Listing 12.1 Code snippets for reflection-based standards and frameworks

```
// JPA
@Entity
@Table(name = "user")
public class Book {

    @Id
    @GeneratedValue(strategy = GenerationType.SEQUENCE)
    @Column(name = "id", updatable = false, nullable = false)
    private Long id;

    @Column(name = "title", nullable = false)
    private String title;

    // [...]

}

// JAXB
@XmlRootElement(name = "book")
@XmlAccessorType(XmlAccessType.FIELD)
public class Book {

    @XmlElement
    private String title;

    @XmlElement
    private String author;

    // [...]

}

// SPRING
@RestController
public class BookController {

    @RequestMapping(value = "/book/{id}", method = RequestMethod.GET)
    @ResponseBody
    public Book getBook(@PathVariable("id") long id) {
        // [...]
    }
```

```
    // [...]
```

}

With that under your belt, you'll learn why exports directives won't take you far if you want to allow reflective access to your modules (section 12.1) and what you can do instead (section 12.2). (Note that this only applies to explicit modules—if your code runs from the class path, it isn't encapsulated, so you don't have to worry about any of this.)

But this chapter is about more than "just" preparing modules for reflection: it also covers the other side and discusses how to update reflecting code as well as alternatives and additions to the reflection API (section 12.3). It closes with how you can use layers to dynamically load modules at run time (section 12.4). (These two sections are written for developers who already had those use cases before Java 9, so they require more familiarity with reflection and class loaders than the rest of this chapter.)

By the time you're done, you'll know all about preparing your project for reflection in a modular world, no matter whether it's the one being reflected or over or doing the reflection. You'll also be able to use reflection to dynamically load code at run time, for example to implement a plugin-based application.

12.1   *Why exports directives aren't a good fit for reflection*

Before we get into how to best prepare your code for reflection, it makes sense to discuss why the mechanism discussed so far for exposing classes, the exports directive (see section 3.3), isn't a good fit. There are three reasons:

- It's highly questionable whether classes designed to be used with such frameworks should be part of a module's public API.
- Exporting those classes to a selected module can couple the module to an implementation instead of a standard.
- Exports don't support deep reflection over nonprivate fields and methods.

We'll look at each of these in turn after we discuss how things worked before the module system.

12.1.1   *Breaking into non-modular code*

Let's say you've successfully migrated your application to Java 9+, as described in chapters 6 and 7. You didn't modularize it yet, though, so you're still running it from the class path. In that case, reflection over your code continues to work as in Java 8.

Reflection-based frameworks will routinely create and modify instances of classes by accessing nonpublic types and members. Although it isn't possible to compile code against package-visible or private elements, reflection allows you to use them after making them accessible. The following listing shows a hypothetical persistence framework that uses reflection to create an entity and assign an ID to a private field.

Listing 12.2 Using reflection

```
Class<?> type = ...
Constructor<?> constructor = entityType.getConstructor();
constructor.setAccessible(true);
Object entity = constructor.newInstance();
Field id = entity.getDeclaredField("id");
id.setAccessible(true);
id.set(entity, 42);
```

Whatever the framework needs to do to get that class

Makes the possibly private constructor and field accessible for the following calls

Now imagine the application gets modularized, and suddenly there's a module boundary between your code and those frameworks. What options does the module system, and particularly the `exports` directives, leave you with for making your internal types accessible?

12.1.2 Forcing the publication of internal types

 ESSENTIAL INFO According to the accessibility rules discussed in section 3.3, types need to be public and in an exported package to be accessible. That also holds for reflection; so, without using an `exports` directive, you'll get an exception like the following:

```
> Exception in thread "main" java.lang.IllegalAccessException:
>    class p.X (in module A) cannot access class q.Y (in module B)
>    because module B does not export q to module A
>        at java.base/....Reflection.newIllegalAccessException
>        at java.base/....AccessibleObject.checkAccess
>        at java.base/....Constructor.newInstance
```

That seems to indicate that you have to make the classes that Spring, Hibernate, and so on need to access public, and export the packages containing them. That adds them to a module's public API, though, and because we're so far considering these types to be internal, that's a serious decision to make.

If you're writing a small service with a few thousand lines of code split into a handful of modules, that may not look like a problem. After all, there isn't much chance for large-scale confusion about your modules' APIs and relationships. But it's also not the scenario where you need modules to shine.

On the other hand, if you're working on a larger code base with numbers of lines of code in the six or seven digits, split into dozens or hundreds of modules that are being worked on by a dozen or more developers, things look very different. In that scenario, exporting a package gives other developers a strong signal that it's okay to use those classes outside of the module, and that they were specifically designed to be used across module boundaries—after all, that's what exports are for.

But because the starting point for this exploration was that you preferred, for whatever reason, to *not* make these classes public, you apparently valued their encapsulation. It would be pretty ironic if the module system then forced you to mark something as supported that you didn't even want to be accessible, thus *weakening* encapsulation.

12.1.3 *Qualified exports create coupling to specific modules*

At this point, think back to section 11.3 and consider using a qualified export to make sure only the one module can access these internals. First, kudos for thinking on your feet—this can indeed fix the problem I just described.

It *can* introduce a new one, though. Think about JPA and its various implementations, like Hibernate and EclipseLink. Depending on your style, you may have worked hard to prevent direct dependencies on your chosen implementation, so you won't look forward to hard-coding one into a module declaration with an `exports ... to concrete.jpa.implementation`. If you rely on qualified exports, there's no way around that, though.

12.1.4 *No support for deep reflection*

Having to make types that you'd rather treat as implementation details accessible to other code is bad. But it gets worse.

Say you did settle on an `exports` directive (qualified or not) to let your framework of choice access your classes. Although it's often possible to use reflection-based frameworks with public members only, this is neither always the case nor always the best approach. On the contrary, it's common to rely on deep reflection over private fields or nonpublic methods to not expose framework-related details to the rest of the code base. (Listing 12.1 shows a number of examples and listing 12.2 shows how `setAccessible` is used to achieve access to internals.)

 ESSENTIAL INFO   Fortunately in general—but unfortunately in this scenario—making the type public and exporting its package doesn't grant access to non-public members. If the framework tries to use them by calling `setAccessible`, you'll get an error like this one:

```
> Exception in thread "main" java.lang.reflect.InaccessibleObjectException:
>   Unable to make field q.Y.field accessible:
>   module B does not "opens q" to module A
>       at java.base/java.lang.reflect.AccessibleObject.
    checkCanSetAccessible
>       at java.base/java.lang.reflect.AccessibleObject.
    checkCanSetAccessible
>       at java.base/java.lang.reflect.Field.checkCanSetAccessible
>       at java.base/java.lang.reflect.Field.setAccessible
```

If you really wanted to go this route, you'd have to make all reflectively accessed members public, which makes the earlier "this weakens encapsulation" conclusion much worse.

To summarize, these are the drawbacks of using `exports` directives for code that's primarily supposed to be used reflectively:

- Only allows access to public members, which often requires making implementation details public.
- Allows other modules to compile code against those exposed classes and members.

- Qualified exports may couple you to an implementation instead of a specification.
- Marks the package as being part of a module's public API.

It's up to you which of these four things you find the worst. For me, it's the last.

12.2 Open packages and modules: Designed for the reflection use case

Now that we've established how thoroughly unsuitable `exports` are for making code accessible for reflection-based libraries, what alternative does the module system offer?

The answer is the `opens` directive, and it's the first thing we're going to look at (section 12.2.1) before introducing its qualified variant (akin to `exports … to`; section 12.2.2). To make sure you pick the right tool for the job, we'll also thoroughly compare the effects of exporting and opening a module (section 12.2.3). Last but not least comes the sledgehammer of giving reflective access: open modules (12.2.4).

12.2.1 Opening packages to run-time access

> **Definition: The opens directive**
>
> A package can be *opened* by adding a *directive* `opens ${package}` to the module declaration. At compile time, opened packages are strongly encapsulated: there's no difference between them being opened or not opened. At run time, opened packages are fully accessible, including nonpublic classes, methods, and fields.

The module *monitor.persistence* uses Hibernate, so it opens a package with entities to allow reflection over them:

```
module monitor.persistence {
    requires hibernate.jpa;
    requires monitor.statistics;

    exports monitor.persistence;
    opens monitor.persistence.entity;
}
```

This allows Hibernate to work with classes like `StatisticsEntity` (see listing 12.3). Because the package isn't exported, other *ServiceMonitor* modules can't accidentally compile code against types it contains.

Listing 12.3 Excerpts from `StatisticsEntity`, which Hibernate reflects over

```
@Entity
@Table(name = "stats")
public class StatisticsEntity {

    @Id
    @GeneratedValue(strategy = GenerationType.AUTO)
```

```
    private int id;
```
Hibernate will inject values into these private fields.

```
    @ManyToOne
    @JoinColumn(name = "quota_id", updatable = false)
    private LivenessQuotaEntity totalLivenessQuota;

    private StatisticsEntity() { }
```
Hibernate can also access the private constructor.

```
    // [...]
```

```
}
```

As you can tell, opens was designed specifically for the use case of reflection and behaves very differently from exports:

- It allows access to all members, thus not impacting your decisions regarding visibility.
- It prevents compilation against code in opened packages and only allows access at run time.
- It marks the package as being designed for use by a reflection-based framework.

Beyond the clear technical advantages over exports for this specific use case, I again find the final point the most important one: with an opens directive, you communicate clearly and in code that this package isn't meant for general use, but only for access by a specific tool. If you want, you can even include that tool by opening the package just for its module. Read on to find out how to do that. As section 5.2.3 explains, if you want to give access to resources like configurations or media files that are located in your packages, you also need to open them.

12.2.2 Opening packages for specific modules

The opens directive we've discussed so far allows all modules to reflect over an opened package. That parallels how exports allows all modules to access the exported package. And just as exports can be limited to specific modules (see section 11.3), so can opens.

> **Definition: Qualifying opens**
>
> The opens directive can be *qualified* by following it up with to ${modules}, where ${modules} is a comma-separated list of module names (no placeholders are allowed). To the modules named in an opens to directive, the package will be exactly as accessible as with a regular opens directive. To all other modules, the package will be as strongly encapsulated as if there were no opens at all.

To make encapsulation even stronger, *monitor.persistence* may only open its entity package to Hibernate:

```
module monitor.persistence {
    requires hibernate.jpa;
    requires monitor.statistics;
```

```
    exports monitor.persistence;
    // assuming Hibernate were an explicit module
    opens monitor.persistence.entity
        to hibernate.core;
}
```

In cases where specifications and implementations are separated (for example, JPA and Hibernate), you may find it a little fishy to mention the implementation in your module declaration. Section 12.3.5 addresses that thought—the summary is that this will be necessary until the standards are updated to take the module system into account.

We'll discuss in section 12.2.3 when you may want to use qualified opens, but before we do that, let's formally introduce a command-line option that we used in section 7.1.

Definition: –add-opens

The option `--add-opens ${module}/${package}=${reflecting-module}` opens *${package}* of *${module}* to *${reflecting-module}*. Code in *${reflecting-module}* can hence access all types and members, public and nonpublic ones, in `${package}`, but other modules can't.

When you set *${reading-module}* to `ALL-UNNAMED`, all code from the class path, or more precisely from the unnamed module (see section 8.2), can access that package. When migrating to Java 9+, you'll always use that placeholder—only once your own code runs in modules can you limit open packages to specific modules.

If you're interested in an example, check the one toward the end of section 7.1.4.

Because `--add-opens` is bound to reflection, a pure run-time concept, it only makes sense for the `java` command. Interestingly enough, it's available on `javac`, though, where it leads to a warning:

```
> warning: [options] --add-opens has no effect at compile time
```

My best guess for why `javac` doesn't roundly reject `--add-opens` is that this makes it possible to share the same argument file with module system–related command-line flags between compilation and launch.

> **NOTE** What are argument files? You can put compiler and JVM arguments into a file and add them to a command with `javac @file-name` and `java @file -name`. See the Java documentation for details: http://mng.bz/K1ZK.)

12.2.3 *Exporting vs. opening packages*

The `exports` and `open` directives have a few things in common:

- They make package content available beyond module boundaries.
- They have a qualified variant `to ${modules}` that only gives access to the listed modules.
- They have command-line options for `javac` and `java` that can be used to bypass strong encapsulation if need be.

They're different in when and to what they give access:

- Exported packages give access to public types and members at compile time, making them perfect to define public APIs that other modules can use.
- Opened packages give access to all types and members (including nonpublic ones), but only at run time, making them well-suited to give reflection-based frameworks access to code that's otherwise considered to be module-internal.

Table 12.1 summarizes this. You may also want to flip back to table 7.1 to see how it relates to gaining access to internal APIs with `--add-exports` and `--add-opens`.

Table 12.1 A comparison of when and to what encapsulated, exported, and opened packages give access

Access	Compile-time		Run-time	
Class or member	Public	Nonpublic	Public	Nonpublic
Encapsulated package	✗	✗	✗	✗
Exported package	✔	✗	✔	✗
Opened package	✗	✗	✔	✔

You may wonder whether and how you can combine `exports` and `opens` directives, and qualified and unqualified variants. The answer is simple—any way you like:

- Your Hibernate entities are public API? Use `exports` and `opens`.
- Want to give only a select few of your application modules compile-time access to your Spring contexts? Use `exports ... to` and `opens`.

There may not be an obvious use case for each of the four possible combinations (and I'd even argue that you should design your code so you don't need any of them), but rest assured that if you encounter one, you can arrange these directives accordingly.

When it comes to whether `opens` should be limited to specific modules, my opinion is that it often won't be worth the additional effort. Although qualified exports are an important tool to prevent colleagues and users from introducing accidental dependencies on internal APIs (see section 11.3.3 for more on that), the target audience for qualified opens are frameworks that are completely independent of your code. Whether or not you open a package just to Hibernate, Spring won't start depending on it. If your project uses a lot of reflection over its own code, then things might look different; but otherwise my default is to open—without qualification.

12.2.4 *Opening modules: Reflection closeout*

Finally, if you have a large module with many packages that are exposed to reflection, you may find it tiresome to open each of them individually. Although there's no wild-card like `opens com.company.*`, something close to it exists.

> **Definition: Open module**
>
> By putting the *keyword* open before `module` in the module declaration, an *open module* is created:
>
> ```
> open module ${module-name} {
>     requires ${module-name};
>     exports ${package-name};
>     // no opens allowed
> }
> ```
>
> An open module opens all packages it contains as if each of them were used in an `opens` directive. Consequently, it doesn't make sense to manually open further packages, which is why the compiler doesn't accept `opens` directives in an open module.

As an alternative to using `opens monitor.persistence.entity`, the *monitor.persistence* module could instead be open:

```
open module monitor.persistence {
    requires hibernate.jpa;
    requires monitor.statistics;

    exports monitor.persistence;
}
```

As you can see, open modules are really just a convenience to keep you from having to open dozens of packages manually. Ideally, you'd never be in that position, though, because your modules aren't that large. A scenario with so many opened packages is more likely during a modularization, when you turn a large JAR into a large module before splitting it up. That's also why `jdeps` can generate declarations for open modules—see section 9.3.2.

12.3 *Reflecting over modules*

Sections 12.1 and 12.2 explored how you can expose code to reflection, so that frameworks like Hibernate and Spring can access it. Because most Java applications use such frameworks, you'll encounter that scenario regularly.

Now we're going to switch sides and reflect over modular code. It's good to know how that works, so you can update your understanding of the reflection API; but because writing reflection code is rare for most developers, chances are you won't be doing this regularly. Consequently, this section is more of a discussion of noteworthy aspects of reflecting over modules and their code than a thorough introduction to all involved topics and APIs.

We'll first look at why you won't need to change your reflection code to work with modular code (12.3.1), and why you may switch to a more modern API (12.3.2). Then we'll get to the modules themselves, which have a prominent representation in the reflection API that can be used to query (12.3.3) and even modify (12.3.4) them. We'll finish by looking more closely at how a module can be modified to allow other modules reflective access to it (12.3.5).

12.3.1 *Updating reflecting code for modules (or not)*

Before venturing into new territories, I want to update your reflection knowledge with changes caused by the module system. Although it's good to understand how reflection deals with readability and accessibility, you'll find that there isn't much you need to change in your code. More important is that you inform your users what *they* have to do when creating modules.

NOTHING NEEDS TO BE DONE FOR READABILITY

One thing I've stated repeatedly is that reflection is bound by the same accessibility rules as static access (see section 3.3). First and foremost, that means for code in one module to be able to access code in another module, the first must read the second. Generally speaking, the module graph won't be set up that way, though—Hibernate won't usually read application modules.

 ESSENTIAL INFO   That sounds like the reflecting module needs to add a reads edge from it to the reflected module, and indeed, there is an API for that (see section 12.3.4). But because reflection *always* requires that edge, always adding it would just lead to unavoidable boilerplate, so the reflection API does it internally. In summary, you don't need to worry about readability.

NOTHING CAN BE DONE FOR ACCESSIBILITY

The next hurdle in the way to accessing code is that it needs to be either exported or opened. As thoroughly discussed in section 12.2, that's indeed an issue, albeit one that you, as the author of a reflection library, can do little about. Either the module's owner prepared the package by opening or exporting it, or they didn't.

 ESSENTIAL INFO   The module system doesn't limit visibility: calls like `Class::forName` or reflection to get references to constructors, methods, and fields succeed. Accessibility is limited: if access isn't given by the reflected module, then *invoking* a constructor or method, *accessing* a field, and calls to `AccessibleObject::setAccessible` will fail with an `InaccessibleObjectException`.

`InaccessibleObjectException` extends `RuntimeException`, making it an *unchecked exception,* so the compiler won't force you to catch it. But make sure you do, and on that operation, too—this way, you can provide users with a maximally helpful error message. See listing 12.4 for an example.

> #### Definition: AccessibleObject::trySetAccessible
> If you prefer checking accessibility without causing an exception to be thrown, the `AccessibleObject::trySetAccessible` method, added in Java 9, is there for you. At its core, it does the same thing as `setAccessible(true)`: it tries to make the underlying member accessible, but uses its return value to indicate whether it worked. If accessibility was granted, it returns `true`; otherwise it returns `false`. Listing 12.4 shows it in action.

Listing 12.4 Three ways to handle inaccessible code

```java
private Object constructWithoutExceptioHandling(Class<?> type)
        throws ReflectiveOperationException {
    Constructor<?> constructor = type.getConstructor();
    constructor.setAccessible(true);
    return constructor.newInstance();
}
```

◀── **This call can throw an InaccessibleObjectException, which isn't explicitly handled—the user is left to sort out the problem.**

```java
private Object constructWithExceptionHandling(Class<?> type)
        throws ReflectiveOperationException, FrameworkException {
    Constructor<?> constructor = type.getConstructor();
    try {
        constructor.setAccessible(true);
    } catch (InaccessibleObjectException ex) {
        throw new FrameworkException(createErrorMessage(type), ex);
    }
    return constructor.newInstance();
}
```

◀── (at setAccessible line)

Here the exception is converted into a framework-specific one with an additional error message explaining the context in which it occurred.

```java
private Object constructWithoutException(Class<?> type)
        throws ReflectiveOperationException, FrameworkException {
    Constructor<?> constructor = type.getConstructor();
    boolean isAccessible = constructor.trySetAccessible();
    if (!isAccessible)
        throw new FrameworkException(createErrorMessage(type));
    return constructor.newInstance();
}
```

◀── (at trySetAccessible line)

By using trySetAccessible, the initial exception is prevented, but in this case a framework-specific one is thrown nonetheless.

```java
private String createErrorMessage(Class<?> type) {
    return "When doing THE FRAMEWORK THING, accessing "
        + type + "'s parameterless constructor failed "
        + "because the module does not open the containing package. "
        + "For details see https://framework.org/java-modules";
}
```

Beyond making sure you properly handle the case in which access couldn't be granted, there isn't anything you can do. This makes updating your project for the module system more of a communication challenge than a technical one: users need to be aware which packages your project may need access to and what to do about it. Your documentation is the obvious place to educate them.

Dedicated JPMS page

Going slightly off-topic, I recommend creating a dedicated page in your documentation for the issue of how to prepare a module for use by your project. The more focused it is, the more likely that searching users will find it, so don't bury it in an already-gigantic document. Then spread that resource wide and far, including in your Javadoc and the exception message for failed access.

12.3.2 *Using variable handles instead of reflection*

Java 9 introduced a new API called *variable handles* (extending Java 7's method handles, which few developers have a use case for). It centers around the class `java.lang.invoke.VarHandle`, whose instances are strongly typed references to variables: for example, fields (although it's not limited to that). It addresses use cases from areas like reflection, concurrency, and off-heap data storage. Compared to the reflection API, it offers more type safety and better performance.

Method and variable handles are versatile, complex features that have little to do with the module system, so I won't formally introduce them here. If you even occasionally write code that uses reflection, you should definitely look into them—for a simple example, see the next listing. There's one particularly interesting aspect, though, that I want to discuss in more depth: how variable handles can be used to give access to module internals.

Listing 12.5   Using `VarHandle` to access a field value

Given an object and the name of a field ...

```
Object object = // ...
String fieldName = // ...
```

... this is the typical reflection code to get the type and field.

```
Class<?> type = object.getClass();
Field field = type.getDeclaredField(fieldName);
```

Lookup and VarHandle are part of the method/variable handle API, which is based on lookups.

```
Lookup lookup = MethodHandles.lookup();
VarHandle handle = lookup.unreflectVarHandle(field);
handle.get(object);
```

You've seen that the reflection API requires the user to open some packages, but there's no way for the reflecting framework to express that in code. The user either knows that based on their understanding of the module system or has to learn it from reading your documentation—neither of which are exactly the most robust way to express a requirement. What if the framework code could make that clearer?

Method and variable handles give you the tool for that. Take another look at listing 12.5—see the call to `MethodHandles.lookup()`? This creates a `Lookup` instance that, among other privileges and information, captures the access rights of the caller.

That means all code, regardless of the module it belongs to, that gets hold of that specific `lookup` instance can do deep reflection on the same classes as the code that created the lookup (see figure 12.1). This way, a module can capture its access rights to its own internals and pass them on to other modules.

Your reflecting code can make use of that by requiring the user to pass lookup objects to it; for example, when bootstrapping your framework. When users have to call a method that takes one or more `Lookup` instances, they're bound to read the docs to learn what they're supposed to do. Then they create an instance in each module that needs to be accessed and pass them to you, and you use them to access their module's internals. Listing 12.6 shows how that works.

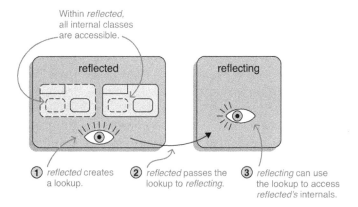

Figure 12.1 The *reflected* module creates a lookup and passes it to *reflecting*, which can then use it to access the same classes and members that *reflected* can access—these include *reflected*'s internals.

Listing 12.6 Using `VarHandle` to access a field value with a private lookup

```
Lookup lookup = // ...
Object object = // ...
String fieldName = // ...

Class<?> type = object.getClass();
Field field = type.getDeclaredField(fieldName);

Lookup privateLookup = MethodHandles
    .privateLookupIn(type,lookup);
VarHandle handle = privateLookup.unreflectVarHandle(field);
handle.get(object);
```

This lookup was created in the module owning object.

By creating a private lookup from the user-provided one, you can access the object's internals from a different module.

The interesting thing about lookups is that they can be passed around between modules. In the case of a standard versus implementation split as with JPA and its providers, the user could pass lookups to JPA's bootstrapping methods, which could then pass them on to Hibernate, EclipseLink, and the like. I think that's a pretty neat way to implement lookups:

- Users are aware that they have to do something, because bootstrapping methods require `Lookup` instances (as opposed to the requirement to open packages, which can't be expressed in code).
- There's no need to change module declarations (unlike with `opens` directives).
- Standards can pass lookups to implementations, thus not forcing users to reference the implementation in code or module declarations (this is also possible for open packages, as section 12.3.5 explains).

That concludes the discussions of using reflection or variable handles to access types that are encapsulated in modules. We'll now turn to the modules themselves and see what information you can get about them.

12.3.3   *Analyzing module properties with reflection*

If you ever tried to analyze a JAR at run time, you found out that doing so isn't convenient. That goes back to the fundamental interpretation of what JARs are: mere containers (see section 1.2). Java doesn't recognize them as first-class citizens like packages and types, so it has no representation at run time that sees them as anything more than just Zip files.

The module system's pivotal change is to align Java's interpretation of JARs with ours as units of code that have names, dependencies, and explicit APIs. Beyond everything we've discussed so far in this book, this should carry all the way to the reflection API, where modules, unlike JARs but like packages and types, should be represented. And indeed they are.

> **Definition: Module and ModuleDescriptor types**
>
> Java 9 introduced the new type `java.lang.Module`, which represents a module at run time. A `Module` instance lets you do the following:
>
> - Analyze the module's name, annotations, exports/opens directives, and service uses
> - Access resources the module contains (see section 5.2)
> - Modify the module by exporting and opening packages or adding reads edges and services uses (if the modifying code is in the same module)
>
> Some of these pieces of information are only available on the equally new type `java.lang.module.ModuleDescriptor`, returned by `Module::getDescriptor`.

One way to get instances of `Module` is to call `getModule` on any `Class` instance, which, no big surprise, returns the module to which that class belongs. The following listing shows how to analyze a module by querying `Module` and `ModuleDescriptor`; the output for some example modules is shown in listing 12.8.

Listing 12.7   Analyzing a module by querying `Module` and `ModuleDescriptor`

```
public static String describe(Module module) {
    String annotations = Arrays
        .stream(module.getDeclaredAnnotations())
        .map(Annotation::annotationType)
        .map(Object::toString)
        .collect(joining(", "));
    ModuleDescriptor md = module.getDescriptor();
    if (md == null)
        return "UNNAMED module { }";

    return ""
        + "@[" + annotations + "]\n"
        + md.modifiers() + " module " + md.name()
        + " @ " + toString(md.rawVersion())
        + " {\n"
```

```
            + "\trequires " + md.requires() + "\n"
            + "\texports " + md.exports() + "\n"
            + "\topens " + md.opens() + "\n"
            + "\tcontains " + md.packages() + "\n"
            + "\tmain " + toString(md.mainClass()) + "\n"
            + "}";
}

private static String toString(Optional<?> optional) {
    return optional.isPresent()
            ? optional.get().toString()
            : "[]";
}
```

Listing 12.8 Output of calling `describe(Module)` **from listing 12.7**

```
> @[]
> [] module monitor @ [] {
>     requires [
>         monitor.observer,
>         monitor.rest
>         monitor.persistence,
>         monitor.observer.alpha,
>         mandated java.base (@9.0.4),
>         monitor.observer.beta,
>         monitor.statistics]
>     exports []
>     opens []
>     contains [monitor]
>     main monitor.Main
> }
>
> @[]
> [] module monitor.persistence @ [] {
>     requires [
>         hibernate.jpa,
>         mandated java.base (@9.0.4),
>         monitor.statistics]
>     exports [monitor.persistence]
>     opens [monitor.persistence.entity]
>     contains [
>         monitor.persistence,
>         monitor.persistence.entity]
>     main []
> }
>
> @[]
> [] module java.logging @ 9.0.4 {
>     requires [mandated java.base]
>     exports [java.util.logging]
>     opens []
>     contains [
>         java.util.logging,
>         sun.util.logging.internal,
```

```
>             sun.net.www.protocol.http.logging,
>             sun.util.logging.resources]
>      main []
> }
>
> @[]
> [] module java.base @ 9.0.4 {
>      requires []
>      exports [... lots ...]
>      opens []
>      contains [... lots ...]
>      main []
> }
```

Some `ModuleDescriptor` methods return information related to other modules: for example, which modules are required, or to which modules packages are exported and opened. These are just module names as strings, not actual `Module` instances. At the same time, many methods of `Module` require such instances as input. So you get strings out, but you need to put modules in—how do you bridge that gap? As section 12.4.1 shows, the answer is layers.

12.3.4   *Modifying module properties with reflection*

In addition to analyzing a module's properties, you can also use `Module` to modify them by calling these methods:

- `addExports` exports a package to a module.
- `addOpens` opens a package to a module.
- `addReads` lets the module read another one.
- `addUses` makes the module use a service.

When looking these over, you may wonder why it's possible to export or open packages of a module. Doesn't that go against strong encapsulation? Didn't we spend all of section 12.2 discussing what the module owner has to do to prepare for reflection because the reflecting code can't break in?

 ESSENTIAL INFO   Here's the thing: these methods are *caller sensitive*, meaning they behave differently based on the code that calls them. For the call to succeed, it either has to come from *within* the module that's being modified or from the unnamed module. Otherwise it will fail with an `IllegalCallerException`.

Take the following code as an example:

```
public boolean openJavaLangTo(Module module) {
    Module base = Object.class.getModule();
    base.addOpens("java.lang", module);
    return base.isOpen("java.lang", module);
}
```

If copied into a `main` method that's executed from the class path (so it runs in the unnamed module), this works fine, and the method returns `true`. If, on the other hand, it runs from within any named module (*open.up* in the following example), it fails:

```
> Exception in thread "main" java.lang.IllegalCallerException:
>     java.lang is not open to module open.up
>     at java.base/java.lang.Module.addOpens(Module.java:751)
>     at open.up/open.up.Main.openJavaLangTo(Main.java:18)
>     at open.up/open.up.Main.main(Main.java:14)
```

You can make it work (again) by injecting the code into the module it modifies, namely *java.base*, with `--patch-module` (see section 7.2.4):

```
$ java
    --patch-module java.base=open.up.jar
    --module java.base/open.up.Main
> WARNING: module-info.class ignored in patch: open.up.jar
> true
```

There you go: the final `true` is the return value from `openJavaLangTo` called with an arbitrary platform module.

Dynamically modifying your own modules' properties isn't something you'll do on a regular basis, even if you're developing a reflection-based framework. So why am I telling you all this? Because as you'll see in the following section, one interesting detail is hidden in here: you can open other modules' packages under certain circumstances.

12.3.5 *Forwarding open packages*

I said that only a module could open one of its packages with `Module:addOpens`, but that's not entirely true. If a module's package is already opened to a set of other modules, then all those modules can also open that package. In other words, modules with reflective access to a package can open that package to *other* modules. What does that mean?

Once again, think about JPA. You may have flinched in section 12.2.2 when it looked as if you needed to open a package either unconditionally or to the module doing the actual reflection, because in the case of JPA, that would mean something like this:

```
module monitor.persistence {
    requires hibernate.jpa;
    requires monitor.statistics;

    exports monitor.persistence;
    // assuming Hibernate were an explicit module
    opens monitor.persistence.entity
        to hibernate.core;
}
```

Wouldn't it be better to open to JPA instead of the specific implementation? That's exactly what's made possible by enabling modules with reflective access to open packages to other modules! This way, JPA's bootstrapping code can open all packages to Hibernate, even those packages that just have reflective access.

So although only the module can add package exports, reads edges, and service uses, the rule for opening packages is relaxed, and all modules to which a package was opened can open it to other modules. For reflection-based frameworks to make use of that, they of course have to be aware of the module system and update their code. In the case of JEE technologies, that could still take a while, though, unless Eclipse adopts a faster release cycle for Jakarte EE (it took more than three years from Java SE 8 to Java EE 8).

Now that we've settled how to reflect over, analyze, and modify an individual module, we can take it to the next level, or rather *layer* as you'll see in the following section, and work with the entire module graph.

12.4   *Dynamically creating module graphs with layers*

In section 12.3, we focused on individual modules: how to reflect over modular code and how to analyze and modify a single module's properties. In this section, we're broadening our scope and looking at entire module graphs.

So far, we've left the creation of module graphs to the compiler or JVM, which generates them before starting its work. From that moment on, the graph is an almost immutable entity that offers no way to add or remove modules.

Although that's fine for many run-of-the-mill applications, there are those which need more flexibility. Think about application servers or plug-in based applications. They need a dynamic mechanism that allows them to load and unload classes at run time.

As an example, let's assume the *ServiceMonitor* application offers an endpoint or a graphical interface with which a user can specify that an additional service has to be observed. That can be done by instantiating the appropriate `ServiceObserver` implementation, but what if that implementation comes from a module that was unknown at launch time? Then it (and its dependencies) would have to be loaded dynamically at run time.

Before the module system, such container applications used bare class loaders for dynamic loading and unloading, but wouldn't it be nice if they, just like compiler and JVM, could also take it to a higher level of abstraction and operate on modules instead? Fortunately, the module system allows just that by introducing the concept of *layers*. The first thing you need to do is to get to know layers, including one that has been around all the time without you knowing (section 12.4.1). The next step is to analyze layers (section 12.4.2) before you dynamically create your own at run time (section 12.4.3).

Note that writing code that deals with layers is even less common than using the reflection API. Here's a simple litmus test: if you've never instantiated a class loader, you're unlikely to use layers any time soon. Accordingly, this section gives you the lay of the land, so you know your way around, but doesn't go into full detail. Still, you may see something you didn't know was possible and end up with some new ideas.

12.4.1 What are layers?

Definition: Module layer

A *module layer* comprises a fully resolved graph of named modules as well as the class loader(s) used to load the modules' classes. Each class loader has an unnamed module associated with it (accessible with `ClassLoader::getUnnamedModule`). A layer also references one or more *parent layers*—modules in a layer can read modules in the ancestor layers, but not the other way around.

Everything we've discussed so far about the resolution and relationships between modules happens *within one module graph*. With layers, it's possible to stack as many graphs as you want, so, conceptually, layers add a third dimension to the two-dimensional concept of module graphs. Parent layers are defined when a layer is created and can't be changed afterward, so there's no way to create cyclic layers. Figure 12.2 shows a module graph with layers.

For *ServiceMonitor*, that means in order to dynamically load the new observer implementation, it needs to create a new layer. Before we come to that in section 12.4.3, let's take a closer look at existing layers and how to analyze them.

Are all modules contained in a layer? Almost. As you've seen, technically speaking, the unnamed modules aren't. And then there are so-called *dynamic modules*, which

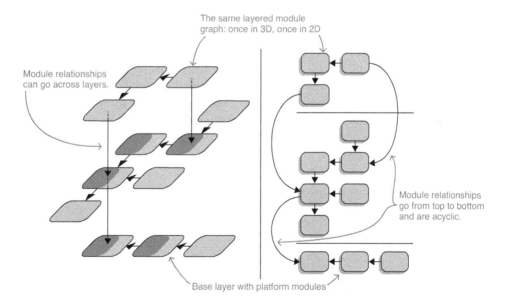

Figure 12.2 With layers, module graphs can be stacked, adding a third dimension to your mental model of the application. Because they don't share class loaders, layers are well-isolated from one another. (Like every good computer science graph, this one may look upside down. Parent layers are below their children because that keeps the layer containing the platform modules at the bottom.)

don't have to belong to a layer, but I'm not covering them in this book. These exceptions aside, all modules are part of a layer.

THE BOOT LAYER

What about all the application and platform modules that were put into a graph throughout this book? They should also belong to a layer, right?

> ### Definition: Boot layer
>
> Indeed they do. When launching, the JVM creates an initial layer, the *boot layer*, which contains the application and platform modules that were resolved based on the command-line options.

The boot layer has no parent and contains three class loaders:

- The *boot class loader* grants all classes it loads all security permissions, so an effort is made by the JDK team to minimize the modules it's responsible for; these are a few core platform modules, chief among them *java.base*.
- The *platform class loader* loads classes from all other platform modules; it can be accessed with the static method `ClassLoader::getPlatformClassLoader`.
- The *system* or *application class loader* loads all classes from the module and class path, which means it's responsible for all application modules; it can be accessed with the static method `ClassLoader::getSystemClassLoader`.

Only the system class loader has access to the class path, so of these three loaders, only its unnamed module will ever be non-empty. Hence, when section 8.2 talks about the unnamed module, it always references the system class loader's.

As you can see in figure 12.3, class loaders aren't islands: each class loader has a parent, and most implementations, including the three just mentioned, first ask the parent to load a class before trying to look it up themselves. For the three boot-layer class loaders, boot is the parent-less ancestor, platform delegates to boot, and system delegates to platform. As a consequence, the system class loader has access to all application and JDK classes from the boot and platform loaders.

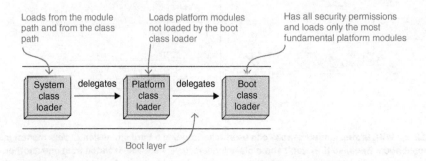

Figure 12.3   Delegation between the three class loaders in the boot layer

12.4.2 *Analyzing layers*

> **Definition: ModuleLayer**
>
> At run time, *layers are represented by* `java.lang.ModuleLayer` instances. They can be queried for the three things a layer is made up of:
>
> - The modules:
>   - The method `modules()` returns the modules the layer contains as a `Set<Module>`.
>   - The method `findModule(String)` searches the layer itself *and* all its ancestor layers for a module with the specified name. It returns an `Optional<Module>` because it may not find it.
> - The layer's parents are returned as `List<ModuleLayer>` by the `parents()` method.
> - Each module's class loader can be determined by calling `findLoader(String)` with a module's name.
>
> Then there's the `configuration` method, which returns a `Configuration` instance—see section 12.4.3 for more on that.

To get hold of a `ModuleLayer` instance, you can ask any module for the layer it belongs to:

```
Class<?> type = // ... any class
ModuleLayer layer = type
    .getModule()
    .getLayer();
```

The last line returns `null` if the type comes from an unnamed module or a dynamic module that doesn't belong to a layer. If you want to access the boot layer, you can call the static `ModuleLayer::boot` method.

So what can you learn from `ModuleLayer` instances? Undoubtedly the most interesting methods are `modules()` and `findModule(String)`, because together with the methods on `Module` (see section 12.3.3), they allow the traversal and analysis of the module graph.

DESCRIBING A MODULE LAYER

Given the `describe(Module)` method in listing 12.7, this is how an entire layer could be described:

```
private static String describe(ModuleLayer layer) {
    return layer
        .modules().stream()
        .map(ThisClass::describe)
        .collect(joining("\n\n"));
}
```

FINDING MODULES IN AND ACROSS LAYERS

It's also possible to determine the presence or absence of specific modules, which can come in handy if the dependency on them is optional (with `requires static`; see section 11.2). In section 11.2.4, I claimed that it would be straightforward to implement a method `isModulePresent(String)` to do that. That makes you put into practice what you learned about layers so far, so let's do it step by step.

At first it seems to be pretty trivial:

```
public boolean isModulePresent(String moduleName) {
    return ModuleLayer
        .boot()
        .findModule(moduleName)
        .isPresent();
}
```

But that only shows whether the module is present in the boot layer. What if additional layers were created, and the module is in another layer? You can replace the boot layer with the layer that contains isModulePresent:

```
public  boolean isModulePresent(String moduleName) {
    return searchRootModuleLayer()
        .findModule(moduleName)
        .isPresent();
}

private ModuleLayer searchRootModuleLayer() {
    return this
        .getClass()
        .getModule()
        .getLayer();
}
```

This way, `isModulePresent` searches the layer containing itself—let's call it `search`—as well as all parent layers. But even that isn't good enough. The module calling that method could be in a different layer, named `call`, which has `search` as an ancestor. (Confused? See figure 12.4.) Then `search` can't look into `call` and hence can't search through all possible modules. No, you need the module of the *caller* to use its layer as the root for your search.

The following listing implements `getCallerClass`, which determines the caller's class with the stack-walking API that Java 9 introduced.

Listing 12.9   New API to walk the call stack

```
private Class<?> getCallerClass() {
    return StackWalker
        .getInstance(RETAIN_CLASS_REFERENCE)

        .walk(stack -> stack
```

Static factory method to get a StackWalker instance where each frame has a reference to the declaring Class

StackWalker::walk expects a function from a Stream<StackFrame> to an arbitrary object. It creates a lazy view of the stack and immediately calls the function with it. The object the function returns is then returned by walk.

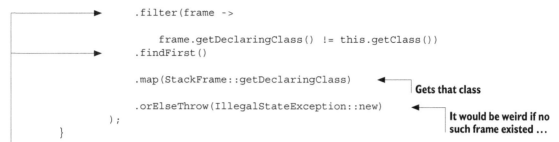

```
                    .filter(frame ->

                        frame.getDeclaringClass() != this.getClass())
                    .findFirst()

                    .map(StackFrame::getDeclaringClass)      ◄─── Gets that class

                    .orElseThrow(IllegalStateException::new)  ◄──
            );                                                    It would be weird if no
    }                                                             such frame existed ...
```

**You're interested in the first frame that comes from a
class that isn't this one (that must be the caller!); you
now have an Optional<StackFrame>.**

With that in your toolbox, the caller's module is at your fingertips:

```java
public  boolean isModulePresent(String moduleName) {
    return searchRootModuleLayer()
        .findModule(moduleName)
        .isPresent();
}

private ModuleLayer searchRootModuleLayer() {
    return getCallerClass()
        .getModule()
        .getLayer();
}
```

That's it for analyzing layers. Now we can finally get to the most exciting part: loading
new code into a running application by create new layers.

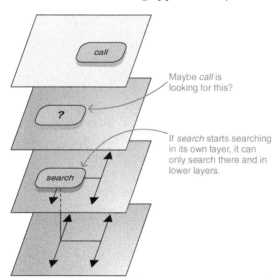

Maybe *call* is
looking for this?

If *search* starts searching
in its own layer, it can
only search there and in
lower layers.

**Figure 12.4   A layer asked to find a module
only scans itself and its parents (in this
graph, that's downward). So if `search`
queries its own layer, it may ignore layers
that *call*, the module initiating the search,
can see, thus running the risk of returning
a wrong result. That's why it's important to
query *call*'s layer.**

12.4.3 *Creating module layers*

Only a fraction of the applications written with Java need to dynamically load code at run time. At the same time, these tend to be the more important ones. Maybe the best-known is Eclipse, with its strong focus on plugins, but application servers like WildFly and GlassFish also have to load code from one or several applications at the same time. As discussed in section 1.7.3, OSGi is also able to dynamically load and unload bundles (its name for modules).

They all have the same fundamental requirements for the mechanism they use to load plugins, applications, bundles, and other new fragments of the running JVM:

- It must be possible to spin up a fragment from set of JARs at run time.
- It must allow interaction with the loaded fragments.
- It must allow isolation between different fragments.

Before the module system, this was done with class loaders. Briefly summarized, a new class loader was created for the new JARs. It delegated to another class loader, such as the system class loader, which gave it access to other classes in the running JVM. Although each class, identified by its fully qualified name, can exist only once per class loader, it can easily be loaded by several loaders. This isolates fragments and gives each the possibility of coming up with its own dependencies without conflicting with other fragments.

The module system didn't change this in any way. Leaving existing class-loader hierarchies intact was one of the driving reasons for implementing the module system below the class loaders (see section 1.7.3). What the module system adds is the notion of layers around class loaders, which enable integration with the modules loaded at launch time. Let's see how you can create one. (You can find the variant of *ServiceMonitor* that creates layers in the branch `feature-layers`.)

CREATING A CONFIGURATION

An important ingredient of a `ModuleLayer` is a `Configuration`. Creating one triggers the module-resolution process (see section 3.4.1), and the created instance represents a successfully resolved module graph. The most bare-bones form to create a configuration is with the static factory methods `resolve` and `resolveAndBind`. The only difference between the two is that the second binds services (see section 10.1.2), whereas the first doesn't.

Both `resolve` and `resolveAndBind` take the same four arguments:

- `ModuleFinder before` is asked to locate modules before looking into the parent configurations
- `List<Configuration>` parents are the configurations of the parent layers.
- `ModuleFinder after` is asked to locate modules after looking into the parent configurations.
- `Collection<String>` roots are the root modules for the resolution process.

Creating a `ModuleFinder` for a module path is as simple as calling `ModuleFinder` `.of(Path...)`. It's common to try to reference as many modules as possible from the parent layer, so the `before` finder is often created without an argument and thus can't find any modules.

For the common case of wanting to create a configuration that has a single parent, it's easier to call the instance methods `resolve` and `resolveAndBind`. They have no `List<Configuration>` parents argument and use the current configuration as parent.

Let's say you want to create a configuration with the boot layer as parent that emulates the launch command `java --module-path mods --module root` but without service binding. For that, you can call `resolve` (so services aren't bound) on the boot layer's configuration (making it the parent) and pass a module finder that looks into the mods directory. The following listing shows that: it creates a configuration that emulates `java --module-path mods --module initial` minus the service binding.

> **Listing 12.10 Emulating `java --module-path mods --module`**

No need to find modules before looking into the parent graph

The finder for modules that don't exist in the parent graph looks into the mods directory.

```
ModuleFinder emptyBefore = ModuleFinder.of();
ModuleFinder modulePath = ModuleFinder.of(Paths.get("mods"));
Configuration bootGraph = ModuleLayer.boot().configuration();
Configuration graph = bootGraph #C
        .resolve(emptyBefore, modulePath, List.of("initial"));
```

Defines the boot layer's configuration as parent by calling resolve on it (resolveAndBind would bind services)

As a second example, let's turn back to the scenario where you want *ServiceMonitor* to start observing new services at run time, for which new `ServiceObserver` implementations need to be loaded. The first step is to create a configuration with the current layer as parent that looks up modules on a specified path.

Because you're using the module system's service infrastructure for your services, you call `resolveAndBind`. You can solely depend on that mechanism to find all the modules you need (and their dependencies), so you don't even need to specify root modules. Here's the implementation.

> **Listing 12.11 Configuration that binds all modules from specified paths**

```
private static Configuration createConfiguration(Path[] modulePaths) {
    return getThisLayer()
        .configuration()
        .resolveAndBind(
            ModuleFinder.of(),
            ModuleFinder.of(modulePaths),
            Collections.emptyList()
        );
}
```

Returns the layer to which the class containing createConfiguration belongs

Called so that services are resolved

You rely on service binding to do the work for you and pull in the desired modules, so you define no root modules.

CREATING A MODULELAYER

As described in section 12.4.1, a layer consists of a module graph, class loaders, and references to parent layers. The bare-bones form to create a module is with the static method defineModules(Configuration, List<ModuleLayer>, Function<String, ClassLoader>):

- You already know how to get Configuration instances.
- The List<ModuleLayer> are the parents.
- The Function<String, ClassLoader> maps each module name to the class loader you want to be in charge of that module.

The method returns a Controller, which can be used to further edit the module graph by adding reads edges or exporting/opening packages before calling layer() on it, which returns the ModuleLayer.

There are several alternative methods you can call that build on defineModules:

- defineModulesWithOneLoader uses a single class loader for all modules. The class loader given as argument to the method becomes its parent.
- defineModulesWithManyLoaders uses a separate class loader for each module. The class loader given as argument to the method becomes the parent of each of them.
- There is a variant of each method that can be called on a ModuleLayer instance and uses that instance as the parent layer; they return the created layer instead of the intermediate Controller.

Continuing your quest to dynamically load ServiceObserver implementations, the next step is to create the actual layer from the configuration. That's fairly simple, as the following listing shows.

Listing 12.12   Creating a layer from a configuration

Creates the configuration as in listing 12.11

getThisLoader returns the class loader that loaded the class containing createLayer.

```
private static ModuleLayer createLayer(Path[] modulePaths) {
    Configuration configuration = createConfiguration(modulePaths);
    ClassLoader thisLoader = getThisLoader();
    return getThisLayer()
        .defineModulesWithOneLoader(configuration, thisLoader);
}
```

The same as getThisLayer in listing 12.11

You only want a single loader for all modules with this layer as the parent, so you call defineModulesWithOneLoader on it.

The final step is to check whether the freshly created layer contains a ServiceObserver that can handle the service you need to observe. To that end, you can use an overload of ServiceLoader::load that expects a ModuleLayer in addition to the service type it looks up. The semantics should be clear: look into that layer (and its ancestors) when locating providers.

Listing 12.13   Discovering service providers in a new layer (and its ancestors)

```
private static void registerNewService(
        String serviceName, Path... modulePaths) {     Creates the layer as in listing 12.1.2
    ModuleLayer layer = createLayer(modulePaths);
    Stream<ServiceObserverFactory> observerFactories = ServiceLoader
        .load(layer, ServiceObserverFactory.class).stream()
        .map(Provider::get);
    Optional<ServiceObserver> observer = observerFactories
        .map(factory -> factory
            .createIfMatchingService(serviceName))
        .flatMap(Optional::stream)
        .findFirst();
    observer.ifPresent(monitor::addServiceObserver);
}
```

Uses the ServiceLoader::load variant   **The rest is service-business-as-usual to**
that accepts the new layer   **find an observer for serviceName.**

If that wasn't enough for you, there are a few more things we've barely touched on that you can do with module layers:

- Create configurations and layers with several parents or several class loaders
- Use layers to load multiple versions of the same module
- Modify the module graph with the `Controller`—for example, to export or open modules—before turning it into a `ModuleLayer`
- Directly load-specific classes from the created layers as entry points into the fragment, as opposed to using JPMS services

You can learn more about these from the excellent Javadoc on the involved methods, particularly in `ModuleLayer` and `Configuration`. Or flip to section 13.3, which makes good use of a few of these possibilities.

Summary

- Modules that code reflects over:
    - In most cases, `exports` directives aren't a good fit for making classes available for reflection, because classes you designed to be used with reflection-based frameworks are rarely suited to be part of a module's public API; with qualified exports, you may be forced to couple your module to an implementation instead of a standard; and exports don't support deep reflection over nonprivate fields and methods.
    - By default, you shouldn't use `exports`, but rather `opens` directives, to open packages for reflection.
    - The `opens` directive has the same syntax as `exports`, but works differently: an opened package isn't accessible at compile time; and all types and members, including nonpublic ones, in an opened package are accessible at run time. These properties are closely aligned with the requirements of reflection-based

frameworks, which makes `opens` directives the default choice when preparing modules for reflection.

- The qualified variant `opens ... to` opens a package just to the named modules. Because it's usually exceedingly obvious which frameworks reflect over which packages, it's questionable whether qualifying `open` directives adds much value.

- If the reflecting framework is split into a standard and its implementations (as with JPA and Hibernate, EclipseLink, and so forth), it's technically possible to only open a package to the standard, which can then use the reflection API to open it to a specific implementation. This isn't yet widely implemented, though, so for the time being, qualified opens need to name the specific implementation modules.

- The command-line option `--add-opens` has the same syntax as `--add -exports` and works like a qualified opens. Opening platform modules from the command line to access their internals is common during a migration to Java 9+, but you can also use it to break into other application modules if you absolutely have to.

- By starting a module declaration with `open module` (instead of just `module`), all packages in that module are opened. This is a good solution if a module contains a lot of packages that need to be opened, but it should be carefully evaluated whether that's really necessary or could be remedied. Ideally, open modules are mostly used during modularization before refactoring a module to a cleaner state that exposes less internals.

- Code that reflects over modules:

  - Reflection is bound by the same accessibility rules as regular code. Regarding having to read the module that you access, the reflection API makes things easier by implicitly adding a reads edge. Regarding exported or opened packages, there's nothing the author of the reflecting code can do about it if a module owner didn't prepare their module for it. (The only solution would be the `--add-opens` command-line option.)

  - This makes it all the more necessary to educate users about strong encapsulation and which packages your module needs access to. Document that well, and make the source easily available.

  - Make sure to properly handle exceptions that are thrown due to strong encapsulation, so you can provide users with an informative error message, possibly linking to your documentation.

  - Consider using variable handles instead of the reflection API. They provide more type safety, are more performant, and give you the means to express your need for access in your bootstrap API by requiring `Lookup` instances.

- A `Lookup` instance offers everybody using it the same accessibility as the module that created it. So when your users create a `Lookup` instance in their module and pass it to your framework, you can access their module internals.

- The new classes `Module` and `ModuleDescriptor` are part of the reflection API and give access to all information regarding a module, such as its name, dependencies, and exported or opened packages. You can use it to analyze the actual module graph at run time.

- Using that API, modules can also modify their own properties and export or open packages or add reads edges to other modules. It's generally not possible to modify other modules, with the exception that every module to which another module's package was opened can open that package to a third module.

- Code that dynamically loads modules:

  - Class loaders are the way to dynamically load code into a running program. This doesn't change with the module system, but it does provide a modular wrapper around class loaders with layers. A layer encapsulates a class loader and a module graph, and creating the latter exposes the loaded modules to all the consistency checks and accessibility rules that the module system offers. Layers can hence be used to provide reliable configuration and strong encapsulation for the loaded modules.

  - When launching, the JVM creates the boot layer, which consists of three class loaders and all platform and application modules that were initially resolved. It can be accessed with the static method `ModuleLayer::boot`, and the returned `ModuleLayer` instance can be used to analyze the entire module graph.

Module versions: What's possible and what's not

This chapter covers

- Why the module system doesn't act on version information
- Recording version information
- Analyzing version information at run time
- Loading multiple module versions

As briefly mentioned in section 1.5.6, the JPMS doesn't support module versions. But then what is `jar --module-version` good for? And didn't section 12.3.3 show that `ModuleDescriptor` can at least report a module's version? This chapter clears things up and looks at module versions from a few different angles.

We'll first discuss in what ways the module system could support versions and why it doesn't do that (section 13.1). It at least allows you to record and evaluate version information, though, and we'll explore that next (section 13.2). Last on the list is the Holy Grail: running different versions of the same module (section 13.3). Although there's no native support for that, there are ways to make it happen with some effort.

By the end of this chapter, you'll have a clear understanding of the module system's limited support for versions. This will help you analyze your application and can even be used to proactively report possible problems. Maybe more important, you'll also know the reasons for the limitations and whether you can expect them to change. You'll also learn how to run multiple versions of the same module—but as you'll see, it will rarely be worth the effort.

13.1 The lack of version support in the JPMS

Java 8 and earlier have no concept of versions. As described in section 1.3.3, that can result in unexpected run-time behavior where the only solution may be to pick different versions of your dependencies than you'd like. That's unfortunate, and when the module system was first conceived, one of its goals was to remedy this situation.

That didn't happen, though. The module system that's now operating in Java is still comparatively blind to versions. It's limited to recording a module's or dependency's version (see section 13.2).

But why is that? Couldn't the module system support having several versions of the same module (section 13.1.1)? If not, couldn't it at least take a bunch of modules and version requirements as input and select a single version for each module (section 13.1.2)? The answer to both questions is "no," and I want to explain why.

13.1.1 No support for multiple versions

A seemingly simple solution to version conflicts would be to allow running two versions of the same JAR. Straightforward. So why can't the module system just do that? To answer that question, you have to know how Java loads classes.

HOW CLASS LOADING PREVENTS MULTIPLE VERSIONS

As discussed when we looked at shadowing in section 1.3.2, the JVM—or, more precisely, its class loaders—identify classes by their fully qualified name, such as `java.util.List` or `monitor.observer.ServiceObserver`. To load a class from the class path, the application class loader scans all JARs until it encounters a class with the specific name it's looking for, which it then loads.

 ESSENTIAL INFO   The critical observation is that it doesn't matter whether another JAR on the class path contains a class with the exact same name—it will never be loaded. In other words, the class loader operates under the assumption that each class, identified by its fully qualified name, exists exactly once.

Turning back to our desire to run multiple versions of the same module, the roadblock is apparent: such modules are bound to contain classes with the same fully qualified name, and without any changes, the JVM would only ever see one of them. What could those changes look like?

CHANGES TO CLASS LOADING THAT WOULD ALLOW MULTIPLE VERSIONS

The first option for allowing several classes with the same name would be to rewrite the entire class-loading mechanism so that an individual class loader could handle that case. That would be a huge engineering task because the assumption that each class loader has at most one class of any given name permeates the entire JVM. In addition to the massive effort, it would also carry a lot of risk: it would be an invasive change and hence would be almost guaranteed to be backward incompatible.

The second option would be to allow multiple classes with the same name to do what, for example, OSGi does: use a separate class loader for each module (see figure 13.1). That would be comparatively straightforward but would also probably cause compatibility issues.

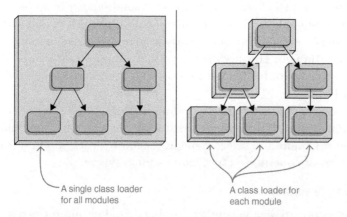

A single class loader
for all modules

A class loader for
each module

Figure 13.1   The JPMS uses the same class loader for all application modules (left), but it's conceivable that it could use a separate loader for each module instead (right). In many cases, that would change the application's behavior, though.

One potential source of problems is that some tools, frameworks, and even applications make specific assumptions about the exact class-loader hierarchy. (By default, there are three class loaders that reference one another—this didn't change in Java 9. The details are explained in the description of the boot layer in section 12.4.1.) Putting each module in its own class loader would considerably change that hierarchy and would probably break most of these projects.

There's another devious detail hidden in changing the hierarchy. Even if you were willing to require projects to adapt to that change to run from the module path, what would happen if they ran from the class path? Would JARs from the class path also each get a separate class loader?

- If so, projects that had trouble with the changed class-loader hierarchy not only wouldn't run as modules, they also wouldn't even run on Java 9+.
- If not, they would need to be aware of two different class-loading hierarchies and correctly interact with each of them, depending on which path they landed on.

None of these impacts on compatibility or migration paths are acceptable if applied to the entire ecosystem.

> **NOTE** The weight of these concerns is different for OSGi. It offers features that most applications that use it can't live without, so their developers can be expected to put in more work. Java 9+, on the other hand, also needs to

work for projects that don't care about the module system. OSGi is opt-in, so if push comes to shove and it doesn't work out for any specific project, it can be ignored. The same is obviously not the case with Java 9+.

 ESSENTIAL INFO Another reason a specific class loader per JAR can be problematic has to do with class equality. Let's assume the same class was loaded by two different class loaders. Their `Class<?>` instances aren't equal, because the class loader is always included in that check. So? Who cares, right?

Well, if you have an instance of each class and compare the two, what's one of the first things that happen in the `equals` comparison? It's `this.getClass() == other.getClass()` or an `instanceof` check. In this case, that will always be false because the two classes aren't equal.

That means with two versions of Guava, for example, `mutimap1.equals(multimap2)` would always be false, no matter what elements the two `Multimap` instances contained. You also couldn't cast an instance of the class from one class loader to the same class loaded from the other, so `(Multimap) multimap2` could fail:

```
static boolean equalsImpl(
        Multimap<?, ?> multimap,          ◀──── Multimap instance on which equals was
        @NullableDecl Object object) {            called. The method is executed in the
    if (object == multimap) {                     context of its class loader.
        return true;
    }                                         ◀──── Object passed to the equals call. It's
    if (object instanceof Multimap) {                assumed to be a Multimap instance from
        Multimap<?, ?> that = (Multimap<?, ?>) object;    a different class loader.
        return multimap.asMap().equals(that.asMap());
    }
    return false;                         object is of type Multimap, but it's from a different class
}                                         loader, so this instanceof check always fails.
```

It would be nice to know how many projects would be tripped up just by that detail. There's no way to know, but my guess is a lot. Compared to that, chapters 6 and 7 are outright benign.

NOTE By the way, everything we've just discussed also applies to split packages (see section 7.2). Wouldn't it be nice if the module system didn't care whether two modules contain the same package and could keep them separate? It would, but that would run into the same problems we just explored.

What we determined so far only means that the module system doesn't allow multiple versions of the same module out of the box. There's no native support, but that doesn't mean it's categorically impossible. Take a look at section 13.3 for ways to make it work.

13.1.2 *No support for version selection*

If the module system can't load several versions of the same module, why can't it at least select the correct versions for us? That, too, is, of course, theoretically possible, but unfortunately isn't feasible—let me explain why.

HOW BUILD TOOLS HANDLE VERSIONS

Build tools like Maven and Gradle work with versioned JARs all the time. They know for each JAR which version it has and which versions its dependencies have. Considering the shoulders of giants on which so many projects stand, it's only natural that they have deep dependency trees that contain the same JARs several times, possibly with different versions.

Although it's nice to know how many different versions require a JAR, that doesn't change the fact that they better not all end up on the class path. If they do, you'll run into problems like shadowing (see section 1.3.2) and outright version conflicts (see section 1.3.3), which will threaten your project's stability.

 ESSENTIAL INFO   When it comes time to compile, test, or launch a project, build tools have to flatten that tree into a list that contains each JAR only once (see figure 13.2). Effectively, they have to *select a version* for each artifact. That's a nontrivial process, particularly if artifacts can define a range of acceptable versions for each dependency. Because the process is nontrivial, it also isn't particularly transparent. It can be hard to predict which versions Maven or Gradle will select, and it isn't surprising that they don't necessarily select the same ones under the same circumstances.

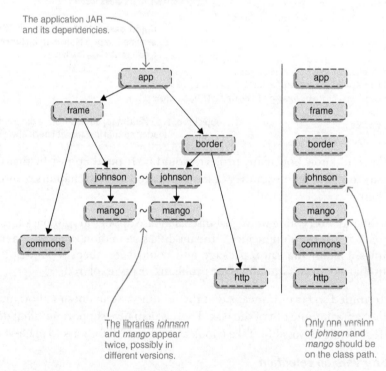

Figure 13.2   An application's dependency tree (left) may contain the same JAR more than once, like `johnson` and `mango`, possibly in different versions. To work on the class path, this tree has to be reduced to a set that contains each JAR only once (right).

WHY THE MODULE SYSTEM DOESN'T SELECT VERSIONS

Now let's leave build tools behind and talk about the module system. As you'll see in section 13.2, modules can record their own version and those of their dependencies. Assuming the module system can't run several instances of the same module, couldn't it select a single version of each?

Let's play this through. In this hypothetical scenario, the JPMS would accept several versions of the same module on the module path. When building the module graph, it would decide for each module which version to pick.

 ESSENTIAL INFO This means the JPMS would now replicate what build tools already do. And because they don't do it exactly the same way, the module system would behave subtly different than most (probably all) of them. Even worse, because Java is based on a standard, the precise behavior would likely have to be standardized, making it difficult to evolve over time.

On top of that would come the effort to implement and maintain the version-selection algorithm. The final nail in the coffin is performance: if the compiler and JVM had to run that algorithm before they could start their actual work, which would measurably increase compile and launch times. As you can see, version selection isn't a cheap feature, and it makes sense that Java isn't adopting it.

13.1.3 *What the future may bring*

In summary, the module system is version agnostic, meaning version information doesn't impact its behavior. That's today. Many developers hope Java will support either of these features in the future. If you're one of them, I don't want to rain on your parade, and however the future looks today doesn't mean it won't happen. I don't see it, though.

 ESSENTIAL INFO Mark Reinhold, chief architect of the Java Platform Group at Oracle and specification lead for the module system, has repeatedly and publicly stated that he doesn't see version support in Java's future. Given the considerable investment such a feature would require, and its dubious payoff, I can understand how he arrived at that decision.

This means we still have to battle versioning problems. Maybe it's my Stockholm syndrome talking, but it's not like those fights are for naught. Working, sometimes hard, to unify version ranges across a project and make sure there's a set of unique JARs that can support the application actually provides benefits.

Imagine you had no incentive to do that. How many more JARs would your project drag onto the class or module path? How much larger would it get, and how much more complicated would debugging be? No, I think allowing conflicting versions to work out of the box would be a horrible idea.

That said, the fact remains that there are cases where a version conflict stops important work dead in its tracks or makes critical updates impossible without having to update tons of other dependencies at the same time. To that end, it would be nice to have a command-line switch like `java --one-class-loader-per-module` that you could try on a rainy day. Alas, it doesn't exist (yet?).

13.2   Recording version information

As we've just covered in detail, the module system doesn't process version information. Interestingly enough, it *does* allow us to record and access that information. That may seem a little weird at first, but it turns out to be helpful when debugging an application.

Let's first look at how to record version information during compilation and packaging (section 13.2.1) before discussing where you see that information and what benefits it provides (section 13.2.2). Recording and evaluating version information is demonstrated in *ServiceMonitor*'s `feature-versions` branch.

13.2.1   Recording versions while building modules

> **Definition: –module-version**
>
> The `javac` and `jar` commands accept the command line option `--module-version ${version}`. They embed the given version, which can be an arbitrary string, in the module descriptor.
>
> Regardless of whether the option is used, if a module is compiled against a dependency that recorded its version, the compiler will add that information to the module descriptor, too. That means a module descriptor can contain the version of the module itself as well as of all dependencies against which the module was compiled.

The `jar` command overrides the module's version if it was present before. So, if `--module-version` is used on both `jar` and `javac`, only the value given to `jar` matters.

Listing 2.5 showed how to compile and package the *monitor* module, but you don't need to flip back. Updating the `jar` command to record the version is trivial:

```
$ jar --create
    --file mods/monitor.jar
    --module-version 1.0
    --main-class monitor.Monitor
    -C monitor/target/classes .
```

As you can see, it's as simple as slipping in `--module-version 1.0`. Because the script compiles and immediately packages the module, there's no need to also add it to `javac`.

To see whether you succeeded, all you need to do is ask `jar --describe-module` (see section 4.5.2):

```
$ jar --describe-module --file mods/monitor.jar

> monitor@1.0 jar:.../monitor.jar/!module-info.class
> requires java.base mandated
> requires monitor.observer
# truncated requires
> contains monitor
> main-class monitor.Main
```

The version is right there in the first line: `monitor@1.0`. Why don't the dependencies' versions show up, though? In this specific case, I didn't record them, but *java.base* definitely has one, and it doesn't appear, either. Indeed, `--describe-module` doesn't print this information—neither the `jar` nor the `java` variant.

To access the versions of a module's dependencies, you need a different approach. Let's look at where the version information appears and how you can access it.

13.2.2 *Accessing module versions*

The versions recorded during compilation and packaging show up in various places. As you've just seen, `jar --describe-module` and `java --describe-module` both print the module's version.

VERSION INFORMATION IN STACK TRACES

Stack traces are also important locations. If code runs in a module, the module's name is printed for each stack frame together with the package, class, and method names. The good news is that the version is included, too:

```
> Exception in thread "main" java.lang.IllegalArgumentException
>     at monitor@1.0/monitor.Main.outputVersions(Main.java:46)
>     at monitor@1.0/monitor.Main.main(Main.java:24)
```

Not revolutionary, but definitely a nice addition. If your code misbehaves for seemingly mysterious reasons, problems with versions are a possible cause, and seeing them in such a prominent position makes it easier to notice them if they're suspicious.

 ESSENTIAL INFO I'm convinced that version information can be a great help. I strongly recommend that you configure your build tool to record it.

MODULE VERSION INFORMATION IN THE REFLECTION API

Arguably the most interesting place to handle version information is the reflection API. (Going forward, you need to know about `java.lang.ModuleDescriptor`. Check out section 12.3.3 if you haven't already.)

 ESSENTIAL INFO As you can see in listing 12.7 and again in listing 13.1, the class `ModuleDescriptor` has a method `rawVersion()`. It returns an `Optional<String>` that contains the version string exactly as it was passed to `--module-version`, or it's empty if the option wasn't used.

On top of that, there's `version()`, which returns an `Optional<Version>`, where `Version` is an inner class of `ModuleDescriptor` that parses the raw version into a comparable representation. If there's no raw version, or if parsing it failed, `Optional` is empty.

Listing 13.1   Accessing a module's raw and parsed version

```
ModuleDescriptor descriptor = getClass()
    .getModule()
    .getDescriptor();
String raw = descriptor
    .rawVersion()
    .orElse("unknown version");
String parsed = descriptor
    .version()
    .map(Version::toString)
    .orElse("unknown or unparsable version");
```

Returns an Optional<String> that's empty if --module-version wasn't used

Returns an Optional<Version> that's empty if rawVersion() is or if the raw version couldn't be parsed

DEPENDENCY VERSION INFORMATION IN THE REFLECTION API

That settles the module's own version. You still didn't see how to access the versions that were recorded for the dependencies, though. Or did you? Listing 12.8, which shows the output of printing pretty much everything a ModuleDescriptor has to offer, contains this snippet:

```
[] module monitor.persistence @ [] {
    requires [
        hibernate.jpa,
        mandated java.base (@9.0.4),
        monitor.statistics]
    [...]
}
```

See @9.0.4 in there? That's part of the output of Requires::toString. Requires is another inner class of ModuleDescriptor and represents a requires directive in a module descriptor.

ESSENTIAL INFO   For a given module, you can get a Set<Requires> by calling module.getDescriptor().requires(). A Requires instance contains a few pieces of information, most notably the required module's name (method name()) and the raw and parsed versions that were compiled against (methods rawCompiledVersion() and compiledVersion(), respectively). The following listing shows code that gets a module's descriptor and then streams over the recorded requires directives.

Listing 13.2   Printing dependency version information

```
module
    .getDescriptor()
    .requires().stream()
    .map(requires -> String.format("\t-> %s @ %s",
            requires.name(),
            requires.rawCompiledVersion().orElse("unknown")))
    .forEach(System.out::println);
```

This code produces output like the following:

```
> monitor @ 1.0
>     -> monitor.persistence @ 1.0
```

```
>       -> monitor.statistics @ 1.0
>       -> java.base @ 9.0.4
# more dependencies truncated
```

And here they are: the versions of the dependencies against which *monitor* was compiled. Neat.

It's fairly straightforward to write a class that uses this information to compare the version against which a module was compiled with the dependency's actual version at run time. It could warn about potential problems, for example, if the actual version is lower, or log all this information for later analysis in case of problems.

13.3 *Running multiple versions of a module in separate layers*

Section 13.1.1 states that the module system has no native support for running multiple versions of the same module. But as I already hinted, that doesn't mean it's impossible. Here's how people did it before the JPMS arrived on the scene:

- Build tools can *shade* dependencies into a JAR, which means all the class files from the dependency are copied into the target JAR, but under a new package name. References to those classes are also updated to use the new class names. This way, the standalone Guava JAR with package `com.google.collect` is no longer needed, because its code was moved to `org.library.com.google.collection`. If each project does that, different versions of Guava can never conflict.
- Some projects use OSGi or another module system that supports multiple versions out of the box.
- Other projects create their own class-loader hierarchy to keep the different instances from conflicting. (This is also what OSGi does.)

Each of these approaches has its own disadvantages, which I'm not going to go into here. If you absolutely *have* to run multiple versions of the same JAR, you need to find a solution that makes the effort worth it for your project.

 ESSENTIAL INFO That said, the module system repackages an existing solution, and that's what I focus on in this section. But although you *can* run multiple versions side by side like this, you'll see that it's somewhat complex, so you may not *want* to. This is less of a recipe and more of a demonstration case.

13.3.1 *Why you need a starter to spin up additional layers*

As discussed in section 12.4, the module system introduces the concept of *layers*, which essentially pair a module graph with class loaders. There's always at least one layer in play: the boot layer, which the module system creates at launch time based on the module path content.

Beyond that, layers can be created at run time and need a set of modules as input: for example, from a directory in the filesystem, which they then evaluate according to the readability rules to guarantee a reliable configuration. Because a layer can't be created if it contains multiple versions of the same module, the only way to make that work is to arrange them in different layers.

ESSENTIAL INFO   That means instead of launching your application, you need to launch a starter that expects the following input:

- Paths to all application modules
- The module's relations, which must consider their different version

It then needs to create a graph of layers-to-be, which are arranged so that each layer contains each module only once, although different layers can contain the same module in multiple versions. The final step is to fill in the actual layers and then call the `main` method.

Developing such a starter as a general solution is a considerable engineering task and effectively means reimplementing existing third-party module systems. Creating a starter that solves only your specific problem is easier, though, so we'll focus on that. By the end of the section, you'll know how to create a simple layer structure that allows you to run two versions of the same module.

13.3.2 Spinning up layers for your application, Apache Twill, and Cassandra Java Driver

Say you depend on two projects, Apache Twill and Cassandra Java Driver. They have conflicting version requirements for Guava: Apache Twill breaks on any version after 13, and Cassandra Java Driver breaks on any version before 16. You've tried everything you can think of to work around the problem, but nothing has worked, and now you want to solve the problem by using layers.

That means the base layer contains only your application starter. The starter needs to create one layer with Guava 13 and another with Guava 16—they need to reference the base layer to have access to platform modules. Then comes a fourth layer with the rest of the application and dependencies—it references both of the other layers the starter creates, so it can look up dependencies in them.

It won't work exactly like that, though. As soon as Apache Twill's dependencies are resolved, the module system will see Guava twice: once in each of the layers the top layer references. But a module isn't allowed to read another module more than once because it would be unclear which version classes should be loaded from.

So you pull these two modules and all of their dependencies into their respective Guava layer, and you're good to go. Almost. Both modules expose their dependency on Guava, so your code needs to see Guava, too; and if that code is in the top layer, you end up in the same situation as before, with the module system complaining about code seeing two versions of Guava.

If you pull your Twill- and Cassandra-specific code into the respective layers, too, you get the layer graph shown in figure 13.3. Now let's create those layers. To do so, assume that you've organized the application modules into three directories:

- `mods/twill` contains Apache Twill with all its dependencies and your modules that directly interact with it (in this example, *app.twill*).

- `mods/cassandra` contains Cassandra Java Driver with all its dependencies and your modules that directly interact with it (in this example, *app.cassandra*).
- `mods/app` contains the rest of your application and its dependencies (in this example, the main module is *app*).

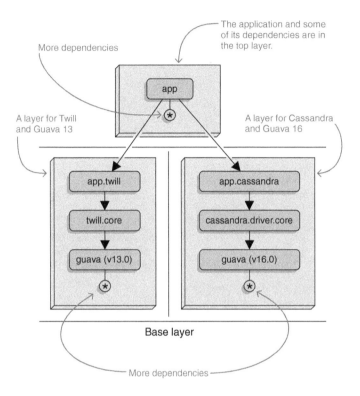

Figure 13.3   Apache Twill and Cassandra Java Driver have conflicting dependencies on Guava. To launch an application using both libraries, each library, including its respective dependencies, has to go in its own layer. Above them is the layer containing the rest of the application, and below the base layer.

Your starter can then proceed as shown in listing 13.3:

1 Create a layer with the modules in `mods/cassandra`. Be careful to pick the right module as root for the resolution process. Pick the boot layer as the parent layer.
2 Do the same for modules in `mods/twill`.
3 Create a layer with the modules in `mods/app`, and pick your main module as root. Use the other two layers as parents; this way, your application's dependency on the modules in `mods/cassandra` and `mods/twill` can be resolved.
4 When that's all finished, get the class loader for the upper layer's main module, and call its `main` method.

Listing 13.3   Starter that creates layers for Cassandra, Apache Twill, and the app

```
public static void main(String[] args)
        throws ReflectiveOperationException {
    createApplicationLayers()
        .findLoader("app")
        .loadClass("app.Main")
        .getMethod("main", String[].class)
        .invoke(null, (Object) new String[0]);
}
```

◄— After the application layers are created, loads the app's Main class and invokes the main method

```
private static ModuleLayer createApplicationLayers() {
    Path mods = Paths.get("mods");

    ModuleLayer cassandra = createLayer(
        List.of(ModuleLayer.boot()),
        mods.resolve("cassandra"),
        "app.cassandra");
    ModuleLayer twill = createLayer(
        List.of(ModuleLayer.boot()),
        mods.resolve("twill"),
        "app.twill");

    return createLayer(
        List.of(cassandra, twill),
        mods.resolve("app"),
        "app");
}
```

◄— Creates one layer for Twill and another for Cassandra, each containing the entire project plus your modules that interact with it

◄— The main application layer starts resolving in your main module and has the twill and cassandra layers as parents.

```
private static ModuleLayer createLayer(
        List<ModuleLayer> parentLayers,
        Path modulePath,
        String rootModule) {
    Configuration configuration = createConfiguration(
        parentLayers,
        modulePath,
        rootModule);
    return ModuleLayer
        .defineModulesWithOneLoader(
            configuration,
            parentLayers,
            ClassLoader.getSystemClassLoader())
        .layer();
}
```

◄— The createLayer and createConfiguration methods are similar to those in section 12.4.3. The main difference is that they specify the root modules for the resolution (not necessary before, because you relied on service binding—here you don't).

```
private static Configuration createConfiguration( #D
        List<ModuleLayer> parentLayers,
        Path modulePath,
        String rootModule) {
    List<Configuration> configurations = parentLayers.stream()
        .map(ModuleLayer::configuration)
        .collect(toList());
    return Configuration.resolveAndBind(
        ModuleFinder.of(),
        configurations,
```

```
        ModuleFinder.of(modulePath),
        List.of(rootModule)
    );
}
```

And that's it! I admit it takes some time, and you'll likely have to fiddle a while to make it work (I had to), but if it's the only solution you're left with, it's worth giving it a try.

Summary

- The `javac` and `jar` commands let you record a module's versions with the `--module-version ${version}` option. It embeds the given version in the module declaration, where it can be read with command-like tools (for example, `jar --describe-module`) and the reflection API (`ModuleDescriptor::rawVersion`). Stack traces also show module versions.

- If a module knows its own version and another module is compiled against it, the compiler will record the version in the second module's descriptor. This information is only available on the `Requires` instances returned by `ModuleDescriptor::requires`.

- The module system doesn't act on version information in any way. Instead of trying to select a specific version for a module if the module path contains several, it quits with an error message. This keeps the expensive version-selection algorithm out of the JVM and the Java standard.

- The module system has no out-of-the-box support for running multiple versions of the same module. The underlying reason is the class-loading mechanism, which assumes that each class loader knows at most one class for any given name. If you need to run multiple versions, you need more than one class loader.

- OSGi does exactly that by creating a single class loader for every JAR. Creating a similarly general solution is a challenging task, but a simpler variant, customized to your exact problem, is feasible. To run multiple versions of the same module, create layers and associated class loaders so that conflicting modules are separated.

Customizing runtime images with jlink

This chapter covers

- Creating images with selected content
- Generating native application launchers
- Judging the security, performance, and stability of images
- Generating and optimizing images

One of the key motivations for discussing modularity in Java has always been what is now called the Internet of Things (IoT). This is true for OSGi, Java's most widely used third-party module system, which set out in 1999 to improve the development of embedded Java applications, and also for Project Jigsaw, which developed the JPMS and aimed to make the platform more scalable by allowing the creation of very small runtimes with just the code an (embedded) application needs.

This is where `jlink` comes in. It's a Java command-line tool (in your JDK's `bin` folder) that you can use to select a number of platform modules and link them into a runtime image. Such a runtime image acts exactly like a JRE but contains only the modules you picked and the dependencies they need to function (as indicated by `requires` directives). During that linking phase, `jlink` can be used to further optimize image size and improve VM performance, particularly startup time.

In the years since Jigsaw's inception, a lot has changed, though. For one thing, disk space in embedded devices no longer comes at such a premium. At the same time, we've seen the rise of virtualization, most prominently with Docker, where container size is once again a concern (although not a major one). The rise of containerization also brought pressure to ease and automate deployment, which today is done a few orders of magnitude more frequently.

And `jlink` helps here, as well. It doesn't stop at linking platform modules—it can also create application images, which include app code as well as library and framework modules. This allows your build process to produce an entirely self-contained deployment unit that consists of your entire app with exactly the platform modules it needs, optimized for image size and performance as you see fit, and launchable with a simple call to a native script.

If you're more of a desktop application developer and your eyes glazed over when I mentioned IoT and Docker, that last bit should have made you sit up. With `jlink`, it's exceedingly easy to ship a single Zip file that users can launch without any further setup. And if you've been using `javapackager`, you'll be delighted to hear that it now calls `jlink` internally, giving you access to all its features (although I won't go into the integration—the `javapackager` documentation has you covered).

So let's start linking! We'll begin with creating runtime images from platform modules (section 14.1) and use that opportunity to explore the linking process in more detail, look into the generated image, and discuss how to pick the right modules. Next up is including application modules and creating custom launchers (section 14.2) before we discuss generating images across operating systems (section 14.3). We close with looking at size and performance optimizations (section 14.4).

To code along, take a look at the `feature-jlink` branch in the *ServiceMonitor* repo. By the end of this chapter you'll know how to create optimized runtime images, possibly including an entire application, for various OSs. That allows you to build a single deployment unit that works out of the box on your servers or your customers' machines.

14.1 Creating custom runtime images

One big use case for `jlink` is the creation of Java runtime images that contain only the modules you need for your application. The result is a tailored JRE that contains exactly the modules your code needs, but nothing else. You can then use the `java` binary in that image to launch your application just like any other JRE.

Customizing the runtime has a few advantages: you can save some disk space (smaller image) and maybe network bandwidth (if you deploy remotely), you're safer (fewer classes mean a smaller attack surface), and you even get a JVM that starts a little more quickly (more on that in section 14.4.3).

> **NOTE** With that said, `jlink` "just" links bytecode—it doesn't compile it to machine code. You might have heard that beginning with version 9, Java experiments with ahead-of-time (AOT) compilation, but `jlink` has nothing to do with that. To learn about AOT in Java, have a look at Java Enhancement Proposal 295 (http://openjdk.java.net/jeps/295).

ESSENTIAL INFO   You can create runtime images tailored to your application as soon as it runs on Java 9+. You don't need to modularize it first.

To understand how to create runtime images with `jlink`, we'll start with the simplest image (section 14.1.1) and then examine the result (section 14.1.2). Next, we'll discuss the special treatment of services (section 14.1.3) before topping off the section with a real-life use case: how to create an image dedicated to running a given application (section 14.1.4).

14.1.1   Getting started with jlink

> **Definition: Required info for jlink**
>
> To create an image, `jlink` needs *three pieces of information*, each specified with a command-line option:
>
> - Where to find the available modules (specified with `--module-path`)
> - Which modules to use (specified with `--add-modules`)
> - Folder in which to create the image (specified with `--output`)

The simplest possible runtime image contains only the base module. The following listing shows how to create it with `jlink`.

Listing 14.1   Creating a runtime image containing only the base module

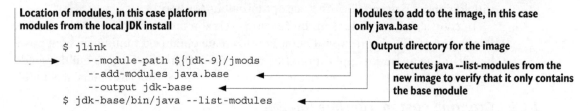

Location of modules, in this case platform modules from the local JDK install

Modules to add to the image, in this case only java.base

Output directory for the image

Executes java --list-modules from the new image to verify that it only contains the base module

```
$ jlink
    --module-path ${jdk-9}/jmods
    --add-modules java.base
    --output jdk-base
$ jdk-base/bin/java --list-modules

> java.base
```

It may seem a little odd that you need to tell `jlink` where to find platform modules. This isn't necessary for `javac` and `java`, so why wouldn't `jlink` know where to find them? The answer is cross-platform linking, which section 14.3 discusses.

> **NOTE**   From Java 10 on, it's no longer necessary to place platform modules on the module path. If it doesn't contain any, `jlink` implicitly loads them from the directory `$JAVA_HOME/jmods`.

 ESSENTIAL INFO   Regardless of whether platform modules are referenced explicitly or implicitly, it's recommended that you only load them from the exact same JVM version as the `jlink` binary. For example, if `jlink` has version 9.0.4, make sure it loads platform modules from JDK 9.0.4.

Given the three command-line options, `jlink` resolves modules as described in section 3.4.1: the module path content becomes the universe of observable modules, and the modules given to `--add-modules` become the root for the resolution process. But `jlink` has a few peculiarities:

 ESSENTIAL INFO By default, services (see chapter 10) aren't bound. Section 14.1.3 explains why and explores what to do about it.

- Optional dependencies with `requires static` (see section 11.2) aren't resolved. They need to be added manually.
- Automatic modules aren't allowed. This becomes important in section 14.2 and is explained there in more detail.

Unless any problems like missing or duplicate modules are encountered, the resolved modules (root modules plus transitive dependencies) end up in the new runtime image. Let's take a look at it.

14.1.2 Image content and structure

First things first: this image takes up only about 45 MB (on Linux; I hear it's even less on Windows) compared to the 263 MB of a full JRE—and that's without the space optimizations discussed in section 14.4.2. So what does the image look like? Section 6.3 introduces the new JDK/JRE directory structure; and as figure 14.1 shows, runtime images created with `jlink` are similar. This isn't a coincidence: the JDKs and JREs you can download are composed with `jlink`.

Note that `jlink` fuses the included modules into `lib/modules` and then omits the `jmods` folder from the final image. This is in line with how the JRE was generated, which also doesn't contain `jmods`. The raw JMOD files are only included in the JDK so that `jlink` can process them: optimizing modules into `lib/modules` is a one-way operation, and `jlink` can't generate further images from the optimized image.

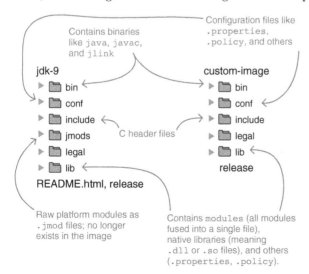

Figure 14.1 Comparison between the directory structure of the JDK (left) and a custom runtime image created with `jlink` (right). The similarity isn't accidental—the JDK is created with `jlink`.

Looking into `bin`, you may wonder which executables you can expect to find there. Turns out that `jlink` is clever and will only generate executables for which the required modules were included in the image. The compiler executable `javac`, for example, comes with the *jdk.compiler* module and won't be available if that module isn't included.

14.1.3 *Including services in runtime images*

If you take a careful look at listing 14.1, it should seem a little odd that the image only contains *java.base*. In section 10.1.2, you learned that the base module uses a lot of services provided by other platform modules and that when services are bound during module resolution, all those providers are pulled into the module graph. So why don't they end up in the image, too?

> **Definition: –bind-services**
>
> To enable the creation of small, deliberately assembled runtime images, `jlink`, by default, performs no service binding when creating an image. Instead, service-provider modules have to be included manually by listing them in `--add-modules`. Alternatively, the *option* `--bind-services` *can be used to include all modules that provide a service* that's used by another resolved module.

Let's pick charsets like ISO-8859-1, UTF-8, or UTF-16 as an example. The base module knows the ones you need on a daily basis, but there's a specific platform module that contains a few other ones: *jdk.charsets*. The base module and *jdk.charsets* are decoupled via services. Here are the relevant parts of their module declarations:

```
module java.base {
    uses java.nio.charset.spi.CharsetProvider;
}

module jdk.charsets {
    provides java.nio.charset.spi.CharsetProvider
        with sun.nio.cs.ext.ExtendedCharsets
}
```

When the JPMS resolves modules during a regular launch, service binding will pull in *jdk.charsets*, so its charsets haven't always been available in a standard JRE. But when you're creating a runtime image with `jlink`, that doesn't happen, so by default images won't contain the *charsets* module. If your project depends on it, you may find out the hard way.

Once you've determined that you depend on a module that's decoupled from the rest via services, you can include it in the image with `--add-modules`:

```
$ jlink
    --module-path ${jdk-9}/jmods
    --add-modules java.base,jdk.charsets
    --output jdk-charsets
$ jdk-charsets/bin/java --list-modules

> java.base
> jdk.charsets
```

> **Definition: –suggest-providers**
>
> Manually identifying service-provider modules can be cumbersome. Fortunately, `jlink` can help you out. The *option* `--suggest-providers` `${service}` *lists all observable modules that provide an implementation of* `${service}`, which must be specified with its fully qualified name.

Say you've created a minimal runtime image containing only *java.base*, and, when executing your application, you run into problems due to missing charsets. You track the problem to *java.base* using `java.nio.charset.spi.CharsetProvider` and now wonder which modules provide that service. Here comes `--suggest-providers` to save the day:

```
$ jlink
    --module-path ${jdk-9}/jmods
    --suggest-providers java.nio.charset.spi.CharsetProvider

> Suggested providers:
>   jdk.charsets
>       provides java.nio.charset.spi.CharsetProvider
>       used by java.base
```

Another good example for silently missing modules is locales. All except the English locales are contained in *jdk.localedata*, which makes them available to the base module via a service. Consider the following code:

```
String half = NumberFormat
    .getInstance(new Locale("fi", "FI"))
    .format(0.5);
System.out.println(half);
```

What does it print? `Locale("fi", "FI")` creates the locale for Finland, and the Finnish format uses floating-point numbers with a comma, so the result will be `0,5`—at least, when the Finnish locale is available. If you execute this code on a runtime image that doesn't contain *jdk.localedata*, like the one you created earlier, you'll get `0.5`, because Java silently falls back to the default locale. Yes, this isn't an error, but silent misbehavior.

As before, the solution is to explicitly include the decoupled module, in this case *jdk.localedata*. But it adds a whopping 16 MB to the image size because it contains a lot of locale data. Fortunately, as you'll see in section 14.4.2, `jlink` can help reduce that additional load.

> **NOTE** When your application's behavior differs between running on generic downloaded Java and on a customized runtime image, you should think about services. Could the misbehavior stem from some feature of the JVM not being available? Maybe its module was decoupled via services and is now missing in your runtime image.

These are some of the services the base module uses and other platform modules provide that you may implicitly depend on:

- Charsets from *jdk.charsets*
- Locales from *jdk.localedata*
- Zip file system from *jdk.zipfs*
- Security providers from *java.naming, java.security.jgss, java.security.sasl, java.smartcardio, java.xml.crypto, jdk.crypto.cryptoki, jdk.crypto.*ec, *jdk.deploy*, and *jdk.security.jgss*

As an alternative to manually identifying and adding individual modules, you can use the blanket `--bind-services`:

```
$ jlink
    --module-path ${jdk-9}/jmods
    --add-modules java.base
    --bind-services
    --output jdk-base-services
$ jdk-base-services/bin/java --list-modules

> java.base
> java.compiler
> java.datatransfer
> java.desktop
# truncated about three dozen more modules
```

This binds all modules that provide a service to the base module, though, and thus creates a fairly large image—this one is about 150 MB without optimizations. You should carefully consider whether that's the way to go.

14.1.4 *Right-sizing images with jlink and jdeps*

So far, you've only created small images consisting of *java.base* and a few other modules. But what about a real-life use case; how would you determine which platform modules you need to sustain a large application? Can't use trial and error, right?

The answer is JDeps. For a thorough introduction, see appendix D—here it suffices to know that the following incantation will list all platform modules your application depends on:

```
jdeps -summary -recursive --class-path 'jars/*' jars/app.jar
```

For this to work, the `jars` folder must contain all JARs required to run your application (your code as well as dependencies; your build tool will help with that), and `jars/app.jar` must contain the `main` method you use to launch. The result will show lots of dependencies between artifacts, but you'll also see lines that show dependencies on platform modules. The following example lists platform modules used by Hibernate Core 5.2.12 and its dependencies:

```
antlr-2.7.7.jar -> java.base
classmate-1.3.0.jar -> java.base
dom4j-1.6.1.jar -> java.base
dom4j-1.6.1.jar -> java.xml
hibernate-commons-annotations-5.0.1.Final.jar -> java.base
```

```
hibernate-commons-annotations-5.0.1.Final.jar -> java.desktop
hibernate-core-5.2.12.Final.jar -> java.base
hibernate-core-5.2.12.Final.jar -> java.desktop
hibernate-core-5.2.12.Final.jar -> java.instrument
hibernate-core-5.2.12.Final.jar -> java.management
hibernate-core-5.2.12.Final.jar -> java.naming
hibernate-core-5.2.12.Final.jar -> java.sql
hibernate-core-5.2.12.Final.jar -> java.xml
hibernate-core-5.2.12.Final.jar -> java.xml.bind
hibernate-jpa-2.1-api-1.0.0.Final.jar -> java.base
hibernate-jpa-2.1-api-1.0.0.Final.jar -> java.instrument
hibernate-jpa-2.1-api-1.0.0.Final.jar -> java.sql
jandex-2.0.3.Final.jar -> java.base
javassist-3.22.0-GA.jar -> java.base
javassist-3.22.0-GA.jar -> jdk.unsupported
jboss-logging-3.3.0.Final.jar -> java.base
jboss-logging-3.3.0.Final.jar -> java.logging
slf4j-api-1.7.13.jar -> java.base
```

All you need to do now is extract those lines, remove the ... -> part, and throw away duplicates. For Linux users:

```
jdeps -summary -recursive --class-path 'jars/*' jars/app.jar
    | grep '\-> java.\|\-> jdk.'
    | sed 's/^.*-> //'
    | sort -u
```

You end up with a neat list of platform modules that your application depends on. Feed those into `jlink --add-modules`, and you'll get the smallest possible runtime image that supports your app (see figure 14.2).

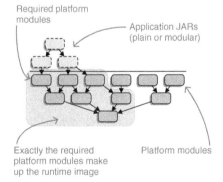

Required platform modules

Application JARs (plain or modular)

Exactly the required platform modules make up the runtime image

Platform modules

Figure 14.2   Given the application JARs (top) and their dependencies on platform modules (bottom), `jlink` can create a runtime image with just the required platform modules.

 ESSENTIAL INFO   There are a few caveats, though:

- JDeps occasionally reports ... -> not found, which means some transitive dependency wasn't on the class path. Make sure the class path for JDeps contains the exact artifacts you use when running your app.
- JDeps can't analyze reflection, so if your code or your dependencies' code interacts with JDK classes by reflection only, JDeps won't pick up on that. That could lead to a required module not making it into the image.

- As discussed in section 14.1.3, `jlink` doesn't bind services by default, but your application may implicitly rely on some JDK-internal providers being present.
- Consider adding the *java.instrument* module, which is needed to support Java agents. It's a must if your production environment uses agents to observe running applications; but even if it doesn't, you may find yourself in a bind where a Java agent is the best way to analyze your problem. Also, it's only about 150 KB, so it's hardly a big deal.

NOTE   Once you've created a runtime image for your application, I recommend you run unit tests and integration tests on it. This will give you confidence that you really included all required modules.

Next up is including application modules in your image—but to do that, your app and its dependencies need to be fully modularized. If that isn't the case, and you're looking for more immediately applicable knowledge, skip to section 14.3 for generating runtime images across OSs or section 14.4 for optimizing your image.

14.2   *Creating self-contained application images*

So far, you've created runtime images *supporting* an application, but there's no reason to stop there. `jlink` makes it easy to create images *containing* the entire application. That means you'll end up with an image containing application modules (the app itself plus its dependencies) and the platform modules needed to support it. You can even create a nice launcher, so you can run your application with `bin/my-app`! Distributing your application just became a lot easier.

> **Definition: Application images**
>
> Even though it's not an official term, I call images including application modules *application images* (as opposed to runtime images) to clearly delineate what I'm talking about. After all, the outcome is more akin to an application than to a general runtime.

ESSENTIAL INFO   Note that `jlink` only operates on explicit modules, so an application depending on automatic modules (see section 8.3) can't be linked into an image. If you absolutely *have* to create an image with your app, have a look at section 9.3.3 on how to make third-party JARs modular, or use a tool like ModiTect (https://github.com/moditect/moditect) that does it for you.

This limitation to explicit modules has no technical grounds—it was a design decision. An application image is supposed to be self-contained, but if it depends on automatic modules, which don't express dependencies, the JPMS can't verify that and a `NoClassDefFoundError` may ensue. Not exactly the reliability the module system strives for.

With the prerequisites settled, let's get going. You'll first create an image that includes application modules (section 14.2.1) before making your life easier by creating launchers (section 14.2.2). Finally, we'll ponder the security, performance, and stability of application images (section 14.2.3).

14.2.1 *Including application modules in images*

All you need to do to create an application image is add application modules to the jlink module path and pick one or more of them as root. The resulting image will contain all required modules (but no others; see figure 14.3) and can be launched with bin/java --module ${initial-module}.

As an example, let's once again turn to the *ServiceMonitor* application. Because it depends on the automatic modules *spark.core* and *hibernate.jpa* and jlink doesn't support those, I had to cut out that functionality. This leaves us with seven modules, all of which depend only on *java.base*:

- *monitor*
- *monitor.observer*
- *monitor.observer.alpha*
- *monitor.observer.beta*
- *monitor.persistence*
- *monitor.rest*
- *monitor.statistics*

I put these into a folder named mods and created an image, as shown in listing 14.2. Unfortunately, I forgot that the observer implementations *monitor.observer.alpha* and *monitor.observer.beta* are decoupled from the rest of the application via services and that they aren't bound by default (see chapter 10 on services and section 14.1.3 on how jlink handles them). Hence I had to try again in listing 14.3 by adding them explicitly. Alternatively, I could have used --bind-services, but I didn't like how large the image became when all JDK-internal service providers were included.

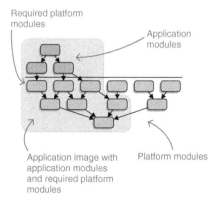

Required platform modules

Application modules

Application image with application modules and required platform modules

Platform modules

Figure 14.3 **Given the application modules (top) and their dependencies on platform modules (bottom), jlink can create a runtime image with just the required modules, including both application and platform code.**

Listing 14.2   Creating an application image containing *ServiceMonitor*

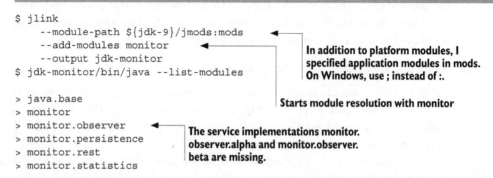

```
$ jlink
    --module-path ${jdk-9}/jmods:mods
    --add-modules monitor
    --output jdk-monitor
$ jdk-monitor/bin/java --list-modules

> java.base
> monitor
> monitor.observer
> monitor.persistence
> monitor.rest
> monitor.statistics
```

In addition to platform modules, I specified application modules in mods. On Windows, use ; instead of :.

Starts module resolution with monitor

The service implementations monitor. observer.alpha and monitor.observer. beta are missing.

Listing 14.3   Creating an application image, this time including services

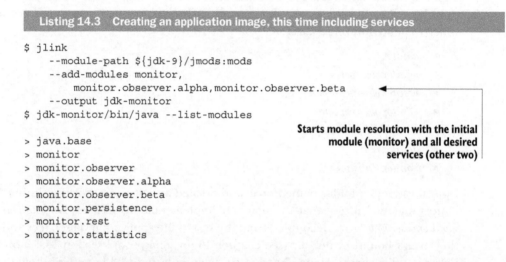

```
$ jlink
    --module-path ${jdk-9}/jmods:mods
    --add-modules monitor,
        monitor.observer.alpha,monitor.observer.beta
    --output jdk-monitor
$ jdk-monitor/bin/java --list-modules

> java.base
> monitor
> monitor.observer
> monitor.observer.alpha
> monitor.observer.beta
> monitor.persistence
> monitor.rest
> monitor.statistics
```

Starts module resolution with the initial module (monitor) and all desired services (other two)

Definition: System modules

Taken together, the platform and application modules that the image contains are known as *system modules*. As you'll see in a minute, it's still possible to add other modules when launching the application.

BEWARE OF RESOLUTION PECULIARITIES!

Remember from section 14.1 that jlink creates a minimal image:

- It doesn't bind services.
- It doesn't include optional dependencies.

ESSENTIAL INFO   Although you'll likely remember to check the presence of your own services, you may forget about your dependencies (that SQL driver implementation, for example) or platform modules (locale data or unusual charsets). The same goes for optional dependencies, which you may want to include but forget that they aren't resolved merely because they're present on the module path (see section 11.2.3). Make sure you really end up with all the modules you need!

The *ServiceMonitor* application uses the Finnish locale to format its output, so it needs to add *jdk.localedata* to the image (see the following listing). This drives up the image size by 16 MB (to 61 MB), but section 14.4.2 shows how to reduce that.

Listing 14.4 Creating the *ServiceMonitor* application image with locale data

```
$ jlink
    --module-path ${jdk-9}/jmods:mods
    --add-modules monitor,
        monitor.observer.alpha,monitor.observer.beta,
        jdk.localedata          ◄
    --output jdk-monitor
```
> The platform module for locales is also added to the image.

USING COMMAND-LINE OPTIONS WHEN LAUNCHING THE APPLICATION

Once you've created the image, you can launch your application as usual with `java --module ${initial-module}`, using the `java` executable in the image's `bin` folder. But because you included your application modules in the image, you don't need to specify a module path—the JPMS will find them inside the image.

After creating the *ServiceMonitor* image in `jdk-monitor`, the application can be launched with a short command:

```
$ jdk-monitor/bin/java --module monitor
```

If you want to, you *can* use the module path, though. In that case, keep in mind that system modules (the ones in the image) will always shadow modules of the same name on the module path—it will be as if those on the module path don't exist. What you can do with the module path is to add *new* modules to the application. These will likely be additional service providers, which allows you to ship an image with your application while still allowing users to easily extend it locally.

Let's say *ServiceMonitor* discovers a new kind of microservice it needs to observe, and the module *monitor.observer.zero* does that. Moreover, the module implements all the right interfaces, and its descriptor declares that it provides `ServiceObserver`. Then, as shown next, you can use the same image from before and add *monitor.observer.zero* via the module path.

Listing 14.5 Launching an application image with an additional service provider

> Places the service provider on the module path

> Instead of really launching the app, looks at the module resolution to see the provider getting picked up (also, to see these options work as with a regular JRE)

```
$ jdk-monitor/bin/java
    --module-path mods/monitor.observer.zero.jar
    --show-module-resolution
    --dry-run
    --module monitor
```

```
> root monitor jrt:/monitor
# truncated monitor's dependencies
> monitor binds monitor.observer.alpha jrt:/monitor.observer.alpha
> monitor binds monitor.observer.beta jrt:/monitor.observer.beta
> monitor binds monitor.observer.zero file://...
```

The jrt: string shows that these modules are loaded from inside the image.   **The additional module is loaded from the module path as indicated by file:.**

 ESSENTIAL INFO   If you want to *replace* system modules, you have to place them on the upgrade module path as described in section 6.1.3. In addition to the special case of the module path, all the other `java` options presented throughout this book work exactly the same in custom application images.

14.2.2 *Generating a native launcher for your application*

If creating an image containing your application and everything it needs, but nothing else, is the cake, adding a custom launcher is the icing. A custom launcher is an executable script (shell on Unix-based OSs, batch on Windows) in the image's `bin` folder that's preconfigured to start the JVM with a concrete module and main class.

> **Definition: –launcher**
>
> To create a launcher, use the `--launcher  ${name}=${module}/${main-class}` *option*:
>
> - `${name}` is the filename you pick for the executable.
> - `${module}` is the name of the module to launch with.
> - `${main-class}` is the name of the module's main class.
>
> The latter two are what you'd normally put after `java --module`. And as in that case, if the module defines a main class, you can leave out `/${main-class}`.

As listing 14.6 shows, with `--launcher  run-monitor=monitor`, you can tell `jlink` to create a script `run-monitor` in `bin` that launches the application with the equivalent of `java  --module  monitor`. Because *monitor* declares a main class (`monitor.Main`), there's no reason to specify that with `--launcher`. If you wanted to, it would be `--launcher run-monitor=monitor/monitor.Main`.

> **Listing 14.6   Creating an application image with a launcher (and taking a peek)**

```
$ jlink
    --module-path ${jdk-9}/jmods:mods
    --add-modules monitor,
        monitor.observer.alpha,monitor.observer.beta
    --output jdk-monitor
    --launcher run-monitor=monitor
```

Generates the image as in listing 14.3 ...

... except for adding a launcher called run-monitor that launches the module monitor (which defines the main class)

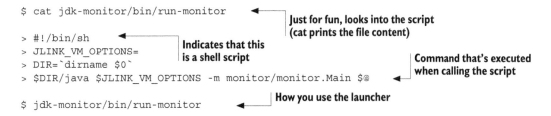

```
$ cat jdk-monitor/bin/run-monitor
```
Just for fun, looks into the script
(cat prints the file content)

```
> #!/bin/sh
```
Indicates that this
is a shell script
```
> JLINK_VM_OPTIONS=
> DIR=`dirname $0`
> $DIR/java $JLINK_VM_OPTIONS -m monitor/monitor.Main $@
```
Command that's executed
when calling the script

```
$ jdk-monitor/bin/run-monitor
```
How you use the launcher

> **NOTE** Did you spot the `JLINK_VM_OPTIONS` in listing 14.6? If there are any command-line options you'd like to specify for your application—for example, tuning the garbage collector—you can put them here.

Using a launcher does have a downside, though: all options you try to apply to the launching JVM will be interpreted as if you'd put them after the `--module` option, making them program arguments instead. That means that when using a launcher, you can't ad hoc configure the module system—for example, to add additional services as discussed earlier.

But I have good news: you aren't forced to use the launcher, and the `java` command is still available. Listing 14.5 works exactly the same if a launcher was created—as long as you don't use it.

14.2.3 Security, performance, and stability

Creating an application image can increase your application's security by minimizing the amount of code available in the JVM and thus reducing the attack surface. As section 14.4.3 discusses, you can also expect small improvements in startup time.

Although that sounds pretty neat, it only fully applies to situations where you have complete control over the application's operation and redeploy regularly. If you ship your image to customers or otherwise have no control over when and how often the image is replaced with a newer one, the tables turn.

> **ESSENTIAL INFO** An image generated with `jlink` isn't built for modifications. It has no auto-update function, and patching it manually isn't a realistic scenario. If users update their system Java, your application image won't be impacted by that. Taken together, it's forever bound to the exact Java version from which you took the platform modules during linking.

The upside is that Java patch updates can't break your application, but the much more serious downside is that your app won't benefit from any security patches or performance improvements the new Java version brings. Let that sink in. If a critical vulnerability is patched in a new Java version, your users will still be exposed until they deploy the new application image that you shipped.

> **NOTE** If you decide to deliver application images, I recommend making this an *additional* delivery mechanism instead of the only one. Let users decide whether they want to deploy an entire image or prefer to run the JARs on their own runtime, over which they have full control and which they can update independently.

14.3   *Generating images across operating systems*

Although the bytecode your application and library JARs contain is independent of any OS, it needs an OS-specific Java Virtual Machine (JVM) to execute them. That's why you download JDKs and runtimes specifically for Linux, macOS, or Windows (for example). It's important to realize that `jlink` operates on the OS-specific plane! Figure 14.4 shows OS-specific pieces.

It's obvious when you think about it: the platform modules `jlink` uses to create an image come from an OS-specific JDK/JRE, so the resulting image is also OS-specific. Thus runtime or application images are always bound to one concrete OS.

Does that mean you have to execute `jlink` on a bunch of different machines to create all the various runtime or application images you need? Fortunately not. As you saw in section 14.1.1, when creating an image, you point `jlink` to the platform modules you want it to include. Here's the thing: those don't have to be for the OS on which you're executing `jlink`!

 ESSENTIAL INFO   If you download and unpack a JDK for a different OS, you can place its `jmods` folder on the module path when running the `jlink` version from your system JDK. The linker will then determine that the image is to be created for that OS and will hence create one that works on it (but, of course, not on another). So given JDKs for all OSs your application supports, you can generate runtime or application images for each of them on the same machine.

I'm running Linux, but say I want to generate an application image for the *Service-Monitor* application that runs on macOS. Conveniently, `jlink` supports such scenarios very well—all you need is a JDK for the target OS.

Turns out the hardest part is to unpack a JDK on an OS it wasn't packaged for. In this case, I have to get into the `*.dmg` file that Oracle distributes for macOS—I won't go into details here, but you can find advice on each of the nontrivial combinations of {`Linux, macOS, Windows`} versus {`rpm/tar.gz, dmg, exe`} with the search engine

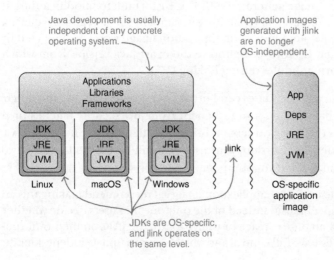

Figure 14.4   **Unlike application, library, and framework JARs (top), application images (right) are OS-specific, like JVMs (bottom).**

of your choice. In the end, I have the macOS JDK in some folder, which I will represent as `${jdk-9-mac-os}`.

Then all I have to do is the same thing as in section 14.2.1, except for replacing my machine's JDK 9 folder (`${jdk-9}`) with the one containing the macOS JDK (`${jdk-9-mac-os}`). This means I'm using the `jlink` executable from my Linux JDK with the `jmods` directory in the macOS JDK:

```
$ jlink
    --module-path ${jdk-9-mac-os}/jmods:mods
    --add-modules monitor,
        monitor.observer.alpha,monitor.observer.beta
    --output jdk-monitor
    --launcher run-monitor=monitor
```

Taking this to my boss should work. (But if it doesn't, I can't even claim that it works on my machine!)

14.4 Using jlink plugins to optimize images

"Make it work, make it right, make it fast," said Kent Beck, creator of extreme programming and author of *Test-Driven Development: By Example* (O'Reilly, 2000). And so, with the nuts and bolts of creating runtime and application images (even across OSs) covered, we'll turn to optimizations. These can considerably reduce image size and slightly increase run-time performance, particularly startup time.

In `jlink`, optimizations are handled by plugins. Hence, it makes sense to first talk about that plugin architecture (section 14.4.1) before making images smaller (section 14.4.2) and faster (section 14.4.3).

14.4.1 Plugins for jlink

A central aspect of `jlink` is its modular design. Beyond the essential steps of determining the correct modules and generating an image for them, `jlink` leaves further processing of the image's content to its plugins. You can see the available plugins with `jlink --list-plugins`, see https://docs.oracle.com/javase/9/tools/jlink.htm for the officially supported ones, or check table 14.1 for a selection (we'll look at each of them in sections 14.4.2 and 14.4.3).

Table 14.1 An alphabetized table of some `jlink` plugins, indicating whether they primarily reduce image size or improve runtime performance

Name	Description	Size	Perf.
class-for-name	Replaces `Class::forName` with static access		✔
compress	Shares string literals, and compresses `lib/modules`	✔	
exclude-files	Excludes files, for example native binaries	✔	

Table 14.1   An alphabetized table of some `jlink` **plugins, indicating whether they primarily reduce image size or improve runtime performance**   *(continued)*

Name	Description	Size	Perf.
exclude-resources	Excludes resources, for example from `META-INF` folders	✔	
generate-jli-classes	Pregenerates method handles		✔
include-locales	Strips all but the specified locales from `jdk.localedata`	✔	
order-resources	Orders resources in `lib/modules`		✔
strip-debug	Removes debug symbols from image bytecode	✔	
system-modules	Prepares the system module graph for quick access		✔

NOTE   The documentation as well as `jlink` itself also lists the *vm* plugin, which lets you pick one of several HotSpot virtual machines (client, server, or minimal) that you want to include in the image. This a theoretical possibility, though, because 64-bit JDKs only ship with the server VM. For most situations, that leaves you with a choice of one.

DEVELOPING PLUGINS FOR JLINK

At the time of book printing, only the supported plugins are available, but that may change in the future when more experimental features are added. The efforts of optimizing images during their creation are still pretty young, and a lot of work is being done here. As a consequence, the plugin API may change in the future and isn't standardized or exported in Java 9+.

That makes developing plugins for `jlink` quite intricate[1] and means you'll have to wait some time before the community really starts contributing plugins. What could those do? First of all, writing `jlink` plugins is a little like writing agents or build-tool plugins—not something that's done during typical application development. It's a specialized task to support specialized libraries, frameworks, and tools.

But let's get back to the question of what community-provided plugins could do. One use case comes from profilers, which currently use agents to inject performance-tracking code into running applications. With a `jlink` plugin, you could do this at link time instead of paying the instrumentation cost while executing your app. If a quick launch matters, that might be a sensible move.

Another use case is enhancing the bytecode of Java Persistence API (JPA) entities. Hibernate, for example, already does that with an agent to track which entities were mutated (so-called *dirty checking*) without having to check every field. Doing it at link

---

[1]   See Gunnar Morling's blog post "Exploring the jlink Plug-in API in Java 9" (http://mng.bz/xJ6B) if you're interested in a walk-through.

time instead of at launch time makes sense, which is why Hibernate already offers plugins for build tools and IDEs that do that during their build process.

As a final example, a really nice, potential `jlink` plugin would be one that indexes annotations at link time and makes that index available at run time. That could considerably reduce startup time for apps scanning the module path for annotated beans and entities. In fact, the plugin tutorial I gave in a footnote does exactly that.

USING JLINK PLUGINS

> ### Definition: Plugin –${name} command-line option
> With the theory out of the way, let's use some of these plugins. But how? It's pretty simple: `jlink` *automatically creates a command-line option* `--${name}` based on each plugin's name. How further parameters are passed depends on the plugin and is described in `jlink --list-plugins`.

Stripping debug symbols is a good way to reduce image size. To do so, create the image with `--strip-debug`:

```
$ jlink
    --module-path ${jdk-9}/jmods
    --add-modules java.base
    --strip-debug
    --output jdk-base-stripped
```

There you go: `lib/modules` just went from 23 MB for just the base module to 18 MB (on Linux).

Ordering the contents of `lib/modules` by putting more important files first can reduce launch time (although I doubt the effect will be noticeable):

```
$ jlink
    --module-path ${jdk-9}/jmods
    --add-modules java.base
    --order-resources=**/module-info.class,/java.base/java/lang/**
    --output jdk-base-ordered
```

This way, module descriptors come first, followed by classes from the `java.lang` package.

Now that you know how to use plugins, it's time to test-drive a few. We'll do that in two sections, the first one focusing on size reductions (section 14.4.2) and the second on performance improvements (section 14.4.3). Because this is an evolving feature and also a rather specialized one, I won't go into full detail—the official `jlink` documentation and `jlink --list-plugins`, although sparse with words, show much more precisely how to use them.

14.4.2 Reducing image size

Let's go through the size-reducing plugins one by one and measure how far they get us. I would have liked to test them on an application image, but *ServiceMonitor* only has about a dozen classes, so that's pointless; and I couldn't find a real application that's freely available and fully modularized, including its dependencies (no automatic modules in images, remember?). Instead, I'll measure the effects on three different runtime images (unmodified size in parentheses):

- *base*—Just *java.base* (45 MB)
- *services*—*java.base* plus all service providers (150 MB)
- *java*—All *java.** and *javafx.** modules, but without service providers (221 MB)

It's interesting that the larger size of *java* compared to *services* doesn't come from the amount of bytecode (lib/modules is a little smaller in *java* than in *services*), but from the native libraries, particularly from the WebKit code bundled for JavaFX's WebView. This will help you understand the plugins' behavior when working to reduce image size. (By the way, I'm doing this on Linux, but proportions should be similar on other OSs.)

COMPRESSING THE IMAGE

> **Definition: compress plugin**
>
> The *compress* plugin aims to reduce the size of lib/modules. It's controlled by the --compress=${value} option, which has three possible values:
>
> - 0—No compression (default)
> - 1—Deduplicate and share string literals (meaning the "text" in String s = "text";)
> - 2—Zip-compress lib/modules
>
> An optional pattern list can be included with --compress=${value}:filter= ${pattern-list}, in which case only files that match the patterns are compressed.

This command creates a compressed runtime image with just the base module:

```
$ jlink
    --module-path ${jdk-9}/jmods
    --add-modules java.base
    --output jdk-base
    --compress=2
```

You obviously don't need to try 0. For 1 and 2, I got the following results:

- *base*—45 MB → 39 MB (1) → 33 MB (2)
- *services*—150 MB → 119 MB (1) → 91 MB (2)
- *java*—221 MB → 189 MB (1) → 164 MB (2)

You can see that the compression rate isn't the same across all images. The *services* image size could be brought down by almost 40%, but the larger *java* image only by 25%. That's because the *compress* plugin only works on lib/modules, but as we discussed, those have almost the same size in both images. Accordingly, the absolute size reduction is similar: about 60 MB for both images, which is more than 50% of the initial size of `lib/modules`.

> **NOTE** Zip-compressing with `--compress=2` will increase startup time—generally speaking, more, the larger the image is. Make sure to measure it if that's important to you.

EXCLUDING FILES AND RESOURCES

> **Definition: exclude-files and exclude-resources plugins**
>
> The plugins *exclude-files* and *exclude-resources* allow the exclusion of files from the final image. The corresponding options `--exclude-files=${pattern-list}` and `--exclude-resources=${pattern-list}` accept a list of patterns against which files that are to be excluded are matched.

As I pointed out when comparing the initial sizes of the *services* and *base* images, it's mainly the native binary for the JavaFX `WebView` that makes *java* larger. On my machine, that's the 73 MB file `lib/libjfxwebkit.so`. Here's how to exclude it with `--exclude-files`:

```
$ jlink
    --module-path ${jdk-9}/jmods
    --add-modules java.base
    --output jdk-base
    --exclude-files=**/libjfxwebkit.so
```

The resulting image is 73 MB smaller. Two caveats:

- This has the same effect as manually deleting the file from the image.
- This makes the *javafx.scene.web* module, which basically contains only the `Web-View`, borderline useless, so it's probably better to just not include that module.

Beyond experimenting and learning, it's bad practice to exclude content that comes with platform modules. Be sure to thoroughly research any decision to do so, because that may impact the JVM's stability.

A much better use of these plugins is to exclude files that your application or dependency JARs contain that you don't need in your application image. These could be documentation, undesired source files, native binaries for OSs you don't care about, configurations, or any of the other myriad things ingenious developers put into their archives. It's also pointless to compare size reductions: you'll save the space the excluded files take up.

EXCLUDING UNNEEDED LOCALES

Locales are something from the platform modules that it *does* make sense to remove. As you discovered in section 14.1.3, the base module can only work with the English locales, whereas the *jdk.localedata* module contains information for all the other locales that Java supports. Unfortunately, these others, taken together, are about 16 MB. That's a little excessive if you need only one or even just a few non-English locales.

> ### Definition: include-locales plugin
>
> Here's where the *include-locales* plugin comes into play. Used as `--include -locales=${langs}`, where `${langs}` is a comma-separated list of BCP 47 language tags (which look like `en-US`, `zh-Hans`, and `fi-FI`), the resulting image will only contain those languages.
>
> This only works if the *jdk.localedata* module makes it into the image, so it doesn't so much *include* additional locales beyond those the base module contains as it *excludes* all other locales from *jdk.localedata*.

Listing 14.4 created an application image for *ServiceMonitor* that includes all of *jdk. localedata* because the app uses the Finnish format for its output. That drove up the image size by 16 MB, which you now know how to push back down. Listing 14.7 uses `--include-locales=fi-FI` to achieve that. The resulting image is marginally larger than the one without *jdk.localedata* (168 KB, to be precise). Success!

Listing 14.7   Creating the *ServiceMonitor* application image with Finnish locale data

```
$ jlink
    --module-path ${jdk-9}/jmods:mods
    --add-modules monitor,
        monitor.observer.alpha,monitor.observer.beta,
        jdk.localedata          ◀
    --output jdk-monitor
    --include-locales=fi-FI
```

All locales except fi-FI (Finnish) are stripped out of jdk.localedata.

The platform module for locales needs to be added to the image—either explicitly (as it is here) or implicitly (by being required or with --bind-services).

How much you can reduce image size by excluding locales depends on how many locales you need. If you deliver an internationalized application to a global audience, you won't be able to save much, but my guess is this isn't the common case. If your app supports only a handful or even a dozen languages, excluding the others will save you almost all of those 16 MB. Whether that's worth the effort is up to you.

STRIPPING DEBUG INFORMATION

When you're debugging Java code in your IDE, you'll usually see nicely formatted, named, and even commented source code. That's because the IDE retrieves the actual sources that belong to that code, ties them to the currently executed bytecode, and conveniently displays them. That's the best-case scenario.

If there are no sources, you may still end up with readable code if, in addition to field and method parameter names (which are always present in bytecode), you see the proper names of variables (which aren't necessarily present). That happens when the decompiled code contains *debug symbols*. This information makes debugging much easier but of course takes up space. And `jlink` allows you to strip out the symbols.

> **Definition: strip-debug plugin**
>
> If the `jlink` plugin *strip-debug* is activated with `--strip-debug`, it will remove all debug symbols from the image's bytecode, thus reducing the size of the `lib/modules` file. This option has no further parameters.

I used `--strip-debug` in section 14.4.1, so I'll spare you the repetition. Let's see how it reduces image sizes:

- *base*—45 MB ⇰ 40 MB
- *services*—150 MB ⇰ 130 MB
- *java*—221 MB ⇰ 200 MB

That's about 10% of the total image size, but remember that this only touches on `lib/modules`, which is reduced by about 20%.

 ESSENTIAL INFO   A word of warning: debugging code without sources and without debug symbols is a hellish task. If you occasionally use remote debugging to connect to a running application and analyze what's going wrong, you won't be happy if you gave away those debug symbols and the few megabytes you saved aren't really important to you. Consider `--strip-debug` carefully!

PUTTING IT ALL TOGETHER

Although excluding files and resources is better left for application modules, the other options work well on pure runtime images. Let's put them all together and try to create the smallest possible images for the three selections of modules. Here's the command for just *java.base*:

```
$ jlink
    --module-path ${jdk-9}/jmods
    --add-modules java.base
    --output jdk-base
    --compress=2
    --strip-debug
```

And here are the results:

- *base*—45 MB ⇰ 31 MB
- *services*—150 MB ⇰ 75 MB (I also removed all locales except `fi-FI`)
- *java*—221 MB ⇰ 155 MB (or 82 MB if you cripple the JavaFX `WebKit`)

Not too bad, eh?

14.4.3 *Improving run-time performance*

As you've seen, there are quite a few ways to reduce an application's or runtime image's size. My guess is, though, that most developers are eagerly awaiting performance improvements, particularly after Spectre and Meltdown have robbed them of some of their CPU cycles.

 ESSENTIAL INFO   Unfortunately, I don't have much good news in this regard: performance optimizations with `jlink` are still in their early stages, and most of the existing or envisioned ones focus on improving startup time, not long-term run-time performance.

One existing plugin, which is turned on by default, is *system-modules*, which precomputes the system module graph and stores it for quick access. This way, the JVM doesn't have to parse and process module declarations, verifying reliable configuration, on every launch.

Another plugin, *class-for-name*, replaces bytecode like `Class.forName("some.Type")` with `some.Type.class`, so the comparatively expensive, reflection-based search for a class by its name can be avoided. We briefly looked at *order-resources*, and there isn't much to add.

The only other performance-related plugin that's currently supported is *generate -jli-classes*. If properly configured, it can move the initialization costs of lambda expressions from run time to link time, but learning how to do that requires a good understanding of method handles, so I won't touch on it here.

And that's all there is regarding performance improvements. I get it if you're disappointed about the lack of big gains in this area, but let me point out that the JVM is already quite optimized. All the low-hanging fruits (and many higher up the tree) have already been picked, and it will take some ingenuity, time, and clever engineering to reach the others. The `jlink` tool is still young, and I'm confident that the JDK development team and the community will make good use of it in due time.

> **Application class-data sharing in Java 10**
>
> Not directly connected to `jlink` is an optimization introduced by Java 10: application class-data sharing.[2] Experiments indicate that it can lead to application launches that are between 10% and 50% quicker. What's interesting is that you can apply this technique *within an application image*, creating an even more-optimized deployment unit.

14.5   *Options for jlink*

For your convenience, table 14.2 lists all the command-line options for `jlink` that this book discusses. More are available in the official documentation at https://docs.oracle .com/javase/9/tools/jlink.htm or with `jlink --help` and `jlink --list-plugins`.

---

2   To learn more, see my blog post "Improve Launch Times on Java 10 with Application Class-Data Sharing," https://blog.codefx.org/java/application-class-data-sharing.

Table 14.2 An alphabetized table of selected `jlink` options, including plugins. The descriptions are based on the documentation, and the references point to the sections in this book that explain in detail how to use the options.

Option	Description	Ref.
`--add-modules`	Defines root modules for inclusion in the image	14.1.1
`--bind-services`	Includes all providers of services that resolved modules use	14.1.3
`--class-for-name`	Replaces `Class::forName` with static access (plugin)	14.4.3
`--compress, -c`	Shares string literals, and compresses `lib/modules` (plugin)	14.4.2
`--exclude-files, --exclude-resources`	Excludes the specified files and resources (plugin)	14.4.2
`--generate-jli-classes`	Pregenerates method handles (plugin)	14.4.3
`--include-locales`	Strips all but the specified locales from *jdk.localedata* (plugin)	14.4.2
`--launcher`	Generates a native launcher script for the application in `bin`	14.2.2
`--list-plugins`	Lists available plugins	14.4.1
`--module-path, -p`	Specifies where to find platform and application modules	14.1.1
`--order-resources`	Orders resources in `lib/modules` (plugin)	14.4.1
`--output`	Generates the image in the specified location	14.1.1
`--strip-debug`	Removes debug symbols from image bytecode (plugin)	14.4.2
`--suggest-providers`	Lists observable providers for the specified services	14.1.3

Summary

- The command-line tool `jlink` creates runtime images from selected platform modules (use `jdeps` to determine which ones an application needs). To benefit from that, the application needs to run on Java 9+, but it doesn't have to be modularized.
- Once the application and its dependencies have been fully modularized (without the use of automatic modules), `jlink` can create application images with it, including the app's modules.
- All calls to `jlink` need to specify the following:
  - Where to find modules (including platform modules), with `--module-path`
  - The root modules for resolution, with `--add-modules`
  - The output directory for the resulting image, with `--output`

- Be aware of how `jlink` resolves modules:
  - Services aren't bound by default.
  - Optional dependencies with `requires static` aren't resolved.
  - Automatic modules aren't allowed.
  - Make sure to add required service providers or optional dependencies individually with `--add-modules` or bind all providers with `--bind-services`.
- Watch out for platform services that you may implicitly depend on without realizing it. Some candidates are charsets (*jdk.charsets*), locales (*jdk.localedata*), the Zip file system (*jdk.zipfs*), and security providers (various modules).
- The runtime image generated by `jlink`
  - Is bound to the OS for which the platform modules chosen with `--module -path` were built
  - Has the same directory structure as the JDK and JRE
  - Fuses platform and application modules (collectively known as system modules) into `lib/modules`
  - Contains only the binaries (in `bin`) for which the required modules were included
- To launch an application image, use either `bin/java --module ${initial-module}` (no module path required, because system modules are automatically resolved) or the launcher created with `--launcher ${name}=${module}/${main-class}`.
- With application images, the module path can be used to add additional modules (particularly those providing services). Modules on the module path with the same name as system modules are ignored.
- Carefully evaluate the security, performance, and stability implications of delivering application images when you aren't able to readily replace them with newer versions.
- Various `jlink` options, which activate plugins, offer ways to reduce image size (for example, `--compress`, `--exclude-files`, `--exclude-resource`, `--include -locales`, and `--strip-debug`) or improve performance (mostly startup time; `--class-for-name`, `--generate-jli-classes`, and `--order-resources`). More can be expected in the future; this area is still in its early phases.
- The `jlink` plugin API isn't yet standardized to ease its evolution in that early phase, which makes it more difficult to develop and use third-party plugins.

Putting the pieces together

This chapter covers

- A bells-and-whistles version of *ServiceMonitor*
- Whether to use modules
- What an ideal module might look like
- Keeping module declarations clean
- Comparing the module system to build tools, OSGi, and microservices

Now that we've covered pretty much everything there is to know about the module system, it's time to wrap things up. In this final chapter, I want to connect the dots and give a few pieces of advice for creating awesome modular applications.

The first step is to show you an example of how the various features discussed throughout the book can come together by applying most of them to the *Service-Monitor* application (section 15.1). Then I'll take a deep dive into a number of more general concerns that will help you decide whether to even create modules, what to aim for when doing so, and how to carefully evolve your module declarations so they stay squeaky clean (section 15.2). I'll close with a review of the technology landscape surrounding the module system (section 15.3) and my vision for Java's modular eco-system (section 15.4).

15.1 Adding bells and whistles to ServiceMonitor

Chapter 2 showed the anatomy of the *ServiceMonitor* application. In section 2.2, you created simple modules that only used plain `requires` and `exports` directives. Since then, we've not only discussed those in detail but also explored the module system's more-advanced features. We've looked at each of them individually, but now I want to put them all together.

To enjoy the *ServiceMonitor* application in all its glory, check out the repository's `features-combined` branch. The following listing contains the declarations for all the modules in *ServiceMonitor*.

Listing 15.1   *ServiceMonitor*, using advanced features presented throughout the book

monitor.observer.utils is geared toward observer implementations, so it's only exported to (some of) them (see section 15.1.2).

The consumer (monitor) and implementations (for example, monitor.observer.alpha) of the observer API are decoupled via services (see section 15.1.3).

```
module monitor.observer {
    exports monitor.observer;
    exports monitor.observer.utils
        to monitor.observer.alpha, monitor.observer.beta;
}

module monitor.observer.alpha {
    requires monitor.observer;
    provides monitor.observer.ServiceObserverFactory
        with monitor.observer.alpha.AlphaServiceObserverFactory;
}

// [...]
```

monitor.observer.beta and monitor.observer.gamma aren't shown here; they look just like monitor.observer.alpha.

```
module monitor.statistics {
    requires transitive monitor.observer;
    requires static stats.fancy;
    exports monitor.statistics;
}
```

Some modules expose types from another module in their API and are unusable without that module, so they imply its readability (see section 15.1.1).

```
module stats.fancy {
    exports stats.fancy;
}
```

stats.fancy isn't present in each deployment, and monitor.statistics reflects that by marking its dependency on that module as optional (see section 15.1.1).

```
module monitor.persistence {
    requires transitive monitor.statistics;
    requires hibernate.jpa;
    exports monitor.persistence;
    opens monitor.persistence.entity;
}
```

Some modules expose types from another module in their API and are unusable without that module, so they imply its readability (see section 15.1.1).

monitor.persistence opens the package containing its persistence entities for reflection (see section 15.1.2).

Neither the Hibernate nor the Spark version that ServiceMonitor uses is modularized, so hibernate.jpa and spark.core are automatic modules (see section 15.1.5).

```
module monitor.rest {
    requires transitive monitor.statistics;
    requires spark.core;
    exports monitor.rest;
}

module monitor {
    requires monitor.observer;
    requires monitor.statistics;
    requires monitor.persistence;
    requires monitor.rest;
    uses monitor.observer.ServiceObserverFactory;
}
```

Some modules expose types from another module in their API and are unusable without that module, so they imply its readability (see section 15.1.1).

The consumer (monitor) and implementations (for example, monitor.observer.alpha) of the observer API are decoupled via services (see section 15.1.3).

Neither the Hibernate nor the Spark version that ServiceMonitor uses is modularized, so hibernate.jpa and spark.core are automatic modules (see section 15.1.5).

If you compare this listing to listing 2.2 or look at figure 15.1, you can see that the fundamental structure of *ServiceMonitor* has stayed pretty much the same. But looking closer, you can see a number of improvements. Let's go over them one by one.

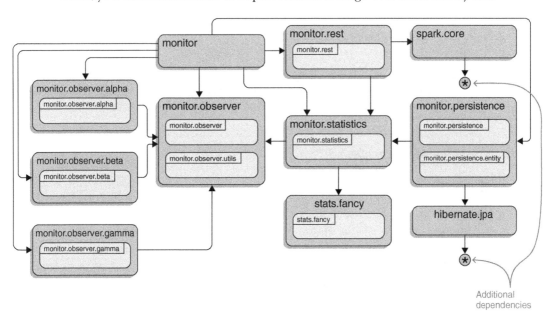

Figure 15.1a Comparison of module graphs for the *ServiceMonitor* application depending on feature use. The first variant only uses plain `exports` and `requires` directives (a), whereas the second makes full use of refined dependencies and exports as well as services (b). (The basic variant has been extended to include the same modules and packages as the advanced one.)

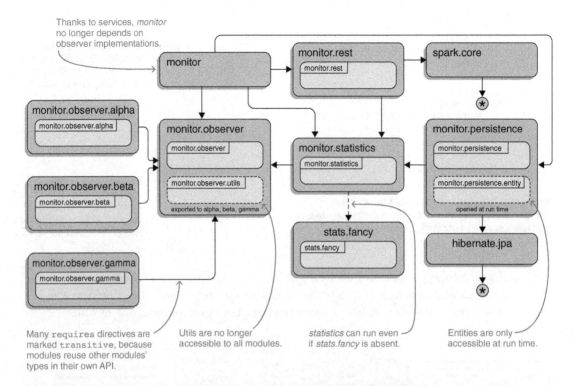

Figure 15.1b   Comparison of module graphs for the *ServiceMonitor* application depending on feature use. The first variant only uses plain `exports` and `requires` directives (a), whereas the second makes full use of refined dependencies and exports as well as services (b). (The basic variant has been extended to include the same modules and packages as the advanced one.)

15.1.1 *Diversified dependencies*

One change that's easy to spot are the `requires transitive` and `requires optional` directives. Although plain `requires` directives are the right choice in most cases, a significant portion of dependencies are a little more complicated.

The most obvious case is optional dependencies, where a module uses types from another module and hence needs to be compiled against it, but the dependency may still be absent at run time. This is exactly the case for *monitor.statistics* and *stats.fancy*, so the dependency is established with a `requires static` directive.

The module system will then enforce the presence of *stats.fancy* when compiling *monitor.statistics* (which makes sense, because otherwise compilation would fail) and will add a reads edge from *monitor.statistics* to *stats.fancy* if the latter made it into the module graph (which also makes sense, because otherwise *monitor.statistics* couldn't access types from *stats.fancy*). But *stats.fancy* may not make it into the module graph, in which case *monitor.statistics* has to handle its absence.

> **Listing 15.2** `Checking` **whether the optional dependency** *stats.fancy* **is present**

```
private static boolean checkFancyStats() {
    boolean isFancyAvailable = isModulePresent("stats.fancy");
    String message = "Module 'stats.fancy' is"
            + (isFancyAvailable ? " " : " not ")
            + "available.";
    System.out.println(message);
    return isFancyAvailable;
}

private static boolean isModulePresent(String moduleName) {
    return Statistician.class
        .getModule()
        .getLayer()
        .findModule(moduleName)
        .isPresent();
}
```

Optional dependencies are discussed in detail in section 11.2.

The other case is a little less obvious than optional dependencies, but no less common—maybe even more so. The module *monitor.rest*, for example, has this method in its public API:

```
public static MonitorServer create(Supplier<Statistics> statistics) {
    return new MonitorServer(statistics);
}
```

But `Statistics` comes from *monitor.statistics*, so any module using *rest* needs to read *statistics* or it can't access `Statistics` and thus can't create a `MonitorServer`. In other words, *rest* is useless to modules that don't also read *statistics*. In the *ServiceMonitor* application, this happens surprisingly often: every module that requires at least one other module and exports a package ends up being in that situation.

That's considerably more frequent than out in the wild and only happens that often because the modules are so small that almost all of their code is public API—it would be surprising if they *didn't* constantly expose their dependencies' types in their own APIs. So although this occurs more rarely in practice, you can still expect to see it on a daily basis—in the JDK, roughly 20% of the dependencies are exposed.

To not keep users guessing about which other modules they need to require explicitly, which is cumbersome and bloats module declarations, the module system offers `requires transitive`. Because *rest* requires `transitive` *statistics*, any module reading *rest* also reads *statistics*, and thus users of *rest* are spared the guesswork. Implied readability is discussed in detail in section 11.1.

15.1.2 *Reduced visibility*

Another change from the application's original versions in section 2.2 is that its modules work harder to reduce their API surface. The updated modules use considerably fewer plain `exports` directives:

- Thanks to services, the observers no longer have to export their implementations.

- By using qualified exports, the package `monitor.observer.utils` in *monitor.observer* is only accessible to a selected set of modules.
- *monitor.persistence* opens its entity package instead of exporting it, thus only making it available at run time.

These changes reduce the amount of code that's readily accessible for any random module, which means developers can change more code inside a module without having to worry about the effects on downstream consumers. Reducing the API surface this way is a boon for the maintainability of frameworks and libraries, but large applications with many modules can also benefit. Section 11.3 introduces qualified exports, and section 12.2 explores open packages.

15.1.3   *Decoupled with services*

The only structural change of the module graph (compared to section 2.2) is that *monitor* no longer directly depends on the observer implementations. Instead, it only depends on the module providing the API, *monitor.observer*, and it uses `Service-ObserverFactory` as a service. All three implementing modules provide that service with their specific implementations, and the module system connects the two sides.

This is much more than just an aesthetic improvement. Thanks to services, it's possible to configure aspects of the application's behavior—which kinds of services it can observe—at launch time. New implementations can be added and obsolete ones can be removed by adding or removing modules that provide that service—no changes of *monitor* are required, and hence the same artifacts can be used without having to rebuild them. To learn all about services, check out chapter 10.

15.1.4   *Loads code at run time with layers*

Although services allow us to define the application's behavior at launch time, we even went one step further. It isn't visible in the module declarations, but by enabling the *monitor* module to create new layers, we made it possible for the application to start observing services at run time for which it didn't even have the `ServiceObserver` implementation when it launched. On demand, *monitor* will create a new module graph and, together with a new class loader, load additional classes and update its list of observers.

> **Listing 15.3   Creating a new layer with the graph created for modules on those paths**

```
private static ModuleLayer createLayer(Path[] modulePaths) {
    Configuration configuration = createConfiguration(modulePaths);
    ClassLoader thisLoader = getThisLoader();
    return getThisLayer()
        .defineModulesWithOneLoader(configuration, thisLoader);
}

private static Configuration createConfiguration(Path[] modulePaths) {
    return getThisLayer()
        .configuration()
        .resolveAndBind(
```

```
        ModuleFinder.of(),
        ModuleFinder.of(modulePaths),
        Collections.emptyList()
    );
}
```

Such behavior is particularly interesting for applications that aren't frequently redeployed and where restarts are inconvenient. Complex desktop applications come to mind, but a web backend that runs on the customer's premises and needs to be comprehensibly configurable could also qualify. For a discussion of what layers are and how to create them, see section 12.4.

15.1.5 Handles dependencies on plain JARs

Another detail that isn't obvious from the module declarations is the modularization status of *ServiceMonitor*'s third-party dependency. Neither the Hibernate version nor the Spark version it uses is modularized yet, and they still ship as plain JARs. Because explicit modules require them, they need to be on the module path, though, where the module system turns plain JARs into automatic modules.

So although *ServiceMonitor* is fully modularized, it can nonetheless depend on non-modularized JARs. Looking at this from the ecosystem-wide perspective, where the JDK modules sit at the bottom and application modules are at the top, this is effectively a top-down modularization effort.

Automatic modules in particular are covered in section 8.3, but all of chapter 8 applies here. If you want to catch up on modularization strategies, check out section 9.2.

15.2 Tips for a modular application

Throughout the book, we've spent a lot of time looking at how to use the module system's various tools to solve individual problems. That's obviously the most important task of a book about the JPMS, but I won't let you go without taking at least a quick inventory of the toolbox as a whole.

The first question is, do you even want to use these tools? Without the metaphor, do you want to create modules (section 15.2.1)? Once that's settled, we'll take a shot at defining what an ideal module might look like (section 15.2.2). We'll then focus on how to keep module declarations in tip-top shape (section 15.2.3) and which changes might break your users' code (section 15.2.4).

15.2.1 Modular or not?

After all you've learned about the module system—its features, its drawbacks, its promises, and its restrictions—maybe you're still asking yourself whether you should modularize your JARs. In the end, only you and your team can answer that for your project, but I can give you my thoughts on the topic.

As I've expressed throughout the book, I'm convinced that the module system offers lots of benefits that are important to libraries, frameworks, and most nontrivial applications. Particularly strong encapsulation, decoupling via services (although that can also be done without modules, albeit less comfortably), and application images stand out to me.

What I like best, though, are the module declarations themselves: they're at all times a true representation of your project's architecture and will provide considerable benefits to every developer and architect who works on those aspects of their system, thus improving its overall maintainability. (I go deeper into this topic in section 15.2.3.)

ESSENTIAL INFO   For those reasons, my default is to start every new project that's developed against Java 9+ with modules. (Theoretically, project-specific reasons could convince me otherwise, but I can't come up with any that might.) If dependencies start making too much trouble when put onto the module path (for example, they could be splitting packages—see section 7.2), it's fairly easy to back out of the module system by using the class path instead of the module path. If you work with modules from the get-go, creating and evolving them will take almost no time, relatively speaking, whereas the improved maintainability will considerably reduce the amount of untangling that needs to be done as the project grows and ages.

   If you're not convinced, give it a try first. Build a demo project with modules or, even better, a small application with real users and requirements. Noncritical, company-internal tools make great guinea pigs.

When it comes to modularizing existing projects, the answer is much more "it depends." The amount of work that needs to be done is much more apparent, but the benefits are just as tangible. In fact, the more work that has to be done, the higher the payoff will usually be. Think about it: which applications are the hardest to modularize? Those that consist of more artifacts, are more entangled, and are less maintainable. But these are also exactly the ones that stand to gain the most from having their structure investigated and worked on. So be careful when somebody assumes the modularization of an existing project has low costs and high benefits (or the other way around).

ESSENTIAL INFO   In the end, a project's expected remaining lifetime can be a tie breaker. The longer the project needs to be maintained, the lower the relative costs and the higher the benefits of modularization. In other words, the longer the remaining lifetime, the more sense modularization makes.

If you're working on a project that has users outside your team, such as a library or a framework, you should also take their needs into account. Even if modularization doesn't seem worth it to you, they stand to benefit considerably from it.

15.2.2 *The ideal module*

Suppose you've made your decision and have gone with modules. What's the ideal module? What are you shooting for when cutting modules and writing declarations? Once again, there's no one-size-fits-all answer, but there are a number of signals you can keep on your radar:

- Module size
- API surface
- Coupling between modules

Before discussing each of these in turn, I want to add that even if you have a notion of what an ideal module is, it's unlikely that you'll churn out one after another. Particularly if you start by modularizing an existing project, chances are you'll create some ugly modules on the way.

If you're working on an application, you don't have to worry about that—you can easily refactor modules as you go. For library and framework developers, life is tougher. As you'll see in section 15.2.4, many refactoring steps can break your users' code, so you have much less freedom to evolve.

Now, let's turn to the three signals you can observe to judge a module's quality: size, surface, and coupling.

KEEP YOUR MODULES SMALL(ISH)

Module declarations give you a great tool to analyze and sculpt the boundaries between modules, but they're relatively blind to what goes on *within* a module. Packages have circular dependencies? All classes and members are public? It's a big ball of mud? That may hurt during development, but your module declarations won't reflect it.

That means the more module declarations you have, the more insight into and control over your code's structure you have (see figure 15.2). On the other hand, there's a one-to-one relationship between modules, JARs, and (typically) build-tool projects, so a higher number of module declarations also means increased maintenance efforts and longer build times. It's clearly a trade-off.

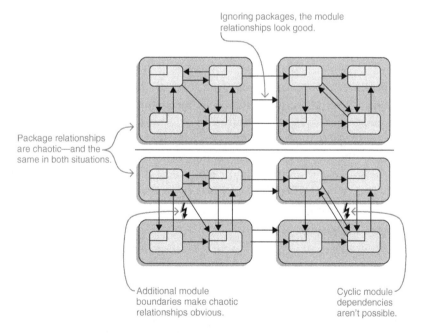

Figure 15.2 These package relationships are arguably somewhat chaotic. With just two modules (top), that doesn't become apparent, though. It's only when trying to create more modules (bottom) that the problems become obvious. The additional module boundaries provided that insight.

Still, as a general rule of thumb, prefer smaller modules over larger ones. Once a module's lines of code get into five digits, you may want to think about cutting it apart; when the module crosses into six digits, I recommend seriously considering it. If it's seven digits, you're likely to have some serious refactoring work ahead of you. (If you have trouble breaking cyclic dependencies between classes, check out section 10.2.5, where you use services to do just that.)

 ESSENTIAL INFO   With all that said, don't trust anybody who tells you there's a correct size for your modules without looking at your project. The only valid answer to "How small or large should modules be?" is, "It depends." Each module should be a cohesive solution to a specific problem. If that problem happens to have a large solution, that's ok—don't start cutting things apart that belong together.

What belongs together? When cutting a cohesive module in two, you're bound to end up with a pretty large API surface between the pieces—which brings us to the next aspect we need to discuss.

KEEP THE API SURFACE SMALL

 ESSENTIAL INFO   The strength of modules is that they can keep their internals to themselves. This allows easier refactoring within the module and a more careful evolution of its public API. Given those benefits, a smaller number of plain `exports` directives is generally preferable. The same is true for qualified exports—the fewer, the better.

How do plain and qualified exports compare? Within a project, there isn't much of a difference. When it comes to entangling two modules, it doesn't really matter whether the export was qualified. That said, a qualification at least indicates that an API may not have been designed for general use, which is useful information, particularly in larger projects.

Libraries and frameworks, unlike applications, always have to think about how their exports impact projects depending on them. In this scenario, a qualified export to other modules within the same project is the same as if the package wasn't exported at all, which is definitely a win. In summary, qualified exports still contribute to the API surface: almost as much as regular exports within a project, but considerably less so across project boundaries.

KEEP COUPLING TO A MINIMUM

Pick two random pieces of code—it doesn't matter whether they're methods, classes, or modules. Everything else being equal, the one with fewer dependencies is more maintainable. The reason is simple: the more dependencies it has, the more changes are in a position to break it.

It goes beyond plain dependencies, though: it's more generally a matter of coupling. If a module not only depends on another, but actively uses all of the dozen packages it exports, the two modules are more tightly coupled. This is even truer if qualified exports are part of the mix, because they essentially say, "This isn't a properly supported API, but I'll let you use it anyway."

ESSENTIAL INFO   This goes beyond individual modules. To understand a system, you not only need to understand the parts (here, modules), but also their connections (here, dependencies and coupling). And if you aren't careful, the system can have many more connections than parts (on the order of the number of modules *squared*; see figure 15.3). Loosely coupled parts are hence a critical ingredient to keeping a system as simple as possible.

One good way to decouple modules are services, as explained in chapter 10. Not only do they break the direct dependency between modules, but they also require you to have a single type through which you can access the entire API. If you don't turn that type into a kraken that connects to dozens of other types, this will greatly reduce the coupling between the modules.

ESSENTIAL INFO   A word of warning: services are neat, but they're harder to predict than plain dependencies. You can't easily see how two pieces of code are connected, and you won't get errors when providers are missing. So don't go overboard and put services everywhere.

This should be the litmus test: Can you create a service type with a reasonably small API? Does it look like it might be used or provided by more than just one module on each side?

If you're unsure, have a look around the JDK. The official documentation lists the services a module uses or provides, and you can use your IDE to look at the user's and implementation's code.

LISTEN TO YOUR MODULE DECLARATION

ESSENTIAL INFO   We've just discussed that modules should be small, should have an even smaller API surface, and should be loosely coupled to their surroundings. In the end, these pieces of advice can be boiled down into a deceptively simple formula: keep cohesion high and coupling low. Looking out for module size, number of `exports`, and number of `requires` as well as the strength of each dependency can help you with that.

The right side is more complicated—not because of more elements, but because of more connections.

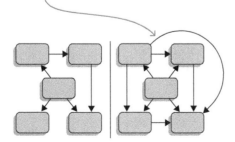

Figure 15.3   Even though both graphs have the same number of nodes, they vary considerably in complexity. The one on the left has about as many edges as nodes, whereas the one on the right has about one edge per pair of nodes. If a new node was added, the left graph would get one or maybe two new edges, whereas the right graph would get about six.

> **NOTE**   Like any set of target numbers, these can be gamed without achieving anything. More important than some numbers is a thought-out overall architecture. Although this book gives you a lot of tools and even some tips for achieving that, it doesn't teach it from the ground up.

Also note that the three signals (size, surface, and cohesion) will often work against one another. As an extreme example, take an application that consists of just one module. It very likely has no API; and with just one artifact, there's not much coupling going on. At the other extreme, a code base where each package is in its own module is full of small modules with small API surfaces. These extremes are, of course, ridiculous, but they illustrate the problem: this is a balancing act.

 ESSENTIAL INFO   In summary, these signals are just, well, signals—you and your team will always have to apply your own good judgment based on the information they provide. But your module declarations can help with that. If they're turning complex and constantly need a lot of changes, they're trying to tell you something. Listen to them.

15.2.3   *Take care of your module declarations*

If you're building a modular project, module declarations are easily the most important `.java` files in your code base. Each of them represents an entire JAR, which will likely consist of dozens, hundreds, or maybe even thousands of source files. Even more than merely representing them, the modular declarations govern how the module interacts with other modules.

So, you should take good care of your module declarations! Here are a few things to look out for:

- Keep declarations clean.
- Comment declarations.
- Review declarations.

Let's take these one by one.

CLEAN MODULE DECLARATIONS

Module declarations are code and should be treated as such, so make sure your code style is applied. Consistent indentation, line length, bracket positions, and so forth—these rules make as much sense for declarations as they do for any other source file.

In addition, I strongly recommend that you structure your module declarations instead of putting directives in random order. All declarations in the JDK as well as in this book have the following order:

1 `requires`, including `static` and `transitive`

2 `exports`

3 `exports to`

4 `opens`

```
5 opens to
6 uses
7 provides
```

The JDK always puts an empty line between blocks to keep them apart—I only do that when there are more than a few directives.

Going further, you could define how to order directives within the same block. Lexicographically is an obvious choice, although for `requires` I first list internal dependencies and then external ones.

> **NOTE** However you decide, if you have a document defining your code style, record the decision there. If you have your IDE, build tool, or code analyzer check such things for you, even better. Try to bring it up to speed so it can automatically check or apply your chosen style.

COMMENTING MODULE DECLARATIONS

Opinions on code documentation, like Javadoc or inline comments, vary wildly, and this isn't the place to make my argument for why it's important. But whatever your team's position on comments is, extend it to module declarations.

If you like the idea that each abstraction has a sentence or a small paragraph explaining its meaning and importance, consider adding a Javadoc comment to each module:

```
/**
 * Aggregates service availability data points into statistics.
 */
module monitor.statistics {
    // ...
}
```

The JDK has such a comment or a longer one on each module.

Even if you don't like writing down *what* a module does, most people agree that documenting *why* a specific decision was made has value. In a module declaration, that could mean adding an inline comment

- To an optional dependency, to explain why the module might be absent
- To a qualified export, to explain why it isn't a public API, but was still made accessible to specific modules
- To an open package, explaining which frameworks are planned to access it

In the JDK, you'll occasionally find comments like this one in *jdk.naming.rmi*:

```
// temporary export until NamingManager.getURLContext uses services
exports com.sun.jndi.url.rmi to java.naming;
```

Generally speaking, my recommendation is this: every time you make a decision that isn't immediately obvious, add a comment. Every time a reviewer asked why some change was made, add a comment. Doing that can help your fellow developers—or yourself two months down the road.

ESSENTIAL INFO   Module declarations present a new opportunity. Never before has it been so easy to properly document the relationships of your project's artifacts in code.

REVIEWING MODULE DECLARATIONS

Module declarations are the central representation of your modular structure, and examining them should be an integral part of any kind of code review you do. Whether it's looking over your changes before a commit or before opening a pull request, wrapping up after a pair-programing session, or during a formal code review—any time you inspect a body of code, pay special attention to `module-info.java`:

- Are added dependencies really necessary? Are they in line with the project's underlying architecture? Should they be exposed with `requires transitive` because their types are used in the module's API?
- If a dependency is optional, is the code prepared to handle its absence at run time? Are there knock-on effects, like missing transitive dependencies that the optional dependency implied readability on?
- Could a new dependency be replaced with a service?
- Are added exports really necessary? Are all public classes in the newly exported packages ready for public use, or do they need to be shuffled around to reduce the API surface?
- If an export is qualified, does that make sense, or is it just a cop-out to get access to an API that was never meant to be public?
- Is the type used as a service designed to be an integral part of the application's infrastructure?
- Were any changes made that can negatively affect downstream consumers that aren't part of the build process? (See section 15.2.4 for more on that.)
- Is the module declaration styled and commented according to the team's requirements?

A diligent review is particularly important because IDEs offer quick fixes that let developers edit declarations at a distance by exporting packages or adding dependencies with a simple command. I appreciate those features, but they make careless editing more likely; thus it's all the more important to ensure that nothing sneaks by unnoticed.

> **NOTE**   If you have a code-review guide, a commit check list, or any other document that helps to keep code quality high, you may want to add an item about module declarations.

Investing time into reviewing module descriptors may sound like a lot of additional work. First, I would argue whether it's *a lot*, particularly compared to the effort that goes into developing and reviewing the rest of the code base. More important, though, I don't see it as an additional task—instead I see it as an opportunity.

ESSENTIAL INFO   Never before has it been so easy to analyze and review your project's structure. And not the white-board sketch that was photographed and uploaded to your team's wiki a few years ago; no, I'm talking about the real deal, the actual relationships between your artifacts. The module declarations show you the naked reality instead of outdated good intentions.

15.2.4 Breaking code by editing module declarations

As with any other source file, changing a module declaration can have unintended and possibly breaking effects on other code. More than that, though, the declaration is the distillation of your module's public API and so has a much higher impact than any random class.

If you develop an application and all consumers of your module are part of the same build process, then breaking changes can't slip by unnoticed. Even for frameworks and libraries, such changes can be detected with thorough integration tests.

ESSENTIAL INFO   Still, it helps to be aware of which changes are more likely to cause problems and which are usually benign. Here's a ranked list of the more troublesome ones:

1 New module name
2 Fewer exported packages
3 Different provided services
4 Editing dependencies

As you'll see, all of these changes can cause compile errors or unexpected run-time behavior in downstream projects. As such, they should always be considered breaking changes, so if you use semantic versioning, a major version bump is in order. This doesn't mean making other changes in your module declarations can't also cause problems, but they're much less likely; so, let's focus on these four.

IMPACT OF A NEW MODULE NAME

Changing a module's name will immediately break all modules that depend on it—they will need to be updated and rebuilt. That's the least of the problems it can cause, though.

Much more dangerous is the modular diamond of death (see section 3.2.2) it may create when some project transitively depends on your module twice: once with the old name and once with the new name. That project will have a hard time including your new version in its build and may well have to resort to eschewing the update just because of the changed name.

Be aware of this, and try to minimize renames. You may still have to do it occasionally, in which case you can try to mitigate the effects by creating an aggregator module with the old name (explained in section 11.1.5).

IMPACT OF EXPORTING FEWER PACKAGES

It should be obvious why "unexporting" packages causes problems: any module that uses types in these packages will fail to access them at compile time and run time. If you want to go this route, you should first deprecate those packages and types to give your users time to move away from them before they're removed.

This only fully applies to plain `exports` directives:

- Qualified exports usually only export to other modules you control, which are likely part of your build and thus updated at the same time.
- Open packages are usually geared toward a specific framework or piece of code that's intended to reflect over them. That code is rarely part of your users' modules, so they won't be impacted by closing the package.

Generally speaking, I wouldn't consider removing qualified exports or opened packages a breaking change. Specific scenarios may go against that rule of thumb, though, so watch out for them and think things through when making such a change.

IMPACT OF ADDING AND REMOVING SERVICES

With services, the situation is a little less clear-cut. As described in section 10.3.1, service consumers should always be prepared to handle the absence of service providers; similarly, they shouldn't break when an additional provider is suddenly returned. But that only really covers that applications shouldn't crash because the service loader returned the wrong number of providers.

It's still conceivable, maybe even likely, that an application misbehaves because a service was there in one version and isn't in another. And because service binding happens across all modules, this may even impact code that doesn't directly depend on you.

IMPACT OF EDITING DEPENDENCIES

The last point on the list, dependencies in all their forms, is also a gray area. Let's start with `requires transitive`. Section 11.1.4 explains that users should only rely on a dependency you let them read if they use it in the direct vicinity of your module. Assuming you stopped exposing the dependency's types and your users updated their code, removing `transitive` from the `exports` directive shouldn't impact them.

On the other hand, they may not know about or heed that recommendation, so keeping them from reading that dependency still requires them to update and rebuild their code. Hence I'd still consider it a breaking change.

It's also possible to come up with scenarios where removing or even adding other dependencies can cause problems, even though that shouldn't be observable from outside your module:

- Adding or removing plain `requires` directives changes optional dependency resolution and service binding.
- Making a dependency optional (or going the other way) can also change which modules make it into the module graph.

So although `requires` and `requires static` can change the module graph and thus impact modules that are totally unrelated to you, this isn't a common case. By default, I wouldn't consider such changes to be breaking.

> **NOTE** Although all that may sound awful and complex, it isn't any more so than when you're editing classes that are part of a public API. You just don't have an intuition yet for how changes to the module declaration impact other projects. It will come over time.

15.3 The technology landscape

After I first introduced the module system in section 1.4, I thought you might have a few questions about how it relates to the rest of the ecosystem. As you may recall, they went like this:

- Don't Maven, Gradle, and others already manage dependencies?
- What about OSGi? Why not just use that?
- Isn't a module system overkill in times where everybody writes microservices?

I'll answer these in a minute, but first I want to introduce you to what Java 9+ has to offer beyond the module system. These benefits come as a package, after all, and if you're skeptical about one, maybe the benefits of the other can sway you.

15.3.1 Maven, Gradle, and other build tools

The Java ecosystem is in the lucky position to have a few powerful, battle-tested build tools like Maven and Gradle. They're not perfect, of course, but they've been building Java projects for more than 10 years, so they clearly have something going for them.

As the name implies, a build tool's main job is to build a project, which includes compiling, testing, packaging, and distributing it. Although the module system touches on a lot of these steps and requires some changes in the tools, it doesn't add any capabilities to the platform that make it compete with them in this area. So when it comes to *building* a project, the relation between the Java platform and its build tools remains much the same.

> ### Build tools on Java 9+
>
> I can't speak for all build tools, but Maven and Gradle have already been updated to work properly with Java 9+ and the module system. The changes are largely internal, and creating modular JARs instead of plain JARs requires nothing more than adding a `module-info.java` to your source folder. They take it from there and mostly just do the right thing.
>
> For details on how your build tool of choice interacts with the module system or other new Java features (like multi-release JARs—see appendix E), look at its documentation. One thing I want to mention explicitly is that you'll likely have to add some command-line options when migrating to Java 9+, so you may want to brush up on how to do that.

If you want to learn more about Gradle, check out Manning's very hands-on *Gradle in Action* (Benjamin Muschko, 2014, www.manning.com/books/gradle-in-action). Unfortunately, I can't recommend any book on Maven that I've had the chance to at least flip through.

DEPENDENCY MANAGEMENT

Build systems usually perform another task, and now Java 9+ performs it, too: dependency management. As section 3.2 discusses, reliable configuration aims at making sure dependencies are present and unambiguous, so that the application becomes more stable—Maven or Gradle will do the same for you. Does that mean the module system replaces build tools? Or is it too late to the game, and these features are useless? On the surface, it seems as though the module system duplicates the build tools' functionality; but when you look closer, you can see that the overlap is small.

First, the module system has no way to uniquely identify or locate artifacts. Most notable is that it has no concept of versions, which means given a few different versions of the same artifact, it can't pick the right one. This situation will result in an error precisely because it's ambiguous.

And although many projects will choose a module name that has the chance to be unique (like reversing a domain name the project is associated with), there is no instance like Maven Central to ensure that, which makes the module name insufficient for uniquely identifying a dependency. Speaking of remote repositories like Maven Central, the module system has no capabilities to connect to them. So although both the module system and build tools manage dependencies, the former performs on a level that's too abstract to replace the latter.

Build systems do have a considerable shortcoming, though: they ensure that dependencies are present during compilation and can even deliver them to your doorstep, but they don't manage the application's launch. If the tool is unaware of an indirectly required dependency (due to use of Maven's `provided` or Gradle's `compileOnly`), or a library gets lost on the way from build to launch, you'll only find out at run time, most likely by a crashing application. The module system, on the other hand, manages direct and transitive dependencies not only at compile time but also at run time, ensuring reliable configuration across all phases. It's also better equipped to detect ambiguities like duplicate artifacts or artifacts containing the same types. So even when you zoom in on dependency management, both technologies are different; the only overlap is that both list dependencies in some form.

ENCAPSULATION, SERVICES, AND LINKING

Moving away from dependency management, we quickly find features of the module system that build tools can't compete with. Most notable is strong encapsulation (see section 3.3), which enables libraries to hide implementation details from other code at compile time and run time—something Maven or Gradle can't even dream of promising. This strictness will take a while to get used to, but in the long run, the JDK, frameworks, libraries, and even large applications will benefit from clearly distinguishing supported and internal APIs and making sure the latter aren't accidentally relied on. In my opinion, strong encapsulation alone is worth the move to the module system.

Looking over the more-advanced features, two particularly interesting ones stand out as being beyond the build tools' reach. First, the module system can operate as a service registry in the *service locator pattern*, allowing you to decouple artifacts and to implement applications that make it easy to use plugins (see chapter 10). Second is the ability to link desired modules into a self-contained runtime image, giving you the opportunity to make deployments slimmer and easier (see chapter 14).

In summary, except for a small overlap in dependency management, build tools and the module system don't compete but should instead be seen as complementary. Figure 15.4 shows this relationship.

15.3.2 *OSGi*

The Open Service Gateway initiative (OSGi) is shorthand for both an organization (the OSGi Alliance) and the specification it creates. It's also somewhat imprecisely applied to the different implementations of that specification, which is how I use it in this section.

OSGi is a module system and service platform on top of the Java Virtual Machine that shares parts of its feature set with the JPMS. If you know a few things about OSGi or have been using it, you may wonder how it compares to Java's new module system, and maybe whether it's replaced by it. But you may also wonder why the latter was even developed—couldn't Java just use OSGi?

NOTE This section may be a little tough if you only know OSGi by hearsay— that's not a problem, because this isn't required reading. If you still want to follow along, start by imagining that OSGi is similar to the module system. The rest of this section will then shine light on some of the important differences.

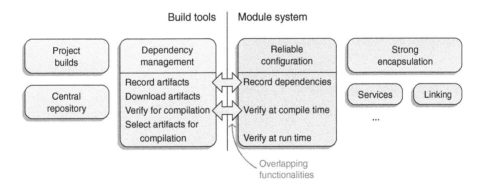

Figure 15.4   Build tools (left) and the module system (right) have very different feature sets. The only similarities are that both record dependencies (build tools by globally unique identifiers plus versions; the JPMS just by module names) and can verify them for compilation. Their handling of dependencies is very different, and beyond that they have virtually nothing in common.

I'm not an OSGi expert, but during my research I paged through Manning's *OSGi in Depth* and liked it (Alexandre de Castro Alves, 2011, www.manning.com/books/osgi-in-depth). Consider turning to it if you need more than the Java Platform Module System can offer you.

WHY DOESN'T THE JDK USE OSGI?

Why doesn't the JDK use OSGi? The technical answer to this question comes down to the way OSGi implements its feature set. It heavily leans on class loaders, which we briefly discussed in sections 1.2 and 1.3.4, and of which OSGi creates its own implementations. It uses one class loader per bundle (modules are called *bundles* in OSGi) and in this way controls, for example, which classes a bundle can see (to implement encapsulation) or what happens when a bundle is unloaded (which OSGi allows—more on that later).

What may seem like a technical detail has far-reaching consequences. Before the JPMS, Java placed no limitations on the use of class loaders, and using the reflection API to access classes by name was common practice.

If the JPMS required a specific class-loader architecture, Java 9+ would drastically break the JDK, many existing libraries and frameworks, and critical application code. Java 9+ still poses migration challenges, but incompatibly changing the class-loader API would be even more disruptive and not replace these challenges but come on top of them. As a consequence, the JPMS operates below class loaders, as shown in figure 15.5.

Another consequence of using class loaders for module isolation is that although OSGi uses them to reduce the *visibility* of classes, they can't reduce *accessibility*. What do I mean by that? Say a bundle *lib* contains a type `Feature` from a package that isn't exported. Then OSGi makes sure code in another bundle *app* can't "see" `Feature`, meaning, for example, that `Class.forName("org.lib.Feature")` will throw a `ClassNotFoundException`. (`Feature` isn't visible.)

But now assume *lib* has an API that returns a `Feature` as an `Object`, in which case *app* can get an instance of the class. Then *app* can call `featureObject.getClass().newInstance()` and create a new `Feature` instance. (`Feature` is accessible.)

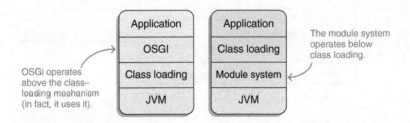

Figure 15.5   OSGi (left) is built on top of the JVM, which forced it to use existing functionality, mainly the class-loading infrastructure, to implement its feature set. The module system (right), on the other hand, was implemented within the JVM and operates below class loading, keeping systems built on top of it working as before.

As discussed in section 3.3, the JPMS wants to ensure strong encapsulation, and what OSGi has to offer isn't strong enough. If you create a situation like earlier, with two JPMS modules *app* and *lib* and a type `Feature` that *lib* contains but doesn't export, *app* can successfully get a class instance with `Class.forName("org.lib.Feature")` (it's visible) but can't call `newInstance()` on it (it isn't accessible). Table 15.1 juxtaposes the differences of OSGi and JPMS.

Table 15.1   OSGI's visibility and JPMS's accessibility limitations

	OSGi	JPMS
Limits visibility (`Class::forName` fails)	✔	✘
Limits accessibility (`Class::newInstance` fails)	✘	✔

CAN THE JPMS REPLACE OSGI?

Can the JPMS replace OSGi? No.

The JPMS was primarily developed to modularize the JDK. It covers all the modularity basics—some of them, like encapsulation, arguably better than OSGi—but OSGi has a lot of features the JPMS doesn't need and thus doesn't have.

To name a few, with OSGi, due to its class-loader strategy, you can have the same fully qualified type in several bundles. This also makes it possible to run different versions of the same bundle at the same time. In that vein, with OSGi, exports and imports can be versioned, letting bundles express what version they are and which versions their dependencies should be. If the same bundle is required in two different versions, OSGi can make that work.

Another interesting difference is that in OSGi, a bundle usually expresses dependencies on packages instead of bundles. Although both are possible, the former is the default. This makes dependencies more robust with regard to replacing or refactoring bundles, because it doesn't matter where a package comes from. (In the JPMS, on the other hand, a package must be in one of the required modules, so moving a package into another module or exchanging one module for another with the same API will cause problems.)

A big feature set of OSGi revolves around dynamic behavior, where its roots as an Internet of Things service gateway clearly show and where the implementation via class loaders enables powerful capabilities. OSGi allows bundles to appear, disappear, and even be updated at run time, exposing an API that lets dependencies react accordingly. This is great for applications running across multiple devices but can also come in handy for single-server systems that want to reduce downtime to a minimum.

The bottom line is that if your project is already using OSGi, chances are high that you're relying on features the JPMS doesn't have. In that case, there's no reason to switch to Java's native module system.

DOES OSGI OBVIATE THE JPMS?

Does OSGi obviate the JPMS? No.

Although what I just presented sounds a lot like OSGi is better than the JPMS for every use case, OSGi has never seen wide adoption. It has carved out a niche and is successful in it, but it has never become a default technology (unlike IDEs, build tools, and logging, to name a few examples).

The main reason for that lack of wide adoption is complexity. Whether it's perceived or real, whether it's inherent to modularity or accidental to OSGi, is secondary to the fact that the majority of developers see OSGi's complexity as a reason not to use it by default.

The JPMS is in a different position. First, its reduced feature set (particularly, no version support, and dependencies on modules, not packages) makes it less complex. In addition, it benefits from being built into the JDK. All Java developers are exposed to the JPMS to some degree, and more senior developers in particular will explore how it can help them with their projects. This more intense use will also spur good tool integration.

So if a team already has the skills and tools and is already running on top of the JPMS, why not go all the way and modularize the entire application? This step builds on existing knowledge, incurs less additional complexity, and requires no new tools, while giving a lot of benefits.

In the end, even OSGi stands to profit from the JPMS, because Java 9+ will put modularity on the map much as Java 8 did with functional programming. Both releases are exposing mainstream Java developers to new ideas and are teaching them an entirely new skill set. At some point, when a project stands to benefit from functional programming or more powerful modularity, its developers climb enough of the learning curve to evaluate and maybe use "the real thing."

ARE JPMS AND OSGI COMPATIBLE?

Are JPMS and OSGi compatible? In a sense, yes. Applications developed with OSGi can run on top of Java 9+ just as they did on earlier versions. (To be more precise, they will run in the *unnamed module*, which section 8.2 explains in detail.) OSGi incurs no migration efforts, but the application code faces the same challenges as other code bases.

In another sense, the verdict isn't in yet. Whether OSGi will allow us to map bundles to JPMS modules is still an open question. For now, OSGi uses no capabilities of the JPMS and continues to implement its features itself. It's also not clear whether adapting OSGi to the JPMS would be worth the considerable engineering cost.

15.3.3 Microservices

The relationship between the module system and microservices architecture has two very different aspects:

- Are microservices and the module system in competition? How do they compare?
- Does the module system concern you if you go with microservices?

We'll look at both in this section.

If you're not familiar with the microservices architecture, you can safely skip this section. If you want to learn more, there are tons of great microservice books out there. To back up my claims, I skimmed Manning's *Microservices in Action* and can recommend it (Morgan Bruce and Paulo A. Pereira, 2018, www.manning.com/books/microservices-in-action).

MICROSERVICES VS. THE JPMS

In general, it's fair to say that the module system's benefits have a larger effect, the bigger the project is. So when everybody is talking about microservices, isn't a module system for large applications the proverbial lipstick on a pig? The answer depends on how many projects will end up being structured as microservices, and that is, of course, a huge discussion in itself.

Some believe microservices are the future and sooner or later all projects will start out that way—it's all microservices! If you're in that camp, you may still implement your services in Java 9+, and the module system will affect you, but, of course, much less than it affects monolithic projects. We'll discuss that in the next section.

Others have a more cautious opinion. Like all architecture styles, microservices have both advantages and disadvantages, and a trade-off must be made between them with the project's requirements in mind. Microservices shine particularly brightly in rather complex projects that have to sustain high loads, where their ability to scale is almost unrivaled.

This scalability is paid for with operational complexity, though, because running a multitude of services requires much more knowledge and infrastructure than putting a handful of instances of the same service behind a load balancer. Another drawback is that getting service boundaries wrong, which is more likely the less the team knows about the domain, is more expensive to fix in microservices than in a monolith.

The critical observation is that the price for the complexity (Martin Fowler calls it the *microservices premium*) must always be paid, but the benefits are only reaped once a project is large enough. This factor has convinced many developers and architects that most projects should start as a monolith and move toward splitting off services, maybe eventually ending in microservices, once circumstances require it.

Martin Fowler, for examples, relates the following opinions of his colleagues (in https://martinfowler.com/bliki/MonolithFirst.html; emphasis mine):

> *You shouldn't start a new project with microservices, even if you're sure your application will be big enough to make it worthwhile. [...] The logical way is to design a monolith carefully, paying attention to modularity within the software, both at the API boundaries and how the data is stored. Do this well, and it's a relatively simple matter to make the shift to microservices.*

By now, the emphasized phrases should be familiar: careful design, modularity, boundaries—these are all properties that the module system promotes (see section 1.5). In a microservice architecture, service dependencies should be clear (cue reliable configuration) and ideally decoupled (service loader API); furthermore, all requests must go through public APIs (strong encapsulation). Carefully using the module system can lay the groundwork for a successful migration to microservices if and when the time for that comes. Figure 15.6 shows the importance of this careful design.

Notwithstanding the module system's focus on larger projects, even small services can benefit from embracing modules.

MICROSERVICES WITH THE JPMS

If your project went with microservices and you're implementing some of them on top of Java 9+ because you want to benefit from improved security and performance, you'll necessarily interact with the module system because it's operating within the JVM that's running your code. One consequence is that the potentially breaking changes discussed in chapters 6 and 7 still apply to the services in question and need to be mended. It's also likely that most of your dependencies will be turned into modules over time, but as section 8.1.3 describes, that doesn't force you to package *your* artifacts as modules.

If you decide to keep all JARs on the class path, strong encapsulation isn't enforced between them. So within that set of JARs, access to internal APIs as well as reflection, for example from frameworks into your code, will continue to work. In this scenario, your exposure to the module system is limited to the changes it had on the JDK.

The other route you could take would be to use your services and dependencies as modules, at which point you'd be fully integrated into the module system. Of its various benefits, the most relevant may end up being the scalable platform briefly described in section 1.5.5 and thoroughly explored in chapter 14, which allows you to use `jlink`.

With `jlink`, you can create a small runtime image with just the right set of platform modules to support your application, *including your modules*, which can cut image size by up to 80%. Furthermore, when linking the required modules together, `jlink` can analyze the bytecode with the knowledge that it sees the entire application and can thus apply more aggressive optimizations, leading to even smaller image sizes and slightly

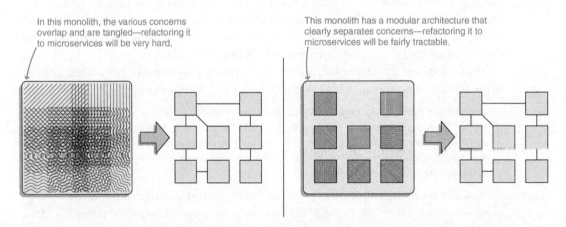

Figure 15.6 Given two hypothetical migrations of a monolithic application to microservices, would you rather start with a sizable square of mud (left) or a properly modularized code base (right)?

improved performance. You also get other benefits: for example, being sure you only use your dependencies' public APIs.

15.4 Thoughts on a modular ecosystem

Java 9+ is a massive release. Although lacking in new language features, it packs a lot of powerful improvements and additions. But all of those improvements are eclipsed by the Java Platform Module System. It's easily both the most anticipated and the most contentious feature of Java 9+, not least because of the migration challenges it causes.

Despite the sometimes-rocky start on the way to the modular future, well-known libraries and frameworks were quick to support Java 9+, and since then there's been no sign of that trend slowing down. What about older, less-well-supported projects? Although some may find new maintainers, even if just to get them to work on a current Java release, the long tail of Java projects may thin out.

That will surely disgruntle some developers whose code bases depend on such projects. That's understandable—nobody likes having to change working code without apparent benefit. At the same time, the exodus of some incumbents will give other projects the chance to sweep up their users. And who knows? Maybe they'll see a benefit from switching after all.

Once the big wave of upgrading to Java 9+ is behind us and projects start raising their baseline to Java 9+, you'll begin to see more and more modular JARs being publicly available. Thanks to the module system's support for incremental and decentralized modularization, this process requires comparatively little coordination between projects. It also gives you the opportunity to start modularizing your project right now.

To what end? Unlike more flashy features like lambda expressions and streams in Java 8 or local variable type inference in Java 10, the module system's effect on your code base will be subtle. You won't be able to look at a few lines of code and be content with its beauty. You won't notice suddenly that you're having more fun when coding.

No, the module system's benefits are on the other end of the spectrum. You'll catch more errors early due to reliable configuration. You'll avoid missteps due to having better insight into your project architecture. You won't so readily entangle your code, and you won't accidentally depend on your dependencies' internals.

It's the moody parts of software development that the JPMS will improve. The module system is no panacea: you still have to put in the hard work to properly design and arrange your artifacts; but with the module system on hand, this effort will have fewer pitfalls and more shortcuts along the way.

As more and more of the ecosystem's artifacts become modular, this effect will only get stronger, until one day we'll ask ourselves how we ever coded without the module system. What was it like, back in the day when the JVM turned our carefully designed dependency graph into a ball of mud?

It will feel strange, thinking back. As strange as writing a Java class without `private`. Can you imagine what that would be like?

Summary

- Design your module system carefully.
- Microservices and the JPMS complement each other.
- OSGi and the JPMS also complement each other.

And now—thank you very much for reading this book. It was a pleasure to write for you. I'm sure we'll see each other again!

appendix A:
Class-path recap

A book discussing the module system of course focuses on the module path (see section 3.4). But the class path is still fully operational; and because you can use it side by side with the module path, it plays an important role during incremental modularizations. In other words, it still pays to know how it works.

A.1   Using the class path to load application JARs

> **Definition: Class path**
>
> The *class path* is a concept related to the compiler and the virtual machine. They use it for the same purpose: to search the listed JARs for types that they require but that aren't in the JDK. (It can also be used with class files, but you can ignore this case for the purpose of learning about the module system.)

Let's look at this book's example *ServiceMonitor* application as an example. It consists of multiple subprojects and has a few dependencies. In this scenario, all subprojects except the last one, *monitor*, have already been built and are present in the jars directory.

The following listing shows how to compile, package, and launch the application using the class path. Except for the new variants of some of the command-line options (for example, using `--class-path`, not `-classpath`), these are exactly the same commands as before Java 9.

Listing A.1   Compiling, packaging, and launching using the class path

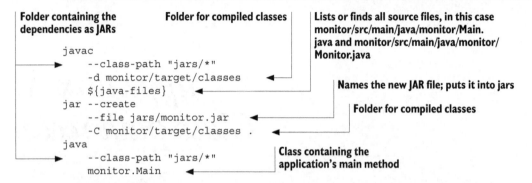

Folder containing the dependencies as JARs

Folder for compiled classes

Lists or finds all source files, in this case monitor/src/main/java/monitor/Main. java and monitor/src/main/java/monitor/ Monitor.java

```
javac
    --class-path "jars/*"
    -d monitor/target/classes
    ${java-files}
jar --create
    --file jars/monitor.jar
    -C monitor/target/classes .
java
    --class-path "jars/*"
    monitor.Main
```

Names the new JAR file; puts it into jars

Folder for compiled classes

Class containing the application's main method

Both the compiler and the runtime search the class path for the types they need. Which ones those are differ, though:

- *Compiler*—The compiler requires types that the code under compilation refers to. These are a project's direct dependencies, or more precisely those types in the direct dependencies that are referenced from a file under compilation.

- *Virtual machine*—The JVM requires all types that the executed bytecode refers to. In general, these are a project's direct and indirect dependencies; but due to Java's lazy approach to class loading, it can be considerably fewer than that. Only types referenced by the code that is actually running are required, meaning a dependency can be missing if the code using it isn't executed. The JVM also allows code to search JARs for resources.

Both `javac` and `java` have command-line options `-classpath`, `-cp`, and, since Java 9, `--class-path`. They generally expect a list of files, but it's possible to use paths and wildcards that then get extended to such a list.

A.2   *The class path since Java 9*

 ESSENTIAL INFO   Regarding Java 9 (and later versions), it's important to stress that the class path isn't going away! It operates exactly as it did in earlier Java versions, and if applications that compiled on such a version didn't do anything problematic (see chapters 6 and 7), they will continue to compile on Java 9 and beyond with the same commands.

Taking this backward compatibility into account, the question remains how the module system deals with types on the class path. In short, they all end up in the *unnamed module*, which the module system spins on the fly. This is a regular module, but it has some peculiarities, one of which is that it automatically reads all resolved modules. This is also true for modules that end up on the class path—they'll be treated just like plain JARs, and their types will end up in the unnamed module as well, ignoring whatever their module declaration has to say. The unnamed module and modules on the class path are part of the migration story, which section 8.2 tells in full detail.

appendix B:
High-level introduction to the reflection API

Reflection allows code to inspect types, methods, fields, annotations, and so forth at run time and to defer the decision about how to use them from compile time to run time. Toward that end, Java's reflection API offers types like Class, Field, Constructor, Method, Annotation, and others. With them, it's possible to interact with types that weren't known at compile time: for example, to create instances of an unknown class and call methods on them.

Reflection and its use cases can quickly become complex, and I'm not going to explain it in detail. Instead, this appendix is intended to give you a high-level understanding of what reflection is, what it looks like in Java, and what you or your dependencies can use it for.

Afterward, you'll be ready to get started using it or work through longer tutorials, such as Oracle's *The Reflection API* trail at https://docs.oracle.com/javase/tutorial/reflect. More important, though, you'll be prepared to understand the changes the module system makes with regard to reflection, which section 7.1.4 and particularly chapter 12 explore.

Instead of building from the ground up, let's start with a simple example. The following snippet creates a URL, converts it to a string, and then prints that. Before resorting to reflection, I used plain Java code:

```
URL url = new URL("http://codefx.org");
String urlString = url.toExternalForm();
System.out.println(urlString);
```

I decided *at compile time* (meaning, when I was writing the code) that I wanted to create a URL object and call a method in it. Even though that's not the most natural way to do it, you can split the first two lines into five steps:

1 Reference the URL class.

2 Locate the constructor taking a single string parameter.

3 Call it with http://codefx.org.

4 Locate the method toExternalForm.

5 Call it on the url instance.

The following listing shows how to implement those five steps with Java's reflection API.

> **Listing B.1   Reflectively creating a URL and calling toExternalForm on it**

The Class instance for the class to operate on is the gateway to reflection.

Fetches the constructor that takes a String argument

```
Class<?> urlClass = Class.forName("java.net.URL");

Constructor<?> urlConstructor
    = urlClass.getConstructor(String.class);
Object url =
    urlConstructor.newInstance("http://codefx.org");

Method toExternalFormMethod =
    urlClass.getMethod("toExternalForm");
Object methodCallResult =
    toExternalFormMethod.invoke(url);
```

Uses it to create a new instance with the given string as a parameter

Fetches the toExternalForm method

Invokes the method in the instance that was created earlier

Using the reflection API is, of course, more cumbersome than writing the code directly. But this way, details that used to be baked into the code (like using URL, or which method is called) become a string parameter. As a consequence, instead of having to settle on URL and toExternalForm at compile time, you could decide which type and method to pick later, when the program is already running.

Most use cases for this occur in "frameworky" environments. Think about JUnit, for example, which wants to execute all methods that are annotated with @Test. Once it finds them, it uses getMethod and invoke to call them. Spring and other web frameworks act similarly when looking for controllers and request mappings. Extensible applications that want to load user-provided plugins at run time are another use case.

B.1   *Fundamental types and methods*

The gateway into the reflection API is Class::forName. In its simple form, this static method takes a fully qualified class name and returns a Class instance for it. You can use that instance to get fields, methods, constructors, and more.

To get a specific constructor, call the getConstructor method with the types of the constructor arguments, as I did earlier. Similarly, a specific method can be accessed by calling getMethod and passing its name as well as the parameter types.

The call to getMethod("toExternalForm") didn't specify any types because the method has no arguments. Here's URL.openConnection(Proxy), which takes a Proxy as a parameter:

```
Class<?> urlClass = Class.forName("java.net.URL");
Method openConnectionMethod = urlClass
    .getMethod("openConnection", Proxy.class);
```

The instances returned by calls to getConstructor and getMethod are of type Constructor and Method, respectively. To call the underlying member, they offer methods like Constructor::newInstance and Method::invoke. An interesting detail of the latter is that you need to pass the instance on which the method is to be called as the first argument. The other arguments will be passed on to the called method.

Continuing the openConnection example:

```
openConnectionMethod.invoke(url, someProxy);
```

If you want to call a static method, the instance argument is ignored and can be null.

In addition to Class, Constructor, and Method, there is also Field, which allows read and write access to instance fields. Calling get with an instance retrieves the value that field has in that instance—the set method sets the specified value in the specified instance.

The URL class has an instance field protocol of type String; for the URL http://codefx.org, it would contain "http". Because it's private, code like this won't compile:

```
URL url = new URL("http://codefx.org");
// no access to a private field ~> compile error
url.protocol = "https";
```

Here's how to do the same thing with reflection:

```
// `Class<?> urlClass` and `Object url` are like before
Field protocolField = urlClass.getDeclaredField("protocol");
Object oldProtocol = protocolField.get(url);
protocolField.set(url, "https");
```

Although this compiles, it still leads to an IllegalAccessException on the get call, because the protocol field is private. But that doesn't have to stop you.

B.2   *Breaking into APIs with setAccessible*

One important use case for reflection has always been to break into APIs by accessing nonpublic types, methods, and fields. This is called *deep reflection*. Developers use it to access data that an API doesn't make accessible, to work around bugs in their dependencies by twiddling with the internal state, and to dynamically populate instances with the correct values—Hibernate does this, for example.

For deep reflection, you need to do nothing more that call setAccessible(true) on a Method, Constructor, or Field instance before using it:

```
// `Class<?> urlClass` and `Object url` are like before
Field protocolField = urlClass.getDeclaredField("protocol");
protocolField.setAccessible(true);
Object oldProtocol = field.get(url);
protocolField.set(instance, "https");
```

One challenge when migrating to the module system is that it takes away reflection's superpowers, meaning calls to setAccessible are much more likely to fail. For more on that and how to remedy it, check chapter 12.

B.3   *Annotations mark code for reflection*

Annotations are an important part of reflection. In fact, annotations are *geared toward* reflection. They're meant to provide metainformation that can be accessed at run time and is then used to shape the program's behavior. JUnit's @Test and Spring's @Controller and @RequestMapping are prime examples.

All important reflection-related types like Class, Field, Constructor, Method, and Parameter implement the AnnotatedElement interface. Its Javadoc contains a thorough explanation of how annotations can relate to these elements (directly present, indirectly present, or associated), but its simplest form is this: the getAnnotations method returns the annotations present on that element in form of an array of Annotation instances, whose members can then be accessed.

But in the context of the module system, how you or the frameworks you depend on process annotations is less important than the underlying fact that they only work with reflection. That means any class you see that has some annotations on it will at some point be reflected over—and if that class is in a module, that won't necessarily work out of the box.

appendix C:
Observing the JVM
with unified logging

Java 9 introduced a unified logging architecture. It pipes the messages the JVM generates through a single mechanism and allows you to select which messages to show with the intricate command-line option -Xlog.

You can use it to observe the JVM's behavior, debug an application if it misbehaves, or look for possible performance improvements. As you know from your own projects, logging has a wide and amorphous area of application, so I won't explain this with a single use case, but will instead look at the mechanism as a whole.

Using -Xlog can initially be a bit intimidating, but we'll examine it step by step, exploring each aspect of the option. Here we'll be looking at the mechanism in general—section 5.3.6 shows how to use it to debug a modular application.

NOTE This mechanism is universal within the JVM and has many more applications than just monitoring the module system. Class loading, garbage collection, interaction with the operating system, threading—you can analyze all of that and much more by using the right flags. Note that this includes neither JDK messages, such as the ones Swing logs, nor your application's messages—this is purely about the JVM itself.

C.1   What is unified logging?

The JVM-internal, unified logging infrastructure is similar to other logging frameworks like Java Util Logging, Log4j, and Logback that you might have used for applications. It generates textual messages, attaches some metainformation like tags (describing the originating subsystem), a log level (describing the importance of the message), and time stamps, and prints them somewhere. You can configure the logging output according to your needs.

> **Definition: -Xlog**
>
> The `java` option `-Xlog` activates logging. This is the only flag regarding this mechanism—any further configuration is immediately appended to that option. Configurable aspects of logging are as follows:
>
> - Which messages to log (by tag and/or by log level)
> - Which information to include (for example, time stamps and process IDs)
> - Which output to use (for example, into a file)
>
> The rest of this appendix looks at each of them in turn.

Before doing anything else, let's have a look at the kind of messages `-Xlog` produces, as shown in figure C.1. Execute `java -Xlog`, and look at the output—of which there are *a lot*. (You didn't give `java` enough details to launch an application, so it helpfully lists all options. To get rid of that wall of text, I run it with `-version`, which outputs the current Java version.)

One of the first messages tells you that the HotSpot virtual machine begins its work:

```
$ java -Xlog -version

# truncated a few messages
> [0.002s][info][os          ] HotSpot is running with glibc 2.23, NPTL 2.23
# truncated a lot of messages
```

It shows how long the JVM has been running (2 ms), the message's log level (`info`), its tags (only `os`), and the actual message. Let's see how to influence these details.

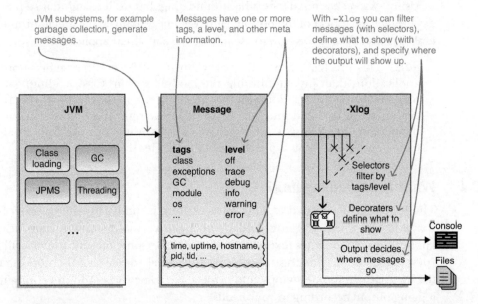

Figure C.1 **Many JVM subsystems (left) generate messages (middle), and the `-Xlog` option can be used to configure what messages get to be seen, which information they include, and where they show up (right).**

C.2 *Defining which messages should be shown*

You can use the log level and tags to define exactly what the logs should show by defining pairs of <tag-set>=<level>, which are called *selectors*. All tags can be selected with all, and the level is optional and defaults to info. Here's how to use it:

```
$ java -Xlog:all=warning -version

# no log messages; great, warning free!
```

Let's try another tag and level:

```
$ java -Xlog:logging=debug -version

> [0.034s][info][logging] Log configuration fully initialized.
> [0.034s][debug][logging] Available log levels:
>    off, trace, debug, info, warning, error
> [0.034s][debug][logging] Available log decorators: [...]
> [0.034s][debug][logging] Available log tags: [...]
> [0.034s][debug][logging] Described tag combinations:
> [0.034s][debug][logging]  logging: Logging for the log framework itself
> [0.034s][debug][logging] Log output configuration:
> [0.034s][debug][logging] #0: stdout [...]
> [0.034s][debug][logging] #A: stderr [...]]
```

Lucky shot! I had to truncate the output because there's so much of it, but trust me, there's a lot of helpful information in those messages. You don't have to take that route, though: -Xlog:help shows the same information, but it's more beautifully formatted (as you'll see later).

A surprising detail (at least at first) is that messages only match a selector if their tags *exactly* match the given ones. Given *ones*? Plural? Yes, a selector can name several tags by concatenating them with +. Still, a message has to contain exactly those to be selected.

Hence, using gc (for garbage collection) versus gc+heap, for example, should select different messages. This is indeed the case:

```
java -Xlog:gc -version

[0.009s][info][gc] Using G1

java -Xlog:gc+heap -version

[0.006s][info][gc,heap] Heap region size: 1M
```

You can define several selectors at once—they just have to be separated with commas:

```
java -Xlog:gc,gc+heap -version

[0.007s][info][gc,heap] Heap region size: 1M
[0.009s][info][gc      ] Using G1
```

Using this strategy, it's cumbersome to get all messages that contain a certain flag. Luckily, there's an easier way to do that: the wildcard *, which you can use with a single tag to define a selector that matches all messages containing that tag:

```
java -Xlog:gc*=debug -version
```

```
[0.006s][info][gc,heap] Heap region size: 1M
[0.006s][debug][gc,heap] Minimum heap 8388608
 Initial heap 262144000  Maximum heap 4192206848
# truncated about two dozen message
[0.072s][info ][gc,heap,exit          ] Heap
# truncated a few messages showing final GC statistics
```

Using logging and selectors, there are three easy steps to get to know a subsystem of the JVM:

1 Find interesting tags in the output of java -Xlog:help.
2 Use them with -Xlog:${tag_1}*,${tag_2}*,${tag_n}* to display all info messages that were tagged with any of them.
3 Selectively switch to lower log levels with -Xlog:${tag}*=debug.

That settles which messages you see. Now let's look at where they might go.

C.3   *Defining where messages should go*

Compared to the nontrivial selectors, the output configuration is simple. You put it after the selectors (separated by a colon), and it has three possible values:

- stdout—The default output. On the console, that's the terminal window, unless redirected. In IDEs, it's often shown in its own tab or view.
- stderr—The default error output. On the console, that's the terminal window, unless redirected. In IDEs it's usually shown in the same tab/view as stdout, but printed in red.
- file=<filename>—Defines a file to pipe all messages into. Including file= is optional.

Unlike with common logging frameworks, it's unfortunately not possible to use two output options simultaneously.

Here's how to put all debug messages in the file application.log:

```
java -Xlog:all=debug:file=application.log -version
```

More output options are available that allow log file rotation based on file size and number of files to rotate.

C.4   *Defining what messages should say*

As I said earlier, each message consists of text and metainformation. Which of these additional pieces of information the JVM will print is configurable by selecting *decorators*, which are listed in table C.1. This happens after the output location and another colon.

Let's say you want to print the time stamp, the uptime in milliseconds, and the thread ID for all garbage-collection debug messages to the console. Here's how to do that:

```
java -Xlog:gc*=debug:stdout:time,uptimemillis,tid -version
```

```
# truncated messages
[2017-02-01T13:10:59.689+0100][7ms][18607] Heap region size: 1M
```

Table C.1 The decorators available for the `-Xlog` option. Information is always printed in this order. The descriptions are based on the documentation.

Option	Description
`level`	The level associated with the log message
`pid`	The process identifier
`tags`	The tag-set associated with the log message
`tid`	The thread identifier
`time`	Current time and date in ISO-8601 format
`timemillis`	The same value as generated by `System.currentTimeMillis()`
`timenanos`	The same value as generated by `System.nanoTime()`
`uptime`	Time since the start of the JVM in seconds (e.g., 6.567s)
`uptimemillis`	Milliseconds since the JVM started
`uptimenanos`	Nanoseconds since the JVM started

C.5 *Configuring the entire logging pipeline*

Formally, the `-Xlog` option has this syntax:

```
-Xlog:<selectors>:<output>:<decorators>:<output-options>
```

Each of the parameters following `-Xlog` is optional, but if you use one, you have to use all the others that come before it. Selectors are pairs of tag sets and log levels. This part is also called the *what-expression*, a term you'll encounter when the configuration isn't syntactically correct. You can define the target location for the log messages with `output` (in short, the terminal window or a log file) and use decorators to define what information the messages should include. (And yes, annoyingly, the output mechanism and further output options are split, with decorators in between.)

For more details, see the online documentation at http://mng.bz/K1Gj or the output of `java -Xlog:help`:

```
java -Xlog:help

-Xlog Usage: -Xlog[:[what][:[output][:[decorators][:output-options]]]]
        where 'what' is a combination of tags and levels on the form
            tag1[+tag2...][*][=level][,...]
        Unless wildcard (*) is specified, only log messages tagged with
            exactly the tags specified will be matched.

Available log levels:
    off, trace, debug, info, warning, error

Available log decorators:
    time (t), utctime (utc), uptime (u), timemillis (tm), uptimemillis (um),
    timenanos (tn), uptimenanos (un), hostname (hn), pid (p), tid (ti),
    level (l), tags (tg)
```

Decorators can also be specified as 'none' for no decoration.

Described tag combinations:
    logging: Logging for the log framework itself

Available log tags:
    [... many, many tags ...]
    Specifying 'all' instead of a tag combination matches all tag
     combinations.

Available log outputs:
    stdout, stderr, file=<filename>
    Specifying %p and/or %t in the filename will expand to the JVM's PID and
    startup timestamp, respectively.

Some examples:
    [... a few helpful examples to get you going ...]

appendix D: Analyzing a project's dependencies with JDeps

JDeps is the *Java Dependency Analysis Tool*, a command-line tool that processes Java bytecode—.class files or the JARs that contain them—and analyzes the statically declared dependencies between classes. The results can be filtered in various ways and can be aggregated to the package or JAR level. JDeps is also fully aware of the module system.

All in all, it's a useful tool for examining the various sometimes-nebulous graphs I talk about so much in this book. More than that, it has concrete applications when migrating and modularizing a project, like analyzing its static dependencies on JDK-internal APIs (section 7.1.2), listing split packages (section 7.2.5), and drafting module descriptors (section 9.3.2).

For this exploration, I encourage you to follow along, preferably with one of *your* projects. It will be easiest if you have a JAR of your project and next to it a folder with all of its transitive dependencies. If you're using Maven, you can achieve the latter with the *maven-dependency-plugin*'s copy-dependencies goal. With Gradle, you can use a Copy task, setting from to configurations.compile or configurations.runtime. A quick search will help you with the details.

As my sample project, I picked Scaffold Hunter:

> *Scaffold Hunter is a Java-based open source tool for the visual analysis of data sets with a focus on data from the life sciences, aiming at an intuitive access to large and complex data sets. The tool offers a variety of views, e.g. graph, dendrogram, and plot view, as well as analysis methods, e.g. for clustering and classification.*
>
> —http://scaffoldhunter.sourceforge.net

I downloaded the 2.6.3 release Zip file and copied all dependencies into `libs`. When showing output, I abbreviate `scaffoldhunter` (in package names) and `scaffold-hunter` (in file names) to `sh` to make it shorter.

D.1   Getting to know JDeps

Let's start with getting to know JDeps: where to find it, how to get the first results, and where to go for help. You can find the JDeps executable `jdeps` in your JDK's bin folder since Java 8. Working with it is easiest if it's available on the command line, for which you may have to perform some setup steps specific to your OS. Make sure `jdeps --version` works and shows that the most recent version is running.

The next step is to grab a JAR and set JDeps loose on it. Used without further command-line options, it will first list the JDK modules the code depends on, including a mention of `not found` for all code that's neither part of the JAR nor part of the JDK. That's followed by a list of package-level dependencies, organized as `${package} -> ${package} ${module/JAR}`.

Calling `jdeps scaffold-hunter-2.6.3.jar` results in the following overwhelming output. You can see that Scaffold Hunter depends on the modules *java.base* (of course), *java.desktop* (it's a Swing application), *java.sql* (data sets are stored in SQL data bases), and a few others. This list of dependencies is followed by the long list of package dependencies, which is a little too much to take in:

```
$ jdeps scaffold-hunter-2.6.3.jar

# remember, "sh" is short for "scaffold-hunter" (in
# file names) and "scaffoldhunter" (in package names)
> sh-2.6.3.jar -> java.base          ◀──┐
> sh-2.6.3.jar -> java.datatransfer      │
> sh-2.6.3.jar -> java.desktop           │   JDK modules the project depends on
> sh-2.6.3.jar -> java.logging
> sh-2.6.3.jar -> java.prefs
> sh-2.6.3.jar -> java.sql
> sh-2.6.3.jar -> java.xml
> sh-2.6.3.jar -> not found                     Package dependencies
>    edu.udo.sh -> com.beust.jcommander  not found ◀── within and across JARs
>    edu.udo.sh -> edu.udo.sh.data       sh-2.6.3.jar
>    edu.udo.sh -> edu.udo.sh.gui        sh-2.6.3.jar
>    edu.udo.sh -> edu.udo.sh.gui.util   sh-2.6.3.jar
>    edu.udo.sh -> edu.udo.sh.util       sh-2.6.3.jar
>    edu.udo.sh -> java.io               java.base
>    edu.udo.sh -> java.lang             java.base
>    edu.udo.sh -> javax.swing           java.desktop
>    edu.udo.sh -> org.slf4j             not found
# truncated many more package dependencies
```

"not found" indicates that dependencies weren't found, which isn't surprising as I didn't tell JDeps where to look for them.

Now it's time to tune the output with the various options. You can list them with `jdeps -h`.

D.2   *Including dependencies in the analysis*

An important aspect of JDeps is that it allows you to analyze your dependencies as if they were part of your code. A first step to that goal is placing them on the class path with `--class-path`, but that only enables JDeps to follow the paths into your dependencies' JARs and rids you of the `not found` indicators. To analyze the dependencies as well, you need to make JDeps recurse into them with `-recursive` or `-r`.

To include Scaffold Hunter's dependencies, I executed JDeps with `--class-path 'libs/*'` and `-recursive`, the result of which can be seen next. In this specific case, the output begins with a few split-package warnings that I'm going to ignore for now. The following module/JAR and package dependencies are as before but now are all found, so there are many more of them:

```
$ jdeps -recursive
    --class-path 'libs/*'
    scaffold-hunter-2.6.3.jar

# truncated split package warnings
# truncated some module/JAR dependencies
> sh-2.6.3.jar -> libs/commons-codec-1.6.jar
> sh-2.6.3.jar -> libs/commons-io-2.4.jar
> sh-2.6.3.jar -> libs/dom4j-1.6.1.jar
> sh-2.6.3.jar -> libs/exp4j-0.1.38.jar
> sh-2.6.3.jar -> libs/guava-18.0.jar
> sh-2.6.3.jar -> libs/heaps-2.0.jar
> sh-2.6.3.jar -> libs/hibernate-core-4.3.6.Final.jar
> sh-2.6.3.jar -> java.base
> sh-2.6.3.jar -> java.datatransfer
> sh-2.6.3.jar -> java.desktop
> sh-2.6.3.jar -> java.logging
> sh-2.6.3.jar -> java.prefs
> sh-2.6.3.jar -> java.sql
> sh-2.6.3.jar -> java.xml
> sh-2.6.3.jar -> libs/javassist-3.18.1-GA.jar
> sh-2.6.3.jar -> libs/jcommander-1.35.jar
# truncated more module/JAR dependencies
>    edu.udo.sh -> com.beust.jcommander  jcommander-1.35.jar
>    edu.udo.sh -> edu.udo.sh.data       sh-2.6.3.jar
>    edu.udo.sh -> edu.udo.sh.gui        sh-2.6.3.jar
>    edu.udo.sh -> edu.udo.sh.gui.util   sh-2.6.3.jar
>    edu.udo.sh -> edu.udo.sh.util       sh-2.6.3.jar
>    edu.udo.sh -> java.io               java.base
>    edu.udo.sh -> java.lang             java.base
>    edu.udo.sh -> javax.swing           java.desktop
>    edu.udo.sh -> org.slf4j             slf4j-api-1.7.5.jar
# truncated many, many more package dependencies
```

No more "not found" JAR dependencies

No more "not found" sources for package dependencies

This makes the output all the more overwhelming, so it's high time to look at how you can make sense from so much data.

D.3   *Configuring JDeps' output*

There are various ways to configure JDeps' output. Maybe the best option to use in a first analysis of any project is -summary or -s, which only show dependencies between JARs, as shown here:

```
$ jdeps -summary -recursive
--class-path 'libs/*'
scaffold-hunter-2.6.3.jar

# truncated split package warnings
# truncated some module/JAR dependencies
> sh-2.6.3.jar -> libs/javassist-3.18.1-GA.jar
> sh-2.6.3.jar -> libs/jcommander-1.35.jar
> sh-2.6.3.jar -> libs/jgoodies-forms-1.4.1.jar
> sh-2.6.3.jar -> libs/jspf.core-1.0.2.jar
> sh-2.6.3.jar -> libs/l2fprod-common-sheet.jar
> sh-2.6.3.jar -> libs/l2fprod-common-tasks.jar
> sh-2.6.3.jar -> libs/opencsv-2.3.jar
> sh-2.6.3.jar -> libs/piccolo2d-core-1.3.2.jar
> sh-2.6.3.jar -> libs/piccolo2d-extras-1.3.2.jar
> sh-2.6.3.jar -> libs/slf4j-api-1.7.5.jar
> sh-2.6.3.jar -> libs/xml-apis-ext.jar
> sh-2.6.3.jar -> libs/xstream-1.4.1.jar
> slf4j-api-1.7.5.jar -> java.base
> slf4j-api-1.7.5.jar -> libs/slf4j-jdk14-1.7.5.jar
> slf4j-jdk14-1.7.5.jar -> java.base
> slf4j-jdk14-1.7.5.jar -> java.logging
> slf4j-jdk14-1.7.5.jar -> libs/slf4j-api-1.7.5.jar
# truncated more module/JAR dependencies
```

Table D.1 lists various filters that give different perspectives on the dependencies.

Table D.1   A short description of some of the options that filter JDeps' output

Option	Description
--api-only or -apionly	Sometimes, particularly if you're analyzing a library, you only care about a JAR's API. With this option, only types mentioned in the signatures of public and protected members of public classes are examined.
-filter or -f	Followed by a regular expression, *excludes* dependencies on classes that match the regex. (Note that unless -verbose:class is used, output still shows packages.)
-filter:archive	In many cases, dependencies *within* an artifact aren't that interesting. This option ignores them and only shows dependencies *across* artifacts.
--package or -p	Followed by a package name, only considers dependencies *on* that package, which is a great way to see all the places where those utils are used.
--regex or -e	Followed by a regular expression, only considers dependencies *on classes* that match the regex. (Note that unless -verbose:class is used, output still shows packages.)

Output on the command line is a good way to examine details and drill deeper into interesting bits. It doesn't make for the most intuitive overview, though—diagrams are much better at that. Fortunately, JDeps has the `--dot-output` option, which creates .dot files for each of the individual analyses. These files are pure text, but other tools, such as Graphviz, can be used to create images from them. See the following listing and figure D.1 for an example.

Listing D.1 Visualizing artifact dependencies

```
$ jdeps -recursive
    --class-path 'libs/*'
    --dot-output dots
    scaffold-hunter-2.6.3.jar
$ dot -Tpng -O dots/summary.dot
```

Specifying --dot-output dots tells JDeps to create .dot files in the dots folder.

Graphviz provides the dot command, which is used here to create a summary.dot.png in dots.

Dot files and Graphviz

The .dot file is plain text and a great intermediate representation to edit. With some regular expressions, you can, for example, remove the *java.base* module from the bottom (makes the graph simpler) or the versions from the JAR's names (makes the graph leaner). For more on Graphviz, check out https://graphviz.gitlab.io.

D.4 Drilling deeper into your project's dependencies

If you want to see more details, `-verbose:class` lists dependencies between classes instead of aggregating them at the package level. Sometimes, listing only direct dependencies on a package or class isn't enough, because they may not be in your code but rather in your dependencies. In that case, `--inverse` or `-I` might help. Given a specific package or regex to look for, it tracks the dependencies back as far as they go, listing

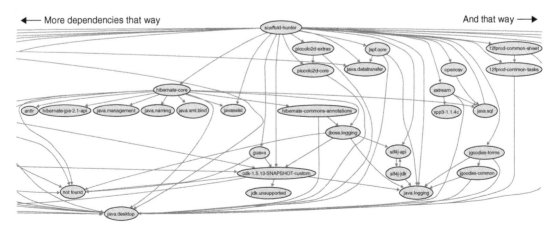

Figure D.1 The result of listing D.1 is a large, complicated, but still approachable dependency graph. This is just a cleaned-up part of it. Don't worry about the details; create one for your project, instead.

the artifacts along the way. Unfortunately, there seems to be no straightforward way to see the result at the level of classes instead of artifacts.

If you're only interested in the dependencies exposed in a library's public API, you can use `--api-only` for that. With it, only types mentioned in the signatures of public and protected members of public classes are examined. There are a few more options that might help you in your specific case—as mentioned, you can list them with `jdeps -h`.

D.5   *JDeps understands modules*

Just as the compiler and the JVM can operate on a higher level of abstraction thanks to the module system, so can JDeps. The module path can be specified with `--module-path` (note that -p is reserved: it's not shorthand for this option) and the initial module with `--module` or `-m`. From there, you can do the same kinds of analyses as earlier:

```
$ jdeps -summary -recursive
    --module-path mods:libs
    -m monitor

# truncated some module dependencies
> monitor -> java.base
> monitor -> monitor.observer
> monitor -> monitor.observer.alpha
> monitor -> monitor.observer.beta
> monitor -> monitor.persistence
> monitor -> monitor.rest
> monitor -> monitor.statistics
> monitor.observer -> java.base
> monitor.observer.alpha -> java.base
> monitor.observer.alpha -> monitor.observer
> monitor.observer.beta -> java.base
> monitor.observer.beta -> monitor.observer
> monitor.persistence -> java.base
> monitor.persistence -> monitor.statistics
> monitor.persistence -> hibernate.jpa
> monitor.rest -> java.base
> monitor.rest -> monitor.statistics
> monitor.rest -> spark.core
> monitor.statistics -> java.base
> monitor.statistics -> monitor.observer
> slf4j.api -> java.base
> slf4j.api -> not found
> spark.core -> JDK removed internal API
> spark.core -> java.base
> spark.core -> javax.servlet.api
> spark.core -> jetty.server
> spark.core -> jetty.servlet
> spark.core -> jetty.util
> spark.core -> slf4j.api
> spark.core -> websocket.api
> spark.core -> websocket.server
> spark.core -> websocket.servlet
# truncated more module dependencies
```

Beyond that, there are some Java 9 and module-specific options. With `--require ${modules}`, you can list all modules that require the named ones. How to use `--jdk-internals` to analyze a project's problematic dependencies is explained in section 7.1.2. Section 9.3.2 explains how `--generate-module-info` and `--generate-open-module` can be used to create first drafts of module descriptors. As mentioned in passing, JDeps will also always report all split packages it finds—a problem discussed in detail in section 7.2.

An interesting option is `--check`, which gives different perspectives on a module's descriptor (see figure D.2):

- It starts by printing the actual descriptor, followed by two hypothetical ones.
- The first of those, which is described as the *suggested descriptor*, declares dependencies on all modules whose types are used in the checked module.
- The second, described as a *transitive reduced graph*, is similar to the first but removes those dependencies that can be read due to implied readability (see section 9.1). This means it's the smallest set of dependencies that yields a reliable configuration.
- Finally, if the module declares any qualified exports (see section 9.3), `--check` will output those that aren't used within the universe of observable modules.

The hypothetical descriptors `--check` creates can also be viewed separately with the two options `--list-deps` and `--list-reduced-deps`, respectively. They also work with the class path, in which case they reference the unnamed module (see section 8.2).

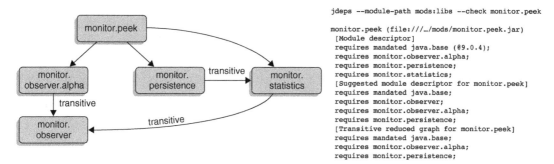

Figure D.2　At left you can see *monitor.peek* (introduced in section 11.1.1) and its transitive dependencies, some of which imply readability on other modules. At right, JDeps suggests including *monitor.observer* in the list of dependencies (because its types are directly referenced). Additionally, it lists the absolute minimum set of modules on which *monitor.peek* needs to depend to be reliable, making full use of implied readability.

appendix E:
Targeting multiple Java versions with multi-release JARs

It's never easy to decide which Java version to require for your project. On the one hand, you want to give users the freedom of choice, so it would be nice to support several major versions, not just the newest one. On the other hand, you're dying to use the newest language features and APIs. From Java 9 on, there's a new JVM feature, *multi-release JARs* (MR-JARs), that helps you reconcile these opposing forces—at least, under some circumstances.

MR-JARs allow you to ship bytecode for different Java versions in the same artifact. You can then rely on the JVM to load the classes that you compiled for the most recent version it supports. Starting with a project that runs successfully on your minimally required version, you can selectively improve it on newer JVMs by using more resilient and performant APIs—without being forced to raise your project's baseline.

 ESSENTIAL INFO Of course, you'll only ever need to consider MR-JARs if you don't have full control over the JVM version running your project. This is always the case for libraries and frameworks and often for desktop applications or web backends that your users host themselves. If, on the other hand, you administer the machines that run your application, you can use a newer JVM and forego the complexities of MR-JARs.

With all of that out of the way, let's explore this handy new feature. We'll start with creating a simple MR-JAR before looking at how it's structured internally. We'll end with some recommendations for when and how to use MR-JARs.

E.1   Creating a multi-release JAR

> **Definition**
>
> *Multi-release JARs* (MR-JARs) are specially prepared JARs that contain bytecode for several major Java versions. How that bytecode is loaded depends on the JVM version:
>
> - Java 8 and earlier load version-unspecific class files.
> - Java 9 and later load version-specific class files if they exist, or otherwise fall back to version-unspecific ones.

To prepare for an MR-JAR, you need to split source files by the Java version they target, compile each set of sources for the corresponding version, and place the resulting .class files into separate folders. When packaging them with jar, you add the baseline class files as usual (directly or with -C; check section 4.5.1) and use the new option --release ${release} for each other bytecode set.

Let's look at an example. Say you need to detect the currently running JVM's major version. Java 9 offers a nice API for that, so you no longer have to parse a system property. (Section 6.5.1 gives a glimpse of it, but the details aren't important here.) By deploying an MR-JAR, you can use that API if you're running on Java 9 or later.

The hypothetical app has two classes, Main and DetectVersion; and the goal is to have two variants of DetectVersion, one for Java 8 and earlier and another for Java 9 and later. These two variants need to have the exact same fully qualified name (which can make it challenging to work with them in your IDE)—assume you place them into two parallel source folders, src/main/java and src/main/java-9.

Figure E.1 shows how to organize the sources, and listing E.1 shows how to compile and package them into an MR-JAR. Note the two compilation steps and the separate output folders. The end result is shown in figure E.2.

Listing E.1   Compiling and packaging sources for different Java versions into a JAR

Compiles the code in src/main/java for Java 8 (or earlier) into classes

Compiles the code in src/main/java-9 for Java 9 into classes-9

```
javac --release 8
    -d classes
    src/main/java/org/codefx/detect/*.java
javac --release 9
    -d classes-9
    src/main/java-9/module-info.java
    src/main/java-9/org/codefx/detect/DetectVersion.java
jar --create
    --file target/detect.jar
    -C classes .
    --release 9
    -C classes-9 .
```

When packaging the bytecode into a JAR, packages default bytecode from classes as usual.

Includes classes specifically for Java 9

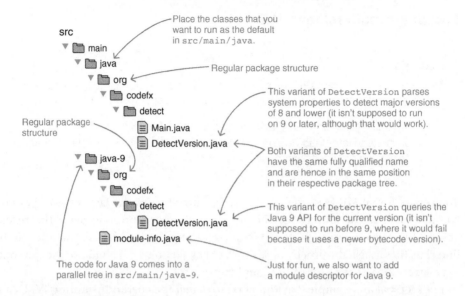

Figure E.1   One possible way to lay out the source code for a MR-JAR. The most important detail is that the version-dependent code, here `DetectVersion`, has the same fully qualified name in all variants.

This simple example creates two variants of `DetectVersion`, one for the minimally required Java 8 and another for Java 9. Formalizing that to the general case of creating a feature with several classes for several versions is surprisingly complex and tedious, so I'll spare you the formal version. Instead, section E.3 leaves you with a rule of thumb.

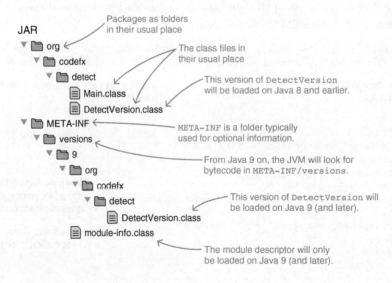

Figure E.2   The JAR resulting from listing E.1

E.2   Internal workings of MR-JARs

How does an MR-JAR work? It's pretty straightforward: it stores version-unspecific class files in its root (as usual) and version-specific files in `META-INF/versions/${version}`.

 ESSENTIAL INFO   JVMs of version 8 and earlier don't know anything about `META-INF/versions` and load the classes from the package structure in the JAR's root. Consequently, it's not possible to distinguish between versions before 9.

Newer JVMs, however, first look into `META-INF/versions` and, only if they don't find a class there, into the JAR's root. They search backward from their own version, meaning a Java 10 JVM looks for code in `META-INF/versions/10`, then `META-INF/versions/9`, and then the root directory. These JVMs thus shadow version-unspecific class files with the newest version-specific ones they support.

In addition to the folders in `META-INF/versions`, an MR-JAR can also be recognized by looking at the plaintext file `META-INF/MANIFEST.MF`: in MR-JARs, the manifest has an entry `Multi-Release: true`.

E.3   Usage recommendations

Now that you know how to create MR-JARs and how they work, I want to give you some recommendations for how to make the most out of them. More precisely, I'll give you tips on these topics:

- How to organize source code
- How to organize bytecode
- When to use MR-JARs

E.3.1   Organizing the source code

 ESSENTIAL INFO   I propose two guidelines when organizing source code for MR-JARs:

- The code for the oldest supported Java version goes in the project's default root directory: for example, `src/main/java`, not `src/main/java-X`.
- The code in that source folder is *complete*, meaning it can be compiled, tested, and deployed as is without additional files from version-specific source trees like `src/main/java-X`. (Note that if you're offering a feature that only works on a newer Java version, having a class that only throws errors stating "`Operation not supported before Java X`" counts as complete. My recommendation is to not leave it out, leading to an uninformative `NoClassDefFoundError`.)

These aren't technical requirements; nothing stops you from targeting Java 11 and putting half of the code in `src/main/java` and the other half, or even all of it, in `src/main/java-11`. But that will only cause confusion.

By sticking to the guidelines, you keep the source tree's layout as simple as possible. Any human or tool looking into it sees a fully functioning project that targets the required JVM version. Version-dependent source trees then selectively enhance that code for newer versions.

How do you verify whether you got it right? As I said earlier, a formal description is complex, so here's that rule of thumb I promised. To determine whether your particular layout works, mentally (or actually) undertake the following steps:

1 Compile and test the version-independent source tree on the oldest supported Java version.
2 For each additional source tree:
   a Move the version-dependent code into the version-independent tree, replacing files where they have the same fully qualified name.
   b Compile and test the tree on the newer version.

If that works, you got it right.

Of course, your tools also have to work with the source layout you choose. Unfortunately, at the time of writing, IDEs and most build tools don't have good support for this layout, and you might be forced to compromise. As an alternative solution, consider creating separate projects for each Java version.

E.3.2   *Organizing the bytecode*

 ESSENTIAL INFO   A straight path leads from that source tree structure to my proposal for organizing the bytecode in the JAR:

- The bytecode for the oldest supported Java version goes into the JAR's root, meaning it's not added after `--release`.
- The bytecode in the JAR's root is complete, meaning it can be executed as is without additional files from `META-INF/versions`.

Once again, these aren't technical requirements, but they guarantee that everybody looking into the JAR's root sees a fully functioning project compiled for the required JVM version with selective enhancements for newer JVMs in `META-INF/versions`.

E.3.3   *When to use MR-JARs*

How do MR-JARs help you solve the dilemma of picking the required Java version? First, and to state the obvious, preparing a MR-JAR adds quite a bit of complexity:

- Your IDE and build tool must be configured appropriately to allow easy work on source files with the same fully qualified name that are compiled against different Java versions.
- You need to keep multiple variants of the same source file in sync, so that they keep the same public API.

- Unit testing gets more complicated because you might end up writing tests that only run or pass on specific JVM versions.
- Integration testing gets more cumbersome because you need to consider testing the resulting artifact on each Java version for which the MR-JAR contains bytecode.

 ESSENTIAL INFO That means you should carefully consider whether you want to create MR-JARs. There should be a considerable payoff for going down this road. (Maybe you can raise the required Java version after all.)

Also, MR-JARs aren't a good fit for using convenient new language features. As you've seen, you need two variants of the involved source files, and there's no good argument on the basis of convenience if you have to keep a source file with the inconvenient variant. Language features will also quickly pervade a code base, leading to a lot of duplicate classes. This isn't a good idea.

APIs, on the other hand, are the sweet spot for MR-JARs. Java 9 introduced a number of new APIs that solve existing use cases with more resilience and/or better performance:

- Detecting the JVM version with `Runtime.Version` instead of parsing system properties (see section 6.5.1)
- Analyzing the call stack with the stack-walking API instead of creating a `Throwable` (this book doesn't cover that API, but developers of your logging framework are already using it)
- Replacing reflection with variable handles (see section 12.3.2)

If you want to use a newer API on a newer Java release, all you need to do is encapsulate your direct calls to it in a dedicated wrapper class and then implement two variants of it: one using the old API, another using the new one. If you've accepted the complexities outlined before, then this is straightforward.

index

Modern Java in Action
Lambdas, streams, functional and reactive programming
by Raoul-Gabriel Urma, Mario Fusco, Alan Mycroft

ISBN: 9781617293566
592 pages
$54.99
September 2018

Functional Programming in Java
How functional techniques improve your Java programs
by Pierre-Yves Saumont

ISBN: 9781617292736
472 pages
$49.99
January 2017

Cloud Native Patterns
Designing change-tolerant software
by Cornelia Davis

ISBN: 9781617294297
400 pages
$49.99
May 2019

For ordering information go to www.manning.com

MORE TITLES FROM MANNING

Spring in Action, Fifth Edition

by Craig Walls

> ISBN: 9781617294945
> 520 pages
> $49.99
> October 2018

Spring Microservices in Action

by John Carnell

> ISBN: 9781617293986
> 384 pages
> $49.99
> June 2017

Event Streams in Action
Real-time event systems with Kafka and Kinesis

by Alexander Dean, Valentin Crettaz

> ISBN: 9781617292347
> 344 pages
> $44.99
> May 2019

For ordering information go to www.manning.com

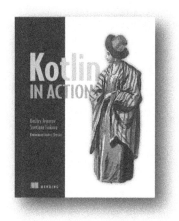

Kotlin in Action

by Dmitry Jemerov and Svetlana Isakova

ISBN: 9781617293290
360 pages
$44.99
February 2017

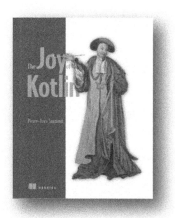

The Joy of Kotlin

by Pierre-Yves Saumont

ISBN: 9781617295362
480 pages
$49.99
April 2019

Enterprise Java Microservices

by Ken Finnigan

ISBN: 9781617294242
272 pages
$49.99
September 2018

MORE TITLES FROM MANNING

Kubernetes in Action
by Marko Lukša

   ISBN: 9781617293726
   624 pages
   $59.99
   December 2017

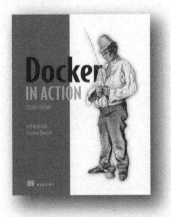

Docker in Action, Second Edition
by Jeff Nickoloff and Stephen Kuenzli

   ISBN: 9781617294761
   350 pages
   $49.99
   August 2019

Docker in Practice, Second Edition
by Ian Miell and Aidan Hobson Sayers

   ISBN: 9781617294808
   384 pages
   $49.99
   February 2019

For ordering information go to www.manning.com